The Five-Fold
MINISTRY GIFTS

The Five-Fold
MINISTRY GIFTS

*Understanding the Gifts
of Christ in Light of God's Purpose*

Clement C. Butler

THE FIVE-FOLD MINISTRY GIFTS
Understanding the Gifts of Christ in Light of God's Purpose

Copyright © 2021 Clement C. Butler. All rights reserved. Except for brief quotations in critical publications or reviews, no part of this book may be reproduced in any manner without prior written permission from the publisher. Write: Permissions, Wipf and Stock Publishers, 199 W. 8th Ave., Suite 3, Eugene, OR 97401.

Wipf & Stock
An Imprint of Wipf and Stock Publishers
199 W. 8th Ave., Suite 3
Eugene, OR 97401

www.wipfandstock.com

PAPERBACK ISBN: 978-1-7252-9801-9
HARDCOVER ISBN: 978-1-7252-9802-6
EBOOK ISBN: 978-1-7252-9803-3

Unless otherwise indicated, Scripture references are taken from the King James Version of the Bible.

Please send comments and questions to approvedworkmanministries@yahoo.com

Please visit our website: www.approvedworkmanministries.com

Follow us on Twitter @242teacher

CONTENDERS FOR THE FAITH

CONTENTS

Introduction xi
Foreword xiii

1. The Essence of Ministry: Understanding God's Why 1
   God's Why 3
   In the Beginning 6
   The Kingdom of God and the House of God 7
   Separation from the Kingdom of God and the House of God 13
   Realignment to God's Purpose 16
   Gathering Us Together 18
   A Son Restored 20

2. God's Purpose: Predestination, Spiritual Blessings, and
   Enlightenment 22
   Ephesians: The Overview 24
   Spiritual Blessings 25
   Spiritual Blessings (Insight Into God's Purpose) 27
   Enlightenment: The Spirit of Wisdom and Revelation 40
   The Hope of His Calling 44
   The Riches of the Glory of His Inheritance in the Saints 46
   The Exceeding Greatness of His Power toward us who
      Believe 48

3. The Message of Unity 51
   The Basis of Unity 52
   Quickened: United with the Father 53
   The Course of this World 54
   The Prince of the Power of the Air 55
   Quickened Together with Christ 56
   Unity in Christ 58
   The Circumcision and the Uncircumcision 61
   Outsiders No Longer 66

    The Middle Wall of Partition Has been Removed............................. 71
    Gender Biases (Male/Female) 76
    Religious, Social, and Ethnic Differences 77
    The Sabbath.. 77
    The Priesthood and the Law... 79
    One New Man and a New Creature....................................... 80
    One Body.. 82
    We Both Have Access by One Spirit unto the Father........................ 85
    Fellow-Citizens with the Saints and of the Household of God......... 86

4. The Mystery of Christ: The Message of God's Purpose and Unity........ 89
    Dispensation Defined 90
    Mystery Defined 92
    The Manifold Wisdom of God... 94

5. Precursor To The Gifts Of Christ 97
    Grace According to the Measure of the Gift of Christ..................... 101
    The Ministry of Jesus Christ... 105
    Gave Gifts to Men 113

6. The Importance of Structure 115
    Moses and the Israelites..116
    Leadership Replacement...118
    Growth and Unity 120
    Reconciliation of Doctrine and Unity................................... 123
    The Gentiles 123
    The Matter of Circumcision 127
    Apostles and Prophets 131
    Diversity Yet Unity... 134

7. The Gift of Christ Explained: Apostle....................................... 136
    Apostle Defined.. 137
    Christ as an Apostle.. 139
    Qualifications for an Apostle 142
    To be a Witness of Christ's Resurrection 144
    Responsibilities and Functions of an Apostle 146
    Proof of Apostleship 167

    Apostolic Relationship with the Church 169
    False Apostles.. 172

8. The Gift of Christ Explained: Prophet 176
    Prophet Defined 179
    Prophecy and Prophesying Defined 180
    The Gift of Prophecy versus the Office of the Prophet.................... 183
    Understanding Spiritual Gifts.. 188
    Spiritual Gifts and Charity 191
    The Purpose of Prophecy 196
    False Prophets.. 200
    The More Sure Word of Prophecy 204
    Christ as a Prophet 206

9. The Gift of Christ Explained: Evangelist 208
    Evangelist Defined 209
    The Work of an Evangelist from a Scriptural Perspective................211
    Jesus Christ and Him Crucified 214
    Christ: The Power of God 217
    Christ: The Wisdom of God 219
    Christ as an Evangelist 223
    Jesus and Nicodemus.. 226
    Jesus and His Disciples 229
    The Evangelist versus Evangelism 230
    Evangelism: The Ministry of Reconciliation 233
    Making Disciples.. 234

10. The Gift of Christ Explained: Pastor 236
    The Inception of the Church 236
    The Concept of Titles... 239
    Bishop, Pastor, and Elder.. 242
    Qualifications of a Pastor, Elder, or Bishop 250
    Responsibilities of a Pastor... 256
    Additional Responsibilities of a Pastor... 261
    Jesus as a Pastor (The Good Shepherd).. 263
    Good Shepherd versus Hireling 268
    "The" Shepherd.. 271

>   Misleading Concepts of Pastors and the Church.............................. 272
>   Are Pastors a Covering?.. 272
>   Deacons.. 276
>   The Purpose of the Local Church... 277

11. The Gift of Christ Explained: Teacher 281
    Teacher: The Distinction.. 281
    Teacher Defined.. 283
    Aquila and Priscilla... 286
    Qualifications and Responsibilities of a Teacher 287
    False Teachers 293
    Jesus as a Teacher... 296
    Preaching versus Teaching... 298

12. The Collective Purpose of the Gifts of Christ..................................... 301
    For the Perfecting of the Saints 304
    For the Work of the Ministry 322
    For the Edifying of the Body of Christ... 328

13. The Unity of the Faith and Maturity Based on the Standard of Christ's Fullness 336
    The Unity of the Faith 340
    The Proper Structure Promotes Unity 345
    Principles of the Unity of the Faith 347
    The Measure of the Fullness of the Stature of Christ..................... 350
    The Transformation Process.. 355
        Present our Bodies as a Living Sacrifice, One that is Holy.... 356
        Do Not be Conformed to this World... 360
        Renewing of the Mind 362

14. A Unified and Mature Body: A Glorious Church................................ 369
    No More Children.. 370
    Winds of Doctrine versus Speaking the Truth in Love 372
    Fitly Joined Together... 374
    A Glorious Church 377

Conclusion... 379
References... 381

INTRODUCTION

Are you called to the ministry of Jesus Christ? Are you functioning in the capacity of an apostle, a prophet, an evangelist, a pastor, or a teacher? If the answer to these questions is yes, this is the ideal book for you. Well, actually, this book is designed for every believer whether you are in a leadership capacity or not, for we are all stakeholders in the Father's purpose.

Over the years, I have heard many teachings on the gifts of Christ, which are commonly referred to as the five-fold ministry gifts. However, unlike those offerings, this text takes a more unconventional approach in discussing the purpose of the gifts. Based on established thinking, it is common to begin the conversation about the gifts with Ephesians 4:12. As a fundamental passage, it provides great insight and says the gifts are given for the perfecting of the saints, the work of the ministry, and the edifying of the body of Christ. Nevertheless, to have a greater appreciation for the gifts, they must be examined from the perspective of God's purpose.

Using the analogy of a movie, starting at Ephesians 4:12 is the equivalent of arriving 40 minutes into a film and asking everyone, "What did I miss?" At this stage in the movie, the context of the story has already been revealed. Therefore, from your vantage point, the plot seems obscure. However, with God's purpose as a starting point, it's akin to watching the opening scene, appreciating all the details, and seeing the storyline gradually unfold.

In providing a comprehensive view of the gifts, this book is divided into three distinct segments. The first section begins by first establishing the foundation or the reason the gifts are appointed in the first place. Therefore, it starts by asking the simple yet profound question, "why?" In answering this question, we will discuss the Father's original intent for humanity and what He predetermined for us before the foundation of the world. This approach not only reveals the heart and mind of the Father, but it also identifies His purpose. Furthermore, in doing so, we will discover that one of the hallmarks of God's purpose is the message of unity. With the gifts existing to fulfill the Father's purpose, anyone who takes up the mantle of ministry has to subscribe to this premise. They must be the purveyors of unity, not the promoters of division.

Additionally, this section includes a discussion on the importance of structure and its relevance to the functioning of the gifts. After establishing this footing, the second part of the book involves a detailed explanation of the qualifications and responsibilities of each of the gifts. Beginning with the office of the apostle, this text leaves no stone unturned in addressing the specifics of each gift. Moreover, included in this section is a discussion on how Christ functioned in each of the gifts. This serves as a benchmark for those who operate in His stead.

Finally, the third portion of the book appeals to the collective responsibilities of the gifts and how they function in unison to accomplish the Father's purpose. At last, our journey places us at the threshold of Ephesians 4:12 where the three shared objectives are tabled with intricate detail. As mentioned, the gifts of Christ are collectively bestowed for the perfecting of the saints, the work of the ministry, and the edifying of the body of Christ. Furthermore, as Ephesians 4:13 outlines, both the gifts and these objectives are intended to accomplish two specific goals:

1. The body of Christ attains to the unity of the faith
2. The body of Christ reaches the standard of Christ's maturity

In unison, these two goals produce a unified, glorified body, which is a manifestation of the Father's purpose.

In addressing the purpose of the gifts of Christ, this book takes a systematic approach and is extensive in discussing this subject. Having said that, to truly glean from its pages, it may have to be read more than once. Moreover, based on the offerings of this book, it is not only beneficial for those who function in the gifts but also for the entire body of Christ. Undoubtedly, after reading this book, your perspective regarding the ministry gifts will be transformed, and your life will be tremendously impacted. If you are looking for a text that addresses the gifts of Christ from a holistic point of view, this is definitely the book for you.

FOREWORD

Clement Butler is an authentic teacher of spiritual life. I always enjoy listening to him, for his delivery is most often organized, practical, and refreshing.

Some years ago, I was invited along with other prominent pastors to speak to a gathering of young people in a park. Instead of speaking, I placed Clement in my slot because I knew he had the ability to hold one's attention in a skillful and spell-binding manner. His delivery was indeed excellent.

Clement is the author of several books; all of which I say are very well written. This book, in particular, *The Five-fold Ministry Gifts: Understanding the Gifts of Christ in Light of God's Purpose* is a masterpiece. It is no dead work. When reading the manuscript, I could hardly put it down. I totally enjoyed it and found it to be quite informative and life-changing.

I highly recommend this book because it unfolds an amazing account of a person's highest identity in God's family of people, the true house of God, the kingdom of God. And finally, it reaches why God has established a unique governmental order for his divine family. After reading the manuscript, I acquired a well-rounded perspective of love and unity.

Dr. Betty Cleare-Pratt

This book is dedicated to the memory of my friend Kevin P. Cash

THE ESSENCE OF MINISTRY: UNDERSTANDING GOD'S WHY

IDENTIFYING THE WHY

It was 2015. I had recently returned from Puebla City, Mexico after completing an intense four-day course for a certificate in meeting management (CMM). Above all, achieving the certification is an indication that an individual is ready to assume a leadership role as a meeting professional in the Meetings and Convention Industry. Having obtained my designation as a Certified Meeting Professional (CMP) a few years earlier, I felt the course was a natural progression in advancing my career as a Conference Services Manager.

As a prerequisite for the certification, I had to complete a paper identifying and implementing an operational improvement for the convention business at the resort where I worked. The objective of the paper was to incorporate what I learned during the course and apply it to a real-life scenario. Therefore, taking into consideration that Conference Planning and Conference Services at my workplace are distinct departments, at different locations, and with separate personnel, I decided to write a paper on the benefits of integrating the two departments.

After preparing my first draft, I met with Nadia, a colleague from our Process Improvement department. On reading my notes, the first thing she asked me was "why?" "Why do you want to implement a system, which combines Conference Planning and Conference Services?" My answer was, "To enhance communication and increase efficiencies in the operation." On hearing my answer to the first question, she again asked "why," and I replied, "To improve our service delivery and overall customer service." After she asked the same question a few more times, based on my replies, it became apparent that she was prodding me to get to the root purpose for the proposed change.

Before this meeting, I never truly appreciated the importance of asking the seemingly simple question "why?" However, through this enlightening exercise, I could properly analyze the situation and come up with a meaningful application for my department. By first determining the "why," I was better equipped to shape the "what." Consequently, the paper was completed with great success, and I was awarded the certification.

The strategy of this endeavor is not limited to problem-solving alone. Rather, it is appropriate for a broad range of applications. For example, before we can have an earnest discussion regarding what is commonly referred to as the five-fold ministry gifts or the gifts of Christ they must first be considered within the context of purpose. In fact, as a principle, things are better understood within the framework of the purpose for their existence. The word "purpose" according to the *Free Dictionary* by Farlex is defined as, "the object toward which one strives or for which something exists." It is the ultimate goal of our efforts.

In general, purpose is usually determined by first asking the question, "why?" However, as it pertains to the ministry gifts, I find there seems to be a greater concentration on asking "what" they are rather than "why" they exist. The "what" speaks of the qualifications, the specifics of how they function, and the responsibilities of the gifts. Additionally, "what" is more concerned with titles. On the other hand, the "why" provides a deeper cause and defines the purpose for which they are allocated in the first place. The "why" takes you back to the intent of the One who gave them. Therefore, purpose is the why behind the function. Once we answer the "why," the "what" is much easier to define.

As a matter of structure, we will spend the first portion of this book defining God's why. This will shed light on His overall purpose and the reasons for the existence of the gifts. Once this has been established, we will pivot and discuss in detail the specifics of each of the gifts of Christ. Finally, in the last section, we will table the collective responsibilities of the gifts and their cumulative purpose.

Based on the present condition of the church, it seems many who function in leadership capacities lack a true understanding of God's purpose or comprehensive knowledge of Scripture, which reflects that purpose. Let me be clear; this has nothing to do with whether or not the call of God is on their lives, but it is primarily a statement based on ignorance. As a principle, whenever God's people are ignorant of what His purpose is, whatever is established caters more to human glory than the fulfillment of the Father's purpose. This also includes those who have a genuine zeal for God, but that fervor of spirit is not according to knowledge (Romans 10:1-3). Therefore, to be impactful in ministry, it is imperative to understand God's purpose. This includes the reason He made the earth, why He created humanity, and what His eternal purpose is for His sons. In particular, Jesus was effective in ministry because He understood and was engaged in the Father's purpose.

In Luke 2:15, while addressing His parents He said, "Do you not know I must be about my Father's business?" Hence, as ministers, our appointment and effectiveness in ministry are dependent on understanding and executing the Father's purpose. Let me say unequivocally, God's purpose is neither defined within the confines of religion nor exhibited through religious expressions. Rather, it is based on what He predetermined for humanity before the foundation of the world.

GOD'S WHY

Whenever the discussion of the five-fold ministry gifts emerges, the tendency is to begin the discussion at Ephesians 4:11-16, which says:

11. And he gave some, apostles; and some, prophets; and some, evangelists; and some, pastors and teachers;
12. For the perfecting of the saints, for the work of the ministry, for the edifying of the body of Christ:

13. Till we all come in the unity of the faith, and of the knowledge of the Son of God, unto a perfect man, unto the measure of the stature of the fulness of Christ:
14. That we henceforth be no more children, tossed to and fro, and carried about with every wind of doctrine, by the sleight of men, and cunning craftiness, whereby they lie in wait to deceive;
15. But speaking the truth in love, may grow up into him in all things, which is the head, even Christ:
16. From whom the whole body fitly joined together and compacted by that which every joint supplieth, according to the effectual working in the measure of every part, maketh increase of the body unto the edifying of itself in love.

In analyzing the components of this passage, we can conclude the following concerning the purpose of the five-fold ministry gifts. Christ gives apostles, prophets, evangelists, pastors, and teachers for the following:

- For the perfecting of the saints
- For the work of the ministry
- For the edifying of the body of Christ
- Until we (the church) all attain the unity of the faith
- Until we (the church) all come to the knowledge of the Son of God unto a perfect man, unto the measure of the stature of the fullness of Christ
- That we (the church) be no more children tossed to and fro and carried about with every wind of doctrine, by the sleight of men, and cunning craftiness, whereby they lie in wait to deceive
- That we (the church) speak the truth in love
- That we (the church) grow up into Him or become like Christ
- Consequently, there will be unity in the entire body based on the contribution of every part according to God's effectual working in every member. The result will be a mature and glorified body that grows and edifies itself in love.

While this passage is meaningful and answers the first "why," we should be compelled to ask the question again. Much like the exercise regarding my certification based on the content of Ephesians Chapter 4, we must again ask the question "why?" This will assist us in understanding that the gifts are a part of a grander design. Therefore, we need to know the primary purpose of their existence. It's similar to accepting a job without understanding the goals of the company. While Ephesians Chapter 4 provides an itemized list of the ministry gifts and their responsibilities, it does not adequately take into account the heart and mind of the Father. As mentioned earlier, "why" is determined by analyzing purpose, and Scripture makes it clear that in the aggregate, God has a purpose.

> According to the eternal purpose which He (God) purposed in Christ Jesus our Lord. (Ephesians 3:11)

Not only does Ephesians 3:11 provide the perspective that God has a purpose, but it also says His purpose is eternal in scope. The word "eternal" is not limited to being everlasting or without end. It also means immutable or unchanged by time. Thus, God instituted His plan in the realm of eternity, and it is incapable of changing. By comparison, while companies may adjust their business plans from time to time depending on market forces or changes in the economic environment, God's plan is unchangeable or constant. In fact, Isaiah 46:10 says the end or the fulfillment of His purpose has been determined from eternity. This also incorporates the concept of predestination, which means that before the foundation of the world, the Father decided our destinies. Therefore, the "why" is based on what the Father predetermined from the position of eternity. Hence, a fundamental question to ask is how do the gifts fit in with the eternal purpose of the Father? Furthermore, Ephesians 3:11 conveys that God's eternal purpose is orchestrated in Christ Jesus. Hence, once we determine what Christ came to do or His purpose, then the eternal purpose of the Father or "His why" becomes more apparent.

For the church to be effective, we have to both understand and be in alignment with God's purpose. Religion is more concerned with "how" and "what"; whereas, God's purpose is more involved with "why." Once the church conveys "why," it does what it does, people will be more inspired. As a principle, people are more interested in why you do something as opposed to what you do (Simon Sinek). Inasmuch as "what" can be ritualistic, ceremonial, and based on external performances, "why," on the other hand, is the expression of the heart and mind. In this regard, the conversation surrounding leadership in ministry is often conducted in isolation with little consideration for God's original purpose. Based on the details presented in my books *God's Eternal Purpose Volumes One and Two*, it was concluded that in principle, Yahweh's purpose surrounds a kingdom agenda. Basically, this plan is two-dimensional in that it includes the establishment of God's kingdom on the earth, along with a family of sons who conform or transform to the image of Jesus Christ. Based on this premise, the Father's overall purpose involves both a kingdom concept and a family concept. Thus, this represents "God's why" and is consequently the message of Scripture in its entirety; it is the subject of every promise, covenant, prophecy, and blessing contained in the Bible.

In accordance with the kingdom and family agenda, the Father instituted spiritual blessings for humanity, which we will discuss in the next chapter. However, the initial manifestation of the Father's purpose is evident in the first chapters of the book of Genesis. This book is foundational because it reveals the Father's original design for humanity and contains the seed of all Scripture. From the beginning, we see the institution of both a kingdom and family agenda.

IN THE BEGINNING

When Genesis 1:1 uses the term, "in the beginning," this serves solely as an introduction to the concept of time as we know it. This expression is a marker or an indicator of when time began because prior to this, the concept of time did not exist. Notice it says, "In the beginning God created." This stands to reason that He existed before "the beginning" or before time began. Therefore, anything that is subjected to time is also subjected to Him. In fact, Isaiah 57:15 points out that God dwells in eternity, which is not subjected to the notion or vicissitudes of time. Furthermore, Scripture reveals that certain components of the plan of God were carried out before the foundation of the world or before time began. To constitute this, Scripture uses words such as predestination or foreordained (Ephesians 1:4; Revelation 13:8). We will further this discussion in Chapter 2.

God created the concept of time to fulfill His kingdom purpose or to manifest what He had already predetermined in eternity. In essence, the concept of time represents a detour from eternity. Hence, time is a temporary instrument and once God's purpose is fulfilled, there will be a return to eternity and the idea of time will cease to exist. Ephesians 1:10 refers to this as the dispensation of the fullness of time or when time is complete. Another term for this is "the restitution of all things" (Acts 3:21). Therefore, when I use the term, "in the beginning" or "from the beginning," it is in reference to the introduction of time, which coincides with creation. Please see the diagram below for a summary of this concept.

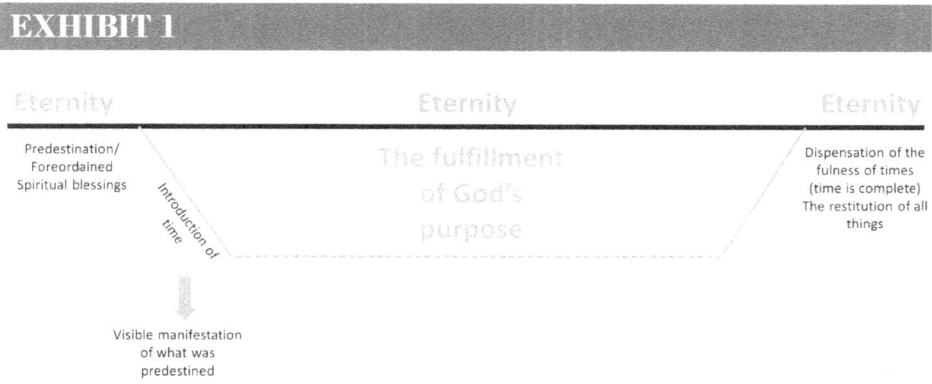

THE KINGDOM OF GOD AND THE HOUSE OF GOD

From the beginning, when God created the earth and subsequently man (humanity), He made a kingdom environment on the earth. Understanding this is fundamental because it sets the premise for the Father's purpose throughout the ages. This kingdom agenda is evident from Genesis 1:26, which states that man was given dominion over the earth. Of note, the word "dominion" is associated with the concept of kingdom rule rather than the tenets of democracy. The details of Genesis Chapter 1, therefore, represent a visible manifestation of God's kingdom agenda, which He had already predetermined in eternity.

> And God said, Let us make man in our image, after our likeness: and let them have dominion over the fish of the sea, and over the fowl of the air, and over the cattle, and over all the earth, and over every creeping thing that creepeth upon the earth. (Genesis 1:26)

The word "dominion" means:

- Control or the exercise of control
- The power to govern
- Sovereignty
- A territory or sphere of influence or control; a realm
- The territory subject to the control of a government

Based on the context of Genesis 1:26, combined with the definition of the word "dominion," we can conclude that in the beginning when God created the earth, He gave humanity government control over the territory called Earth. In principle, God set up His government on Earth and placed His son here in order to expand His kingdom dominion on Earth. He was in reality colonizing Earth with the kingdom of heaven. Additionally, it is important to note that as it pertains to our original purpose, when God created man, He made him in the capacity of a son (Luke 3:38). This establishes the premise that from the beginning, God's design was for humanity to have a relationship with Him. This also creates the concept of a Father-son affiliation. Consequently, from the beginning, we are presented with two circumstances relative to the purpose of God: a kingdom environment, as well as a family atmosphere, which then constitutes a house.

In short, from the beginning, there was the kingdom of God and the house of God. However, the kingdom and the house/family are interrelated as there is no distinct separation between the two. In fact, the house, which consists of the family, is an essential component of the kingdom. Therefore, in relation to the kingdom of God, the basic principle is that to *be a part or inheritor of the Kingdom, you must be a member of the house.* This is why Jesus told Nicodemus in John 3:3, "Except a man be born again, he cannot see (or partake) of the kingdom of God." Hence, without being a member of the house, you cannot be a part or an inheritor of the kingdom. Furthermore, in order to be a part of the house and be counted for an inheritance, you have to be a son. Hence, Adam in his capacity as a son was both a member of the kingdom of God, as well as a member of the house of God.

To order to have a better appreciation for the dynamics that existed from the beginning, it is necessary to examine the words "king," "kingdom," "father," "son," and "house," along with their attributes. In particular, the words "king" and "kingdom" provide us with a kingdom perspective; whereas "father," "son," and "house" point to the notion of family.

KING

- One that is supreme or preeminent
- A monarch (one who reigns over a state or territory)
- A male sovereign who is the official ruler of an independent state or nation

Some of the attributes of a king are as follows:

- Kings are not voted or elected to power and therefore cannot be voted out of power
- A king's reign is consistent with his life
- A king's authority is absolute.
- A king is the embodiment of the government of his kingdom

In many democracies, the three branches of government are the executive, the legislative, and the judiciary. For a democracy to function effectively and in the interest of the separation of powers, power is distributed among the three branches. However, in a monarchy, the king embodies all three branches, and his power is absolute and unquestionable. 1 Timothy 1:17 in acknowledgement of God as King says, "To the King eternal, immortal, invisible, the only wise God, be honor and glory forever and ever." In addition, Isaiah 57:15 refers to Him as, "The High and Lofty One who inhabits eternity." Therefore, with God being both King and eternal, His reign or His dominion is everlasting. He had no predecessor or successor. Moreover, with dominion being the inherent right of the King, when God bestowed this privilege to humanity (Genesis 1:26), He essentially created a kingdom environment on Earth and extended His government influence on Earth.

KINGDOM

The acknowledgement of God as King brings us to the discussion of His kingdom. Whereas democracy is the government of the people, by the people, and for the people, a kingdom is distinctly different. According to *Merriam-Webster's Dictionary*, the word "kingdom" means:

- A politically organized community or major territorial unit having a monarchical form of government headed by a king or queen

As it pertains to God's kingdom, Scripture speaks of the kingdom of God and the kingdom of heaven. While there is much debate on whether the two are the same, Scripture offers the perspective that they both refer to the same thing and are used interchangeably in the Gospels for identical discussions. For example, Luke 6:20 says, "Blessed be ye poor: for yours is the kingdom of God." However, Matthew 5:3, in referencing the same conversation says, "Blessed are the poor in spirit: for theirs is the kingdom of heaven." First, the expression kingdom of God acknowledges the fact that God has a kingdom. As a King, it ascribes kingdom ownership or dominion to Him.

In support of this, the term kingdom of heaven identifies the extent or range of the kingdom over which God rules. In 1 Kings 8:27, Solomon, while dedicating the temple said, *"But will God indeed dwell on the earth? Behold, the heaven and heaven of heavens cannot contain thee."* Also, Deuteronomy 10:14 says, *"Behold, the heaven and the heaven of heavens is the LORD'S thy God, the earth also, with all that therein is."* Furthermore, the phrase kingdom of heaven creates a comparison between the kingdoms of the earth, which are limited in scope, and God's heavenly kingdom, which is infinite. For example, at the height of its power, the Kingdom of Great Britain covered an area of almost one-quarter of the world's population and basically the same percentage of the earth's total land area. It was an identifiable realm or territory. In describing the expanse of the empire, the phrase, "The empire on which the sun never sets," was often used. This was an indication that the sun was always shining on at least one of its territories. Despite the vastness of the kingdom of Great Britain, it could still be defined. However, to identify the magnitude of God's kingdom, the word "heaven" is used making it boundless.

In summary, the kingdom of God conveys who the government belongs to while the kingdom of heaven explains the extent of His dominion. To put it another way, one is possessive and the other is descriptive. Now that we have a better understanding of the kingdom position that existed from the beginning, let us look at the family environment, which points to the house of God.

FATHER

With the kingdom as a foundation, from this premise came the existence of a family. A monarchial form of government is family-based and rulership is a family affair. In accordance with Scripture, this consists of a Father and sons, which therefore constitutes a house. As stated earlier, Luke 3:38 identifies Adam as "the son of God" from the perspective of creation. Hence, this designates God as Father and consequently produced a Father-son relationship. The word "father" means the following:

- Head or founder of a household or family
- One who imparts life and is committed to it
- One in intimate connection and relationship
- The progenitor of a people
- A person who has originated or established something

Father, therefore, constitutes a household or family with an atmosphere of intimacy and relationship. Indeed, many acknowledge God as Creator, but from the perspective of a son, Father speaks of something far more significant. Therefore, from the beginning, God's intent was not only to have a kingdom environment but also to have a family. This household consisted of a family of sons.

SON

The identification of Adam as a son is noteworthy because it represents God's intent and purpose for humanity based on what He predetermined in eternity. In fact, it serves as the highest designation that can be attributed to us. Being a son is significant because as it pertains to a family, it carries with it a certain status, along with specific responsibilities and particular benefits. The magnitude of a son includes the following:

- A son is one who is in the role of his father to fulfill the father's life and purpose
- A son is an extension and a representative of the father
- A son declares his father's generation
- A son signifies a relationship
- A son denotes citizenship
- Inheritance is designated for sons

In consideration of the attributes of a son, Adam in this capacity was both a citizen of the kingdom of God and a member of the family/house of God. As God's representative on Earth, he was an extension of the Father to represent Him and fulfill His purpose. It is important to note that according to Scripture, the name "Adam" included both males and females. Therefore, the designation of a "son" in a kingdom environment and in relation to the house of God is not based on gender but pertains to all humanity. Thus, the concept of unity has always been incorporated into God's purpose.

1. This is the book of the generations of Adam. In the day that God created man, in the likeness of God made he him;
2. Male and female created he them; and blessed them, and called their name Adam, in the day when they were created. (Genesis 5:1-2)

HOUSE

For the most part, when we think of the word "house," the common reference surrounds a physical structure or building. However, based on its predominant use in Scripture, and in alignment with God's purpose, the word "house" means the following:

- A household
- A family
- A family of descendants
- All the persons forming one household (family)

Therefore, as it pertains to God's purpose, a house is an entity associated with both a family and a kingdom. For example, at present, the House of Windsor headed by Queen Elizabeth II is the reigning house of the United Kingdom and other commonwealth countries. Hence, the royal family represents both the house and the constituents of the kingdom. Similarly, the acknowledgement of God as Father and Adam in the capacity of a son signified a household or family. In addition, as this family existed in a kingdom environment it also made them a royal family.

To provide a better perspective of this affiliation, let us consider the words of the Davidic covenant. In 2 Samuel 7:16, the Lord said, "And thine house and thy kingdom shall be established for ever before thee: thy throne shall be established forever." There is always a correlation between the house and the kingdom or in this instance, the house of God and the kingdom of God.

Interestingly, purpose always answers the question: "Why am I here?" Therefore, from the beginning, God's purpose was to establish His kingdom on Earth and have a family or house of sons who represent Him and reflect His image. Wow! What an important statement, for throughout time, this purpose of unity and being reflections of the Father's image has not changed. This will become more apparent as we progress through this study.

SEPARATION FROM THE KINGDOM OF GOD AND THE HOUSE OF GOD

Based on the Father's original design, humanity belonged to both the kingdom of God and the house of God. As a son of the Father's house, Adam (humanity) enjoyed unity or oneness with the Father as well as a relationship, fellowship, and communion. However, as a result of disobedience, when Adam sinned, the result was death as mentioned in Genesis 2:15-17:

> 15. And the LORD God took the man, and put him into the garden of Eden to dress it and to keep it.
> 16. And the LORD God commanded the man, saying, Of every tree of the garden thou mayest freely eat:
> 17. But of the tree of the knowledge of good and evil, thou shalt not eat of it: for in the day that thou eatest thereof thou shalt surely die.

The death mentioned in the above passage refers to spiritual death and all its attributes, which also include physical death. Ephesians 2:1 refers to spiritual death as being dead in trespasses and sins. At its core, spiritual death simply means separation from God. Therefore, when Adam sinned, the following occurred relative to God's original purpose for humanity.

- Humanity was no longer citizens or constituents of the kingdom of God
- The kingdom dominion that was bestowed to humanity over the earth as an inheritance was forfeited and we no longer had dominion
- We became estranged from the Father's house or family and consequently lost our positions as sons
- Humanity lost unity or oneness with the Father along with relationship, fellowship, and communion with Him.

In summing up the consequences of the above, God's kingdom's influence on Earth was interrupted and another kingdom or government was introduced. Consequently, humanity became sons or citizens of this kingdom. Additionally, we also became sons of another house or family. This kingdom or dominion to which humanity was now subjected is referred to as the power or kingdom of darkness (Colossians 1:13). Furthermore, the change in house or family was a result of humanity being adopted by another father resulting in a change of heritage and relationship.

From a spiritual perspective, the characteristics and behaviors of the son will always be a reflection of the father with whom they are affiliated. This was evident in Jesus' conversation with the Pharisees in John 8:44 when He said to them, "Ye are of your father the devil, and the lusts of your father ye will do." Nevertheless, collectively, humanity now belonged to another kingdom and house. The diagram below provides a summary of this discussion.

EXHIBIT 2

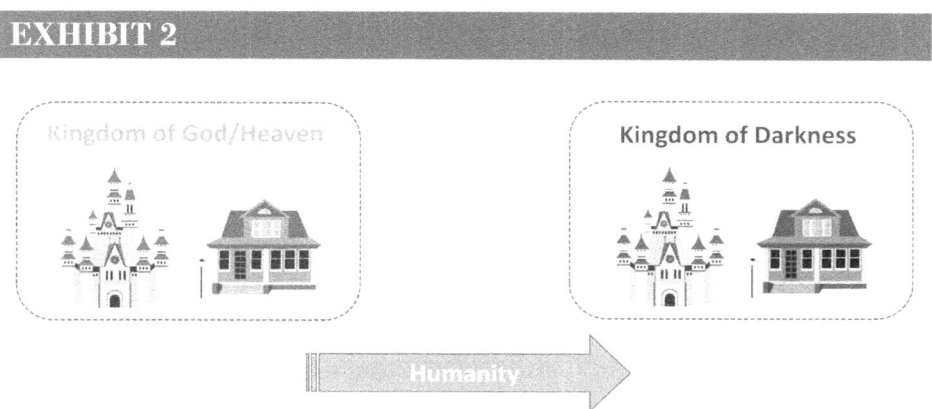

As a result of sin, humanity changed kingdoms, houses, and citizenship.
We were adopted by another father.
We became members of another family.

This entire scenario represented "somewhat of a detour" from God's original purpose for humanity but obviously, not in the true sense of the word. Nevertheless, from the point of man's disobedience in Genesis Chapter 3, the main objective of the rest of the Bible was dedicated to realigning humanity to God's original purpose. This involved reinstating humanity to God's kingdom and the Father's house. However, recall that before the foundation of the world, the Father had already predetermined the destiny of humanity. Hence, with this being immutable or unchangeable, humanity's realignment to God's kingdom and house was definite. In fact, the spiritual blessing that the Father predetermined in Christ before the world began served as a guarantee of this fulfillment (Ephesians 1:3-14). Before man's disobedience, the Father created a package of blessings for us in accordance with His determinate counsel. He did it based on His determined purpose for us.

REALIGNMENT TO GOD'S PURPOSE

The word "realignment" means to put back in proper order or to have a new orientation. It is the act of restoring something to its previous position or state. In using a practical example, whenever an organization determines that it needs realignment, it is communicating that it must go back to its core values or original purpose. It is simply reacquainting its stakeholders with its "why." This also requires a change in culture. This is often necessary because, over the years, influences are introduced to the organization that cause the company to veer from its original purpose. One of the tools used to accomplish realignment is the company's vision and mission statement.

In short, the vision statement expresses an organization's ultimate goal and the reason for its existence. It states the company's "why." The mission statement supports the vision and defines how the organization plans to accomplish the vision. It says who and how. Similarly, God's vision or purpose from the beginning has not changed. According to Scripture, it is the establishment of His kingdom on Earth with a family of sons who reign and rule with Him. Therefore, Christ came proclaiming the vision of the Father. He supported this by being the "who" and "how." He made it possible for humanity to be realigned with the original purpose of the Father. Hence, Jesus came with the following mandate:

- The reestablishment of the kingdom of God on Earth. Consequently, humanity could become citizens of God's kingdom
- Reinstatement of humanity into the Father's house. This was accomplished by His death and adoption into the family of God by the Spirit of adoption
- The restoration of humanity to our original position as sons of God
- Reconciliation of humanity with the Father (by atonement) thereby once again creating unity, oneness, relationship, fellowship, and communion with Him

Christ came with God's "why," which was established from the beginning and predetermined before the world or time began. He came as the last Adam (1 Corinthians 15:45-47) in the volume of the Scriptures to fulfill the original purpose of the Father. *He did not come with a new idea; He came to realign humanity to God's purpose.* For this reason, throughout the New Testament and in harmony with God's original purpose, we see words with the prefix "re" meaning "do again" or "go back" to the original state. For example, there are words such as "repent," "redemption," "restore," "reformation" "restitution," and "reconciliation." These all indicate a return to what was originally predetermined by the Father.

In recognition of God's purpose, Jesus' signature message throughout the Gospels was concerning the kingdom of God. In fact, from the onset, this was abundantly clear as His initial declaration in Matthew 4:17 was, "Repent: for the kingdom of heaven is at hand." The word "repent" basically means to change your mind based on a feeling of regret or remorse. Notice that Jesus didn't just come with the call for repentance, but this was accompanied by the message of the kingdom of heaven. Therefore, in principle, Jesus' message was, "Change the way you think for God's original idea of the kingdom is being reintroduced." Thus, the message He taught was directed at changing or realigning the minds of the people in accordance with the culture of the kingdom of heaven. In doing so, Jesus introduced the teaching in Matthew Chapter 5 which said, "Ye have heard…but I say unto you." In essence, He was saying, "You have been conditioned and programmed to think a certain way, and it is reflected in your behavior. However, based on the core values of the kingdom of God, I am here to conduct a reorientation. The purpose of this is to harmonize the way you think and your behavior with the principles of the kingdom of God.

In the aggregate, the predominant message of Matthew, Mark, and Luke is the kingdom of God or the kingdom of heaven. With precision, they are abundantly clear in communicating the culture and nature of the kingdom. To explain the kingdom, they all use an array of natural and everyday examples. For the most part, they begin with the expression, "The kingdom of heaven or the kingdom of God is like such and such." On the other hand, the concentration of the Gospel of John is also the kingdom of God but particularly, the perspective of the Father-Son relationship within a kingdom environment. With greater concentration, this Gospel conveys the message of the house of God or the Father's house. More so than any of the other Gospels, John is dedicated to portraying Christ as the Son in a family atmosphere. Therefore, even in the communication of the Gospels, the original purpose of the Father is evident. Combined, the four Gospels declare both the message of the kingdom of God and the message of the Father's house.

In summary, not only was Jesus reintroducing the kingdom of God on Earth, but this also included the assignment of restoration. Christ was therefore charged with the responsibility of restoring humanity to His kingdom and the Father's house or the family of God. However, a sacrifice was required to make the reconciliation possible.

GATHERING US TOGETHER

In harmony with God's original purpose, John 11:52 says that Jesus' purpose through His death was to "gather together in one the children of God that were scattered abroad." Concisely, this verse embodies everything that has been presented to this point as it pertains to the purpose of God. With sin separating us from God, this verse echoes the same message of reconciliation and restoration. The term "gather together" means to join in one those previously separated or divided. Therefore, as humanity was separated from the Father, His kingdom, and His house, Jesus was tasked with reuniting us with Him. Furthermore, the word "children" in the verse is the Greek word *teknon*, which means sons. Thus, the verse reiterates the fact that the purpose of Jesus' death was to reunite the sons with the Father. Consequently, He was simply reintroducing God's agenda from the beginning.

As a son, the first Adam was responsible for forfeiting the kingdom dominion he was given and alienating humanity from the family of God. Therefore, when the last Adam (Jesus Christ) came, also in the capacity of a Son, He came representing the kingdom of God and the Father's house or family. As the representative of the Father's house, He says in John 14:2, "In my Father's house are many mansions: if it were not so, I would have told you. I go to prepare a place for you." This was really a message of restoration to the family of God. In essence, He was saying, "You have the opportunity of dwelling in or being a member of My Father's house. However, only sons have the privilege of being regarded as members of the family. To incorporate you into My Father's family, I have to go away or die." Thus, Jesus prepared a place for us or restored us to the Father's house through His death. His sacrifice made it possible for humanity to be restored to our highest designation of sons.

Evidently, John 14:2 has nothing to do with going to heaven or "mansions" in heaven. Rather, it is the message of reconciliation and restoration with the Father and the Father's house or family. Through Christ, we can once again be members of the family of God. For more on this please check out my book, *Are There Really Mansions in Heaven? It's a Family Affair*. Romans 8:15 says once we receive the Holy Spirit or the Spirit of adoption, which makes us sons of the Father's house, we cry Abba, Father. Galatians 4:6-7 adds,

6. And because ye are sons, God hath sent forth the Spirit of his Son into your hearts, crying, Abba, Father.
7. Wherefore thou art no more a servant, but a son; and if a son, then an heir of God through Christ.

The diagram below provides a summary of this discussion.

EXHIBIT 3

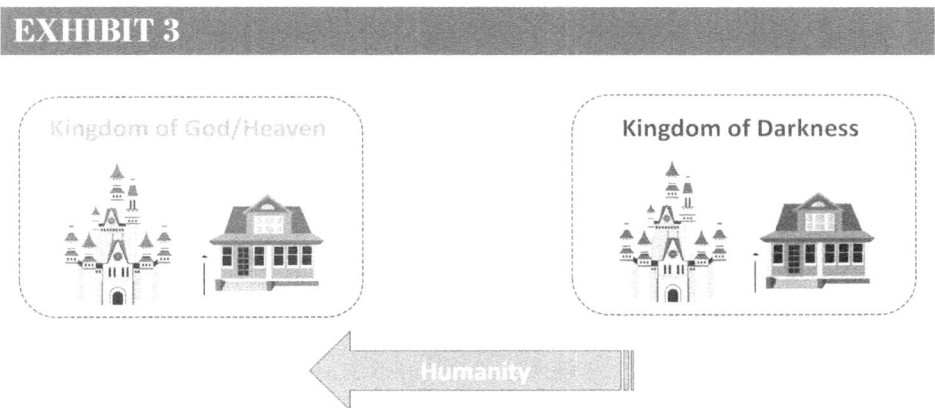

As a result of Christ's sacrifice, He made it possible for humanity to change kingdoms, houses, and citizenship.
We can be adopted by the Father.
We can become members of His house/family.

A SON RESTORED

In consideration of the Father's original purpose and the message of humanity's restoration as a son, Jesus offers a parable in Luke 15:11-32, which adequately encapsulates this position. With Jesus' principal message being the kingdom of God, this account, which is commonly referred to as *The Prodigal Son*, is a practical illustration that speaks of a son being restored to both the Father's house and the kingdom of God. Therefore, this parable serves as the perfect summation of all we have discussed in this chapter.

The parable describes the disposition of a son who forfeits his inheritance and becomes estranged from his father's house. After going through a period of destitution and hopelessness, something transformed his manner of thinking. He no longer saw himself as a son but took on the disposition of a servant. Therefore, not only did he lose his inheritance, but he also resigned himself to be less than he was intended to be. Consequently, with this adopted thinking, he said, "How many hired servants of my father's house have bread enough and to spare, and I perish with hunger?"

With a repentant heart he said, "I will go to my father and say to him, "Father, I have sinned against heaven and before thee, and am no more worthy to be called thy son, make me as one of thy hired servants" (Luke 15:18). What is interesting is that when he decided to return to his father, he was thinking he was not worthy to be restored to the position of a son. Nevertheless, being a son was his inherent position, so even though his disposition had changed, the father's intent for him did not.

Anticipating his son's return, the father, while seeing him afar off had compassion on him, ran to him, fell on his neck, and kissed him. This is a demonstration of the father's love and sympathy for his son. His kiss was not only a sign of affection but also one of reconciliation and forgiveness. Despite the son's conviction that he was no longer worthy to be called a son, the father had a different perspective. In fact, as an indication of complete restoration as a son, the father placed the best robe on him, put a ring on his finger and shoes on his feet. In particular, the ring was a sign of dignity and favor, which further validated his restoration as a son. Moreover, to celebrate his son's return, the father had the fatted calf killed saying, "My son was dead and is alive again; he was lost and is found." This statement is again repeated after the elder son took exception to the festivities commemorating the return of the son.

In its entirety, this declaration of the father captures the message of reconciliation and restoration of a son to the Father's house and the kingdom of God. It speaks of unity with the Father in accordance with His purpose from the beginning.

The intent of this chapter was to provide an understanding of God's "why" by explaining His purpose for humanity. Before we get consumed in the "what" as it pertains to ministry gifts, the "why" must be prioritized. With the kingdom of God and the family of God as the foundation, it is within this context that the gifts exist. Hence, the purpose of the gifts is best understood based on what the Father predetermined for humanity before the foundation of the world. If we do not know the destiny He has determined for those in Christ, it would be difficult to be the agent to assist in fulfilling it. In other words, if we are ignorant of the specifics of His purpose, then our effectiveness as leaders will be impaired. On that note, in the next chapter, we will discuss in greater detail what the Father has predetermined for humanity or the spiritual blessings in Christ.

GOD'S PURPOSE: PREDESTINATION, SPIRITUAL BLESSINGS, AND ENLIGHTENMENT

THE BOOK CONTEXT

It is imperative that leaders, in particular, understand the big picture to be effective in ministry. In its entirety, the Word of God represents the written documentation of God's purpose and His intent for humanity. It is a comprehensive offering, which reveals the Father's heart and mind. Therefore, acquaintance with His purpose for us requires a firm understanding of Scripture.

Contrary to the practice and opinion of many, the Bible is not a storybook from which to extract mere moral lessons or a colorful sermon. Indeed, the Bible contains many illustrations of human behavior to aid us in our daily lives. However, embedded in the accounts is the significance of God's purpose or His grand design. Most importantly, it is the blueprint for His purpose. Therefore, while looking at the trees, let us not miss the importance of the forest.

On that note, 2 Timothy 3:16 says, "All Scripture is given by inspiration of God." The term "inspiration of God" is the Greek word *theopneustos*, which means divinely breathed in. Therefore, to communicate His purpose or His "why" to humanity, the Father breathed the contents of Scripture into certain individuals. 2 Peter 1:20 puts it another way and says holy men spoke as they were moved by the Holy Spirit. Hence, contained in Scripture is a detailed conveyance of God's why.

When we read the Word of God, we are actually reading His purpose and intent. Additionally, within the overall framework of the purpose of God, each book of the Bible is designed to convey a certain message or a predominant subject. Like pieces of a puzzle or parts of a whole, they all contribute a particular component resulting in a complete picture. Within the discipline of rightly dividing the Word of God, this principle is referred to as "The Book Context." This simply means that each book of the Bible has a predominant theme running through its chapters. For example, the focus of the book of Galatians is to highlight the differences between the things related to the Spirit and those associated with the flesh. Throughout the book, there is great consistency in expressing this distinction with its usage of statements, examples, and allegories. One of the pivotal questions that summarize the general theme of the book is Galatians 3:3, which says, "Are you so foolish? Having begun in the Spirit, are you now made perfect by the flesh?" Therefore, as it pertains to fulfilling the purpose of the Father, the book serves as an admonishment for His sons to walk in the Spirit as opposed to walking after the flesh.

In a similar fashion, the book of Ephesians subscribes to precise communication relative to the purpose of God. Hence, to understand the five-fold ministry gifts mentioned in Ephesians Chapter 4, attention first has to be given to the dominant discussion of the book of Ephesians. In this regard, the underlying theme of the book of Ephesians centers on the message of God's purpose and unity in Christ. Therefore, what distinguishes it from the other books is that it is very deliberate in specifically announcing the precise details and intent of God's purpose. It provides insight into the mind of God and enlightenment that there is indeed a masterplan. In my opinion, Ephesians stands at the crossroad of Scripture, taking into account all that has been predetermined by the Father and bringing it into focus. It compresses His eternal purpose into six concise chapters and says that the main objective of the Father is *unity in Christ.* Undoubtedly, anyone who is persuaded that they are called by God to function in ministry, especially in a leadership capacity, must have a good understanding of what Ephesians is expressing. It contains the mind of the Father and the mandate for those chosen to fulfill His purpose. How can you function as an apostle, prophet, evangelist, pastor, or teacher if you are ignorant concerning God's eternal purpose?

As stated, to be effective in a corporate environment, employees must embrace and embody the vision and mission of the company. However, if they are unaware of what they are, they will not align with the company's goals even though they are employees. In this regard, the book of Ephesians represents God's mission and vision statement for His leaders and humanity in general.

When it comes to gifts of Christ, the attention is often directed toward Ephesians Chapter 4 with little consideration for the context of the entire book. However, it is important to note that the exchange in Ephesians Chapter 4 exists within the environment of what is being discussed in the entire book. In other words, the *passage context* exists within the *book context*. Therefore, to have a proper perspective of the purpose of the gifts, it behooves us to examine the entire context of Ephesians.

EPHESIANS: THE OVERVIEW

- Ephesians Chapter 1 provides the perspective that God has a predetermined plan for humanity before the world began. This is defined within the context of spiritual blessings in Christ.
- Ephesians Chapter 2 informs us that God's plan is for all humanity (Jews and Gentiles). It promotes the message of unity by emphasizing one body and one house.
- Ephesians Chapter 3 says the plan of God that was previously a mystery or hidden is now being revealed. It summarizes all the elements of the plan of God as "God's eternal purpose." Additionally, it is based on the plan of God that ministers are appointed.
- Ephesians Chapter 4 continues the concept of unity and states that to accomplish what He has predetermined, Christ gave gifts to humanity. Therefore, there is a correlation between God's eternal purpose and the purpose of the gifts.

- Ephesians Chapter 5, in conveying the message of unity, uses the practical relationship of a marriage between a man and a woman to illustrate the relationship between Christ and the church. Furthermore, in highlighting the relationship between Christ and the church, Christ's purpose is to have a glorious church or bride, one that is holy and without blemish.
- Ephesians Chapter 6 after providing righteous instructions for various relationships, admonishes believers to put on the whole armor of God to stand against the craftiness of the devil.

As we progress throughout this book, Ephesians will serve as a compass for the overall discussion of the gifts of Christ.

SPIRITUAL BLESSINGS

Again, I reiterate that the gifts of Christ exist to fulfill the purpose of the Father. Therefore, to properly function in the gifts, we have to understand His purpose. In this regard, Ephesians Chapter 1 takes us into the mind of the Father and reveals what He predetermined for humanity. From the onset, the epistle begins with the acknowledgment that the Father did something significant on our behalf. It says that "He hath blessed us with all spiritual blessings in heavenly places in Christ." First, the word "blessings" is the Greek word *eulogia* from which we get the English word eulogy, which means a formal expression of praise, approval, or commendation. Hence, before the foundation of the world, the Father made a favorable decree on our behalf or blessed us. Furthermore, in the interest of not dismissing the importance of any word, Ephesians 1:3 indicates specifically that the Father *hath* blessed us. This is an indication of an action that was taken; it describes an occurrence as opposed to a continuous action. Consequently, there are no further blessings that the Father has to prescribe for humanity as the blessings have already been bestowed.

In reality, everything we can petition Him for, He has already granted. Furthermore, the "spiritual blessing" mentioned in the verse is a singular blessing and points to *one of something*. Hence, even though there are several components to the blessing, it is still a solitary comprehensive blessing. In other words, it is all-inclusive. Additionally, with the inclusion of the word "all," the blessing is indeed holistic in that God left nothing out. This also means that He does not need to amend or improve what He originally determined. Therefore, the Father *has already* prescribed a single comprehensive blessing for humanity in heavenly places in Christ Jesus.

In using a practical example, the word "comprehensive" when used to explain auto insurance means that it covers a wide array of events relative to your motor vehicle. Unlike third-party insurance, which is limited in scope, comprehensive insurance is all-encompassing protection for your motor vehicle. Moreover, Ephesians states that the blessings are distinctly *in* Christ, which speaks of a place or position. Therefore, to be a beneficiary of the blessings, you must be *in* Christ or unified with Him. Being in Christ is the same as "putting on Christ" or "being one spirit with Him." Hence, even though the blessings have already been prescribed for humanity, to be a partaker of the blessings, you must be in Christ, for outside of Him blessings do not exist.

Additionally, the inclusion of the adjectives "spiritual" and "heavenly" to describe the type of blessings creates a contrast between blessings that are natural and earthy. In today's religious environment with an enormous focus on material blessings, the premise is established that as it pertains to God's purpose, the prevailing principle is spiritual blessings. To be clear, spiritual blessings are those designed to benefit our human spirits. As we will discover in reviewing the components of the blessings, they all enrich us spiritually. In addition, they are in heavenly places, which reinforces the fact that the benefits supersede those of an earthly nature. Moreover, these blessings are not based on merit but are in accordance with what the Father determined before the foundation of the world.

The term, "before the foundation of the world" not only signifies the blessings were foreordained before time began but that they were also not decided based on human endeavors. On that note, Isaiah 46:10 reveals that God established the end of His plan from the beginning and from ancient times the things that are not yet done. Therefore, in eternity past, before Genesis 1:1 declared the words, "in the beginning," the Father established His purpose for humanity and therefore ordained spiritual blessings for us. The blessings were bestowed according to His eternal purpose. *When God created humanity, He did so based on these blessings.* Hence, the Father ordained spiritual blessings for humanity, and contained within these blessings was His purpose. In truth, the blessings are His purpose.

Another example of this format is provided in the account of Isaac and Jacob in Genesis Chapter 27. In Genesis 27:28-29 when Isaac blessed Jacob, contained within the blessing was his destiny. Now that we understand that the spiritual blessings reveal God's purpose for humanity, let us look at the blessings in detail to get a perspective of the Father's purpose for us. However, keep in mind that these blessings are only realized in Christ.

SPIRITUAL BLESSINGS (INSIGHT INTO GOD'S PURPOSE)

As we examine each of the spiritual blessings, it will become apparent that collectively, they provide a detailed picture of the Father's purpose, which He orchestrated through Christ. As a single offering, they are indeed comprehensive in that they embrace every promise and covenant of the Father. As mentioned earlier, they are specifically designated as spiritual blessings because their objective is higher than natural blessings. They are customized for our inner man.

> A. ***The Father chose us in Him before the foundation of the world that we should be holy and without blame before Him in love.*** The first spiritual blessing is the fact that the Father chose us; to be chosen by Him is a blessing. The word "chosen" is the Greek word *eklegomai*, which means to pick or choose for one's self. Therefore, before the foundation of the world, the Father selected humanity for Himself. Furthermore, not only did He choose us, but He did so in a specific capacity, which is holy and without blame because of His love. In other words, the Father made the determination that we would be like Him and therefore possess His very nature and character. In essence, He simply wanted to duplicate Himself through humanity. 2 Peter 1:3-4 is

a great companion scripture to this blessing and provides a significant overview of what the Father did.

> 3. According as his divine power hath given unto us all things that pertain unto life and godliness, through the knowledge of him that hath called us to glory and virtue:
> 4. Whereby are given unto us exceeding great and precious promises: that by these ye might be partakers of the divine nature. (2 Peter 1:3-4)

The exceeding great and precious promises that are based on spiritual blessings made it possible for humanity to share in the Father's divine nature. As a result of being born of the Father, we can be like Him. Consequently, when the Father looks at us, He sees a reflection of Himself. Notice that Ephesians 1:4 says our condition of being holy and without blame before God is a result of the Father's love for us. This also means that when He sees us, He does so from the perspective of His love. Therefore, despite man's disobedience, the position of the Father has not changed. Additionally, this specific blessing of the Father choosing us sets the premise for all those mentioned in the remainder of Ephesians Chapter 1.

This blessing also involves being transformed into the image or character of Jesus Christ. The Father choosing us to be holy and without blame before Him in love is positional, but it also has a functional aspect to it, for the Lord also predetermined we would be conformed to the image of Jesus Christ (Romans 8:29). This speaks of transformation and maturity, which is necessary to manifest His character. This will be discussed in detail in Chapter 13.

B. ***The Father predestinated us unto the adoption of children by Jesus Christ to Himself.*** Not only did the Father choose us, but this blessing indicates that He did so in a specific capacity. The word "predestinated" means to foreordain for a divine purpose or to determine the future of something beforehand. The word points to the fact that God settled our destinies in advance. Hence, before the foundation of the world or before time began, the Father determined that all humanity would be adopted as His children. He predestinated us unto the adoption of children by Jesus Christ unto Himself. To be clear, this predestination is not limited to a selective group of people. Rather, it is designed for all humanity.

Adopting us as children also places God in the capacity of Father and humanity in the position of sons. Therefore, this spiritual blessing carries with it the significance of a relationship with God within the framework of a family or household. The word "adoption" is the Greek word *huiothesia*, which is a combination of two words, *huios* meaning "son" and *tithemi* meaning "placement." Hence, it means the placement or installation of a son.

Before the foundation of the world, God had an installation ceremony where He adopted us as His sons. Adoption is a legal term that means the voluntary act of legitimately taking a child and caring for him/her as your own. Thus, Scripture uses the word "adoption" in reference to us as sons of God because it is a formal and legal declaration that God is our Father. We have complete rights as children including inheritance.

Being a son of God is a spiritual blessing and a privileged position. Accordingly, 1 John 3:1 says, "Behold, what manner of love the Father hath bestowed upon us, that we should be called the sons of God." In accordance with God's purpose, as sons born of His incorruptible seed (Holy Spirit), we inherently receive the genes and characteristics of our Father (1 Peter 1:23). Consequently, we are also made partakers of His divine nature (2 Peter 1:4) capable of being holy and without blame before Him in love.

Romans 8:15 says that the adopting agent is the Spirit of adoption or the Holy Spirit. Once we receive Him, we become sons and consequently cry Abba, Father. Being a son speaks of several things including a relationship with the Father, being members of His house or household, as well as citizens of His kingdom. As mentioned previously, in terms of designations, a son is the highest appointment humanity can be assigned and is not gender-specific. In addition, a son is an extension and representative of the Father. Therefore, when the question is asked in Psalm 8:4, "What is man, that thou art mindful of him?" The answer is that from eternity, before the world began, the Father considered us sons who possess His nature. When He thinks of us, He sees His eternal purpose. He sees us as members of His house and citizens of His kingdom. This is all according to the good pleasure of His will. In other words, this is what He wanted to do, and it pleased Him.

C. Moreover, Ephesians 1:6 in accordance with the spiritual blessings says that *the Father hath made us accepted in the beloved or Jesus Christ*. As with the other components of the blessing, the language used here also denotes that the act occurred in time past. The word "accepted" means that He has highly favored us or honoured us with blessings in Christ. This is a general statement of the Father's love and consideration for us. It also means that the Father has endued us with special honour and pursued us with grace. As mentioned, this act of acceptance was not based on what we did but in keeping with His purpose. According to human standards, the act of acceptance is generally based on conformity to a particular norm. However, the Father accepted us in Christ before we were even created. This, therefore, represents a significant component of the spiritual blessing.

D. In continuing with the comprehensive nature of the spiritual blessings, Ephesians 1:7 says that "*we have redemption through His blood, the forgiveness of sins according to the riches of His grace.*" Therefore, the spiritual blessings bestowed by the Father also include redemption through the blood of Christ and forgiveness of sins. This is indeed extraordinary because not only did the Father choose us, adopt us as sons, and accept us in Christ before the foundation of the world, but He also made provision for restoration and reconciliation. 1 Peter 1:18-20 says,

18. Forasmuch as ye know that ye were not redeemed with corruptible things, as silver and gold, from your vain conversation received by tradition from your fathers;
19. But with the precious blood of Christ, as of a lamb without blemish and without spot:
20. *Who verily was foreordained before the foundation of the world, but was manifest in these times for you.*

Before time began, Christ was foreordained to take away our sins. Therefore, Adam's transgression did not take God by surprise and He did not have to execute a contingency plan based on what transpired in Genesis Chapter 3. The Father did not have to enact an amendment to His purpose. The spiritual blessings God had already predetermined for humanity took into account Adam's transgression and the transgressions of all humanity. For this reason, Romans 5:16 says the free gift of grace is of many offenses to justification. Without question, redemption is a significant spiritual blessing, for without it, there would be no adoption into the family of God and consequently, we would not be sons. Unfortunately, we do not often consider redemption as a spiritual blessing, but it is.

The word "redeem" means the following:

- To deliver, buyback, or ransom
- To restore to honour worth or reputation
- To recover possession or ownership by payment of a price
- To recover from captivity especially by a money payment

In the context of salvation, it was the payment made to restore humanity from the power of sin's dominion. As a result of Adam's disobedience, humanity became members of another house and citizens of another kingdom. Consequently, we became slaves to sin or as Romans 7:14 puts it, we were "sold under sin." Therefore, a price had to be paid for our freedom or to restore humanity to the Father's house and His kingdom. Hence, in keeping with what was already done before the foundation of the world, Christ offered Himself as the payment to redeem us to the Father. Because the Father had already chosen us in Him, He also provided assurances for us. Therefore, through Christ's sacrifice, Colossians 1:13 says that the Father delivered us from the power or kingdom of darkness and translated us into the kingdom of His dear Son.

The inclusion of forgiveness in Ephesians 1:7 strengthens the discussion of redemption because it also speaks of being pardoned. The pardoning of sins refers to letting the offense go as if it had never been committed. This is in the same context as atonement, for Christ's act of redemption also has the power of reconciliation. From a human perspective, I could redeem you, but I do not necessarily have to restore you. Generally speaking, redemption says I paid the price to ransom you from the power that held you captive. However, redemption coupled with atonement speaks of something more significant. The word "atone" means to reconcile, which is to reestablish a close relationship, to reunite, or to restore harmony. Hence, it provides realignment with the original purpose. It is a condition that says the offense never occurred; therefore, there is a complete restoration.

Despite Adam's transgression, this speaks of the reinstatement of our status as sons in accordance with God's original purpose. For example, in our judicial system when a person previously convicted of an offense is pardoned and his/her record expunged, in the eyes of the law, the conviction has been erased. The Father has already chosen us and made us accepted in the beloved; thus, within His plan is the provision of reconciliation. This is why redemption and forgiveness are spiritual blessings. Furthermore, when we forgive others who have wronged us, we are, in fact, bestowing blessings upon them. We release them from debt and restore the relationship to its original state. Therefore, if the relationship has not been restored to its original state, then true reconciliation has not occurred.

According to riches of God's grace, Ephesians 1:9 says that the Father has made known unto us the mystery of His will according to His good pleasure, which He purposed in Himself. This is so amazing.

The word "will" in this instance is not a demand but signifies a gracious disposition toward something or a pleasure toward what is liked. Therefore, what the Father purposed or His will is based on the expression of His delight toward us. In fact, as the verse says, it is based on His good intent that He designed beforehand and purposed in Himself. Consequently, it is this will that He made known unto the church. What was once a mystery or a hidden thing has now been made known. In essence, the packaging of everything that we have discussed to this point can be categorized as "the mystery of God's will." Ephesians 3:9 puts it another way and says, "And to make all men see what is the fellowship of the mystery, which from the beginning of the world hath been hid in God who created all things by Jesus Christ." Therefore, once the Father determined His purpose or ordained spiritual blessings for humanity, He hid it in Himself or made it a mystery until the time to make it known. Hebrews 9:10 refers to this as the time of reformation.

In most cases, a well-constructed plan has a fundamental goal or an achievable end. God's purpose is no different. In this regard, Ephesians 1:10 reveals the culmination of God's plan, which He determined before time began. It says, "That in the dispensation of the fullness of times He might gather together in one all things in Christ, both which are in heaven, and which are on earth; even in him." On this note, while the church seems concerned with cultivating disunity by denominational isolation, in the end, the Father's primary purpose involves unity. One of the hallmarks of being in Christ as stated in Galatians 3:28 is that gender (male/female), ethnicity, and social status do not exist. Therefore, unity in the body or unity of the faith can only be accomplished when we are both aware of and aligned with the Father's purpose. This will be further detailed in Chapter 13. However, let us consider what Ephesians 1:10 is conveying.

First, recall from Chapter 1 of this book that God dwells in eternity, which is not subjected to time. However, He introduced the concept of time to facilitate the fulfillment of His kingdom purpose or the spiritual blessing that was ordained before time began. Within the overall concept of time, the Father has ordained seasons to fulfill His purpose. To this end, Acts 1:7 speaks of the times and seasons, which the Father has fixed by His own authority. Therefore, in the overall plan of God, He has determined particular times and seasons for which certain aspects of His plan would be revealed or carried out. An example of this in Scripture is Galatians 4:4-5, which says, "But when *the fullness of the time was come* God sent forth His Son, made of a woman, made under the law, to redeem them that were under the law, that we might receive the adoption of sons." Hence, at the set time determined by the Father, He sent Jesus into the world to redeem humanity, so we might be adopted as sons. Other instances are Mark 1:15 and Luke 21:24, which speak of an appointed time for the accomplishment of a specific purpose. Therefore, once God's overall purpose has been fulfilled, the notion of time will be irrelevant and cease to exist. Moreover, all the appointed seasons will be fulfilled. This is referred to in Ephesians 1:10 as the dispensation of the fullness of times or when the concept of time is complete. At this point, the Father is going to do something significant. He will gather together in one all things in Christ. This includes all things in heaven and on Earth. This speaks of a united fellowship where God is all in all (1 Corinthians 15:24-28). Specifically, this will occur at the end of the millennial reign of Christ when He shall deliver up the kingdom to the Father, having put an end to all rule, authority, and power. The word "dispensation" refers to the administration or management of a house or household affairs. Therefore, the administration of God will no longer be based on the concept of time or seasons but rather, from the perspective of eternity.

According to Genesis 1:14, the primary purpose of the lights in the firmament is to divide the day from the night. They are also given for time, signs, seasons, days, and years. In other words, they determine the time and seasons. However, Revelation 21:22 in reference to the New Jerusalem says the city will have no need for the sun or the moon, for the glory of God and the light of the Lamb are the light thereof. Therefore, because the concept of time will then be irrelevant, and the glory of God will provide light, these celestial bodies will no longer be necessary. Time will be complete. The Father's purpose from before time began was unity; this will be fully realized at the end of Christ's thousand-year reign, which is at the threshold of eternity.

E. After taking a slight detour to expound on the objective of the Father's overall purpose, Ephesians 1:11 continues the discussion on spiritual blessings and adds, "In whom (Christ) also we have obtained an inheritance being predestinated according to the purpose of Him who worketh all things after the counsel of His own will." As a component of the spiritual blessing, the Father decided before the world began that we would receive an inheritance. However, this endowment is premised on humanity being in the capacity of sons because inheritance is specifically designed for sons, which again is not gender-specific. Therefore, without first being designated as sons, there is no inheritance.

At this point, it should be evident that the elements of the spiritual blessings are in a particular succession. For instance, Ephesians 1:5 says we have been adopted by the Father, which makes us sons. As we are born of the Father, this also supports the perspective of a household or family environment. Therefore, as sons who have been redeemed and are now members of His household and kingdom, this makes us eligible for the inheritance mentioned in Ephesians 1:11. This is why Hebrews Chapter 9 says Christ not only provided eternal redemption but also eternal inheritance (Hebrews 9:11-15).

The inheritance is a constituent of the spiritual blessings mentioned in Ephesians 1:3; this means it is of the same nature as the blessings. Therefore, just as the blessings are spiritual so is the inheritance. Hence, the inheritance in harmony with the context of the chapter has nothing to do with natural or earthy possessions. As sons of God, by birthright, we are heirs and joint-heirs with Christ. For this reason, this speaks specifically about inheriting the kingdom of God, reigning, and ruling with Christ.

As a premise, the verse also adds that God works all things after the counsel of His own will. He is His own advisor and His will is the force that governs His effectual working. To make sound decisions, we sometimes seek the advice of others; however, as it pertained to God's will for humanity, He consulted with Himself and made His own determination. Another example of this is Acts 2:23, which says that the determinate counsel and foreknowledge of God delivered up Christ. This signifies that the purpose of the Father has specific boundaries and is clearly defined. Furthermore, God's predetermination is based on His foreknowledge, which as we have concluded is the awareness of something before it exists or occurs.

F. Additionally, not only did the Father bestow upon us an inheritance, but **He also sealed us with the Holy Spirit of promise, which Ephesians 1:14 refers to as the earnest of our inheritance until the redemption of the purchased possession.** This is certainly a loaded blessing, but what exactly does it mean?

First, let us examine the word "sealed" as it provides a practical illustration of the function of the Holy Spirit, relative to our inheritance. To appreciate what it means to be *sealed*, a somewhat nostalgic assessment is required. During ancient times, letters were sealed with wax, which bore the signature stamp of the owner. This practice was done in the interest of security or perseverance, as well as to identify the owner thereby conveying the authenticity of the letter. In essence, the seal served as the owner's trademark and verification that the letter came from him/her. Similarly, the Holy Spirit functions as a seal for believers thereby securing or preserving us for our inheritance. Moreover, the Spirit serves as the Father's trademark on our lives and the authentication or verification that we belong to Him. This is what Romans 8:9 means when it says, "Now if any man have not the Spirit of Christ, he is none of His." Therefore, the true testament that we belong to God is the presence and function of the Holy Spirit in our lives. 2 Timothy 2:19 says. "Nevertheless the foundation of God standeth sure, having this seal, the Lord knoweth them that are His. And, Let everyone that nameth the name of Christ depart from iniquity." Hence, functional righteousness or walking in righteousness is a manifestation of those who have the Holy Spirit or who bear the Father's seal.

In addition to serving as the seal of our inheritance, the Holy Spirit also serves as the earnest of our inheritance. The word "earnest" speaks of money or part of the purchase price given as a down payment and serves as an assurance that the full amount will be paid. Practically speaking, it is the same principle as placing a deposit on merchandise with the intent that the balance will be paid and the item collected at the appointed time. Similarly, the Holy Spirit functions as a pledge of our inheritance until the redemption of the purchased possession. In the context of the passage, what is the purchased possession? 1 Corinthians 6:19-20 says, "Know ye not that your body is the temple of the Holy Ghost which is in you, which ye have of God, and ye are not your own? For ye are bought with a price: therefore glorify God in your body, and in your spirit, which are God's."

As sons of God, we have been purchased or redeemed by the precious blood of Christ (1 Peter 1:18-21). Therefore, when we become born again, the Father essentially purchases us; our bodies and spirits belong to Him. At salvation, our spirits are quickened or made alive; however, we are subjected to a mortal body. In other words, our spirits have been redeemed but not our physical bodies. This is what Romans 8:20 means when it says the creature or the new man was made subject to vanity which refers to our mortal bodies. Hence, even though 2 Corinthians 5:17 says that in Christ we are new creatures, we still have the same earthy tabernacle.

According to 1 Corinthians 6:17, being born again also represents being joined to the Father or being one spirit with Him. Incorporating this with our previous discussion, being one with the Father is equivalent to being sealed or having His trademark. Therefore, the Lord will return for those who are one with Him or who bear His seal. However, as human beings, we are presently subjected to this mortal body. The redemption of the purchased possession will be complete when our mortal bodies are changed from mortal to immortality. In this regard, Romans 8:21 says, "The creature itself (the new man) also shall be delivered from the bondage of corruption (our mortal bodies) into the glorious liberty of the children of God." This is what 2 Corinthians 5:1 means when it says, "For we know that if our earthly house of this tabernacle were dissolved, we have a building of God, an house not made with hands, eternal in the heavens." This also speaks of being transformed when corruption shall put on incorruption. To this, 1 John 3:2 adds, "It does not appear what we shall be, but we know that when He shall appear, we shall be like Him, for we shall see Him as He is." In fact, all of creation is groaning for this very purpose.

Additionally, Romans 8:23 says, "And not only they, but ourselves also, which have the firstfruits of the Spirit, even we ourselves groan within ourselves, waiting for the adoption, to wit, *the redemption of our body.*" Hence, once the physical body has been redeemed, the transaction regarding us as the purchased possession will be completed. Seeing that flesh and blood cannot inherit the kingdom of God, which is our inheritance, corruption, therefore, must put on incorruption (1 Corinthians 15:50).

In summary, when the Lord purchased us, the transaction involved both our spirits and bodies, but the redemption was not complete as it did not include the transformation of our physical bodies. The Father regenerated our spirits when we received the Holy Spirit. This represented a down payment or seal as a guarantee that the purchase would be completed. Therefore, at the resurrection, when mortal puts on immortality, the redemption of the purchased possession will be finalized. However, the Lord can only complete the purchase for those He has left a deposit. Can you imagine going to the store to complete the purchase of an item and there is no record a deposit was left? This simply means you have no claim of ownership.

Not only did God establish His purpose, but He also provided His Holy Spirit as a guarantee for the fulfillment of His purpose. This reminds me of the circumstances surrounding the promise God made to Abraham. Hebrews 6:13 says that when God made the promise to Abraham, because He could swear by no greater, He swore by Himself. Hebrews 6:17 points out that He did this to show the inheritors of the promise the unchangeability of what He had determined. Hence, not only did God make the promise, but He also became its guarantor thereby interposing Himself in the plan.

As I mentioned at the beginning of this chapter, the book of Ephesians provides tremendous insight concerning God's purpose, which He hid in Himself before the world began. Therefore, what was once termed as the unsearchable riches of Christ is now being declared. The epistle is a revelation of God's why, His manifold wisdom and purpose for humanity. In summarizing what has been discussed to this point, the communication centered on the topic of spiritual blessings, which are shown in the diagram below.

EXHIBIT 4

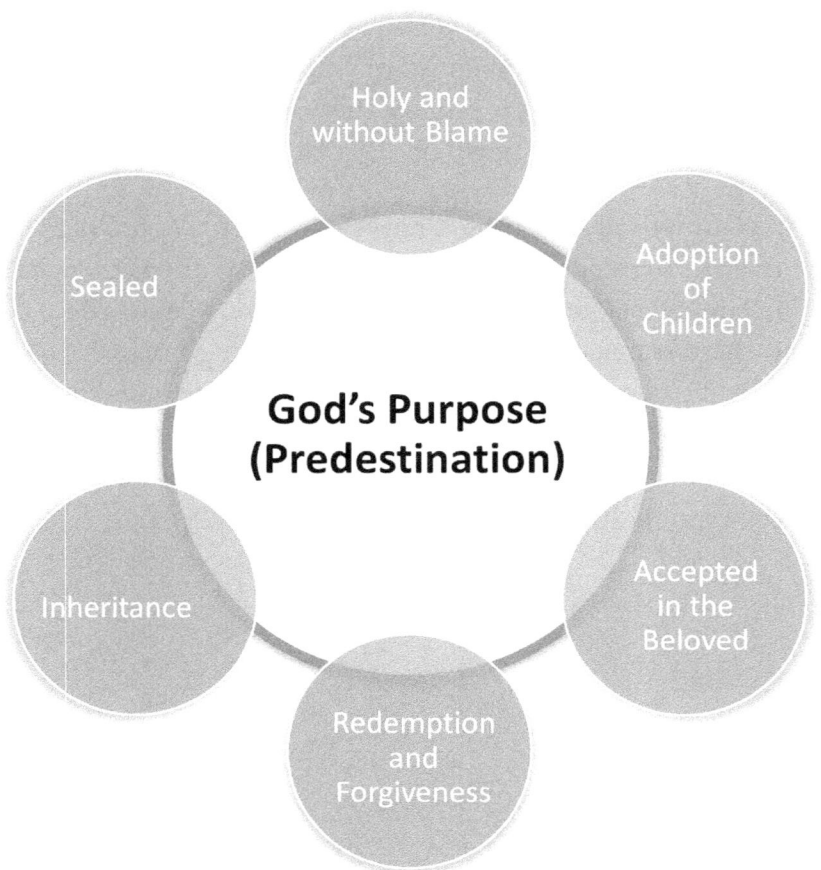

After outlining the details of the Father's purpose or the spiritual blessings, which He has determined for humanity, the apostle Paul then offers a prayer for believers.

ENLIGHTENMENT: THE SPIRIT OF WISDOM AND REVELATION

15. Wherefore I also, after I heard of your faith in the Lord Jesus, and love unto all the saints,

16. Cease not to give thanks for you, making mention of you in my prayers;
17. That the God of our Lord Jesus Christ, the Father of glory, may give unto you the spirit of wisdom and revelation in the knowledge of him:
18. The eyes of your understanding being enlightened; that ye may know what is the hope of his calling, and what the riches of the glory of his inheritance in the saints,
19. And what is the exceeding greatness of his power to us-ward who believe, according to the working of his mighty power,
20. Which he wrought in Christ, when he raised him from the dead and set him at his own right hand in the heavenly places,
21. Far above all principality, and power, and might, and dominion, and every name that is named, not only in this world, but also in that which is to come:
22. And hath put all things under his feet, and gave him to be the head over all things to the church,
23. Which is his body, the fulness of him that filleth all in all. (Ephesians 1:15-23)

The above petition is a classic example of a distinct difference between being knowledgeable of God's purpose and truly apprehending it. Paul had already outlined the Father's purpose earlier in the chapter, but he knew that alone was not enough. Therefore, He was advancing the conversation regarding God's purpose. Hence, after providing extensive details of God's purpose and spiritual blessings, he says, "I continuously appeal to the Father on your behalf." He prayed for them to come into the fullness of what God has purposed. Again, this is evidence that the development of God's people extends beyond the initial step of teaching or providing knowledge. With this in mind, Paul is saying, "Now that you know what the Father's purpose for you is, now that the curtain has been drawn, and you have insight into His heart and mind, my prayer is that you receive the spirit of wisdom and revelation in the knowledge of Jesus Christ." This is how we gain knowledge or understanding of the truth. Paul was not praying for God to give them anything new. He simply wanted them to be aware of what the Father had already done. Enlightenment removes the veil and causes us to experience the fullness of what the Father has determined for us.

Notice specifically that the spirit of wisdom and revelation pertains to having an understanding of Jesus Christ. This is because the blessings are directly related to Him. However, part of the challenge resides in a lack of awareness about what Christ came to do. Based on the context of Ephesians Chapter 1, everything the Father has predestinated for us is orchestrated through Christ. Therefore, as a Son, Christ is the representative of the Father to fulfill His life and purpose. Hence, to come into the fullness of what the Father has purposed and predetermined for us, we need the spirit of wisdom and revelation in the knowledge of Him.

What is the spirit of wisdom and revelation? First, the spirit of wisdom speaks of insight not obtained through natural means or based on human intelligence. It is an understanding that comes exclusively from divine insight. Furthermore, the spirit of revelation refers to the unveiling of something that was previously hidden but is now visible or known. Therefore, combined, they refer to receiving spiritual awareness beyond human comprehension or perception. Hence, once we are aware of what Christ came to do for us, something transpires within us. Ephesians 1:18 says the eyes of our understanding or our minds become enlightened; there is enlightenment. The diagram below provides a visual of this process.

EXHIBIT 5

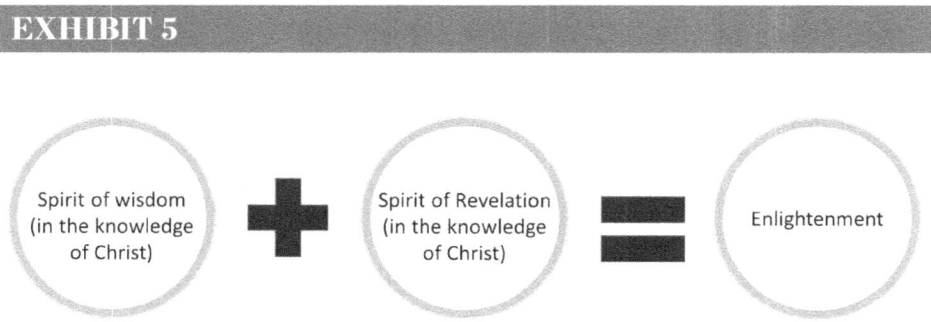

Providing a recap, first, we discussed that in the aggregate, God has a purpose. Then we detailed the specific spiritual blessings, which constitute that purpose. Next, Ephesians 1:18 says we need enlightenment to come into that purpose. Enlightenment, therefore, brings illumination to all the Father has predetermined and the spiritual blessings He has bestowed upon us.

The word "enlightened" means to illuminate or to bring to light. In simple terms, it means to know or understand. It is the ability to see. The word "enlightenment" has the prefix "en" which means "with" or "in." This is paired with the word "light," which means that which makes vision or understanding possible. Therefore, enlightenment provides understanding or illumination on the inside or in the heart/mind.

Enlightenment is a word that is often used in many circles to characterize a certain experience associated with awakening. For example, it was used to define an intellectual and philosophical movement in Europe during the 17th and 18th centuries. Also referred to as the Age of Reason, it was marked by the belief that science and logic provide more understanding than tradition or religion. Furthermore, the word is also used in Buddhism and Hinduism, to describe an awakening or a state of existence in which an individual transcends desire and suffering and attains nirvana or freedom. In particular, these perspectives of enlightenment are solely based on the human will and knowledge of self, which makes it a humanistic doctrine. However, as it pertains to the fulfillment of God's purpose, enlightenment is the product of receiving the spirit of wisdom and revelation in the knowledge of Jesus Christ. Once we are aware of or understand Christ's purpose then enlightenment occurs. It is a knowledge not based on intellect or the human will but one that influences and transforms our lives into the image of Christ.

Additionally, Matthew 13:15 in harmony with Ephesians 1:18 also explains how enlightenment occurs. It is agreed that we understand with our hearts or our minds. However, for the heart to have understanding, it requires eyes that can see and ears that can hear. Hence, as a principle, when our eyes are single, our entire bodies will be full of light or enlightened. A single eye, according to Matthew 6:22-23, speaks of being whole and dedicated to a single purpose, which is the will of God. It is a condition of being undivided. However, if the heart is torn between the things of God and the things of this world, then there can be no enlightenment. I would dare say the church is not apprehending God's purpose because it is serving both God and mammon. Consequently, there is no singleness of eye and enlightenment. Further to that, leaders in the body of Christ through their faith and prosperity messages have created a culture of wantonness in believers resulting in the pursuit of worldly things rather than the attainment of God's purpose. For more regarding this topic, please refer to my book *Faith: Who Hath Bewitched You*? What is interesting is that once we have been enlightened, it will be evident. Therefore, enlightenment carries with it a certain awareness.

1. We will know the hope of His calling.
2. We will know the riches of the glory of His inheritance in the saints.
3. We will know the exceeding greatness of His power toward us who believe.

In a more concise communication, Ephesians Chapter 1 is actually saying that as a result of enlightenment, we can apprehend that for which we have been apprehended by Christ (Philippians 3:12). Why did Christ apprehend us or take possession of us? The word "apprehend" speaks of purpose. Being apprehended by the Father is one thing. However, when we apprehend or understand why we have been apprehended, enlightenment occurs. Our purpose then becomes one with God's purpose, and we make it our own. In short, we comprehend God's "why." This is also what Philippians 3:14 refers to as "the mark for the prize of the high calling of God in Christ."

1. THE HOPE OF HIS CALLING

Enlightenment results in knowing the hope of the Father's calling. Categorically, the hope of His calling when compared to the pursuit of earthly endeavors or achievements is certainly a higher occupation. In general terms, a calling is a vocation or what you have been called to. In this instance, the word "calling" speaks to what we have been appointed or predestined to as sons of God. Additionally, the word "hope" means expectation. Therefore, we will know the expectation that He has predetermined for us or in simple terms, His purpose for humanity. It speaks of understanding or coming into the fullness of all the Father has ordained for us.

When the Father called or appointed us, what was His expectation? Was it one of mediocrity or greatness? At the risk of being repetitive, enlightenment results in us apprehending that for which we have been apprehended. Specifically, this surpasses the position of salvation and points to attaining the measure of the fullness of the stature of Christ (Ephesians 4:13). Enlightenment takes us on the journey from being children or babies to mature sons.

The fact that the Lord has made a predetermination for us represents a portion of the equation; however, when we are enlightened concerning the hope He has called us to, a metamorphosis occurs. We are changed from glory to glory into the image of Christ.

Notice particularly, it does not say the hope of our calling but rather, "the hope of His calling." Therefore, it is a position of purpose. Hence, once there is an awareness of His predetermined purpose, this translates to an understanding of what our purpose is. Moreover, we cannot realize our true purpose and potential without first having insight into and embracing His purpose. As believers, we hear countless teachings regarding understanding your purpose or living your best life. However, as sons of God, this is all predicated on embracing what He has predetermined for us. We must apprehend and align with the destiny He has already determined for us. The following diagram provides the transition of coming into purpose.

EXHIBIT 6

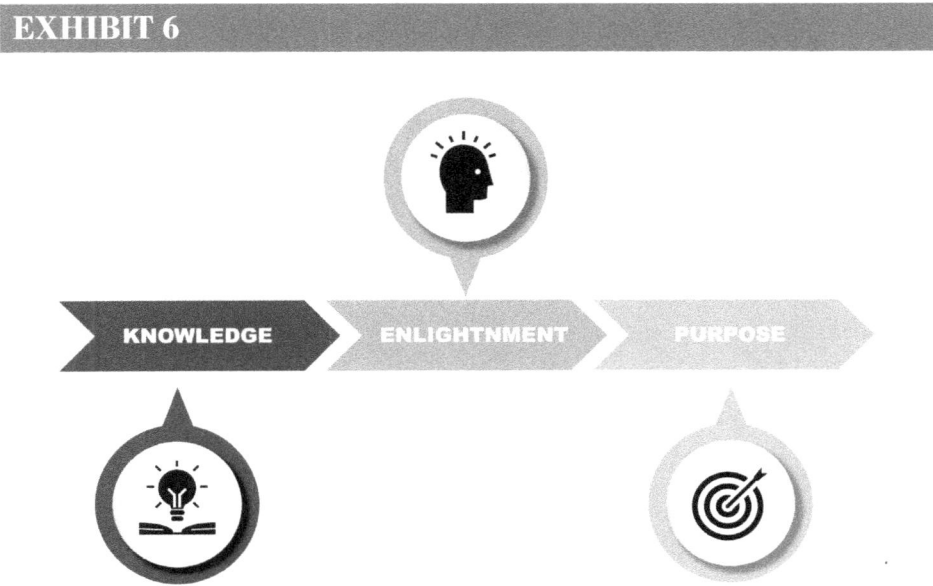

Earlier in this chapter, what the Father has called us to was outlined. Isn't it ironic that while in conversation with others, they sometimes convey a destiny for us that is greater than what we have prescribed or envisioned for ourselves? They see the potential in us that we have yet to attain. Similarly, the Father has ordained our destiny because our potential is based on the spiritual blessings He has already provided. Therefore, His expectation is in harmony with what He has already bestowed upon us. It is simply a matter of being enlightened.

Sometimes we have unrealistic expectations of people, but God does not. Based on the aggregate of the blessings and His destiny for us, He has set the expectation that His sons would come to the measure of the fullness of the stature of Christ. Therefore, if we have expectations of ourselves that are contrary to what the Father has ordained, it is because our eyes are not single, and we are serving two masters. We have not been enlightened. Also, some church leaders have set lower expectations for the sons of God thereby limiting and, in some cases, hindering them from realizing the Father's purpose. This is similar to the operation of the Pharisees in Luke 11:52, who took away the key of knowledge. They did not enter, and they hindered those who were entering.

It is not enough to simply be apprehended by Christ. Salvation is not the destination but is the beginning of the journey. It requires a certain disposition to know the hope of our calling or to apprehend that for which we have been apprehended. Based on Philippians Chapter 3, the requirement is counting as loss the things we have gained for the excellency of the knowledge of Jesus Christ. This includes letting go of fleshly affiliations, social status, and self-righteousness. The conversation on attaining the maturity of Christ will also be discussed in detail in Chapter 13.

2. THE RICHES OF THE GLORY OF HIS INHERITANCE IN THE SAINTS

Another consequence of being enlightened is knowing the riches of the glory of Christ's inheritance among the saints. Why does it require enlightenment to understand this? Recall Ephesians 1:11 says that as sons of the Father, we have obtained an inheritance that He has predetermined for us. As discussed earlier, this inheritance pertains to the kingdom of God, which is also our birthright.

To emphasize the magnitude of the inheritance, the passage uses the term "riches of the glory." The word "glory" speaks of magnificence, excellence, or the complete weight of honour. Hence, coupled with the word "riches," the phrase "riches of glory" conveys the wealth of the complete weight or the abundance of the inheritance. In other words, the inheritance represents the abundance of the Father and that abundance is rich. Therefore, the term is used to accentuate its value. It says how rich and glorious it is, especially when compared to that which is earthly or what this world has to offer. To this end, if we do not know the value of something, there is a tendency to despise it or choose something of lesser value over it.

If we are not enlightened or if the flesh veils our minds, we will not understand the magnitude of our inheritance and, therefore, seek fleeting alternatives. For example, Hebrews Chapter 12 relays the account of Esau who sold his birthright/inheritance for one morsel of meat. Because of the cravings of the flesh, Esau rejected his birthright choosing short-term satisfaction over the abundance of his inheritance. Furthermore, in the principle Jesus gave in John 6:27, He admonishes us not to labor for meat due to its perishing nature but to focus on laboring for that which endures to everlasting life. Moreover, in defining Esau's actions, Hebrews 12:16 depicts Esau as a fornicator or profane person, which characterizes him as living after the flesh. However, by comparison, Hebrews 11:24-26 in reference to Moses says:

24. By faith Moses, when he was come to years, refused to be called the son of Pharaoh's daughter;
25. Choosing rather to suffer affliction with the people of God, than to enjoy the pleasures of sin for a season;
26. Esteeming the reproach of Christ greater riches than the treasures in Egypt: for he had respect unto the recompence of the reward.

To put this passage into perspective, Egypt at the time of Moses was a great civilization and as the son of Pharaoh's daughter, he had tremendous prominence. By comparison, Moses placed greater value on suffering affliction with the people of God and the benefits of an eternal reward than on the advantages of having the riches of Egypt. It truly requires enlightenment to come to this conclusion. Therefore, those who choose the riches of this world and worldly pleasures over the rewards of God, lack enlightenment.

Additionally, this illumination also creates the disposition of being a stranger or pilgrim on Earth. Just like Abraham, we too are looking for a city whose builder and maker is God (Hebrews 11:10). This establishes a contrast between pursuing what is earthy and that which is heavenly. Once we have an appreciation for the enormity of our inheritance, the things of this world will indeed grow strangely dim. When we make a reasonable comparison, we echo the sentiments of David in Psalm 84:10: "I'd rather be a door keeper in the house of my God, than to dwell in the tents of wickedness."

3. THE EXCEEDING GREATNESS OF HIS POWER TOWARD US WHO BELIEVE

The third item resulting from the eyes of our understanding being enlightened is an awareness of the exceeding greatness of God's power toward us. Before we get into the specifics of what this statement is saying, notice that it does not just say "the greatness of His power." Rather, it uses the adjective "exceeding" to describe the greatness of God's power. This takes into account the enormity of what the Father has done for us. By itself, the word "greatness" conveys that something is outstanding or superior in quality, and in most cases, it does not require an additional qualifier. However, to express the limitless degree of the Father's greatness, the passage uses the word "exceeding," which means extraordinary, exceptional, or to surpass. It points to something that is far beyond what is ordinary or usual. Furthermore, the word "power" speaks of the inherent ability residing in someone by virtue of his or her very nature. It is the strength or force that someone is capable of exerting. Therefore, to describe the power of God that works in us, the phrase "exceeding greatness" is used. It is the abundance or the full packaging of the Father's ability, which is directed toward us and resides in us.

After describing the magnitude of His power toward us, the passage then offers a vivid illustration of the type of power being referenced. Sometimes as a promotion of their power, countries display their military might to support their declaration of greatness. In essence, they are saying their claim of greatness is not limited to mere words; there is a visual manifestation. Similarly, to ensure there is a precise understanding of what He has invested in us, it says that the power which the Father has given us is the same degree that was demonstrated in raising Christ from the dead. *The power required to resurrect Christ from the dead is the same power that now resides in us.*

Additionally, it is also the measure of power exhibited in seating Christ in heavenly places at the right hand of the Father. This depicts a status of equal honour and authority with the Father. Hence, it is the power of resurrection as well as position. It is a position far above all principalities, powers, might, dominions, and every name that is named, not only in this world but also in that which is to come. Therefore, the exceeding greatness of the power the Father gave to us incorporates both resurrection power, as well as a position of honour. Ephesians 2:4-6 echoes the same sentiment:

4. But God, who is rich in mercy, for his great love wherewith he loved us,
5. Even when we were dead in sins, hath quickened us together with Christ, (by grace ye are saved;)
6. And hath raised us up together, and made us sit together in heavenly places in Christ Jesus.

As sons of God, united with Him, we are also seated at the right hand of the Father in Christ Jesus, in heavenly places. What an awesome display of the power of God toward us. In summarizing this discussion on enlightenment let us revisit the three consequences of being illuminated. The "hope of His calling" speaks to **who we are**. It points to the character and purpose He has predetermined for us. The "riches of the glory of His inheritance in the saints" signifies **what we have**. It draws attention to that which is heavenly and eternal above that which is earthy and temporal. Finally, the "exceeding greatness of His power in us" exemplifies **what He has done for us**. It speaks of the enormous degree of power and honour the Father has given us. Therefore, despite the spiritual blessings and all the Father has predetermined for us, until our minds are illuminated, we will not come into the awareness of what He has done.

Based on what we have discussed in this chapter, it should be apparent that Ephesians is indeed progressive in its mandate for ministers of the gospel. It sets the parameters with what the Father has predetermined for us before the foundation of the world. It reveals not only His purpose, but it also gives us a glimpse of His heart and mind. Furthermore, the spiritual blessings He has ordained for humanity provide the assurance that what He has purposed will be fulfilled. It provides a great foundation for the purpose and perspective of ministry. Therefore, as ministers in a leadership capacity, not only are we responsible for imparting what the Father has predetermined, but it also behooves us to labor so that His people apprehend that for which they have been apprehended by Christ. For what is the benefit of knowing His purpose but not coming into its fullness?

CHAPTER 3

THE MESSAGE OF UNITY

GOD'S PURPOSE IS FOR ALL HUMANITY

In the previous chapter, the emphasis surrounded predestination and the fact that relative to God's purpose, He predetermined a specific destiny for humanity. Additionally, to realize this purpose, He also foreordained spiritual blessings, which highlight the specifics of His purpose. These blessings then become the mechanism for humanity to realize what the Father had predestined. What is interesting is that before the foundation of the world, when God chose us in Him, nationalities did not exist; denominations did not exist; ethnicities did not exist; gender did not exist, and social status did not exist. Thus, what He predestinated and the accompanying blessings were ordained for all humanity, which makes His purpose one of unity and His message is oneness. This is indeed a powerful statement. Unity is defined as the following:

- The quality or state of being united or joined as a whole
- Oneness or a condition of harmony
- Having a common purpose, objective, or aim
- Being of the same substance, essence, or character

Therefore, after Ephesians Chapter 1 lays the foundation regarding God's fundamental purpose for humanity in a general sense, the emphasis of Ephesians Chapter 2 is designed to communicate that His plan is for all humanity. It is not intended for a particular ethnic group, gender, or denomination but for everyone. Hence, anyone who is teaching otherwise is not promoting God's purpose. His purpose has always been that of oneness. Therefore, for ministers who operate in the leadership gifts, the two pillars offered in Ephesians involve *the message of God's purpose,* as well as *the message of unity.* In fact, these two tenets are interrelated and should not be taught in isolation. Unfortunately, teaching them in seclusion coupled with a misinterpretation of the scriptures has given rise to denominationalism and disunity within the body of Christ. The result is a gospel that is used to divide people with various denominations, promoting what they consider to be God's purpose. This is indeed a narrow-minded perspective only designed to create walls of division. However, as we have determined, the Father's purpose and message are of unity.

A religious denomination is defined as a subgroup within a religion that operates under a common name and identity. Additionally, these groups are known for specific doctrines, traditions, and values that are often distinct from other denominations. Examples of some of the most notable denominations in Christianity include the Roman Catholics, the Eastern Orthodox, Methodists, Baptists, Presbyterians, Anglicans, and Lutherans, etc. While unity within these denominations may be apparent, within the entire body, it is lacking. Generally speaking, the concept of denominationalism within Christianity fosters an environment of disunion or division; whereas, adherence to God's purpose engenders unity.

THE BASIS OF UNITY

Before embarking on the message of oneness, Ephesians Chapter 2 begins by continuing the discussion on the exceeding greatness of God's power, which was introduced in Ephesians Chapter 1. It is important to note that when studying Scripture, the conversation from chapter to chapter is uninterrupted. The separation by chapter and verse only provides convenience for reference purposes when studying and referring to Scripture. Therefore, Chapter 2 simply offers a more detailed explanation of the exceeding greatness of God's power towards us mentioned in Ephesians Chapter 1.

1. And you hath he quickened, who were dead in trespasses and sins;
2. Wherein in time past ye walked according to the course of this world, according to the prince of the power of the air, the spirit that now worketh in the children of disobedience:

3. Among whom also we all had our conversation in times past in the lusts of our flesh, fulfilling the desires of the flesh and of the mind; and were by nature the children of wrath, even as others.
4. But God, who is rich in mercy, for his great love wherewith he loved us,
5. Even when we were dead in sins, hath quickened us together with Christ, (by grace ye are saved;)
6. And hath raised us up together, and made us sit together in heavenly places in Christ Jesus:
7. That in the ages to come he might shew the exceeding riches of his grace in his kindness toward us through Christ Jesus.
8. For by grace are ye saved through faith; and that not of yourselves: it is the gift of God:
9. Not of works, lest any man should boast.
10. For we are his workmanship, created in Christ Jesus unto good works, which God hath before ordained that we should walk in them. (Ephesians 2:1-10)

QUICKENED: UNITED WITH THE FATHER

Before highlighting the reality of being united with each other, the scripture first establishes the principle on which unity is based. In that vein, *it is important to understand that before we can be united with each other, we must first be united to the Father.* Hence, the basis of our unity is unity with the Father, which is the same as being one spirit with Him (1 Corinthians 6:17). This is accomplished by the exceeding greatness of God's power toward us; this made us one with Him. *Additionally, unity of the faith can only be achieved among those who have unity of the Spirit.*

Because of Adam's transgression, all humanity became dead *in* sin. Consequently, we were separated from God, which is also referred to as spiritual death. This also meant we were separated from both the Father's house and His kingdom. Therefore, to be reunited with the Father or become one spirit with Him again, we must be made alive. Thus, to explain this process, Ephesians 2:1 uses the word "quickened," which means to make alive or to cause to live. Hence, the quickening spoken of here is the same resurrection power mentioned in Chapter 1.

Being born again is the demonstration of the exceeding greatness of God's power toward us. This is significant because as mentioned, it not only includes life, but it is also a position of honour with Christ. Furthermore, in referring to the definition of unity, being quickened makes us one with the Father whereby we are of His very substance. Thus, we share a common purpose with Him.

THE COURSE OF THIS WORLD

To explain what it means to be dead in trespasses and sins and why we needed quickening, Ephesians 2:2 mentions the influence that once governed our lives. It says in time past, we conducted or regulated our lives according to the course of this world. What exactly does this mean? The word "course" in this passage is the Greek word *aion*, which refers to a period of time or age. Additionally, the word "world" is the Greek word *kosmos*, which includes the aggregate of earthly things, world affairs, as well as its government. According to 1 John 2:16, the affairs or influences of the world are summarized into three distinct categories. It speaks of:

- The lusts of the flesh
- The lust of the eyes
- The pride of life

Hence, when Ephesians 2:2 says that we walked according to the course of this world or age, these were the governing influences that orchestrated our lives. Based on the time in which we live or from generation to generation, enticements can vary, but they still represent the governing influence of the world. In short, walking according to the course of the world means the world is the benchmark for how we manage our lives or behave. The world is our advisor. Whatever is popular, customary, or accepted based on the world is common practice for us. Furthermore, the statement concerning government provides the insight that at present, there is a dominion or authority, which presently dictates the affairs on the earth. Colossians 1:13 refers to this regime as the power or kingdom of darkness and those who are subjects of this kingdom regulate their lives in accordance with its government mandate.

THE PRINCE OF THE POWER OF THE AIR

On the subject of government, Ephesians 2:2 adds that the prince of the power of the air is the one who orchestrates the influences of the world that we just discussed; he is the spirit that works in the children of disobedience. Therefore, on the earth, there are presently two influences at work:

1. The Spirit of God who produces obedience and the fruit of righteousness in the sons of God
2. The spirit of the devil that is effective in the sons of disobedience

Furthermore, with the usage of the word "prince," this bolsters the perspective of a government or kingdom because a ruler governs every kingdom. To support this, Jesus referred to the devil as the prince of this world (John 12:31, John 14:30, and John 16:11). Additionally, 2 Corinthians 4:4, points out that the devil is also the god of this world. To be clear, he is not the god of the earth, for Psalm 24:1 certifies that the earth belongs to the Lord. However, the devil, as the god of this world, exercises government control over it and sets its agenda. He influences its values, ideas, culture, goals, and opinions and this is reflected in the actions of those who belong to him. Therefore, Ephesians 2:2 says that the devil or the prince of the power of the air is the spirit that is active in the children of disobedience. They are held captive to this influence, and he has dominion over them.

Moreover, Ephesians 2:3 says that in times past, this same inspiration cultivated in us a lifestyle of the lusts of the flesh. As a result, we fulfilled the desires of the flesh and mind. This influence governed our thoughts, as well as our actions. Additionally, our very nature and state of mind was one of wrath or retribution. This was our disposition, which is in stark contrast to the nature of peace. The word "nature" refers to the fundamental qualities of a person or thing; it is the identity or essential character by birth, origin, or constitution. Therefore, the inclusion of the word "nature" indicates our actions or behaviors were automatic responses based on our genetic constitution. Seeing that our past character was a reflection of our birth, for that to change, we had to experience a new birth or be quickened. Additionally, the term, "dead *in* trespasses and sins," speaks of being under the dominion of sin, which is the same as being a slave to sin or sold under sin (Romans 6:1, Romans 7:15). This means that under this government, we had no independence from sin but behaved in accordance with our nature. However, through Jesus Christ, we are now free from the dominion of sin. Subsequently, we are now dead *to* sin. Hence, there is a distinction between being *dead in sin* and being *dead to sin*. For more on this discussion, please refer to my book *God's Eternal Purpose Volume Two, Chapter Five: Are you Reigning?*

Nevertheless, despite what our nature was and regardless of the governing influence that we were subjected to, God's rich mercy and great love were still committed toward us. Romans 5:8 says, "But God commended His love toward us, in that while we were yet sinners, Christ died for us." If spiritual death resulted in separation from God, then life as a result of the exceeding greatness of His power brings about unity with the Father. Furthermore, Colossians 1:13 indicates that through Christ, we were also translated from one kingdom or dominion to another kingdom or dominion. We are delivered from the kingdom of darkness to the kingdom of God. Therefore, we are subjected to a different agenda and influence from that of the world. This is what Jesus meant when He said in John 14:30, "The prince of this world cometh, and hath nothing in me." In other words, his influence does not move or entice me. The values, ideas, cultures, goals, and opinions of the kingdom of God are in stark contrast to those of the kingdom of darkness and the world. Being quickened or born again means new life and this life follows a different governing influence.

QUICKENED TOGETHER WITH CHRIST

Not only did the Father quicken us, but Ephesians 2:5 says that *He quickened us together with Christ*. Therefore, when Christ was resurrected from the dead, we were as well. We were made alive together with Christ; it was a simultaneous act. Hence, as it pertains to Christ's death, resurrection, and exaltation, the occurrences that transpired with Christ also happened concurrently to us. In that regard, not only did the Father raise us up together with Christ, but He also exalted us with Him. Ephesians 2:6 says that He also made us to sit in heavenly places in Christ. Recall that Ephesians 1:20 identifies this position as at the right hand of the Father far above all principalities, powers, might, and dominion, and every name that is named, not only in this world but also in that which is to come. Therefore, as believers in Christ, this is our current position. As a parallel witness in Scripture, this is the same message conveyed in Romans 6:3-7. To obtain a more comprehensive perspective of what transpired when we were quickened, it is necessary to examine the account offered in Romans Chapter 6. This exercise is referred to as *Scripture reconciled with Scripture.*

3. Know ye not, that so many of us as were baptized into Jesus Christ were baptized into his death?
4. Therefore we are buried with him by baptism into death: that like as Christ was raised up from the dead by the glory of the Father, even so we also should walk in newness of life.
5. For if we have been planted together in the likeness of his death, we shall be also in the likeness of his resurrection:
6. Knowing this, that our old man is crucified with him, that the body of sin might be destroyed, that henceforth we should not serve sin.
7. For he that is dead is freed from sin. (Romans 6:3-7)

Overall, the context of Romans Chapter 6 surrounds being dead to sin and alive unto God. It speaks of what occurred during salvation thereby allowing believers to walk in "newness of life." Whereas Ephesians 2:1 is general with its usage of the word "quicken" in explaining salvation, Romans 6:3-7 provides elaborate details of what transpired when we were born again. Notice in referring to salvation, the passage uses the word "baptism." To be clear, this is not in reference to water baptism but rather, being baptized into Christ is a euphemism for being born again or quickened. When we accept Christ, we are baptized or immersed in Him. Hence, to be baptized into Christ means we identify with Him; it is a statement of being fully committed to Him.

Additionally, the passage says we were also baptized into His death or we died with Him. This speaks to the fact that our old man or nature, which was a servant of sin, was also crucified with Christ. Consequently, Romans 6:7 says, "For he that is dead is freed from sin." This act liberated us from sin, and it no longer has dominion over us. Subsequently, we were also buried with Christ. As a result of our connection with Him, just as Christ was raised from the dead, we were as well. We are resurrected to walk in "newness of life," a life that is qualitatively different. The person that the prince of the power of the air exercised dominion over has been crucified, is dead, and no longer exists. The new creature (2 Corinthians 5:17) that exists based on the resurrection is no longer subjected to the dominion of death. Therefore, the doctrine of the dual nature of the sons of God is nothing short of damnable heresy.

Recall at the beginning of this chapter it was stated that before we can be united with each other, we must first be united with the Father. When we were quickened, we experienced the exceeding greatness of His power and were united with Him. Consequently, we were also unified with the Father's house and His kingdom. This is the unity Jesus spoke about in John 14:2 when He said in His Father's house or family there are many mansions or dwelling places, I go to prepare a place for you. Through His death, Christ prepared a place for us to dwell in the Father's family or to be members of His household. Jesus' message in John Chapter 14 was one of unity. He made it possible for us to be united with the Father. Again, for more on John 14:2 please refer to my book, *Are There Really Mansions in Heaven? It's a Family Affair*. In order to come into the understanding of the unity that exists in Christ, Ephesians 1:17 says the eyes of our understanding must be enlightened. There has to be an appreciation that as believers in Christ, we are all united in Him. Not only were we crucified, buried, and resurrected with Him, but we are also now seated *together* in heavenly places with Him. This is the position and condition of everyone who has been quickened. In Christ, we are all united.

UNITY IN CHRIST

Notice, on the overall subject of unity, Ephesians Chapter 2 takes a systematic approach. With unity as a backdrop, the first portion of Ephesians Chapter

2 establishes the fact that as believers, we are all united in Christ. With this as a foundation, the latter portion of Ephesians Chapter 2 continues the conversation of unity with greater specificity. It conveys the message that despite the ethnic, religious, and other differences, which once created a division in humanity, in Christ, these no longer exist. Because we are all in Christ and Christ is not divided, there is unity among those who are in Him. Unfortunately, many believers are more acquainted with the concept of being united in Christ than they are with being united with each other. Therefore, Ephesians Chapter 2 serves to eliminate the concept of division in the church on the grounds of ethnicity and religious ideology, replacing it with the message of unity.

On the subject of the ethnicity of all believers, 1 Peter 1:23 offers a compelling perspective. It states that as believers, we are quickened or born again of incorruptible seed. The word "seed" is used in this passage because Genesis 1:11 established the principle that every seed produces after its kind. When Adam sinned, he took on the nature of sin; therefore, his seed became corruptible.

With all of humanity being in the loins of Adam, we were all subjected to sin and death. Hebrews 7:9-10, provides the reference for this principle in relation to Abraham. Hence, when Adam reproduced, his offspring reflected the nature of his seed. Therefore, the term "corruptible seed" embraces not only the heritage and ethnicity of our natural parents but also the nature of sin that was transferred through the seed. This is why Psalm 51:5 says we were shaped in iniquity and in sin did our mother conceive us. For this reason, in order for God to produce a new creature capable of walking in "newness of life," the seed had to be different. Because every seed produces after its kind, to produce different fruit, the seed had to change. Hence, we were born again, not of *corruptible seed* but of *incorruptible seed*. Therefore, as believers, we not only took on a different heritage and ethnicity but also a different nature.

According to Galatians 3:28, the ethnicity of the incorruptible seed unlike the corruptible seed, does not contain national, gender, or social differences but rather the essence of Christ. Furthermore, as we are born of different seed, we also have a different Father and belong to a different family.

Romans 8:15-17 says we are the children of God and have been adopted by the Holy Spirit into one family. Moreover, in this family, we have been positioned as sons and God is our Father. Therefore, as new creatures in Christ, whose citizenship is in heaven, natural affiliations including ethnicity, no longer define who we are. *We have the same Father and hence the same ethnicity.* Therefore, while believers seem to be engaged in the subject of race and ethnicity in the church, which contributes to division, the fact is we are all born of the same seed.

Nevertheless, to emphasize the message of unity, Ephesians 2 highlights the conditions that once existed between Jews and Gentiles or the circumcision and the uncircumcision. These circumstances fostered an atmosphere of division or disunity between humanity and created walls of separation. From a scriptural perspective, the Bible in its entirety identifies three general groups of people. Therefore, regardless of all the groups of people mentioned in Scripture, they can all be categorized as Jews, Gentiles, or the church. The Jews are natural descendants of Abraham and are also referred to as Israelites. The Gentiles are a broad classification of people that includes every ethnicity and nation other than Israel. Finally, the church is a combination of both Jews and Gentiles who believe in Christ and have been quickened or born again. However, unlike the other two groupings, the church does not subscribe to ethnicity, gender, or natural lineages.

11. Wherefore remember, that ye being in time past Gentiles in the flesh, who are called Uncircumcision by that which is called the Circumcision in the flesh made by hands;
12. That at that time ye were without Christ, being aliens from the commonwealth of Israel, and strangers from the covenants of promise, having no hope, and without God in the world:
13. But now in Christ Jesus ye who sometimes were far off are made nigh by the blood of Christ.
14. For he is our peace, who hath made both one, and hath broken down the middle wall of partition between us;
15. Having abolished in his flesh the enmity, even the law of commandments contained in ordinances; for to make in himself of twain one new man, so making peace;

16. And that he might reconcile both unto God in one body by the cross, having slain the enmity thereby:
17. And came and preached peace to you which were afar off, and to them that were nigh.
18. For through him we both have access by one Spirit unto the Father.
19. Now therefore ye are no more strangers and foreigners, but fellowcitizens with the saints, and of the household of God;
20. And are built upon the foundation of the apostles and prophets, Jesus Christ himself being the chief corner stone;
21. In whom all the building fitly framed together groweth unto an holy temple in the Lord:
22. In whom ye also are builded together for an habitation of God through the Spirit. (Ephesians 2:11-22)

To say the obvious, the letter to the Ephesians is addressed not to Jews or Gentiles but to the church, which is a union of both groups. Ephesians 1:1 says, "Paul, an apostle of Jesus Christ by the will of God, to the saints which are at Ephesus and the faithful in Christ Jesus." Therefore, the characterization of Gentiles in Ephesians 2:11 is based on natural affiliation and is simply used as a reference to draw a comparison. It asserts that in time past, they were considered Gentiles according to the flesh. The term "time past" is used because, as it pertains to the church, there is a new classification of people who are not identified by natural relationships. Hence, prior to its discussion of unity, the passage first makes the distinction that once existed between Jews and Gentiles. It points out that before there was oneness, there was division along ethnic, cultural, and religious lines. Having already addressed the subject of ethnicity, let us turn our attention to the general classification of the Circumcision and the Uncircumcision.

THE CIRCUMCISION AND THE UNCIRCUMCISION

THE NATURAL PERSPECTIVE OF CIRCUMCISION

Ephesians 2:11, in describing the Jews and the Gentiles, uses the terms "Circumcision and Uncircumcision." In fully committing ourselves to this subject, we will discuss both the natural and spiritual implications of these designations. As it pertains to the flesh and in accordance with the context of this discussion, circumcision refers to the removal of the foreskin of a male's penis. While in today's environment the practice of circumcision is predominately for health and hygiene benefits, its scriptural significance is much broader. The Jews generally referred to themselves as the Circumcision; therefore, the Gentiles by default were categorized as the Uncircumcision. Consequently, the very practice of circumcision created a distinction between the two groups of people. The circumcision ritual was performed on every male Israelite at eight days old, as well as those who were bought by Israelites as they were included in their households (Genesis 17:11-13). On the other hand, this was not the practice among the Gentile nations. To truly appreciate the basis for the designations of circumcision and uncircumcision, it is necessary to refer to the book of Genesis and its implementation.

In Genesis 12:1-3, God called Abram (Abraham) and made several promises to him. After promising to make of him a great nation and bestowing several personal blessings, the Lord said to him in Genesis 12:3, "In thee shall all the nations of the earth be blessed." Of note, this component of the promise serves not only as the nucleus of the gospel, but it is also the foundation for the message of unity; however, this point will be developed later.

In Genesis 15:5, God reassures Abraham of His initial promise and says his descendants shall be as the stars in the sky. In response, Genesis 15:6 says Abraham believed in the Lord and therefore, He counted it to him for righteousness. In other words, based on the principle of his belief and not works, God considered Abraham as righteous. Now, this is where it gets interesting! According to Romans 4:5, this event created the basis of righteousness by faith, which is in opposition to righteousness by works or righteousness by the Law. Additionally, based on the condition Abraham was in when he was considered righteous, it makes the conversation of the circumcision and the uncircumcision even more intriguing. In this regard, Romans 4:9 asks, "Cometh this blessedness then upon the circumcision only or upon the uncircumcision also? For we say that faith was reckoned to Abraham for righteousness."

The question that is being asked is, is righteousness only for the Jews, or is it also for the Gentiles? To answer this question, it has to be determined when Abraham was considered righteous. In this regard, Romans 4:10 asks the question, "How was it (righteousness) reckoned? When he was in circumcision or in uncircumcision? Not in circumcision, but in uncircumcision." In plain language, the passage is stating that Abraham was considered righteous while he was in a state of uncircumcision, which represented the Gentiles. Consequently, after he was deemed righteous, the Lord then introduced circumcision, which was a seal or token of the covenant, and this depicted the Jews. Thus, in Abraham, we have the righteousness of all humanity. Romans 4:11-12 provides a wonderful summation of this discussion:

11. And he received the sign of circumcision, a seal of the righteousness of the faith which he had yet being uncircumcised: that he might be the father of all them that believe, though they be not circumcised; that righteousness might be imputed unto them also:
12. And the father of circumcision to them who are not of the circumcision only, but who also walk in the steps of that faith of our father Abraham, which he had being yet uncircumcised.

This entire exchange not only reveals the wisdom of the Father, but it is also the hallmark of the message of unity. In simplicity, the Lord orchestrated His plan of unity for all humanity through Abraham, for in him, we see the fatherhood of both the Jews and Gentiles, along with the blessings of righteousness by faith. Furthermore, this is in harmony with the promise of Genesis 12:3 where the Lord said to Abraham, "In thee shall all the nations of the earth be blessed." In other words, all humanity and not just one group of people would be the beneficiaries of this blessing.

First, Galatians 3:8 indicates that when the Lord made this promise, which is one of righteousness, He was in fact preaching the gospel to Abraham. Therefore, the gospel of Jesus Christ is itself a message of unity to be a blessing to all humanity. Furthermore, Galatians 3:16 adds more substance to the dialogue by stating that God made the promise, not only to Abraham but also to his seed, meaning Jesus Christ. Hence, it is through Jesus Christ that the blessing of the promise and unity is realized. Moreover, Acts 3:26 affirms that the promise God made to Abraham is one of righteousness when it says, "Unto you first God, having raised up His Son Jesus, sent Him to bless you, in turning away everyone of you from his iniquities." Additionally, Galatians 3:14 says that the blessing of Abraham is also the promise of the Holy Spirit, which quickens us and consequently frees us from the dominion of sin. Recall from our previous discussion that this is also the same as being baptized into Christ.

26. For ye are all the children of God by faith in Christ Jesus.
27. For as many of you as have been baptized into Christ have put on Christ.
28. There is neither Jew nor Greek, there is neither bond nor free, there is neither male nor female: for ye are all one in Christ Jesus.
29. And if ye be Christ's, then are ye Abraham's seed, and heirs according to the promise. (Galatians 3:26-29)

In this example, the dividing classifications of circumcision and uncircumcision that were used to separate humanity have been eliminated. In fact, with Abraham, the Lord actually used the entire exercise as a demonstration of unity. Let us now examine circumcision from a spiritual perspective.

THE SPIRITUAL PERSPECTIVE OF CIRCUMCISION

So far, we have discussed circumcision from the perspective of the flesh; however, the scripture informs us that there is one of greater significance. Therefore, while some religions place emphasis on the fleshly ritual, the one of the spirit is more substantial. Hence, from a spiritual point of view, the designation of circumcision and uncircumcision still has relevance, as we will discover. In Philippians 3:3, Paul reclassifies the perspective of what it means to be called "the circumcision." He says, "For we are the circumcision, which worship God in the spirit, and rejoice in Christ Jesus, and have no confidence in the flesh." He was making a distinction between two groups of people who regarded themselves as the "the circumcision." One group observed the ritual of the flesh and consequently placed confidence in the flesh. These were the natural Israelites, whom we have already discussed. However, in relation to the circumcision of Christ, Paul identified himself with another group. This group consisted of both Jews and Gentiles whose circumcision was not according to the flesh but of the Spirit.

10. And ye are complete in him, which is the head of all principality and power:
11. In whom also ye are circumcised with the circumcision made without hands, in putting off the body of the sins of the flesh by the circumcision of Christ:
12. Buried with him in baptism, wherein also ye are risen with him through the faith of the operation of God, who hath raised him from the dead.
13. And you, being dead in your sins and the uncircumcision of your flesh, hath he quickened together with him, having forgiven you all trespasses. (Colossians 2:10-13)

Therefore, the group Paul was referring to in Philippians 3:3 is those whose circumcision is made without hands. The phrase "without hands," means that it is not a natural process. Hence, it is a circumcision of the Spirit and not of the flesh. As discussed, the practice of circumcision in the natural sense involved the removal of the foreskin from the male's penis. *In principle, this procedure pertained to the removal of flesh.* According to the precepts of rightly dividing the Word of God, this exercise is identified as "a type." In short, a type is a person, place, or thing mentioned in the Old Testament, which prefigures and represents a future person, place, or thing of similar characteristics in the New Testament. Therefore, natural circumcision, which was made by hand prefigured and represented the spiritual circumcision of Christ made without hands.

Just as natural circumcision involved the removal of flesh, the circumcision of Christ is a spiritual procedure that involves putting away the body of the sins of the flesh. Romans 6:6 refers to this as "the old man being crucified." The circumcision of Christ is also the same as being baptized into Christ. Our old man that was the servant of sin and the flesh was crucified with Christ. Consequently, we were also resurrected with Him and walk in "newness of life." Therefore, those who are now truly *the circumcision* are those who have been quickened and are no longer the servants of sin (Romans 6:7).

The body of sin or the flesh has been removed through the circumcision of Christ. Hence, while religion emphasizes the natural process, it is the spiritual operation that truly matters.

The principle of circumcision offered in Genesis 17:11 is that it was a token or sign of the covenant between the Lord and Israel. Additionally, Genesis 17:13 says that the covenant was an everlasting covenant and therefore has eternal benefits. With the pillars of the covenant being eternal redemption and eternal inheritance (Hebrews 9:11-15), the true heirs of the promise are not those who are circumcised in the flesh but those of the circumcision of Christ. For this reason, the circumcision of Christ serves as the seal of the covenant between God and His people. Thus, being born again is a sign of being in a covenant relationship with the Father. Hence, those who are only circumcised in the flesh and not with the circumcision of Christ have no share in this covenant. In truth, those who have not experienced the circumcision of Christ can actually be regarded as the uncircumcised, for they are not heirs of the promise. Again, I reiterate Galatians 3:29, "And if ye be Christ's, then are ye Abraham's seed, and heirs according to the promise."

Isn't it interesting that whereas the circumcision in the flesh was once used to foster division between humanity, the circumcision of the Spirit creates unity? Through the circumcision of Christ, we are united in Him.

OUTSIDERS NO LONGER

Do you sometimes wish you belonged to a certain group, club, or institution? Often, being a member has a certain prestige attached to it. Furthermore, being excluded and denied the benefits of the group can sometimes cause us to feel like outsiders.

In continuing the conversation of unity, Ephesians Chapter 2 highlights the other disparities that once existed between the Jews and Gentiles. One group enjoyed a certain privileged position and many advantages, while the other was marginalized. When compared to the Jews, Ephesians 2:12 says the following concerning those who were Gentiles:

- They were without Christ
- They were aliens from the commonwealth of Israel
- They were strangers from the covenants of promise
- They had no hope
- They were without God in the world

In combination, the above exclusions paint a clear picture of what it meant to be exempt from the things of God. First, the Gentiles were without Christ, or they were separated from Christ. Additionally, they were aliens or foreigners from the commonwealth of Israel. The word "commonwealth" is the Greek word *politeia*, which refers to the administration of civil affairs and citizenship; it speaks of government and the rights of a citizen. Therefore, the Gentiles as a group were precluded from the overall benefits of being citizens of Israel. Furthermore, contingent on this status, the Gentiles as foreigners were not shareholders in the covenants of promise. Moreover, these all equated to having no hope and being without God in the world.

Taken together, the Gentiles as a group were excluded from the advantages reserved for the Jews. However, there is a specific reason why Ephesians highlights the status of those who were once Gentiles. It is not to express a sense of deficiency or to promote one group over the other but rather, its purpose is to show that the playing field has now been leveled. It is to pinpoint that where there was once exclusion, there is now inclusion and unity. Additionally, it is to emphasize that the dispensation or God's management of His household affairs has changed. Interestingly, the things that were seemingly reserved for one group were, in fact, predetermined for all humanity. They are components of the same purpose or spiritual blessings that were foreordained for all humanity before the foundation of the world. However, in the orchestration of His plan, God chose one group to facilitate His purpose until it was time to include everyone.

When God called Abraham in Genesis Chapter 12, He promised him that He would make of him a great nation and then entered a covenant relationship with him. However, in Genesis 15:13, the Lord also forecasted that his seed would be in bondage to the Egyptians for a period of 400 years. Therefore, when the Lord appeared to Moses in Exodus 3:6, He said to him, "I am the

God of thy Father, the God of Abraham, the God of Isaac, and the God of Jacob." The Lord used this title while introducing Himself to remind Moses of His covenant relationship with His people. For this reason, after the Israelites left Egypt, the Lord said to them in Exodus 19:5, "And ye shall be unto me a kingdom of priests, and a holy nation." Hence, they were God's chosen people. Deuteronomy 7:6 reinforces this and says, "For thou art an holy people unto the Lord thy God: the Lord thy God hath chosen thee to be a special people unto himself, above all people that are upon the face of the earth." Additionally, Romans 3:1 says that the Jews enjoyed an advantage because unto them were committed the oracles of God; they were entrusted with His word, which included His promises, and this was indeed a privileged position. Romans 9:4-5 provides a great summary of the position enjoyed by Israel:

4. Who are Israelites; to whom pertaineth the adoption, and the glory, and the covenants, and the giving of the law, and the service of God, and the promises;
5. Whose are the fathers, and of whom as concerning the flesh Christ came, who is over all, God blessed forever. Amen.

Based on the above, it is evident that the Jews were distinguished from all other nations and favored. They were regarded as a peculiar group of people. On the other hand, none of these advantages pertained to the Gentiles. Ephesians 2:12 referred to them as strangers, for they had no share in the things pertaining to God. In short, they were outsiders.

Furthermore, as a general classification by the Jews, Gentiles were also considered unclean (Acts 10) and on occasion, they were even referred to as dogs in a comparative sense. This was evident during Jesus' encounter with a Gentile woman in Matthew Chapter 15 who petitioned Him for the healing of her daughter. Therefore, to make a comparison between the privileged position of the Jews to that of the Gentiles, Jesus said in Matthew 15:26, "It is not meet to take the children's bread and to cast it to dogs." Nevertheless, her response not only revealed that she understood the principle of what He was saying, but it was also a demonstration of her faith. In response, she said, "Truth, Lord: yet the dogs eat of the crumbs which fall from the masters' table." Interestingly, she did not allow her position at the time to determine her destiny or that of her daughter. This is because faith does not take an account of your current position. Upon hearing her response, Jesus marveled at her faith and her daughter was immediately healed.

Even Samaritans who were classified as half-Jew, half-Gentile were ostracized by the Jews. In John Chapter 4, during Jesus' interaction with a Samaritan woman at a well, He asks her for a drink of water. Knowing He was a Jew, she responded and said in John 4:9, "How is it that thou, being a Jew, askest drink of me, which am a woman of Samaria? for the Jews have no dealings with the Samaritans." As a general policy, the Jews had no association with the Samaritans. Hence, the deep divisions between Jews and Gentiles were evident along ethnic, social, cultural, and religious lines. However, that was about to change.

Whenever the word "but" is introduced in a conversation, it not only negates everything which was previously said, it also introduces a statement that contrasts what was mentioned. It serves as a reversal of ideology. Hence, after stating the position of those who were previously classified as Gentiles, Ephesians 2:13, says, "But now in Christ Jesus ye who sometimes were far off are made nigh by the blood of Christ." Therefore, because of Christ's sacrifice, the status of those who were previously Gentiles has changed. Whereas they were once outsiders or considered to be of a lower position, they are now brought near. The term "made nigh," speaks of having a relationship and consequently being a partaker as a result of a change in position. Thus, those who previously had no affinity with God and were exempt from the privileges afforded to Israel, now have a different arrangement. In fact, in this new position, labels do not exist, and the designations of Jew and Gentile no longer exist.

To be clear, Ephesians 2:12 starts the conversation with Gentiles being excluded from Israel and all that pertained to them. However, when Ephesians 2:13 says that former Gentiles are now made nigh or have a relationship with the Father through the blood of Christ, it is not saying they are now included with natural Israel. For through Christ's sacrifice, a completely new entity has been created. Furthermore, based on this perspective, the scripture has redefined what it means to be an Israelite. To eliminate dependency on their natural heritage,

Paul, in the book of Romans, offers an enlightening perspective on what it means to truly be an Israelite. Romans 9:6-8 establishes the premise that those who are truly Israel are not those born after the flesh but rather those who are born of the Spirit.

> 6. Not as though the word of God hath taken none effect. For they are not all Israel, which are of Israel:
> 7. Neither, because they are the seed of Abraham, are they all children: but, In Isaac shall thy seed be called.
> 8. That is, they which are the children of the flesh, these are not the children of God: but the children of the promise are counted for the seed. (Romans 9:6-8)

As witnessed in our discussion on circumcision, the more significant perspective of what it means to be an Israelite pertains more to spiritual birth as opposed to natural birth. In this regard, the above passage is clear that being an Israelite is not based on being born after the flesh or dependent upon the natural seed. On the contrary, it submits that being an Israelite is actually predicated on being a child of promise. In a nutshell, being a child of the promise is equivalent to being born of the Spirit. To support this position, Galatians Chapter 4 makes a comparison between Isaac and Ishmael who were both sons of Abraham. Despite both sons being the seed of Abraham, they each represented something different. Isaac depicted being born after the Spirit, while Ishmael portrayed being born after the flesh (Galatians 4:21-31).

After making the analogy, Paul says in Galatians 4:28, "Now we, brethren as Isaac was, are the children of promise." Therefore, to identify what it means to be a son of God or in this instance, considered truly Israel, the requirement is to be born of the Spirit. For this reason, the designation of Israel in Romans Chapter 9 is in essence spiritual Israel and not natural Israel, hence, the conclusion, "For they are not all Israel, which are of Israel." In other words, Israel in its true sense embraces all those born of the Spirit and this transcends natural birth. In this regard, everyone born of the Spirit of God is an Israelite. This reinforces Galatians 3:29, which says, "And if ye be Christ's then are ye Abraham's seed and heirs according to the promise."

Through Christ, those who were once outsiders are now citizens of Israel and of the kingdom of God. In light of this, 1 Peter 2:9-10 says to the church, "But ye are a chosen generation, a royal priesthood, an holy nation, a peculiar people; that ye should shew forth the praises of him who hath called you out of darkness into his marvellous light: Which in time past were not a people, but are now the people of God: which had not obtained mercy, but now have obtained mercy." Based on these qualifiers, the church is indeed regarded as Israel from a spiritual perspective.

THE MIDDLE WALL OF PARTITION HAS BEEN REMOVED

Through Christ's death, He removed the impediment that served as a dividing wall between humanity. Ephesians 2:14 contributes to the conversation of unity by stating that Christ has broken down the middle wall of partition between Jews and Gentiles. With these two groups of people representing the essential division in humanity, removing the wall made it possible for the creation of one people and therefore unity. In the news today, there is a lot of discussion regarding walls. Without the political infusion, the general purpose of a wall is to serve as a boundary between people. Symbolically, it represents barriers, which seem impossible to cross and overcome. Unlike a gate, which signifies protection or security, the primary function of a wall is to create division and legitimize differences. What precisely is the middle wall of partition mentioned in Ephesians 2:14?

Some contend that the wall of partition was in reference to the soreg. This was a low retaining wall that surrounded the temple and served as a boundary or a line of separation between the Jews and Gentiles. Specifically, this partition prohibited Gentiles and non-purified Jews from entering the temple courts. In fact, there were signs posted on the soreg in Greek and Latin that warned unauthorized people from entering the Holy Temple under the penalty of death. For example, in Acts 21:27-28, when the Jews saw Paul in the temple, they stirred up the people and they took hold of him. They accused him of bringing Greeks into the temple thereby polluting it.

According to John 12:20 and Acts 8:27, Greeks also came to Jerusalem to worship; however, they were restricted to the court of the Gentiles, which was the outermost court in the temple during the time of Christ. This was also the section where Jesus drove out the money changers and those that sold the animals for sacrifice in John 2:13-16. It should be noted that the soreg was instituted by the Jews and was not based on God's design for the temple. Therefore, to some, it would seem practical that this wall of partition was the one spoken of in Ephesians 2:14. However, based on the context of the passage, the middle wall of partition spoken of here is not in reference to the soreg. First, the soreg was *not* implemented by God and therefore had no significance in the conversation. Along these lines, there were many doctrines and practices instituted by the religious establishment, which Jesus referred to as the traditions of men (Matthew 15:1-9). However, the focus of Ephesians Chapter 2 is specifically the ordinances implemented by the Lord, which separated Jews from Gentiles. Therefore, the passage utilizes the word "wall" in a legitimate sense because it prohibited humanity from becoming one. Wherefore, it requires understanding what separated Jews from Gentiles to appreciate what the wall of partition was. I would also dare say that the wall of partition not only separated Jews from Gentiles but also, in an absolute sense, humanity from God.

Through Christ's sacrifice, He broke down the middle wall of partition thereby making Jews and Gentiles one. He did away with it and deprived it of its authority. What authoritative principle divided Jews and Gentiles and created division between humanity? In describing the wall, Ephesians 2:15 uses the word "enmity," which means animosity or the reason for opposition. Therefore, in addition to its dividing function, the wall also created conditions of adversity. In plain language, Ephesians 2:15 says that the enmity or the wall was *the law of commandments contained in ordinances*. Therefore, the word "wall" is being used in a figurative sense. The Law and all its ordinances were the obstacles or barriers that divided humanity. Hence, to have a proper perspective of the context of this passage, an understanding of the Law is required.

For clarity, the Law was comprehensive and basically covered three categories or components. It comprised of ceremonial laws, civil laws, and moral laws.

The Five-Fold Ministry Gifts

The ceremonial laws included everything pertaining to Israel's worship. They entailed the sacrificial offerings for sin (Leviticus 1-7); the Sabbath (Leviticus 23:3); priestly rules and responsibilities (Leviticus 10:8-20); regulations for the priests (Leviticus 21, 22); dietary restrictions (Leviticus 11:1-47); circumcision, what qualified as uncleanness (Leviticus 12, 13, 14); and the Feasts of the Lord.

The civil laws incorporated everything related to Israel's daily life and legal system. They covered how justice was meted out (Leviticus 24:17-23; laws concerning property redemption (Leviticus 25); justice for the poor (Leviticus 19:15); correct scales in commerce practices (Leviticus 19:35); robbery, extortion, bearing false witness and restitution (Leviticus 6:1-7).

Finally, the moral laws took into account the commands from God to regulate human behavior. These laws also embraced some of the civil laws and included stealing, defrauding your neighbor, and loving your neighbor as yourself (Leviticus 19); they also incorporated incest, adultery, sacrificing children to idols, and homosexuality (Leviticus 18).

In particular, the civil and moral components of the Law have been incorporated in the New Testament (Ephesians 4:28; Ephesians 5:3) and are still relevant today. In fact, they have also been adopted as the law in many modern societies as they serve as the foundation for justice and moral living. However, the ceremonial components of the Law, which pertained to the priests, sacrifices, circumcision, dietary restrictions, the feasts, and the Sabbath, etc. were fulfilled through Jesus Christ by His death on the cross. In this regard, Colossians 2:13-17 says:

> 13. And you, being dead in your sins and the uncircumcision of your flesh, hath he quickened together with him, having forgiven you all trespasses;
> 14. Blotting out the handwriting of ordinances that was against us, which was contrary to us, and took it out of the way, nailing it to his cross;
> 15. And having spoiled principalities and powers, he made a shew of them openly, triumphing over them in it.
> 16. Let no man therefore judge you in meat, or in drink, or in respect of an holyday, or of the new moon, or of the sabbath days:

17. Which are a shadow of things to come; but the body is of Christ.

The term "blotting out" in the above passage means to obliterate or to erase. This is synonymous with the phrase, "took it out of the way." In both instances, the action is in reference to removing the handwriting of ordinances or decrees that was against us, which was contrary to us. Specifically, the handwriting of ordinances pointed to the ceremonial components of the Law. How was the Law an adversary to humanity? To answer this question, the purpose of the Law has to be determined. First, Romans 3:20 says, "Therefore by the deeds of the law there shall no flesh be justified in his sight: for by the law is the knowledge of sin."

Furthermore, Galatians 3:24 says, "Wherefore the law was our schoolmaster to bring us unto Christ, that we might be justified by faith." In principle, the Law was implemented to provide an awareness of sin, but it could not provide deliverance from it (Hebrews 10:1-4). This is also evident in the account of Romans Chapter 7, where frustration and wretchedness were expressed because, as an instrument of deliverance, the Law was ineffective. For this reason, these ordinances functioned as adversaries to humanity. To be clear, the Law was not sin as mentioned in Romans 7:7, but it made sin apparent. It did this so that the entire world would be guilty before God (Romans 3:19). The Law allowed sin to be imputed or charged and the conclusion was that both Jew and Gentile were all under sin (Romans 3:9). Furthermore, the Law also operated as a schoolmaster or supervisor responsible for safety and manners along with discipline. However, because of its inability to redeem from sin, the schoolmaster was only instituted until the time of reformation (Hebrews 9:10) or until Christ brought true righteousness.

Therefore, through Christ's sacrifice, He removed what was contrary to us by fulfilling the righteousness of the Law. This is why Jesus said in Matthew 5:17, "Think not that I am come to destroy the law, or the prophets: I am not come to destroy, but to fulfil." Thus, following the ceremonial aspects and pattern prescribed in the Law, Jesus as High Priest entered into the holy place with His own blood and obtained eternal redemption for us (Hebrews 9:12). By fulfilling what the sacrifices of the Law could not accomplish, He blotted out or erased the handwriting of ordinances that were in opposition to us. Romans Chapter 8 provides a meaningful summary of this discussion.

3. For what the law could not do, in that it was weak through the flesh, God sending his own Son in the likeness of sinful flesh, and for sin, condemned sin in the flesh:
4. That the righteousness of the law might be fulfilled in us, who walk not after the flesh, but after the Spirit. (Romans 8:3-4)

As we progress in our understanding of the middle wall of partition, it is important to recognize the scriptural relationship that exists between Ephesians 2:14-15 and Colossians 2:14. For instance, the term "took it out of the way" used in Colossians 2:14, in reference to the ceremonial ordinances, means that Christ took them *out of the midst or middle*. This is equivalent to Ephesians 2:14, which says that Christ broke down the middle wall of partition, which was also in the midst of Jews and Gentiles. Therefore, this is further validation that Scripture's usage of the phrase "middle wall of partition" is representative of the ceremonial ordinances and not the soreg.

As mentioned previously, the wall being a middle partition has a two-fold meaning. Not only did the ceremonial components of the Law serve as a barrier between Jews and Gentiles, but they also functioned as an obstacle between humanity and the Father. Because of sin, humanity was separated from the Father and the ceremonial laws were incapable of providing reconciliation. However, when Christ died, thus, fulfilling the requirements of the Law, Matthew 27:51 says that the veil of the temple was rent in two—from top to bottom. The veil in the temple was situated between the holy place and the most holy place. As long as the veil stood, eternal redemption and unity with the Father were impossible. However, through Jesus' sacrifice, we now have the boldness to enter the holiest of all. This means that access or unity with the Father is now possible. The removal of the soreg did not accomplish this unity.

In continuing with the comparison between the two passages, notice that Ephesians 2:15 uses the word "enmity" to describe the obstruction or the law of commandments contained in ordinances. The word enmity means hostility or reason for opposition. Similarly, to express the identical sentiment, Colossians

2:14 uses the word "contrary," which is the same as an adversary. Therefore, through His sacrifice, Christ simultaneously removed the obstruction that prohibited the union between the Jews and the Gentiles, as well as the obstacle that could not facilitate unity with the Father.

The opposite of enmity is harmony; therefore, once the impediment is removed, the outcome is peace. Again, I reiterate the principle offered at the beginning of this chapter, which is that for there to be unity between humanity, there must first be unity with the Father. Let us look at several instances where the ceremonial components of the Law are/were used to foster division.

GENDER BIASES (MALE/FEMALE)

The ceremonial ordinances of the law were instruments that created enmity. Like a wall in a metaphoric sense, they separated people from each other thereby prohibiting unity. In using this as an example, any doctrine or practice that fosters division in the body of Christ represents a wall and therefore has to be abolished. An example of this would be doctrines that contain gender biases, which marginalize women and prohibit them from speaking in the church or attaining leadership roles. Whereas Galatians 3:28 speaks of the removal of walls, many seek to construct their own based on a misunderstanding of the scriptures.

Galatians conveys that in Christ, social, ethnic, and gender walls have all been removed, for we are all one. For more insight into this topic, please refer to my book, *Freedom: The True Perspective about Women in Ministry*. On the other hand, this principle does not pertain to the righteous requirements outlined in Scripture regarding holy living, for there are some who have perverted the gospel of Christ. If a doctrine related to true holiness creates divisions in the church, then this is different. In short, perversion of the gospel occurs when there is an amalgamation of the things pertaining to the flesh and the things of the Spirit to accommodate and satisfy human desires. This was the basis of Paul's contention with the Galatians where the gospel was perverted or corrupted to the point that it seemed like another gospel (Galatians 1:6-7).

RELIGIOUS, SOCIAL, AND ETHNIC DIFFERENCES

Interestingly, many doctrinal challenges that have created divisions in the church have their basis in the ceremonial components of the Law. Another practical scriptural example of this is in Paul's epistle to the church of Galatia. In Galatians 2:11-21, he recounts his exchange with Peter while in Antioch and his fellowship with the Gentiles. Prior to the arrival of certain Jews, Peter ate with the Gentiles and made no distinction between him and them. Having understood from the vision he received in Acts Chapter 10 regarding the Gentiles, he certainly was of a different persuasion. In fact, by his own admission, he said in Acts 10: 34-35, "Of a truth I perceive that God is no respecter of persons: but in every nation he that feareth Him, and worketh righteousness, is accepted with Him." Based on the vision, Peter was fully aware that the wall which divided Jews and Gentiles had been removed and there was now unity. However, once certain Jews arrived, out of fear and intimidation, he separated himself from the Gentiles and made a distinction. In essence, he reestablished the social and ethnic wall that had already been removed. As a result, Barnabas and the other Jews that were with them were also caught up in the hypocrisy.

THE SABBATH

Additionally, there are divisions in the church concerning doctrine related to the keeping of the Sabbath. Not only has this resulted in the formation of entire denominations, but it has also fueled the belief that those who do not observe the Sabbath are in error. When we carefully examine the book of Hebrews, it is evident that the ceremonial categories of the Law dominate the landscape of the book. However, systematically, the book details how all the ordinances find their fulfillment in Christ. For example, the book addresses the topic of the Sabbath in chapters three and four explaining what it truly means to enter God's rest. On this note, the signature statement regarding the Sabbath is Hebrews 4:10, which says, "For he that is entered into His rest, he also hath ceased from his own works, as God did from His." This is connected to Jesus' statement in Matthew 11:28 which says, "Come unto me, all ye that labour and are heavy laden, and I will give you rest." Therefore, the main objective of the Sabbath is for humanity to enter into God's rest.

To have a better understanding of the Sabbath, we have to look at its implementation, which is recorded in the book of Genesis. In Genesis 2:1-3, when God finished creating the heavens and the earth, on the seventh day, He ceased from His works. He did not rest because He was tired, but He did this to establish a principle, which is rest speaks to the fact that labour has ended. Therefore, He was establishing the rule *that at the end of labour comes rest*. This is an important principle to remember to understand the Sabbath. Furthermore, the Lord also blessed the Sabbath and made it holy. By blessing and sanctifying the Sabbath, the Lord was also indicating that when you get to this place of rest, you are blessed and sanctified.

Primarily, the Law and its ceremonial practices represented righteousness by works. In essence, the Law depicted labour, which could not bring true redemption and sanctification (Hebrews 10:1-10). Furthermore, Romans Chapter 4 says the Law could not produce a state of blessedness. On the other hand, righteousness by faith accomplishes something totally different. In this regard, Romans 4:7 says, "Blessed are they whose iniquities are forgiven, and whose sins are covered." Therefore, righteousness by faith results in true redemption and sanctification. Additionally, it also means we are blessed. Recall from the principle of Genesis Chapter 2 that these are all associated with a state of rest. Because the Law was incapable of producing this type of rest, Jesus spoke of providing rest for all who labour and are heavy laden (Matthew 11:28-30). The Law represented labour; therefore, it could not produce righteousness. As a consequence, the people were heavily burdened. Trying to fulfill the Law was a tedious exercise that still resulted in being short or devoid of the glory of God.

However, through Christ, righteousness is attainable without works or labour, which again represents the Law. Thus, Romans 9:4 says, "For Christ is the end of the law for righteousness to everyone that believeth." Therefore, Christ represents an end to labouring for righteousness or righteousness of the Law. Consequently, this produces a state of rest. This is what Hebrews 4:10 means when it says, "For he that is entered into his rest, he also hath ceased from his own works, as God did from His." Hence, once we are baptized into Christ, the old man is crucified resulting in true righteousness or "newness of life". With the concept of labouring for righteousness coming to an end, we enter God's rest. In all reality, Christ then is the fulfillment of the Sabbath. Furthermore, in this place of rest, we are also in a position of sanctification and blessing. This then is the realization of the principle the Lord established from the beginning, which was that at the end of labour comes rest.

Entering God's rest is the equivalent of attaining righteousness by faith. It is righteousness without works or labour. It is righteousness without the Law. Entering God's rest also means we attain the glory of God. In addition, for believers, entering God's rest has a functional application. This is when we do not live unto ourselves but unto God. This is the admonishment Hebrews 4:11 speaks of; this rest requires sacrifice and effort. While many are focused on the observance of a particular day, Scripture emphasizes that the true Sabbath speaks of something more significant. For the purpose of this discussion, this was a condensed offering on the Sabbath. However, for more on this topic, please see my book *God's Eternal Purpose Volume Two, Entering Into His Rest*.

THE PRIESTHOOD AND THE LAW

As it pertains to the ceremonial components of the Law, there must be an understanding that the priesthood and the Law functioned together or worked in tandem. In fact, Hebrews 7:11 says that under the Levitical priesthood, the people received the Law. Therefore, the practice of the Law was only relevant under the Levitical priesthood. However, Hebrews chapters six and seven speak of a different priesthood. They both conclude that the order of Christ's priesthood, which is after the order of Melchisedec, is better than that of the Levitical order. For this reason, Hebrews 7:12 says, "For the priesthood being changed, there is made of necessity a change also of the Law." Seeing that the priesthood and the Law operated as a partnership, when the priesthood changed, the Law also was disestablished. In other words, with Christ's priesthood being after the order of Melchisedec, the Law, because it was weak and unprofitable, was also abolished. This is the same position expressed in Ephesians 2:15 where Christ abolished in His flesh the law of commandments contained in ordinances. Therefore, by virtue of a better priesthood, Christ also became the surety of a better testament, which is established on better promises. Under the Melchisedec priesthood, the instrument that is connected to it is a better testament and this contains better promises than what the Law provided.

Furthermore, based on Christ's position as High Priest, Hebrews 8:3 says, "Every high priest is ordained to offer gifts and sacrifices; wherefore it is of necessity that this man have somewhat also to offer." Therefore, following the pattern outlined by the high priest under the Levitical priesthood in the earthly tabernacle, Christ, as a minister of the sanctuary and the true tabernacle in heaven offered a better sacrifice. Hebrews 10:1 points out that the Law was only a shadow of good things to come and consequently could not take away sin. However, in relation to Christ, Hebrews 10:5 says, "When He cometh into the world, He saith, Sacrifice and offering thou wouldest not, but a body hast thou prepared me." Thus, Christ, being a High Priest of good things to come, by a greater and more perfect tabernacle, entered the holy place with His own blood and obtained eternal redemption for humanity. Unlike the sacrifices of the Law, which resulted in temporary redemption, Christ's sacrifice brought about eternal redemption (Hebrews 9:12). Additionally, this also resulted in eternal inheritance (Hebrews 9:15). In conclusion, the ceremonial components of the Law not only created an atmosphere of enmity, but they were also ineffective in producing righteousness and reconciling humanity to God and consequently, to each other.

ONE NEW MAN AND A NEW CREATURE

In addition to union with the Father, Ephesians 2:15 states that in removing the middle wall of partition, Christ also united Jews and Gentiles thereby creating one new man and making peace. As a principle, once the reason for opposition has been removed, then peace abounds. Therefore, peace is also a product of unity. This is one reason Jesus is referred to as the Prince of Peace (Isaiah 9:6). Seeing that the wall produced hostility, then the removal of the wall results in peace or harmony. Similarly, the key to promoting unity and peace in the body of Christ is to remove the walls or partitions that divide its members. As previously mentioned, this could pertain to doctrine or practices that foster an atmosphere of disunity. Notice specifically that Ephesians 2:15 uses the term, "one new man." The product of the union does not consist of Jewish believers and Gentile believers but rather, a new man without any prior ethnic affiliation. On this note Colossians 3:10-11 says:

10. And have put on the new man, which is renewed in knowledge after the image of him that created him:
11. Where there is neither Greek nor Jew, circumcision nor uncircumcision, Barbarian, Scythian, bond nor free: but Christ is all, and in all.

For different reasons, the concept of categorizing people into various groups is a pervasive practice. In today's society, humanity is divided based on skin color, wealth, religion, politics, family heritage, education, and many other factors. It is a mechanism used to highlight differences, which then fosters an environment of disunity. Hence, whenever there is division, God's purpose and unity are not the focus. This also contributes to idolatry or the exaltation of personalities above the Word of God.

Unfortunately, this culture of classifying people has also infected the church and the consequences are the same. However, as mentioned previously, in Christ, the elements that are used to divide humanity in a general sense are non-existent. Galatians 3:28 in echoing the same sentiments of Colossians 3:10-11 says that we are all one in Christ. It dismisses the notion of dividing factors such as ethnicity, social status, and gender. Specifically, there is no such thing as a black church or a white church but simply the church of Christ. This also extends to the discussion of denominationalism, for the very concept itself breathes division.

The criteria used by the world to engender division or create walls are based on identifying each other after the flesh. The measurement used is connected to skin color, gender, ethnicity, height, weight, and the other factors mentioned above. Therefore, if we are using these principles to identify and classify believers, we are following the same pattern of the world and not seeing from the perspective of the Father. When the Father sees us, He sees a new creature. He does not see us through the lens of nationality, ethnicity, gender (male/

female), or social status, for these are all fleshly identifiers. Being in Christ speaks of being in union with or being one with Christ. Therefore, when the Father sees us, He sees Christ. 2 Corinthians 5:17 says "If any man be in Christ, he is a new creature."

The term "new creature" speaks of being a new creation or species, one that did not exist before. Concerning this new creature, 2 Corinthians 5:16 says, "Wherefore henceforth know we no man after the flesh." The word "know" means to perceive with the senses or to have regard for. Therefore, this new creature is not subjected to labels associated with the flesh. Hence, if believers are being defined based on the perception of our natural senses, which results in fleshly labels, we are still making identifications based on the flesh and not seeing from the Father's perspective. This is also the impetus that fosters division. On the other hand, the absence of these identifications in the body of Christ cultivates an atmosphere of unity. We will revisit this discussion regarding the new creature in Chapter 13 during the exchange on the unity of the faith.

ONE BODY

In continuing with the message of unity, Ephesians 2:16 says the Father has also reconciled us in one body. The word "one" speaks of a single entity that is undivided and characterized by unity.

> 12. For as the body is one, and hath many members, and all the members of that one body, being many, are one body: so also is Christ.
> 13. For by one Spirit are we all baptized into one body, whether we be Jews or Gentiles, whether we be bond or free; and have been all made to drink into one Spirit. (1 Corinthians 12:12-13)

The body of Christ or the church is a single united entity though it is comprised of many members from diverse backgrounds. The principal message of the passage is that despite the diversity of the members, there is only *one* body. As stated previously, it is unfortunate that this recognition of unity seems to be more apparent within denominational circles than with the body as a whole. Notice it says that by one Spirit, we are all baptized into one body. It is the Holy Spirit or the Spirit of adoption by which we become sons of God and members of the same family.

To explain how the church functions as a single entity, the preceding scripture uses the illustration of a human body. This is based on the principle of Romans 1:20, which says that we understand spiritual or invisible things based on the example of natural or created things. Just as all the parts of a human body have specific roles and are vital to the proper functioning of the entire body, so it is for each member of the body of Christ. All members of the body are dependent on each other and all are specifically designed for the body to function as one. The Lord tailored the body after this manner to prevent division in the body and that all members would equally care for one another.

14. For the body is not one member, but many.
15. If the foot shall say, Because I am not the hand, I am not of the body; is it therefore not of the body?
16. And if the ear shall say, Because I am not the eye, I am not of the body; is it therefore not of the body?
17. If the whole body were an eye, where were the hearing? If the whole were hearing, where were the smelling?
18. But now hath God set the members every one of them in the body, as it hath pleased him.
19. And if they were all one member, where were the body?
20. But now are they many members, yet but one body.
21. And the eye cannot say unto the hand, I have no need of thee: nor again the head to the feet, I have no need of you.
22. Nay, much more those members of the body, which seem to be more feeble, are necessary:
23. And those members of the body, which we think to be less honourable, upon these we bestow more abundant honour; and our uncomely parts have more abundant comeliness.
24. For our comely parts have no need: but God hath tempered the body together, having given more abundant honour to that part which lacked:

25. That there should be no schism in the body; but that the members should have the same care one for another.
26. And whether one member suffer, all the members suffer with it; or one member be honoured, all the members rejoice with it.
27. Now ye are the body of Christ, and members in particular. (1 Corinthians 12:14-27)

Furthermore, the body of Christ is one because it consists of members who are joined to the Lord or one spirit with Him (1 Corinthians 6:17). To explain this unity with the Father from a natural perspective, Ephesians 5:30 uses a practical illustration. It offers an example of the unity that exists between a husband and his wife. In Genesis 2:23 when the Lord created Eve to be Adam's wife, Adam said, "This is now bone of my bones and flesh of my flesh." The language used here is the acknowledgment that they were one and of the same substance. Similarly, the church is one with Christ and of the same substance. Therefore, just as a wife, the church as a collective are members of Christ's body, of His flesh, and of His bones. Just as a man who is joined to his wife is one flesh, the church is joined to the Lord and is one spirit with Him. Furthermore, as one body, not only are we joined to the Lord, but we are also members one of another. Romans 12:5 says, "So we, being many, are one body in Christ, and everyone members one of another."

Being united with the Father, we are also *to the same degree* united with each other. It is a simultaneous unity. Again, in using the natural example of the unity of a husband and wife, Ephesians 5:29 says, "For no man ever hated his own flesh; but nourisheth and cherisheth it, even as the Lord the church." Therefore, as we are members of one body, we should not have contempt for one another but rather nourish and cherish each other as we do our own bodies. Often, Ephesians Chapter 5 is highlighted to describe the union and relationship between a husband and his wife. While this is significant and useful, it is important to note that the overarching conversation is really the union between Christ and the church. It is the message of oneness and that we are connected to Him and each other.

Just as the new man in Christ is not identified by divisive labels neither is the body to which they belong. Hence, the body of Christ does not consist of

Catholics, Anglicans, Baptists, Seventh Day Adventists, etc., but collectively those who have been reconciled to the Father. In fact, these designations by themselves represent walls and work in opposition to the message of unity.

Recall that the word "reconcile" means to bring back to a former state of harmony or to reestablish a close relationship. The definition itself speaks of unity. When Adam sinned, the relationship with the Father was severed. Unity was lost and humanity became estranged from His house and His kingdom. Furthermore, the ceremonial performances and sacrifices of the law were ineffective in producing reconciliation or relationship with the Father. Therefore, through Jesus' sacrifice, He made it possible for reconciliation and unity.

WE BOTH HAVE ACCESS BY ONE SPIRIT UNTO THE FATHER

The reason we now have access to the Father is because of our relationship. The word "access" also speaks of admission or the ability to have an audience with someone of high rank. It is similar to meeting the criteria for official clearance. Prior to Christ's death, only the high priest on the Day of Atonement went behind the veil into the holiest of all, which is where the presence of God was. He went with the blood of bulls and goats, which he offered for himself and for the sins of the people. According to Hebrews 9:8, this was an indication that the way or access to the holiest of all was not made manifest. However, Christ, as a High Priest of good things to come, entered the heavenly tabernacle with His own blood and obtained eternal redemption for us. As a result of Christ's sacrifice, the veil of the temple was torn thus providing access to the holiest of all and the presence of God. Consequently, Hebrews 10:19-22 says:

19. Having therefore, brethren, boldness to enter into the holiest by the blood of Jesus,
20. By a new and living way, which he hath consecrated for us, through the veil, that is to say, his flesh;
21. And having an high priest over the house of God;

22. Let us draw near with a true heart in full assurance of faith, having our hearts sprinkled from an evil conscience, and our bodies washed with pure water.

FELLOW-CITIZENS WITH THE SAINTS AND OF THE HOUSEHOLD OF GOD

In continuing with its message of unity, Ephesians 2:19 speaks of being fellow-citizens and members of God's household. Recall that Ephesians 2:12 says the Gentiles were once aliens or foreigners from the commonwealth of Israel. However, through Christ's death, both Jews and Gentiles have been reconciled into one body. Therefore, as members of this one unified body, former Jews and Gentiles are now fellow-citizens and members of the household of God. In its entirety, this is a statement of unity, equality, and reconciliation. Furthermore, in Ephesians 2:19, two dynamics are being presented, for it encapsulates both the kingdom of God, as well as the family of God.

The Greek word for fellow-citizen is *sympolites* and it means possessing the same citizenship as others or belonging to the same community. It affords everyone the same rights and privileges of citizenship. To be clear, in the kingdom of God former Jews do not hold a position of advantage over former Gentiles. They are both equal and possess identical benefits of citizenship. The church is not governed by the principles of natural ethnicity. Recall Romans 9:8, which establishes the tenet that the identification of true Israel or the people of God is not associated with fleshly birth but rather spiritual birth.

Additionally, former Gentiles are also fellow-citizens of the household of God. The word "household" is the Greek word *oikeios,* which means belonging to a house or family. It speaks of being a relative or kindred. We are all members of one family. Remember that when God created Adam, He made him in the capacity of a son. He was also a representative and extension of the Father to fulfill his purpose. Moreover, in this position, he was both a citizen of the kingdom of God and a member of the family/house of God. He also had a relationship with the Father and enjoyed unity with Him. However, when Adam sinned, humanity was separated from both the Father's kingdom and

His house. Unity with the Father was also lost. Therefore, Christ's death made it possible for humanity to be reconciled to the Father. This refers to being reinstated as citizens of His kingdom and also as sons of His family. This is the message of Ephesians 2:19.

In furthering the discussion of unity, Ephesians 2:21 refers to the church as a building that is fitly framed together. The term "fitly framed together" means to join closely together or to organize compactly. With the verse using the illustration of a building, it speaks of a carpenter who constructs the framework of a building meticulously joining each piece to create a seamless durable structure.

The consistent communication of this chapter based on the context of Ephesians Chapter 2 is the message of unity. In Christ, nationalities do not exist; social status does not exist and gender (male/female) classifications do not exist. The walls that were used to divide humanity and produce contention have been abolished, for we all are one. To truly appreciate this reality, it requires going beyond the veil of our flesh and not taking account of each other after the flesh. Based on the path we are taking, you may wonder how this approach directly relates to the five-fold ministry or the gifts of Christ. As I mentioned at the beginning of Chapter 2, the classic mistake many make in discussing the gifts of Christ is to make a beeline directly to Ephesians Chapter 4. However, that method circumvents the overall context of Ephesians and the meaningful principles offered in the chapters that precede it. Striving for mastery in any endeavor requires discipline, and this approach certainly calls for that. As we progress through this study and gather the puzzle pieces along the way, in the end, you will have an appreciation for the completed picture. So far, we have discussed God's "why" or His purpose, which He predetermined before the foundation of the world. This was followed by a detailed offering of the spiritual blessings in Christ, which provide a greater definition of the Father's purpose.

As leaders in the body of Christ and representatives to fulfill the Father's purpose, it is imperative to have a comprehensive understanding of what His objective is. For how can you effectively carry out a mission without knowing what the purpose is? Additionally, the significance of this particular chapter cannot be overstated. In its entirety, the discussion centered on the topic of unity from various aspects. Therefore, the purpose of this chapter was to lay the foundation for the exchange on the unity of the faith, which is a fundamental purpose of the gifts. Hence, by the time Ephesians Chapter 4 mentions the unity of the faith, the book has already created an atmosphere of unity.

CHAPTER 4

THE MYSTERY OF CHRIST: THE MESSAGE OF GOD'S PURPOSE AND UNITY

Having revealed the details of God's purpose and that it is one of unity in Christ, Ephesians Chapter 3 uses this as a backdrop and creates a headline. It says what we have been discussing all along is really *the mystery of Christ*. Notice that the chapter opens with the words, "For this reason." Therefore, Paul packages all that was said in the first two chapters and gives it a consolidated theme. Hence, the conversation of God's purpose and unity sets the foundation for the dialogue of Ephesians Chapter 3.

1. For this cause I Paul, the prisoner of Jesus Christ for you Gentiles,
2. If ye have heard of the dispensation of the grace of God which is given me to you-ward:
3. How that by revelation he made known unto me the mystery; (as I wrote afore in few words,
4. Whereby, when ye read, ye may understand my knowledge in the mystery of Christ)
5. Which in other ages was not made known unto the sons of men, as it is now revealed unto his holy apostles and prophets by the Spirit;
6. That the Gentiles should be fellowheirs, and of the same body, and partakers of his promise in Christ by the gospel. (Ephesians 3:1-6)

In this chapter, Paul sets his gaze specifically on former Gentiles to ensure they understand the magnitude of what has transpired. According to Galatians 2:7-8, Paul asserts that as a matter of stewardship, the gospel of the Gentiles was entrusted to him while the gospel of the Jews was committed to Peter. Therefore, in his capacity as the Apostle to the Gentiles, Paul says something significant has occurred for our benefit, and he has been given the responsibility of communicating it to us. Despite having already laid out the details of the mystery in the first two chapters, he offers a captioned encore in Chapter 3. Thus, in the fashion of a grand announcement, he says, "If ye have heard of the dispensation of the grace of God, which has been given to me for you." This is a major development, and I want to make sure that you are fully aware. To have an appreciation of the context of the passage, it is important to understand the word "dispensation." According to *Merriam-Webster's Dictionary*, dispensation means the following:

DISPENSATION DEFINED

- The act of dispensing. The notion here is that someone has something that they dispense (distribute) to someone else. This principle gives the connotation of administration or management
- Permission to break a law or an official promise; an exemption from a law
- The act of providing something to people; a formal authorization
- Divine ordering or administration of worldly affairs
- A system of principles, promises, and rules ordained and administered. For example, the administrations of Law and Grace

Additionally, dispensation is the Greek word *oikonomia* and it means the following:

- The management of a household or household affairs (*oikos*, "a house," *nomos*, "a law")
- Stewardship
- A general state or ordering of things; specifically, a system of revealed commands and promises regulating human affairs
- A "dispensation" is not a period or epoch (a common, but erroneous, use of the word), but a mode of dealing, an arrangement, or administration of affairs

In principle, dispensation pertains to the administration of the plan of God as opposed to a period of time. It speaks to the management of His household or household affairs. A dispensation manifests itself within times and seasons, but it is not necessarily related to time. The main element of dispensation is administration and management. It reflects the particular way God has made known His dealings with humanity at appointed seasons. In focusing on one of the aforementioned definitions, which is the management of a household or household affairs, let us look at a practical example.

As we are aware, certain laws govern each house, and they can vary depending on the house. On that note, Hebrews 3:1-6, speaks of two distinct houses. It highlights the house that Moses belonged to Israel, as well as the house of Christ: the church. The administration of the house of Israel was the Law, and the management of the house of Christ is grace. The distinction in the rules that govern each of these houses is most evident in Matthew chapters five to seven during what is commonly referred to as "The Sermon of the Mount." While introducing new management or principles for the administration of His house, Jesus used the contrasting phrase, "You have heard...but I say unto you." In other words, the laws that governed the house of Moses are not the principles by which my house is managed.

Because the rules managing the house of God have changed, the systems regulating human behavior have as well. To be clear, God is constant, and He does not change. His purpose, which He predetermined before the foundation of the world, remains the same. However, His manner of dealing with humanity changes in the progression of the fulfillment of His purpose. This is what Acts 1:7 means when it refers to the times or the seasons, which the Father hath put in his own power. Hence, at particular seasons or what the scripture refers to as the fullness of the time, there are specific manifestations of God's plan (Galatians 4:4). Therefore, when Paul speaks of the dispensation of the grace of God, he is referring to the management or administration of God's grace governing the church or His house.

Paul is saying that he has been given stewardship or appointed as a manager of the administration of God's grace. Hence, everything offered in Ephesians represents the details of the administration of God's grace. Thus, God's grace is manifold. Furthermore, the administration of grace is significantly different from the previous administration of the Law. It includes unity for all humanity; it has the components of eternal redemption and eternal inheritance, which is the consolidated promise in Christ. In addition, the benefits of the promise are for all humanity, for the Gentiles who were once excluded are now joint-heirs. Similar to Paul, those who have been bestowed the gifts of Christ have also been appointed as managers or administrators of God's grace. Therefore, to be an effective manager, there must be an understanding of the details of the plan. Hence, ministers must be aware of God's purpose for humanity and that His purpose exists within the framework of unity.

MYSTERY DEFINED

As mentioned at the beginning of this chapter, Paul captions the discussion of Ephesians Chapter 3 as the mystery of Christ. Normally, when we hear the word "mystery," the notion is that it is something beyond our understanding or what we cannot comprehend. However, the word "mystery" in this context does not refer to that which is presently unknown or hidden but rather, something that was previously a secret but is now revealed. Ephesians 3:9 declares that when the Lord determined His purpose from before the foundation of the world, He hid it in Himself thereby making it a mystery. Why did He do this? 1 Corinthians 2:7-10 provides us with the answer.

7. But we speak the wisdom of God in a mystery, even the hidden wisdom, which God ordained before the world unto our glory:
8. Which none of the princes of this world knew: for had they known it, they would not have crucified the Lord of glory.
9. But as it is written, Eye hath not seen, nor ear heard, neither have entered into the heart of man, the things which God hath prepared for them that love him.
10. But God hath revealed them unto us by his Spirit: for the Spirit searcheth all things, yea, the deep things of God.

First, the mystery of Christ, which is referred to as a hidden mystery (because it was hidden in God), was ordained for our glory. It was hidden because if the rulers of this world knew this was God's intent, they would not have crucified Jesus Christ or the Lord of glory. Therefore, everything the Father determined before the foundation of the world was done so He could bestow upon us His glory or the complete weight of His honour and dignity. He wanted to deposit His very nature into us and for us to exhibit that nature.

Ephesians 1:4 summarizes this glory as being holy and without blame before Him in love or possessing His very nature. Hence, due to the significance of this blessing and to ensure its fulfillment, the Father hid it in Himself. For this reason, 1 Corinthians 2:9 says that eyes did not see, nor did ears hear the things God hath prepared for those who love Him. In other words, the Father kept it a secret. Thus, this verse is not referring to some future unknown but rather to past events, which the Father hid from humanity and everyone else. However, because of a change in administration, the Spirit of God is now revealing what was once hidden. In support of 1 Corinthians 2:7, which says that what the Lord determined before the world was for our glory, Colossians 1:25-27 offers more insight:

25. Whereof I am made a minister, according to the dispensation of God which is given to me for you, to fulfil the word of God;
26. Even the mystery which hath been hid from ages and from generations, but now is made manifest to his saints:
27. To whom God would make known what is the riches of the glory of this mystery among the Gentiles; which is Christ in you, the hope of glory:

Wow! The entire plan of God was designed so we would be carriers of the glory of God. Whereas 1 Corinthians 2:7 reveals that what the Lord predetermined was for our glory, Colossians 2:27 announces how this was accomplished. It says the rich glory of this mystery is *Christ in you the hope of glory*. Therefore, once we receive the Holy Spirit or are quickened, then we receive the nature of the Father. The indwelling Holy Spirit brings with Him the complete estimate or worth of the Father's dignity and honour. We then become the vessels of the Father's glory. On this note, this provides us with the ability to move from glory to glory as we are transformed into the image or character of Christ.

Another definition of dispensation, which was mentioned above, is the permission to break a law or rule. In relation to the Jews and Gentiles, the

Law served as the middle wall of partition between the two groups. Therefore, the dispensation of grace serves as permission to break the standing rule that separated humanity. Where there was enmity, there is now peace; where there was division, there is now unity.

THE MANIFOLD WISDOM OF GOD

> 7. Whereof I was made a minister, according to the gift of the grace of God given unto me by the effectual working of his power.
> 8. Unto me, who am less than the least of all saints, is this grace given, that I should preach among the Gentiles the unsearchable riches of Christ;
> 9. And to make all men see what is the fellowship of the mystery, which from the beginning of the world hath been hid in God, who created all things by Jesus Christ:
> 10. To the intent that now unto the principalities and powers in heavenly places might be known by the church the manifold wisdom of God,
> 11. According to the eternal purpose which he purposed in Christ Jesus our Lord. (Ephesians 3:7-11)

Synonymous with the term "mystery of Christ," is the phrase "the unsearchable riches of Christ." Just like the word "mystery," the word "unsearchable" is not referring to something that cannot be known but rather something that was previously unknown or hidden but is now being revealed. Furthermore, with the inclusion of the word "riches" to describe what was unsearchable, this provides the perspective that what the Father predetermined for us is of tremendous value. Along these lines, Paul adds that his responsibility as a manager is to make all men see what is the fellowship of the mystery.

In the context of this passage, the word "fellowship" refers to the share or participation that one has in anything. Therefore, as a minister, Paul is saying his responsibility is to make all men understand their share of what the Father determined from before the foundation of the world. This begins with having the eyes of our understanding enlightened so that we would know the following:

- The hope of His calling

- What are the riches of the glory of His inheritance in the saints
- What is the exceeding greatness of His power to us-ward who believe

Recall that this embraces who we are, what He has done for us, and who He is in us. Furthermore, with fellowship being a community of people who share common interests or beliefs, the fellowship of the mystery refers to the shared interests that believers have in the mystery of Christ. Based on the approach we have taken, we can conclude that the shared interests involve the blessings of Christ and the message of unity in Him. Therefore, as leaders who have been bestowed the gifts of Christ, this is the fellowship we have been assigned to promote.

The Father also hid what He was doing because He had a specific intent. He wanted to make a grand reveal. His objective is that the church would make His manifold wisdom known to the authorities or angelic hosts in heavenly places. In essence, the very existence of the church, the sons who bare His very nature, is a declaration of the manifestation of God's wisdom. We are the products of the depth of the riches both of the wisdom and knowledge of God (Romans 11:33). When the principalities and powers in heavenly places look at the sons of God, they behold the manifold wisdom of God. Notice that in describing the Father's wisdom, the passage uses the word "manifold," which, like grace, means much variegated or marked with a great variety of colors. Therefore, it speaks of the great diversity of the wisdom of the Father. With the angelic host as an audience, the church has been given the mandate to proclaim God's diverse wisdom. The body of Christ is a manifestation of the principalities and powers in heavenly places of the manifold wisdom of God.

In consideration of what we have been discussing, 1 Peter 1:10-12 provides a great summation of the conversation on the mystery of Christ. It also adds that even the angels are interested in understanding and comprehending the things God has prepared for those who love Him.

10. Of which salvation the prophets have inquired and searched diligently, who prophesied of the grace that should come unto you:
11. Searching what, or what manner of time the Spirit of Christ which was in them did signify, when it testified beforehand the sufferings of Christ, and the glory that should follow.

12. Unto whom it was revealed, that not unto themselves, but unto us they did minister the things, which are now reported unto you by them that have preached the gospel unto you with the Holy Ghost sent down from heaven; which things the angels desire to look into. (1 Peter 1:10-12)

In Psalm 8, David makes a logical comparison in relation to what God has created. He says, "When I consider thy heavens, the work of thy fingers, the moon, and the stars, which thou hast ordained, I am left with a question. When I take into account these great celestial bodies and their splendor, I am forced to ask, 'What is man that thou art mindful of him?'" In other words, by comparison, he seems insignificant. As if that was not enough, David also says, "You made him a little lower than the angels and crowned him with glory and honour. However, despite this, you made him to have dominion over the works of thy hands and put all things under his feet."

When God created Adam (humanity), He made him in His image and likeness, which means He created him to represent Him and function on His behalf. Furthermore, He also created Adam in the capacity of a son, which in a kingdom and family setting is the highest designation that can be bestowed. This means He created humanity as an extension of Himself to fulfill His purpose. In essence, God created humanity because He wanted a family. However, He wanted a family who bears His very nature. Therefore, despite being made a little lower than the angels, humanity has a position of great prominence. This is why Hebrews 2:4 says, "For unto the angels hath He not put in subjection the world to come, whereof we speak."

The "world to come" is in reference to the inheritance of the kingdom of God where humanity will rule and reign with Christ. For this reason, with all the intricacies of the plan of God and the wisdom by which He orchestrated it, the church is declaring to the principalities and powers in heavenly places God's manifold wisdom. What an awesome reality! This declaration by the church and everything that Ephesians has so far addressed is in accordance with the eternal purpose of God, which He purposed in Christ Jesus our Lord. As mentioned in Chapter 1, there is indeed a grand design or purpose that is not only everlasting but is also unchangeable. Undoubtedly, it is God's "why."

CHAPTER 5

PRECURSOR TO THE GIFTS OF CHRIST

THE UNITY OF THE SPIRIT

Finally, we arrive at the threshold of Ephesians Chapter 4 with its direct emphasis on the five-fold ministry gifts. Certainly, we did not take the conventional approach in discussing this topic but rather a systematic one. With all intention, this was done in support of the premise put forth at the beginning of this book that people are more interested in why we do something as opposed to what we do. Recall that the *why* speaks of purpose, and in this instance, it highlights the reason God gave the gifts to humanity in the first place.

Additionally, for those in ministry, particularly in a leadership capacity, the process we undertook provided a greater perspective of the rationale behind the gifts. At this point, one thing should be certain: the gifts do not exist in a vacuum but are entirely connected to the purpose of the One who bestowed them. With God's purpose and the message of unity as a backdrop, Ephesians Chapter 4 continues the message of unity with equal enthusiasm.

1. I therefore, the prisoner of the Lord, beseech you that ye walk worthy of the vocation wherewith ye are called,
2. With all lowliness and meekness, with longsuffering, forbearing one another in love;
3. Endeavouring to keep the unity of the Spirit in the bond of peace.
4. There is one body, and one Spirit, even as ye are called in one hope of your calling;
5. One Lord, one faith, one baptism,

6. One God and Father of all, who is above all, and through all, and in you all. (Ephesians 4:1-6)

After tabling the message of unity in Ephesians chapters two and three, Paul continues the same discussion in Ephesians Chapter 4. In this regard, he admonishes the church to keep the unity of the Spirit in the bond of peace. Because of the significance of unity, notice that he uses the word "endeavoring" in relation to keeping the unity of the Spirit. The word endeavour means to attempt by exertion of effort. On the whole, preserving unity in any forum is a challenge and requires tremendous work. The word also signifies that maintaining unity is a continuous responsibility. What exactly is the unity of the Spirit? In simple terms, it is the unity the Holy Spirit brings.

This is the same message of unity we discussed in detail in Chapter 3 of this book. Specifically, it was highlighted that all believers are one in Christ, and divisions based on ethnicity, gender (male/female), social status, and all attributes related to the flesh are no longer relevant. Additionally, it emphasized there is one body, all believers are fellow-citizens of the kingdom of God, and they are also members of God's household or family. Therefore, these are the elements of the unity the church is to endeavor to maintain.

Moreover, the passage also points out that the unity of the Spirit is preserved in the bond of peace or the connection of oneness. Therefore, in the church, knowing we are one is what binds us together; it is the unifying principle. On the other hand, when we lose sight we are one, division manifests itself. When the connection of being one is broken, unity is the casualty. Hence, as long as we are of the mind that we are one and function as such, we are preserving the unity of the Spirit.

To further emphasize the message of unity, Ephesians Chapter 4 offers a series of compelling phrases to support and promote the concept of unity. The inclusion of these statements highlights the unity of the faith.

There is one body

The statement "one body" is the ultimate declaration of unity. Though the body of Christ has many members, it is a single entity. 1 Corinthians 12:12 in using the human body as an illustration says, "For as the body is one, and hath many members, and all the members of that one body, being many, are one body: so also is Christ." Furthermore, despite the many denominations or fractions that presently exist in the body of Christ, there is indeed only one body. Hence, for the unity of the faith to exist, the body truly has to function as one. Moreover, if there is no unity of the faith, then there can be no unity of the Spirit. The unity of the faith is explained in Chapter 13 of this book.

There is one Spirit
Just as there is only one body, there is also only one Spirit who connects us all. It is by the same Holy Spirit that we are all adopted into the family of God whereby we cry Abba, Father. Additionally, it is the same Holy Spirit who dwells in every believer. It is the same Holy Spirit through which we all have access to the Father. The same Holy Spirit works in every believer. It is the same Spirit who works to manifest the fruit or character of love in our lives.

We are called in one hope of our calling
This refers to the hope of our calling mentioned in Ephesians 1:17. Therefore, before the foundation of the world, the Father predetermined one hope for every believer. Regardless of position or titles, we all have the same destiny. The spiritual blessings in Christ outlined in Ephesians Chapter 1 are ordained for all who accept Jesus. Hence, the Father determined that every believer would be like Him and conform to the image of Jesus Christ. However, when there is no singularity of purpose, the result is fractions and divisions in the body.

There is one Lord
The title "Lord" refers to whom a person or thing belongs. It speaks of ownership, master, or one who has control of a person. Therefore, the reference here is Jesus Christ. He is Lord of the entire body and our allegiance is to Him and Him alone. There should be unity among believers because we all owe our devotion to one Lord and Saviour.

There is one faith
The statement "one faith" speaks to the fact that as it pertains to God's purpose, only one doctrine promotes that objective. Because the Father has a single purpose or "one hope of our calling," the doctrine surrounding that purpose is also singular in nature. However, in the church, just as there is a plurality of denominations, the doctrine or faith they promote is also varied. Again, if there is no unity of the faith, then there is no unity of the Spirit.

There is one baptism
This speaks of being baptized or immersed into Christ and therefore being committed to Him. 1 Corinthians 12:13 says, "For by one Spirit are we all baptized into one body, whether we be Jews or Gentiles, whether we be bond or free; and have been all made to drink into one Spirit."

There is one God and Father who is above all and in us all.
This is both a statement of supremacy and unity. First, despite others that are called gods or that are worshipped as gods, there is truly only one God. Additionally, to the same degree, there is also only one Father. With there being only one God and Father who is above all and in us all, this is also an expression of unity. As believers, we all have the same God and Father. Additionally, in embracing the concept of only one Father, this affirms that as sons of God, we are all members of the same family and household.

Truly, the message of oneness is resounding in the passage and serves as a precursor for the next discussion. In this regard, before highlighting the specifics of the gift of Christ, there is a concerted effort to ensure that the foundation of purpose and unity is fully expressed and understood. Hence, the purpose of the gifts exists within this context. To be clear, in accordance with the format of the chapter, for anyone who embarks on the path of ministry, the disposition of unity is a prerequisite. However, it is unfortunate that many of the conversations surrounding the gifts of Christ are conducted with little regard for unity. Furthermore, the same intensity that is placed on determining the existence of the gift in our lives or functioning in it, should also be placed on promoting the purpose of the gift, which is the unity of the Spirit. For without understanding and adhering to this premise, there can be no unity but rather divisions or fractions.

GRACE ACCORDING TO THE MEASURE OF THE GIFT OF CHRIST

After its persuasive message of unity, Ephesians Chapter 4 embarks on bringing attention to the grace associated with the measure of the gift given to believers.

> 7. But unto every one of us is given grace according to the measure of the gift of Christ.
> 8. Wherefore he saith, When he ascended up on high, he led captivity captive, and gave gifts unto men.
> 9. (Now that he ascended, what is it but that he also descended first into the lower parts of the earth?
> 10. He that descended is the same also that ascended up far above all heavens, that he might fill all things.)
> 11. And he gave some, apostles; and some, prophets; and some, evangelists; and some, pastors and teachers. (Ephesians 4:7-11)

Before addressing what is popularly regarded as the *five-fold ministry gifts*, notice that Ephesians 4:7 specifically uses the term, "gift of Christ." By comparison, when referring to the apostle, prophet, evangelist, pastor, and teacher, the more common phrase is indeed the *five-fold ministry gifts*. However, it is interesting that this specific expression is not mentioned in the above passage. By no means am I suggesting that the term is incorrect but based on Scripture, the phrase "gift of Christ" certainly creates a different perspective. To that point, while speaking with a friend, I replaced the term "five-fold ministry gifts" with "gift of Christ." It was interesting that the substance of the conversation was noticeably different based on this substitution. Furthermore, this was one of the reasons the expression "understanding the gifts of Christ" was included as a subtitle of this book.

Additionally, with the usage of the word "gift," it is clear that what is bestowed is not earned but rather, it is based on the grace of God. Furthermore, the word "gift" also implies that the ability to operate in the gifts did not originate with us but with Christ. Therefore, in the body of Christ, leadership is also a reflection and function of God's grace. Moreover, the gifts are also given to promote the unity of the faith.

According to Ephesians 4:7, everyone is given grace according to the measure of the gift of Christ. What exactly does this mean? With the discussion of unity as a backdrop, Ephesians 4:7 embraces the fact that even though there is overall unity, there are still degrees of distinction. Therefore, even though there is one body, one Spirit, one hope of our calling, one Lord, one faith, one baptism, one God and Father who is above all, through all and in us all, there are still variations based on the grace of God. On that note, variety does not cancel unity, particularly, the unity of the Spirit. In referring to grace, we concluded earlier that grace is multifaceted in that it also includes God's influence in our lives. Recall that in Ephesians 3:8, Paul was given the grace to preach the unsearchable riches of Christ. Hence, based on Ephesians 4:7, the Lord bestows grace or His influence in accordance with the measure of the gift of Christ. The word "measure" is the Greek word *metron,* which refers to the following:

- A rule or standard of judgment
- An instrument for measuring. An instrument for receiving and determining the quantity of something

Based on the definitions of the word "measure," the passage is stating two things. First, what is bestowed by the Lord is according to a certain standard and that principle is consistent with Christ's gift. In simple terms, the functioning of the gifts is based on the standard that Christ exhibited. Hence, Ephesians 4:7 uses the term gift of Christ because they are the gifts He functioned in while on Earth. He was an apostle. He was a prophet. He was an evangelist. He was a pastor, and He was a teacher. Therefore, the model of how the gifts operate is seen in how Christ operated. He is the benchmark or model for the operation of the gifts. They are not based on the standard that we determine or what is decided by denominations or the religious establishment. The gifts are a representation and reflection of who He is and His purpose. I reiterate that when Christ came, He came with God's "why." He came to fulfill the Father's purpose, which He predetermined from before the foundation of the world. Included in this was the restoration of humanity to the kingdom of God and the house of God. Similarly, the gifts Christ bestows are also connected to God's why. They exist in accordance with God's purpose. In addition, they are called the gifts of Christ because when He gives the gifts, He is essentially giving of Himself. He is the personification of the gifts. Therefore, when the world sees the gifts functioning, they are beholding Christ in operation. They should see the consistent standard that Christ demonstrated.

The second perspective offered based on the definition of the word "measure" is in relation to the degree of the gift. The other definition for the word "measure" speaks of a vessel for receiving and determining the quantity of something. Thus, the measure of the gift of Christ not only signifies that Christ is the benchmark for the gifts or that He is the one who confers the gifts, but that He also facilitates the degree by which it is imparted. Christ functioned in all the gifts without measure. However, as leaders, we are given a measure of the gifts; therefore, individuals endowed with gifts are given them at varying levels.

Based on the objective God has called the individual to, He imparts a particular measure to accomplish His purpose. It is important to understand that the same endowment is not conferred upon everyone. It is based on the grace of God. Therefore, comparisons among ministers are not necessary. Even though several believers may be granted the same gift, for example, a teacher, the measurement based on God's purpose for them individually may be different. Nevertheless, despite the measurement, the gift is a manifestation of God's grace and not based on the ability of the receiver. Once we comprehend and embrace this principle, it eliminates envy and division amongst the ministers of the gospel. God is the one who determines the measure of the gift.

In this regard, despite the measure of the gift given to an individual, the presence of the gift will always be evident. For example, while highlighting his apostleship, Paul says in Galatians 2:8, "For He (God) that wrought effectively in Peter to the apostleship of the circumcision, the same was mighty in me towards the Gentiles." In other words, just as God bestowed the gift of apostleship to Peter in relation to the Jews, He similarly conferred the gift of apostleship to Paul with respect to Gentiles. Furthermore, Paul added that when James, Peter, and John who were recognized as pillars in the church *perceived the grace that was given to him*, they gave him and Barnabas the right hand of fellowship. This means the gift in Paul was evident, and they recognized it. Consequently, they accepted them and acknowledged them as partners of the gospel.

Additionally, for those who are bestowed the gift of Christ, the degree of the gift will also be manifested. Throughout the New Testament, many functioned in the capacity of an apostle; however, the measure in each person was not identical. For example, both Paul and Barnabas were apostles as indicated in Acts 14:14. However, as the witness of Scripture provides, the measure of the gift in Paul was dissimilar to the measure in Barnabas. Furthermore, even with both Peter and Paul being apostles, Peter made an acknowledgement in 2 Peter 3:16 concerning Paul. He said in all Paul's epistles, some things are hard to understand, which the unlearned and unstable wrestle with to their own destruction as they do the other scriptures.

To be clear, Peter was not saying that he did not understand what Paul was saying, but simply that because of the tremendous revelation he was given, some of it was not easy to comprehend. This is especially true for those who are unlearned and unstable who twist or pervert the scriptures. Therefore, the statement is also recognition of the authority of Paul in his capacity as an apostle and his impact on the church. Obviously, Peter was familiar with the context of what Paul wrote and fully endorsed it as he stated in 2 Peter 3:1-2. However, it is also evident by his statement that the measure of the gift in Paul was different from the measure in Peter. Yet, despite this distinction, they still operated in the unity of the Spirit and in the bond of peace.

Another example that highlights the varying portion of a gift is in the account of Elijah and Elisha. In 2 Kings Chapter 2, knowing that he would soon be taken away, Elijah the prophet asked Elisha, "What can I do for you before I am taken away?" Elisha's response was, "Let a double portion of thy spirit be upon me." Therefore, after Elijah was taken away, Elisha took up the mantle that fell from him and it was evident that the anointing of Elijah or the gift of a prophet was on him with a greater measure. Despite the fact that they were both prophets, the measure of the anointing they had varied. Nevertheless, the gift was bestowed to accomplish God's purpose and not for Elisha's benefit.

Just as Christ reflected the purpose of the Father while He was on earth, His purpose for giving the gifts is to function in the purpose of the Father. In this vein, those who have the gifts and operate in Christ's stead are to promote the same message He preached. In essence, the gifts serve as a continuation of what He started. With Christ being the basis for comparison in relation to how the gifts function, it would behoove us to examine what He said and did to have a better perspective of the gifts.

THE MINISTRY OF JESUS CHRIST

In Matthew 4:17, Jesus officially launched His ministry with the words, "Repent: For the kingdom of heaven is at hand." Based on what we have discussed to this point, it should be evident that the pronouncement of these words, was the embodiment of God's why. Essentially, He consolidated the Father's intent from before the foundation of the world and in one sentence He outlined God's purpose for humanity. In this regard, what Jesus said wasn't simply the flavor of the month sermon, but this was the consistent message throughout His earthly ministry. In fact, this was the only message He preached.

Furthermore, with these words, He also introduced a particular narrative concerning ministry and ministers. Therefore, by His words and actions, He established the platform for those who would follow in His stead. As a Son, Jesus came as an extension of the Father to fulfill His purpose. Functioning in the gifts was incorporated in that purpose. Hence, as He was the firstborn of many brethren, we as sons of the Father are given the same gifts and kingdom mandate. Therefore, regardless of the gift that is bestowed, our disposition should be that of sons who are extensions of the Father to fulfill His life and purpose. This is in harmony with the question Isaiah asked in Isaiah 53:8,

"Who shall declare His generation?" In other words, who shall represent Him and be a continuation of His purpose?

Concerning the gifts, there are two general points I want to present concerning those who have been conferred the gifts of Christ. The first pertains to a servant's frame of mind and the other addresses religious behavior compared to the message of the kingdom of God.

THE INFLUENCE OF THE WORLD VERSUS BEING A SERVANT

Regardless of the specific gift bestowed by the Father, there is a general posture for all ministers of the gospel, which is the disposition of a servant. Therefore, whether you function in the capacity of an apostle, prophet, evangelist, pastor, or teacher, the character is still that of servitude. I know that in today's environment of celebrities and larger than life egos, this concept seems to be forgotten. However, it is unfortunate that this mentality has also infiltrated the church and is popular among ministers, particularly, those in leadership positions. Nevertheless, Scripture is clear that the source of this influence is from the world and has no place in the kingdom of God. A practical illustration highlighting this circumstance is presented in Matthew 20:20-28:

20. Then came to him the mother of Zebedee's children with her sons, worshipping him, and desiring a certain thing of him.
21. And he said unto her, What wilt thou? She saith unto him, Grant that these my two sons may sit, the one on thy right hand, and the other on the left, in thy kingdom.
22. But Jesus answered and said, Ye know not what ye ask. Are ye able to drink of the cup that I shall drink of, and to be baptized with the baptism that I am baptized with? They say unto him, We are able.
23. And he saith unto them, Ye shall drink indeed of my cup, and be baptized with the baptism that I am baptized with: but to sit on my right hand, and on my left, is not mine to give, but it shall be given to them for whom it is prepared of my Father.

24. And when the ten heard it, they were moved with indignation against the two brethren.
25. But Jesus called them unto him, and said, Ye know that the princes of the Gentiles exercise dominion over them, and they that are great exercise authority upon them.
26. But it shall not be so among you: but whosoever will be great among you, let him be your minister;
27. And whosoever will be chief among you, let him be your servant:
28. Even as the Son of man came not to be ministered unto, but to minister, and to give his life a ransom for many.

According to this account, the mother of James and John came to Jesus, along with her sons with a specific request. She appealed for her sons to sit one on the right and the other on the left of Jesus in His kingdom. In accordance with her petition, she was advocating on their behalf for positions of prominence and glory. Having been persuaded of who He is, they saw an opportunity for positions of greatness.

The basis of this request was self-serving and designed to promote their own interests. However, in response to the appeal, Jesus presents a different perspective. First, He asked them if they would partake of the afflictions and sufferings prescribed for Him. After affirming they would undergo such hardship, Jesus assured them they would indeed experience suffering. However, He concluded that the appointments they sought were not His to give. He pointed out they will be given to those for whom they were prepared by the Father.

When the other ten apostles heard of the request, they were extremely displeased with James and John. Therefore, in response to the entire exchange, Jesus offered a comparison between two governing influences and mindsets. In relation to James and John, He pointed out that their request was motivated or influenced by the rulers of the Gentiles. Furthermore, He added that those who have power and authority exercised dominion or governance over them. To exercise authority over others means you govern or influence their thoughts and values; you set the standard of conformity, which is reflected in their behavior. In essence, He was saying, based on the principles and actions of those in authority in the world, James' and John's minds were conditioned to desire the same thing concerning the kingdom of God. They wanted the same prestige and recognition they witnessed based on the pattern of the world. In essence, they saw the world and its leaders as their benchmark. Isn't it ironic that this same deportment is visible in many ministers of the gospel today? The result is a church leadership that wants to be treated as if they are celebrities having people honour and serve them. However, this posture has no place in the kingdom of God. This is not the purpose of the gift of Christ.

In opposition to this disposition, Jesus offers an alternative perspective and a different governing influence. He says, "But it shall not be so among you: but whosoever will be great among you, let him be your minister." In other words, He was saying, the influence of the rulers of the world will not be the standard you follow. Instead, He communicated the standard of the kingdom of God. Therefore, contrary to what the world promotes, true greatness is not in being served but rather, in being a servant. The word "minister" is the Greek word *diakonos,* which means one who executes the commands of another or in this instance, a servant. Therefore, in comparison to the persuasion of James and John, this frame of mind is certainly the polar opposite.

The pattern of the kingdom of God and ministry is based on the mindset of being a servant, not on the expectation of being served. In highlighting the perspective of a servant, Jesus says, he that desires greatness must be a servant. Hence, Jesus was reconditioning their minds and setting the standard for His ministers and the purpose of ministry. As the benchmark, He said His purpose was not to be served or waited upon but to be a servant. To be clear, leaders who rule well deserve double honour, especially those who labor in the Word and doctrine (1 Timothy 5:17). Additionally, they should be esteemed very highly in love for their work's sake (1 Thessalonians 5:13). However, the celebrity status and stardom mentality that has infiltrated the church is based on the influence of the world and not after God. Thus, it is this posture that Matthew Chapter 20 addresses, and Jesus warns us about. In fact, in the kingdom of God, there is only one celebrity and that is the Lord Jesus Christ. Therefore, at its core, the bestowing of the gift of Christ is for leaders to be servants. They are not granted for self-exaltation, recognition, or fame.

THE RELIGIOUS ESTABLISHMENT VERSUS THE KINGDOM OF GOD

In addition to the characteristics of a servant, the gift of Christ is not to promote a religious agenda. As we have discussed, when God created humanity, He produced a kingdom environment, as well as a family atmosphere. Hence, God's kingdom and His house are the pillars on which His purpose or will is established. Therefore, when Jesus came and proclaimed that the kingdom of heaven is at hand, this was not a religious declaration. To be clear, the kingdom of God is not a religion. Furthermore, even some of the concepts contained within the religion of Christianity are not in harmony with the principles of the kingdom of God. From the beginning, God's purpose never involved the formation of religion as it exists, but rather, the establishment of His kingdom on Earth. Therefore, the tenets of the kingdom of God take precedence over the demonstration of any religious expression, including those under the banner of Christianity.

According to the *Free Dictionary* by Farlex, religion is defined as a specific fundamental set of beliefs and practices generally agreed upon by a number of persons. Religion is therefore identifiable. Moreover, based on this definition, religious ideology can evolve in accordance with the consensus of those involved with it. For example, in 1978, the Church of Jesus Christ of Latter Days Saints or the Mormons adopted what they refer to as the "revelation on the priesthood." In 1852, Brigham Young enacted a policy that men of black African descent could no longer be ordained to the priesthood. However, he also added that at some point in the future, black church members would be afforded all the privileges of those enjoyed by other members. Consequently, in June 1978, after spending many hours seeking the Lord for guidance, the church leaders declared that they received a revelation. Accordingly, they acknowledged that "the long-promised day has come."

The leaders said they were "aware of the promises made by the prophets and presidents of the church who have preceded us." Therefore, they determined that "All of our brethren who are worthy may receive the priesthood." Hence, this policy "rescinded the restriction on priesthood ordination and extended the blessings of the temple to all worthy Latter-day Saints, men and women."

However, from previous discussions, it is clear that in the kingdom of God, ethnicity, and gender identifications are non-existent; yet, in religion, they are often pronounced. Therefore, this previous position and subsequent pivot was a religious posture that is not supported by Scripture and unrelated to God's purpose. Furthermore, based on the premise of Ephesians Chapter 1, the spiritual blessings in Christ were predetermined for all humanity. Hence, a "new revelation" to promote the Father's purpose was not necessary. Additionally, the purpose of the Father is also one of unity, and we are all called to preserve the Spirit of unity in the bond of peace.

Please note that it is not the intention of this inclusion to specifically highlight the Mormons, for there are countless examples of religious behaviors by many denominations that can be emphasized. Conversely, the purpose, as mentioned earlier, is simply to pinpoint that the gift of Christ is not to promote a religious position, but for leaders to fulfill Christ's kingdom mandate.

To be clear, the concept of religion that is being discussed is not the pure religion mentioned in James 1:27. In this instance, pure religion refers to the worship of God that is undefiled or not polluted with the opinions and ideals of man. According to the passage, its hallmarks are caring for and visiting the marginalized along with living a life of holiness. Certainly, by using the word "pure" James makes the distinction between this type of religion and the one that is tainted. An example of this can be seen in how the scribes and Pharisees injected the traditions of men into the worship of God thereby rendering their actions ineffective (Matthew 15:9). Therefore, my usage of religion refers to the vain or fruitless worship of God because it contains the element of the doctrine of men. It is this religion that facilitates divisions. Furthermore, it also works in opposition to preserving the unity of the Spirit, which is a function of the gift of Christ.

Additionally, religion involves ceremonial performances and doctrines that differ depending on the ideologies of the religious group. These differences often result in fractions between humanity because of the opposing views held by the various religious groups. Generally speaking, religion, specifically within the confines of Christianity, can be summarized as man's attempt to define and establish what God's will is. Included in this is also the manner in which He is to be worshipped. However, it is evident from the numerous denominations existing today that a consensus on God's will for humanity is severely lacking. In fact, while admonishing His disciples about how they will be persecuted by the religious establishment, Jesus said that in doing so, these leaders will think they are performing the will of God. This is a clear indication it is not apparent to them that they are operating in contravention of God's purpose.

Evidently, people can be convinced they are doing the will of God but have the wrong persuasion. This is also akin to having a zeal of God but not according to knowledge. In using Romans 12:1-4, the principle is that when people are ignorant of fundamental truth, they establish their own standards and consequently are not in submission to God's principles. This also fosters an environment of self-righteousness. As Romans Chapter 12 demonstrates, there is indeed a zeal or fervency for the things of God but unfortunately, His true purpose is not known. Therefore, in this instance, the substitution is a religious expression that attempts to redefine God's will. When this occurs, the focus is often redirected from God toward man and the result is idolatry along with vain worship. Consequently, what is taught for doctrine is actually the traditions of men (Matthew 15:9) and this is not the purpose of the gift of Christ. Take note that this entire operation explains the basis of how religion functions in the body of Christ. Therefore, regardless of how it is manifested or what form it takes, its seed is revealed by Scripture.

When referring to the behavior of the religious establishment of Jesus' day, there seems to be a notion that those practices are not prevalent amongst the religious leaders of today. However, as we have discussed, the operation of religion remains the same. Based on Jesus' interactions with the scribes, Pharisees, and Sadducees, we have a clear illustration of the purpose, function, and effect of religion. Therefore, the same characteristics highlighted by Jesus are still practiced today and are visible among many leaders. Let us look at some of the attributes of religion that are revealed in Scripture.

    a) It is a practice that creates an environment where people love the praise of men more than the praise of God (John 12:43). This produces idolatry.

b) It is a system where religious leaders who sit in positions of authority say one thing but do the opposite (Matthew 23:2-4). Therefore, it is embedded in hypocrisy.

c) It involves fostering an atmosphere in which leaders enjoy being seen by men. It is based on externalism, rituals, and ceremonies (Matthew 23:5). It is anchored in pageantry and performances.

d) It consists of a structure where religious leaders love to be exalted and given preferential treatment over everyone else (Matthew 23:6). This consists of a celebrity culture and is also related to idolatry.

e) It is a system where the religious leaders love greetings or special attention in public and to be called Rabbi or teacher (Matthew 23:7). It is based on prestige and name or title recognition.

f) It is an environment that uses religious teachings as a tool to suppress the people (Luke 11:52). It is used to hinder God's people.

g) It is a scheme where leaders take advantage of the vulnerable or susceptible for their own profit (Matthew 23:14). It uses deception for gain.

h) It is an approach where the leaders place greater emphasis on the outward appearance rather than on the inward workings of the heart (Matthew 23:25-27). It has a form of godliness with no inward power.

i) It is a system in which the traditions of men hold precedence over the commandments of God (Matthew 15: 1-9). As stated, this results in vain worship.

j) It is a culture that fosters and supports divisions among the people based on ethnicity, social status, and gender (male/female). However, in Christ, these do not exist (Galatians 3:27-28).

Based on the above, it is a recognizable fact that the tenets of religion are the antithesis of the principles of the kingdom of God. In fact, during His dialogue with the religious leaders, Jesus was creating a contrast between the fundamentals of the kingdom of God and those offered by the religious establishment. Furthermore, He was creating a distinguishable culture for those who would take up His mantle. Therefore, for those who operate in Christ's stead, who have been furnished with the gift of Christ, the above characteristics of religion have no place. The gifts are not provided for the purpose of religious expression or to be self-serving but for the unity of the Spirit.

GAVE GIFTS TO MEN

In revisiting Ephesians 4:8, it says, "When He ascended up on high, He led captivity captive, and gave gifts unto men." Hence, those to whom the gifts are bestowed are identified by their functions. Within the confines of religion, some are of the persuasion that the gifts of Christ are only bestowed to men, not women. Therefore, it is their conviction that only men should be apostles, prophets, evangelists, pastors, and teachers. Recall that as a precursor to its conversation on the gifts, Ephesians Chapter 4 is deliberate in its communication on oneness and unity. Consequently, such a conclusion would not only contradict this position but also result in division and gender biases. It would also oppose the concept of the unity of the Spirit.

It should be noted that the word "men" in this passage is a generic term for all humanity; therefore, it includes both men and women. It is the Greek word *anthropos*, from which we get the word "anthropology." According to *Merriam-Webster's Dictionary*, anthropology is the science of human beings. It studies people, especially their history, development, distribution, biological characteristics, and culture. Hence, the gifts Christ gave are given to humanity, which includes both men and women. In addition, as we have discussed, Galatians 3:28 points out that in Christ, there is neither male nor female, but we are all one.

As a point of emphasis, Romans 11:29 says, "For the gifts and calling of God are without repentance." Even though the reference of this verse is directly concerning God's selection of Israel, it establishes a meaningful principle that once the Father bestows a gift, it is permanent. Even in the natural, once gifts are granted, they are irrevocable. Additionally, as we have determined, when Christ gives the gifts mentioned in Ephesians 4:11, He is essentially giving of Himself. He is the gift, therefore when they are given and manifested through believers, we are witnessing Christ.

THE IMPORTANCE OF STRUCTURE

For any purpose to have success, it must be supported by organization. Therefore, when the Father determined His purpose from before the foundation of the world, He also implemented the framework necessary to fulfill it. In this regard, before delving into the gifts individually, it is important to offer a perspective on structure, particularly, as it pertains to the church and its leadership. For any institution or entity to function effectively, it must have a proper organizational structure, and the church is no different. First, the word "structure" is defined as something arranged in a definite or coherent pattern of organization. It is a framework that provides clarity in relation to specific functions and responsibilities.

In the corporate world, schools, and many other institutions, the presence of structure is visible. It is used to promote harmony and order and is the basis for achieving objectives. Unfortunately, when this framework is absent, the result is anarchy and subsequent failure or mediocrity. Indeed, many churches and denominations purport to subscribe to scriptural parameters, especially concerning church structure. However, upon close examination of Scripture, their tenets and practices seem to suggest otherwise. From a leadership perspective, the book of Acts is clear in its pronouncement of how the church ought to operate. Therefore, it is impossible to understand the structure and function of the church without an understanding of the book of Acts. However, let us begin this discussion by examining a familiar example of structure from the Old Testament.

MOSES AND THE ISRAELITES

When it comes to the administration of God's purpose for His people, Scripture provides several illustrations of the significance of structure. For example, Exodus Chapter 18 provides the account of Moses in his capacity as leader and judge of Israel in relation to the matters they brought to him.

> 13. And it came to pass on the morrow, that Moses sat to judge the people: and the people stood by Moses from the morning unto the evening.
> 14. And when Moses' father in law saw all that he did to the people, he said, What is this thing that thou doest to the people? why sittest thou thyself alone, and all the people stand by thee from morning unto even?
> 15. And Moses said unto his father in law, Because the people come unto me to inquire of God:
> 16. When they have a matter, they come unto me; and I judge between one and another, and I do make them know the statutes of God, and his laws. (Exodus 18:13-16)

After observing the system by which Moses settled the disputes of the people, Jethro his father-in-law said, "The thing that thou doest is not good. Thou wilt surely wear away, both thou, and this people that is with thee: for this thing is too heavy for thee; thou art not able to perform it thyself alone." Based on Jethro's observation, he commented that the task of judging the people was too great for one individual. In other words, the process lacked proper structure, which results in exhaustion and frustration, not only for leaders but for the people as well. Conversely, the existence of a meaningful structure accomplishes the opposite, as we will soon discover.

After examining the situation, Jethro offered to revamp the process by which judgment was meted out in Israel. However, first, he acknowledged Moses in his capacity as judge. In this vein, he validated him as the representative to present the matters of the people before God. Therefore, in a conciliatory fashion, he not only certified his position as judge but also affirmed that what he was doing was good. Hence, Jethro was not suggesting that Moses abdicate his leadership function but simply delegate some of the responsibility. Thus, in a skilled manner, Jethro conveyed to Moses that his authority was not being diminished.

Furthermore, included in his organizational advice, Jethro also added the element of empowerment through knowledge. Therefore, he advised Moses to teach the people the ordinances and laws thereby instructing them on how to live and what they must do. Having ignorant constituents never contributes to a good organizational structure. In any public institution, if the necessary information is only reposed in one person or a few individuals, there will never be growth. However, once people are informed, they are enlightened with an awareness, which often makes them better. Additionally, the more information people have the less dependent they are on leadership. Thus, they reduce the burden of leadership. Based on this principle, information is clearly the means by which growth is fostered; unfortunately, the opposite is also true.

In addition to informing the people of the statutes, Jethro advised Moses to select individuals who would function as legislators based on certain criteria. We will find that whenever it pertains to leadership responsibility in relation to God's people, the righteous requirements are always consistent. In this instance, the qualifications for the legislative were that they must fear God, be men of truth, and hate covetousness or dishonest gain. Thus, one of the primary criteria for the implementation of a structure is the establishment of qualifications. Furthermore, in establishing the new framework for judging Israel, Jethro proposed a system where the selected legislators would be appointed as rulers over thousands, hundreds, fifties, and tens. This example also provides insight that proper structure also aids in the development of the next level of leadership. For the task of resolving the matters of the people went from being a solo act to an orchestra.

In addition, Jethro suggested to Moses that the function of the legislators be a permanent position. This brought an element of stability to the structure. Hence, it was not just something to be conducted whenever Moses was inundated but it was to be a permanent fixture. Moreover, the structure also kept leadership involved and engaged in the process. Recall that the intent of the new structure was not to circumvent Moses in his capacity of judge but to reduce the burden of leadership and better serve the people. Hence,

Moses was not removed from the equation of judging Israel but remained an integral part of the organizational structure. Included in the model, the appointed legislators would be responsible for judging the small matters, while the difficult ones would be brought to Moses.

Undoubtedly, based on Jethro's recommendation, we see a definite pattern of organization. After Jethro gave Moses his advice, he said to him, "If thou shalt do this thing, and God command thee so, then thou shalt be able to endure, and all this people shall also go to their place in peace." Notice that despite providing Moses with reasonable advice, he concluded that the final decision rests with God's approval. Overall, Jethro submitted to Moses that the implementation of the proposed structure would be of benefit to both him and the people. Therefore, Moses would be able to persist in his responsibility, and the people would have their matters resolved more efficiently. Fortunately, Moses adhered to the advice from his father-in-law and implemented the organizational structure.

Having discussed the significance of proper structure based on an Old Testament illustration, let us now turn our attention to the book of Acts as it provides several meaningful examples of the significance of organizational structure particularly regarding the church. Specifically, we will examine the concept and benefits of structure concerning the following:

1. Leadership Replacement
2. Growth and Unity
3. Reconciliation of Doctrine and Unity

1. LEADERSHIP REPLACEMENT

Having core leadership intact is essential to the success of any organization. In this regard, the book of Acts accounts that before the eleven apostles could move forward with their mandate, the first thing they did was to ensure the leadership structure was complete. After the death of Judas, there was a leadership vacancy among the apostles, which needed to be addressed to find a replacement. Therefore, in Acts 1:15, we have what can be appropriately categorized as a general assembly. This gathering consisted of about 120 disciples and during this meeting, Judas' replacement was tabled. Peter, in addressing the other apostles and disciples, provides the narrative that what transpired with Judas was based on the fulfilment of prophecy.

20. For it is written in the book of Psalms, Let his habitation be desolate, and let no man dwell therein: and his bishoprick let another take.
21. Wherefore of these men which have companied with us all the time that the Lord Jesus went in and out among us,
22. Beginning from the baptism of John, unto that same day that he was taken up from us, must one be ordained to be a witness with us of his resurrection.
23. And they appointed two, Joseph called Barsabas, who was surnamed Justus, and Matthias.
24. And they prayed, and said, Thou, Lord, which knowest the hearts of all men, shew whether of these two thou hast chosen,
25. That he may take part of this ministry and apostleship, from which Judas by transgression fell, that he might go to his own place.
26. And they gave forth their lots; and the lot fell upon Matthias; and he was numbered with the eleven apostles. (Acts 10:20-26)

Before the selection process began, notice that Peter first outlined the qualifications for the position. Again, every position particularly that of leadership has a certain set of criteria that must be met. The decision was not going to be based on who was popular, which family they belonged to, or any measure associated with the flesh. In this case, the candidates must have been with Jesus from the time He was baptized up to the time of His ascension. In other words, they must have been with Jesus during His entire ministry. This could not be individuals who simply joined because of the feeding of the five thousand or who were only persuaded after His resurrection. Therefore, two foundational requirements were faithfulness and commitment.

Having witnessed what Jesus did and having been taught by Him for three-and-a-half years, the candidates would also have to be of the same mind as the eleven apostles. In other words, they were required to know the culture of the organization and be vested. In his address, not only did Peter highlight the requirements of the job, but he also gave a summary of what the position entailed. He said that the principal responsibility of the office was *to be a witness* with the apostles of the resurrection of Jesus Christ. Of note, this has nothing to do with seeing Christ after His resurrection but on the contrary, it embraces *proclaiming and demonstrating the power of His resurrection*. However, this will be discussed in detail in the next chapter when we examine the qualifications of an apostle.

By functional definition, an apostle's focus from a leadership perspective is teaching about the kingdom of God and being a witness of Christ's resurrection. After Peter presented the qualifications of the office along with its major responsibilities, the assembly then nominated Joseph and Matthias. However, with only one position to be filled, they prayed and sought the Lord for guidance. Thus, by consensus, they chose Matthias and he was numbered with the eleven apostles. Replacing Matthias was about maintaining the leadership structure for the church.

2. GROWTH AND UNITY

Acts Chapter 6 provides a parallel example to the one offered in Exodus Chapter 18 regarding the appointment of the legislators in Israel. Like the previous illustration, this one also speaks of the significance of organizational structure. In studying the book of Acts, one narrative is notably consistent: once there is an adherence to structure or order, growth and unity are always manifested. In this regard, the book of Acts serves as the template for church structure and function.

Having the disposition of "all things common," believers, in addressing the needs of the poor, sold their houses and lands and brought the money to the apostles. As the church was in its infancy, this was the structure that existed at the time, and the apostles were responsible for distributing to everyone based on his or her need (Acts 4:32-37). However, as the church grew, so did the enormity of the task. Hence, combined with their primary responsibilities of prayer and ministry of the Word, the apostles were unsuccessful in properly attending to the needs of the poor.

1. And in those days, when the number of the disciples was multiplied, there arose a murmuring of the Grecians against the Hebrews, because their widows were neglected in the daily ministration.
2. Then the twelve called the multitude of the disciples unto them, and said, It is not reason that we should leave the word of God, and serve tables.
3. Wherefore, brethren, look ye out among you seven men of honest report, full of the Holy Ghost and wisdom, whom we may appoint over this business.
4. But we will give ourselves continually to prayer, and to the ministry of the word.
5. And the saying pleased the whole multitude: and they chose Stephen, a man full of faith and of the Holy Ghost, and Philip, and Prochorus, and Nicanor, and Timon, and Parmenas, and Nicolas a proselyte of Antioch:
6. Whom they set before the apostles: and when they had prayed, they laid their hands on them.
7. And the word of God increased; and the number of the disciples multiplied in Jerusalem greatly; and a great company of the priests were obedient to the faith. (Acts 6:1-7)

Prior to the introduction of this new structure, everything pertaining to the church centered on the apostles. They were directly responsible for everything—from the ministry of the Word to facilitating the needs of the poor. However, based on the above account, the daily distribution to the poor was not an efficient process. Apparently, the Grecians were murmuring against the Hebrews citing that their widows were being neglected in the daily distribution. Hence, the structure that was successful in the beginning proved to be ineffective because of the tremendous growth of the church. Therefore, realizing the dilemma, the apostles (leaders) called the disciples together to restructure the process. Due to inefficiency, it required reorganization.

Notice in the apostles' capacity as leaders, they entrusted the disciples with the responsibility of selecting those who would play a pivotal role in the reorganization. Any time you involve the stakeholders in the decision-making process, it contributes to their empowerment. Moreover, the apostles sanctioned this initiative because they trusted the disciples' judgment. However, even though they entrusted the disciples with the selection, the apostles still provided the criteria for selection. Similar to the example of selecting legislators in the example with Moses, the candidates had to be of righteous character. Acts 6:3 says they had to be of honest report, full of the Holy Ghost and wisdom. Wherefore, once the seven individuals were chosen, the apostles prayed for them and laid their hands upon them. This action signified the approval of those selected thereby granting them the authority to do the work. Consequently, the responsibility of the distribution of goods to the poor was transferred from the apostles and delegated to others.

Because of an inadequate structure, there was complaining, contention, neglect, and the notion of favoritism. In essence, this represented the seeds of division in the church and threatened its unity. However, the restructuring exercise addressed this matter and as a result, several other things followed.

- The Word of God increased.
- The number of disciples multiplied in Jerusalem.
- A great company of priests was obedient to the faith.

Based on this example, the net outcome of having the appropriate structure was increase or growth of the church. Additionally, the adequate structure also allowed for the following:

- The apostles (leaders) were able to focus on their core objectives, which included prayer and preaching the gospel. Indeed, distribution to the poor is important; however, in terms of the leaders' core responsibilities and their primary purpose, the process proved more efficient when it was assigned to others. No one can be everything to everyone.
- Overall, the church (or the organization) experienced success, which is in alignment with its purpose. In this instance, the Word of God increased and there was tremendous growth.
- The next level of leadership was created. The responsibility of good leadership is to reproduce itself. This was particularly evident based

on the accounts of two of the seven who were chosen, namely Stephen and Philip.
- Greater unity among members of the church (the stakeholders) was realized because their needs were met efficiently. The internal conflicts ceased. The seeds of division were eliminated.

All of these were possible as a result of having the proper organizational structure in the church. Therefore, the right structure facilitates success, not only for leadership but for everyone involved.

3. RECONCILIATION OF DOCTRINE AND UNITY

The book of Acts provides another example of why having a proper organizational structure is essential. In this instance, it pertains to the function of church leadership regarding its position on certain subjects and the way doctrinal disputes should be addressed for reconciliation. In particular, this example is concerning the Gentiles and the question of circumcision. Nevertheless, even though the subject matter may be different depending on the situation, the model for reconciliation remains the same. Therefore, regardless of what the topic or doctrine is for consideration, Scripture provides us with the pattern to follow. To have a better appreciation for this point, let us look that the circumstances that led to the discrepancy concerning the Gentiles and circumcision.

THE GENTILES

In Acts Chapter 10, the Lord revealed to Peter that the Gentiles were also included in salvation. This is the same revelation Paul expands on in the book of Ephesians thereby offering more details. Recall that Ephesians 3:6 says the Gentiles are now fellow heirs of the same body and partakers of God's promise in Christ. However, up to the time of Acts Chapter 10, this was unknown, and the gospel was only being preached to the Jews. Therefore, the inclusion of the Gentiles represented a new perspective in relation to the church. To convey a precise message concerning the Gentiles, the Lord in a vision showed Peter a sheet descending from heaven filled with unclean animals. During the vision, a voice said to Peter in Acts 10:13, "Rise, Peter; kill and eat." However, based on the instructions outlined in the Law, Israelites were forbidden from eating unclean animals (Leviticus 11:2-27). Therefore, Peter responded in Acts 10:14 and said, "Not so, Lord; for I have never eaten anything that is common or unclean." However, in response, the voice said to him, "What God hath cleansed, that call not thou common." In other words, the Lord was saying, what I have purified, do not call unclean. Moreover, to send a resounding message, the statement was repeated three times.

In the vision, the illustration of the unclean animals figuratively depicted the Gentiles, for Jews were forbidden to fellowship with them. Hence, the Lord used the vision to indicate that the Gentiles, who were once considered unclean, have been purified. Additionally, He was changing the perspective of Gentiles in the eyes of the Jews. Furthermore, the vision conveyed the message that the distinction between the Jews and Gentiles had been eliminated. Their status and position had changed. Therefore, in Acts 10:34-35, during Peter's encounter with Cornelius who was a Gentile, he said, "Of a truth I perceive that God is no respecter of persons: But in every nation he that feareth him, and worketh righteousness, is accepted with him." Moreover, as Peter preached the Word of God to Cornelius' household, they were all filled with the Holy Ghost and were then baptized.

Eventually, word reached the other apostles and brethren at Jerusalem that the Gentiles had received the Word of God. In other words, the rest of the church leaders became aware that there was a shift from what was traditionally accepted. Consequently, in Acts 11:2 when Peter went to the church at Jerusalem, they contended with him for associating and eating with Gentiles. Like Peter in the previous chapter, their perspective and position regarding the Gentiles were based on what was outlined in the Law. However, Peter rehearsed to the other apostles and brethren the vision from the Lord and all that transpired with Cornelius. Therefore, after hearing the account, they glorified God saying in Acts 11:18, "Then hath God also granted unto the Gentiles repentance unto life." Hence, after Peter met with the other leaders of the church, they accepted the position that the Gentiles were also included.

In this scenario, the leadership of the church tabled the matter regarding the Gentiles and unanimously accepted their inclusion in the body of Christ. As a result of having a proper organizational structure, the church was able to effectively address and resolve the matter. Additionally, this represented a turning point for the church, for now, the gospel would be preached to both Jews and Gentiles. Furthermore, this also constituted the message of unity as Jews and Gentiles were now one, establishing one body and one household (Ephesians 2:11-22). Whereas the Jewish religion had distinctions based on ethnicity, the kingdom of God does not.

Because of the persecution that resulted from Stephen's death (Acts 8:1-2, 4), the disciples were dispersed to various places. Consequently, they preached the gospel wherever they went. Nevertheless, the apostles remained in Jerusalem. Therefore, those who went to Antioch preached the Word of God to the Gentiles; a great number believed and turned to the Lord. Hence, when the leaders (apostles) of the church at Jerusalem heard this report, their response was completely different from the initial occasion. Having already embraced the Gentiles, they sent Barnabas as their representative to support the work. Based on what the church leadership determined in Jerusalem, they validated their decision with action. In reality, this measure also signified the unity that existed in the church. As a result of this cohesion, many more people were added to the church. Again, this is evidence that proper leadership and structure always contributes to both unity and growth. After a time in Antioch, Barnabas went to Tarsus to look for Saul (Paul), and they returned to Antioch where they preached the gospel for an entire year and taught many people (Acts 11:19-26).

In Acts Chapter 13, while in Antioch, the Lord said, "Separate me Barnabas and Saul for the work whereunto I have called them." Therefore, they departed and also took John with them for what is generally considered as Paul's first missionary journey. However, after stops in Seleucia, Cyprus, Salamis, and Paphos, John departed from them and returned to Jerusalem. Nevertheless, Barnabas and Saul journeyed onto Perga, and they eventually returned to Antioch. While in Antioch, they preached the gospel in the synagogue. When they were done, many of the Jews supported them and persuaded them to continue in the grace of God. Furthermore, several Gentiles appealed to

Barnabas and Saul that the same words would be preached to them the next Sabbath. Consequently, the next Sabbath, almost the entire city came to hear the Word of God. However, when the Jews saw the multitude, they were filled with envy. Because of the size of the crowd, they changed their previous position and spoke against Paul, contradicting what he said. It seemed that when the numbers were smaller, the Jews were comfortable with what Paul and Barnabas were preaching; however, when the crowd grew, their disposition changed.

> 46. Then Paul and Barnabas waxed bold, and said, It was necessary that the word of God should first have been spoken to you: *but seeing ye put it from you, and judge yourselves unworthy of everlasting life, lo, we turn to the Gentiles.*
> 47. For so hath the Lord commanded us, saying, I have set thee to be a light of the Gentiles, that thou shouldest be for salvation unto the ends of the earth.
> 48. And when the Gentiles heard this, they were glad, and glorified the word of the Lord: and as many as were ordained to eternal life believed.
> 49. And the word of the Lord was published throughout all the region. (Acts 13:46-49)

Notice that in harmony with divine order, the Lord commissioned Paul and Barnabas to be lights to the Gentiles *after He had established the position regarding the Gentiles with the leadership*. Also, recall that they sent Barnabas to Antioch to support the preaching of the gospel to the Gentiles. Therefore, the mandate given to them aligned with what was already given to the leadership. Hence, after the Jews expelled Paul and Barnabas from Antioch, they went to Iconium preaching the gospel and a great number of both Jews and Gentiles believed. However, the unbelieving Jews stirred up the Gentiles and corrupted their minds against Paul and Barnabas. After a plot to stone them was discovered, they fled to Lystra and Derbe preaching the gospel. After preaching for some time in these two cities, they returned to Iconium and eventually, to Antioch.

During their journey, Acts 14:23 says that they ordained elders in every church and commended them to the Lord. Therefore, not only were Paul and Barnabas operating in accordance with an established structure, but they also facilitated the implementation of the local church structure. They appointed elders or pastors in every church. Furthermore, upon returning to Antioch, they gathered the church together and rehearsed all the Lord had done and how He had opened the door of faith to the Gentiles. Even in the report, they delivered to the church at Antioch, what they said was in support of and in harmony with the established position the Lord gave to the church and its leadership. Notice that having the proper structure in place allowed for the Word of God to be preached effectively, particularly, to the Gentiles. Nevertheless, the inclusion of the Gentiles would eventually create another challenge, which also had to be addressed by the church leadership.

THE MATTER OF CIRCUMCISION

With many Gentiles being added to the church, there arose a dispute regarding the practice of circumcision. The fact that Gentiles were a part of the church was a foregone conclusion and this position was accepted. However, many Jewish believers were of the opinion that the Gentiles still needed to be circumcised to be saved. Moreover, there was a group of Pharisee believers who added adherence to the Law of Moses to the requirements.

1. And certain men which came down from Judaea taught the brethren, and said, Except ye be circumcised after the manner of Moses, ye cannot be saved
2. When therefore Paul and Barnabas had no small dissension and disputation with them, they determined that Paul and Barnabas, and certain other of them, should go up to Jerusalem unto the apostles and elders about this question.
3. And being brought on their way by the church, they passed through Phenice and Samaria, declaring the conversion of the Gentiles: and they caused great joy unto all the brethren.
4. And when they were come to Jerusalem, they were received of the church, and of the apostles and elders, and they declared all things that God had done with them. (Acts 15:1-4)

With the church consisting of both Jews and Gentiles, the matter of circumcision challenged its unity. Those who promoted the doctrine of circumcision in relation to the Gentiles represented the seeds of discord and denominationalism in the body of Christ. For the first time since the inception of the church in Acts Chapter 2, we are presented with teaching that proposed to divide the church. Therefore, as this was a weighty matter, it was determined that Paul, Barnabas, and others should go to Jerusalem to the apostles and elders to settle the issue.

As noted in the previous account, the authority of the apostles and their leadership was firmly acknowledged by the church. Wherefore, when they arrived in Jerusalem, the apostles and elders welcomed them, and they declared all the things God had done through them. With the subject of circumcision being a contentious topic in the church, they once again assembled what can be appropriately described as an apostolic council. Acts 15:6 says, "And the apostles and elders came together for to consider this matter."

First, Peter offered his position based on the vision the Lord gave him and his interaction with Cornelius. This was followed by the testimony of Barnabas and Paul declaring the wonders and miracles God did among the Gentiles through them. Finally, James, while endorsing Peter's position, offered scriptural support, which for the Jews in particular, was a substantial reference. Using a witness from Scripture, he quoted the prophet Amos (Amos 9:11-12) who prophesied concerning the Gentiles. In his closing remark, he offered this conclusion, "Wherefore my sentence is, that we trouble not them, which from among the Gentiles are turned to God: But that we write unto them, that they abstain from pollutions of idols, and from fornication, and from things strangled, and from blood. For Moses of old time hath in every city them that preach him, being read in the synagogues every sabbath day" (Acts 15:19-21.).

Based on the consensus from the council, it was agreed by the apostles and elders that circumcision was not a necessity for salvation. This decision then became the unified position and official communication of the church regarding this subject. This was truly an exercise of preserving the unity of the Spirit in the bond of peace. Furthermore, to show solidarity concerning what was decided, Acts 15:22 says, "Then pleased it the apostles and elders, with the whole church, to send chosen men of their own company to Antioch with Paul and Barnabas; namely, Judas surnamed Barsabas, and Silas, chief men among the brethren." Similar to the determination regarding the Gentiles, not only was there an agreement, but the leaders, along with the entire church provided additional support for the preaching of the gospel and to promote what was decided. Moreover, to ensure there was no ambiguity concerning the position of the church, the leaders also sent letters validating what was decided, commending the brethren, and offering instructions regarding other things.

> 23. And they wrote letters by them after this manner; The apostles and elders and brethren send greeting unto the brethren which are of the Gentiles in Antioch and Syria and Cilicia:
> 24. Forasmuch as we have heard, that certain which went out from us have troubled you with words, subverting your souls, saying, Ye must be circumcised, and keep the law: to whom we gave no such commandment:
> 25. It seemed good unto us, being assembled with one accord, to send chosen men unto you with our beloved Barnabas and Paul,
> 26. Men that have hazarded their lives for the name of our Lord Jesus Christ.
> 27. We have sent therefore Judas and Silas, who shall also tell you the same things by mouth.
> 28. For it seemed good to the Holy Ghost, and to us, to lay upon you no greater burden than these necessary things;
> 29. That ye abstain from meats offered to idols, and from blood, and from things strangled, and from fornication: from which if ye keep yourselves, ye shall do well. Fare ye well. (Acts 15:23-29)

To address the conflict regarding circumcision, the leaders of the church assembled to resolve the matter. In this regard, circumcision represented a doctrinal position the church needed to resolve. Needless to say, because the appropriate organizational structure was in place, everyone knew where to go for resolution. Additionally, because the church's position was resolute with both anecdotes and Scripture, this fostered an atmosphere of unity in the body. Hence, the separate doctrine being promoted, which could have resulted in a denominational schism was rejected by the church. Therefore, as mentioned previously, a proper structure promotes unity; whereas, its absence engenders division. Wouldn't it be great if the entire body of Christ functioned based on this principle?

The latter part of Acts Chapter 15 provides the account of the parting of Paul and Barnabas due to a difference of opinion. In Acts 15:36, Paul entreated Barnabas to revisit the brethren they encountered on their first journey to see how they were doing. However, Barnabas was determined to bring John with them. He had accompanied them at the beginning of their journey. Nevertheless, Paul was opposed to this because John had left them at Pamphylia and was not involved in the work. Because of the sharp contention between the two, Barnabas left with John to Cyprus and Paul took Silas with him through Syria and Cilicia. When Paul returned to Derbe and Lystra, they met Timotheus (Timothy), and he was added to their company. As they journeyed, notice specifically what they did in Acts 16:4-5.

4. And as they went through the cities, they delivered them the decrees for to keep, that were ordained of the apostles and elders which were at Jerusalem.
5. And so were the churches established in the faith, and increased in number daily.

Paul, Silas, and Timothy did not have a separate agenda from what was ordained by the apostles and elders at Jerusalem. They were not promoters of their own positions, but rather that which was determined by leadership. There was singleness of heart, and they understood there was one objective. Therefore, through obedience to the established structure, growth ensued. As a result of proper leadership, the churches in the various cities were established in the faith and increased in number daily. On the contrary, without the appropriate organizational structure, growth cannot be realized, purpose is lost, and unity cannot be achieved. God is a God of structure. Hence, for the church to accomplish His "why," there must be an adherence to His divine order. Unfortunately, much of the anarchy and disunity that exists in the church today is a result of deviation from God's established order and not having the appropriate structures in place. As the example reveals, differences of opinions, especially pertaining to the doctrinal positions of the church will arise. However, when the proper mechanism in terms of organizational structure is in place, there is also the opportunity for resolution.

APOSTLES AND PROPHETS

To accomplish His purpose concerning the church, the Father implemented a specific structure regarding its leadership. With that said, in bestowing the gifts of Christ, included in this endowment is also the concept of organization. As a premise, there are several instances throughout the New Testament where apostles are mentioned in tandem with the prophets. What is significant about these two gifts of Christ that they seem to be referenced with a degree of emphasis over the other gifts? This occurs not only to create a direct association between the two gifts but also to emphasize their significance in the body of Christ.

> 19. Now therefore ye are no more strangers and foreigners, but fellowcitizens with the saints, and of the household of God;
> 20. And are built upon the foundation of the apostles and prophets, Jesus Christ himself being the chief corner stone;
> 21. In whom all the building fitly framed together groweth unto an holy temple in the Lord:
> 22. In whom ye also are builded together for an habitation of God through the Spirit. (Ephesians 2:19-22)

The above passage says that the church or the household of God is built upon the foundation of the apostles and prophets. To be clear, Paul is not stating that apostles and prophets serve as the foundation of the church, for Scripture is clear that as it pertains to the church there is only one foundation. 1 Corinthians 3:11 says, "For other foundation can no man lay than that is laid, which is Jesus Christ." However, in terms of organizational structure, apostles and prophets serve a foundational function for the entire body of Christ. In comparing the church to a building, the strength and integrity of the structure depend on its foundation. It is to provide the base upon which the entire building rests. Moreover, the foundation holds the structure upright, distributes the building's load and supports it. Hence, based on this analogy, the foundational function of an apostle and prophet is to act as the principals of the church. They have a fundamental responsibility in terms of doctrinal truth; therefore, they provide strength and stability to the church. For what it's worth, the church isn't established on the foundation of the pastor. Hence, in relation to structure, the church is not pastoral but apostolic.

Even though apostles and prophets serve a foundational purpose concerning the house of God, Ephesians 2:20 aptly identifies Jesus Christ as the chief cornerstone of that foundation. To get a better understanding of His function in this capacity, let us consider the significance of a cornerstone. Nowadays, cornerstones perform a more decorative or ornamental function in buildings compared to their purpose many years ago.

Historically, the cornerstone, also referred to as the foundation stone, was the first stone laid in the construction of a masonry foundation. It was usually placed in the corner of the building to be a guide to the workers and assist them in the measurement of the building. It was crucial because all the other stones were set in reference to it thereby ensuring that the building was square and stable. Furthermore, as it was one of the largest and most solid stones, the entire weight of the structure rested on it. Therefore, while Scripture concludes that apostles and prophets are indeed important in their foundational assignment, to ensure the house of God is stable and in the correct position, they must align with Jesus Christ. As the cornerstone, He is the reference point of the church and every believer must align with Him. Furthermore, the church gets its correct measurement from Jesus Christ as He is also our standard of measurement. This will be discussed in greater detail in Chapter 13.

Moreover, despite the foundational role apostles and prophets have concerning the church, there is also an established order between them.

> 28. And God hath set some in the church, first apostles, secondarily prophets, thirdly teachers, after that miracles, then gifts of healings, helps, governments, diversities of tongues.

29. Are all apostles? Are all prophets? Are all teachers? Are all workers of miracles?
30. Have all the gifts of healing? Do all speak with tongues? Do all interpret?
31. But covet earnestly the best gifts: and yet shew I unto you a more excellent way. (1 Corinthians 12:28-31)

As a second witness of church structure, the Bible says clearly that based on the Father's design, He established in the church first apostles and secondarily prophets. Notice in this arrangement, Scripture assigns precedence to the apostles; however, the church today has reversed that order and has instead given priority to the pastor. Nevertheless, 1 Corinthians 12:28 says, "And God hath set some in the church, first apostles. The word "first" in this passage is the Greek word *proton* and it means the following:

- First in time or place in any succession of things or persons
- First in rank, influence, or honour
- Principal

Based on the above definition and in harmony with Scripture, the Father has given apostles precedence as it pertains to the church. This is the structure He has instituted. Therefore, for the church to align with God's purpose and fulfill its mandate, it has to be apostolic in nature. Similar to the placement of apostles, which is first, the position of prophets is identified as second or secondarily. The word "secondarily" is the Greek word *deuteros,* which means the following:

- The other of two
- Second in time, place, or rank

In many instances, where the word "second" is used in Scripture, it is in direct association with what was mentioned first. Examples can be found in Matthew 22:39 and 1 Corinthians 15:47. Accordingly, just as the apostle is first in rank as it pertains to the church, prophets being "the other of the two," are second in terms of position. They are next to the apostles in authority and rank. Therefore, as it relates to the structure and function of the church, it is imperative that we have a comprehensive understanding of all the gifts.

However, from a foundational perspective, it is important to understand the function of the apostle and prophet.

In revisiting 1 Corinthians 12:28, it says, "And God hath set some in the church, first apostles, secondarily prophets, thirdly teachers, after that miracles, then gifts of healings, helps, governments, diversities of tongues." Furthermore, according to the witness of Ephesians 2:20, the church is established on the foundation of the apostles and prophets with Jesus Christ being the chief cornerstone. Therefore, as we have discussed previously, the church, based on God's design, is established on apostolic order. However, based on the contemporary constitution, the church seems to be established predominately on pastoral order as opposed to the apostolic mandate outlined in Scripture. The framework offered in the book of Acts and several epistles has seemingly been abandoned and replaced with another system. However, regardless of what may be popular or widely practiced, Scripture ultimately serves as the guideline for church structure. I reiterate that for any organization to fulfill its purpose, proper structure is necessary. For the body of Christ to accomplish God's "why," divine order is a prerequisite. For it is only with a proper organizational structure that the unity of the faith can be preserved.

DIVERSITY YET UNITY

1 Corinthians Chapter 12 creates an analogy by comparing the body of Christ to a physical human body. In doing so, the passage establishes the principle that even though diversity exists, there is still unity in the body. Diversity, therefore, does not signify disunity. This is also evident from the discussion about spiritual gifts stating that despite the diversity of gifts, it is the same Spirit, which distributes to every man as He wills. Hence, the point being emphasized is that regardless of the many members of the body, it is still one body. Thus, the significance of the chapter is the message of unity. It says *one Spirit, many gifts, and one body, many members*. Nevertheless, even though there is unity in the body and each member has a significant role, there still exists a particular order of things. Therefore, for unity to be possible there has to be order.

Notice that before engaging in the discussion about the order of the leadership gifts, the passage is careful to establish the foundation of unity and equality. It also underscores the importance of every member. Hence, in the midst of unity, structure and order still exist. With this as a backdrop, 1 Corinthians 12:28-31 says for the purpose of structure, the gifts within the body have a particular order. The order of the gifts is first apostles, then prophets, thirdly, teachers, and so on.

Having explained the Father's purpose for humanity, which includes the message of unity, we are finally at the juncture to discuss the individual gifts of Christ in detail. As we have conveyed throughout this book, these two components are the fundamental reasons why the gifts are bestowed. Therefore, regardless of the individual responsibilities related to each gift, as a whole, they both express the collective assignment of the gifts. Furthermore, the gifts also exist to provide organizational and functional structure to the church to fulfill the Father's purpose. Hence, when the gifts are absent or ineffective, the body of Christ is left wanting. Each of the gifts is a component of the overall ministry of Jesus Christ, so each one makes a specific contribution to the fulfillment of that purpose. Therefore, as we discuss each gift of Christ, we will discover its relevance to the Father's purpose. Moreover, it should be noted that the Father may bestow more than one gift to an individual; thus, he or she can function in several offices at the same time. For example, Paul functioned in the offices of apostle, evangelist, and teacher (1 Timothy 2:7; 2 Timothy 1:11).

CHAPTER 7

THE GIFT OF CHRIST EXPLAINED: APOSTLE

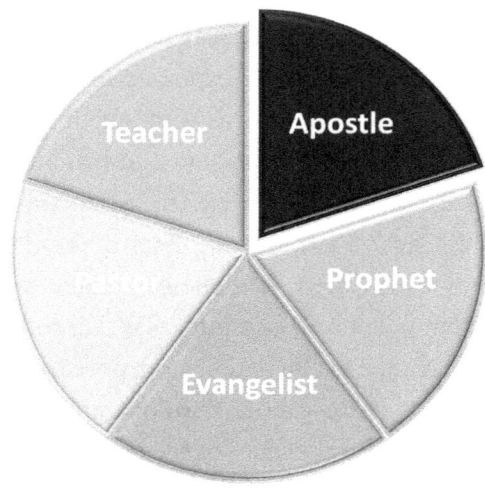

*And he gave some, **apostles**; and some, prophets; and some, evangelists; and some, pastors and teachers" (Ephesians 4:11).*

In discussing the individual gifts of Christ, we will begin with the gift of the apostle. As mentioned in Chapter 5, the gifts are a representation and extension of how Christ functioned while He was on Earth. He was an apostle. He was a prophet. He was an evangelist. He was a pastor. He was a teacher. He is the very essence of the gifts. Therefore, when Christ gives the gifts to humanity, He is giving of Himself to continue the work He started. As the standard, He is the image in the mirror or the reflection of how the gifts ought to function. Therefore, for those who purport to function in the gifts and do not use Christ as a benchmark, this image is a false representation. Hence, for a better understanding of the gifts, a comprehensive explanation of each one will be offered over the next several chapters. This will also include a segment of how Christ functioned in each gift. Additionally, some denominations are of the opinion that the office of the apostle no longer exists. On the other hand, other denominations assign the title with tremendous liberty even though based on Scripture, apostles were a limited number. With that said, in this chapter, we will also reconcile this difference from a scriptural perspective while explaining the roles and responsibilities of an apostle.

APOSTLE DEFINED

The word "apostle" is the Greek word *apostolos*, which means the following:

- A delegate
- A messenger
- One sent forth with orders

According to *Baker's Evangelical Dictionary of Biblical Theology*, an apostle is "The authorization of an individual to fulfill a particular function with emphasis on the one who sends, not on the one who is sent." This concept is often used in a military sense to describe one that is sent with orders. Hence, it resembles the position of a general in an army who has authority but who is also under authority. Therefore, the office of an apostle is not to be taken lightly as they are commissioned to represent the One who sends them.

Today, we live in a spiritual environment where many claim to be apostles with little knowledge of the office or its true function. It is unfortunate that depending on whom you ask, the response of what qualifies one to be an apostle is varied. From experience, we can conclude that when definite guidelines are absent, disarray runs rampant. Some think the office is no longer applicable, but based on Scripture, this perspective is incorrect. According to the premise established in Ephesians Chapter 4, the gift of the apostle is still viable today just as the other gifts of Christ. Ephesians 4:13 says the collective purpose of the gifts is granted until something specific happens. In other words, the gifts all function until certain goals are met. They are "Till we all come in the unity of the faith, and of the knowledge of the Son of God, unto a perfect man, unto the measure of the stature of the fulness of Christ" (Ephesians 4:13). This is the same message of purpose and unity, which serves as the foundation of God's will for humanity. Therefore, until this occurs in the body of Christ, all five components of the gift of Christ are fully functional. In addition to the twelve apostles that Revelation 21:14 classifies as the apostles of the Lamb, there were indeed other apostles in the New Testament. For example, Acts 14:14 mentions that both Barnabas and Paul were also apostles. In addition, Apollos can be added to this list (1 Corinthians 4:6-13), James (Galatians 1:19), along with Andronicus and Junia (Romans 16:7).

As with many things, just as we have the genuine, there is also the counterfeit. As a matter of fact, 2 Corinthians 11:13 speaks of false apostles and deceitful workers who have transformed themselves into the apostles of Christ. Hence, it is evident not everyone who claims the designation of an apostle is truly an apostle of Christ or a recipient of His gift. Moreover, based on the proliferation of those claiming ascension to the office, it appears the adoption of the title is more fashionable than purposeful. With that said, there seems to be a greater focus on status than function. Nevertheless, those who are truly the apostles of Christ must understand the significance of the gift. However, before delving into the specifics of what it means to be an apostle, let us examine the inception of the office with Jesus Christ.

12. And it came to pass in those days, that He went out into a mountain to pray, and continued all night in prayer to God.
13. And when it was day, he called unto him his disciples: and of them he chose twelve, whom also he named apostles. (Luke 6:12-13)

Notice particularly, that Luke 6:13 says Jesus called unto Him His disciples and of them, He chose twelve whom also He named apostles. Based on the account offered in Luke Chapter 10, Jesus, on one occasion, sent out seventy-two disciples. Their purpose was to serve as heralds or an advance team preaching the gospel in preparation for Christ's arrival to that place. Additionally, John Chapter 6 states that after Jesus spoke concerning eating His flesh and drinking His blood, many of His disciples left Him.

66. From that time many of his disciples went back, and walked no more with him.
67. Then said Jesus unto the twelve, Will ye also go away?
68. Then Simon Peter answered him, Lord, to whom shall we go? thou hast the words of eternal life.
69. And we believe and are sure that thou art that Christ, the Son of the living God. (John 6:66-69)

Therefore, based on the two accounts, it is evident that Jesus had many disciples; however, in this initial appointment, from among them, He specifically selected twelve apostles. Thus, the apostles represented a distinct group within His group of followers. Note that in Luke 6:12-13, Jesus made a clear distinction between disciples and apostles. A disciple is a general term and means a pupil, a learner, or simply a follower. On the other hand, an apostle, as the definition indicates, means something different. Hence, this designation is a distinct calling to accomplish a precise purpose.

Incorporated in this selection process is the concept of organization or structure. From a management perspective, choosing leaders is essential for the growth and furtherance of any entity. Therefore, inherent in the selection of apostles was the concept of choosing leaders and providing structure for the church. Before selecting His apostles, observe that Jesus went up to the mountains and prayed all night to the Father. This is evidence that the appointment of leaders requires guidance and in this regard, direction from the Father. Moreover, with Jesus calling and commissioning them specifically as apostles, this established the foundation that the church is apostolic in nature. Notice, He did not call them as pastors but as apostles. We will expand on this principle later in the chapter.

CHRIST AS AN APOSTLE

At its foundation, the apostle is an office instituted by Christ based on His own position and function. In harmony with the definition, Jesus while speaking to the Father, said in John 17:18, "As thou have sent (*apostello*) me into the world, even so have I sent (*apostello*) them into the world." Therefore, in light of the commission He received from the Father, He then appointed the twelve apostles with a similar mandate to continue His purpose. This provides a practical application to the definition of an apostle stated earlier. As a general under authority, Jesus subsequently granted authority to those He chose as apostles. Again, I reiterate that to understand the purpose of an apostle, it is necessary to appreciate how Jesus operated while He was on Earth. As mentioned, He is the template or benchmark for the office of an apostle. Hence, when the Father sent Christ into the world, He sent Him with one specific message, which is the message of the kingdom of God or the kingdom of heaven. This included the restoration of humanity to both the kingdom of God and the family or house of God. In essence, the Father sent Him to accomplish His "why," which was predetermined from before the foundation of the world.

In light of this, when Jesus established His platform for ministry, He said in Matthew 4:17, "Repent; for the kingdom of heaven is at hand." This was the purpose for which the Father sent (*apostello*) Him into the world. Therefore, every teaching or message Jesus communicated was in support of this agenda. As an apostle, He proclaimed and established the mandate of the One who sent Him. Similarly, those on whom the gift of an apostle have been bestowed, are sent (*apostello*) with the same commission. That being the case, it is also fundamental they are purveyors of the same message. In fact, while the apostles were with Jesus, through His teachings, He was constantly preparing them to function in that office. For throughout the Gospels, while providing the principles of the kingdom, He constantly said, "The kingdom of heaven or the kingdom of God was like such and such." Additionally, even after His resurrection, Acts 1:3 says that for a period of forty days, He spoke to them regarding a specific topic: the things *pertaining to the kingdom of God*.

1. The former treatise have I made, O Theophilus, of all that Jesus began both to do and teach,
2. Until the day in which he was taken up, after that he through the Holy Ghost had given commandments unto the apostles whom he had chosen:

3. To whom also he shewed himself alive after his passion by many infallible proofs, being seen of them forty days, and speaking of the things pertaining to the kingdom of God. (Acts 1:1-3)

Thus, we see the consistency of His message, ensuring that those who now function in His stead were equipped with the same doctrine. Consequently, Acts 2:42 says that after Peter's sermon on the Day of Pentecost, the people continued steadfastly in the apostles' doctrine. What then is the apostles' doctrine? It is the same message of the kingdom Jesus promoted while He was on Earth, which was passed on to the apostles. His message and agenda became their message and agenda. Accordingly, one of the indications of an apostle is distinctly the substance of their message, which is the kingdom of God. Therefore, if an alternative message is being offered, it is not the apostles' doctrine or the message from the Father. Furthermore, those spreading that message are not operating in Christ's stead.

As previously stated, Christ established the foundation of how apostles should operate, for He was the principal One sent by the Father. In light of His position, Hebrews 3:1 clearly refers to Him as the Apostle and High Priest of our profession or what we believe. In this regard, the definite article "the" in front of the word "apostle" in Hebrews 3:1, assigns Christ the position of prominence; thus, it affords Him the status of **Chief Apostle.** Therefore, as it pertains to the gospel in which we believe, Jesus Christ is our Chief Apostle. Nowhere else in Scripture is this title ascribed to any other individual. In consideration of all the apostles who exist, it is to be understood He alone is supreme.

Recall that the office of an apostle is based on the gift bestowed by Jesus and this is done in accordance with the measure He has determined. Nevertheless, despite the abundance of the measure that may be conferred, only Christ is the Chief Apostle. In terms of jurisdiction and responsibility, Galatians 2:7 says Peter was given apostleship of the Jews while the apostleship of the Gentiles was committed to Paul. However, despite the measure they were given and the extent of their apostleship and authority, they were not considered chief apostles. Nevertheless, to create a hierarchy among apostles, this mindset exists in the modern church. Howbeit, this is motivated by the pride of life and recognition, which results in vainglory.

The concept of apostles designating themselves as chief apostles is often based on a misunderstanding of 2 Corinthians 11:5. In the passage, Paul says, "For I suppose I was not a whit behind the very chiefest apostles." To be clear, Paul was by no means referring to himself as a chief apostle but was merely making a distinction. The word "chiefest" means greatly or exceedingly and Paul uses the word to describe the more noteworthy apostles. Therefore, with a major theme of 2 Corinthians being Paul's defense of his apostleship, he was simply relaying that compared to the most eminent apostles, based on the measure given to him, he was not inferior to them. Thus, this was more a statement validating his position as an apostle, especially to those who questioned his authority (1 Corinthians Chapter 9).

QUALIFICATIONS FOR AN APOSTLE

What does Scripture say is the requirement for an apostle? Having the understanding that it is indeed a gift, certainly, there isn't anything someone can personally do that unequivocally qualifies him or her for the position. Scripture provides little insight into the qualifications of those Jesus initially selected as the twelve apostles. Obviously, Jesus chose from among the disciples who were with Him. He was familiar with them and their characters. However, after Judas betrayed Him and a replacement was required, the principal requirement for an apostle was specifically outlined. Needless to say, the criteria mentioned here do not negate righteous character because for an apostle, this was an automatic standard.

As previously stated, Scripture is consistent that the overarching qualification for any office in relation to the people of God is righteousness (Exodus 18, 1 Timothy 3:1-13, Titus 1:5-9).

> 21. Wherefore of these men which have companied with us all the time that the Lord Jesus went in and out among us,

22. Beginning from the baptism of John, unto that same day that he was taken up from us, must one be ordained to *be a witness with us of his resurrection.*
23. And they appointed two, Joseph called Barsabas, who was surnamed Justus, and Matthias.
24. And they prayed, and said, Thou, Lord, which knowest the hearts of all men, shew whether of these two thou hast chosen,
25. That he may take part of this ministry and apostleship, from which Judas by transgression fell, that he might go to his own place.
26. And they gave forth their lots; and the lot fell upon Matthias; and he was numbered with the eleven apostles. (Acts 1:21-26)

In selecting someone for the office, the first thing to observe is that the selection was made from those who witnessed what Jesus did and said. They were not newcomers who had recently joined the disciples. Therefore, the selection was strategic and included disciples who had spent a significant amount of time with Christ. By this measure, they were equally qualified as the eleven apostles. Hence, this principle provides us with the first qualification they used in selecting. Thus, apostles must have significant experience and training in the things of God both in doctrine and action. Additionally, many are of the opinion that the primary qualification for an apostle is to have seen Christ after His resurrection. However, is this what the above passage is conveying?

Observe specifically, that Acts 1:22 says the responsibility of an apostle is <u>to be a witness with the other apostles of Christ's resurrection</u>. What does it mean to be a witness of Christ's resurrection? Notice that the passage uses the words "to be," which speaks of a future continuous action. Hence, the commission of apostleship speaks to being a witness or testifying of Christ's resurrection. Therefore, contrary to what is popularly stated, the passage does not say the requirement of an apostle is to see Christ after His resurrection. I am by no means suggesting that those who were appointed did not see Christ after His resurrection, for they certainly did. However, Acts 1:22 does not outline it as a prerequisite or qualification for the office. In 1 Corinthians Chapter 15, Paul, in order to validate Christ's resurrection, provides the account of the many people who saw Him after He rose from the dead.

3. For I delivered unto you first of all that which I also received, how that Christ died for our sins according to the scriptures;
4. And that he was buried, and that he rose again the third day according to the scriptures:
5. And that he was seen of Cephas, then of the twelve:
6. *After that, he was seen of above five hundred brethren at once; of whom the greater part remain unto this present, but some are fallen asleep.*
7. After that, he was seen of James; then of all the apostles.
8. And last of all he was seen of me also, as of one born out of due time.
9. For I am the least of the apostles, that am not meet to be called an apostle, because I persecuted the church of God. (1 Corinthians 15:3-9)

As the above passage states, many saw Christ after His resurrection, but they were not all appointed as apostles. Therefore, that alone is not the determining factor. Additionally, there is no second witness in Scripture to support this criterion. Based on the premise of Ephesians Chapter 4, the designation of an apostle is established fundamentally on being bestowed the specific gift by Christ. Furthermore, as it relates to being an apostle, the emphasis of the church seems more focused on who has seen Christ after His resurrection as opposed to being a witness of His resurrection. Indeed, there is a substantial difference between the two, as we will determine.

TO BE A WITNESS OF CHRIST'S RESURRECTION

First, the word "witness" refers to someone who can testify of what they know from a personal perspective or firsthand account. In reiterating Acts 1:22, the eleven apostles were looking for someone *to be a witness with them of Christ's resurrection*. Therefore, the apostles were looking to ordain or appoint someone to be in companionship with them and testify of Christ's resurrection. In other words, by their words and actions, they would provide empirical evidence of the power of His resurrection. Hence, they were identifying themselves with a particular responsibility, not an event. The responsibility was to demonstrate the reality of the resurrection of Jesus Christ.

32. And the multitude of them that believed were of one heart and of one soul: neither said any of them that ought of the things which he possessed was his own; but they had all things common.

33. And with great power gave the apostles witness of the resurrection of the Lord Jesus: and great grace was upon them all.

34. Neither was there any among them that lacked: for as many as were possessors of lands or houses sold them, and brought the prices of the things that were sold,

35. And laid them down at the apostles' feet: and distribution was made unto every man according as he had need. (Acts 4:32-35)

In Acts Chapter 4 when it says the apostles gave witness of the resurrection of the Lord Jesus, reference is being made to the things they said and did in the name of Jesus. This included healing the lame man at the gate of the temple and preaching the gospel. Therefore, by their very actions, they confirmed that Christ had resurrected from the dead and was indeed alive. Hence, when the apostles spoke of being a witness of the resurrection of Jesus Christ in Acts Chapter 1, they were actually saying the function of the office was to manifest the resurrection of Jesus Christ. The significance of Christ's resurrection also serves as the cornerstone of hope for every believer.

12. Now if Christ be preached that he rose from the dead, how say some among you that there is no resurrection of the dead?
13. But if there be no resurrection of the dead, then is Christ not risen:
14. And if Christ be not risen, then is our preaching vain, and your faith is also vain.
15. Yea, and we are found false witnesses of God; because we have testified of God that he raised up Christ: whom he raised not up, if so be that the dead rise not.
16. For if the dead rise not, then is not Christ raised:
17. And if Christ be not raised, your faith is vain; ye are yet in your sins.
18. Then they also which are fallen asleep in Christ are perished.
19. If in this life only we have hope in Christ, we are of all men most miserable. (1 Corinthians 15:12-19)

The resurrection of Jesus Christ is the foundation on which the entire gospel is based. This encompasses all the components of the spiritual blessings outlined in Ephesians Chapter 1, which the Father predetermined before the foundation of the world. Without His resurrection, there is no partaking of the Father's nature; there is no adoption as sons into the family of God; we are not accepted in the beloved; there is no redemption and forgiveness of sins; there is no sealing by the Holy Spirit or any inheritance; there is no redemption of our physical bodies. For the blessings to be activated, the requirement was Christ's resurrection. Hence, the spiritual blessings are the basis of our gospel and faith. Therefore, without His resurrection, our preaching is meaningless, and everything we believe is empty.

Based on this discussion, Corinthians 15:15 specifically says if there is no resurrection then we are found to be false witnesses of God. In other words, we are testifying or proclaiming something that never happened; we are bearers of an untrue testimony. Hence, to be a witness of Christ's resurrection is to testify of the things that were established as a result of His resurrection. This is what the apostles were referring to when they chose Matthias to be a witness with them of Christ's resurrection. This is the message of the apostle.

Without the resurrection of Christ, there is no restoration to the family of God or the kingdom of God. Therefore, being a witness of Christ's resurrection includes preaching the comprehensive gospel of the kingdom of God. Moreover, notice that despite the qualifications of Joseph and Matthias (both met the requirements for an apostle), the apostles prayed to the Lord for guidance before making a decision just as Jesus did. Again, due to the significant role leadership plays, appointments require direction from the Father.

RESPONSIBILITIES AND FUNCTIONS OF AN APOSTLE

Now that the groundwork concerning apostleship has been provided, let us look at the specific responsibilities and functions of an apostle as outlined in Scripture.

A) THEY SERVE A FOUNDATIONAL PURPOSE IN RELATION TO THE CHURCH

As mentioned at the beginning of this chapter, in terms of administration and leadership, the first office Jesus instituted was the apostle. When He made His selection from among His many disciples, He did not appoint twelve pastors but specifically, twelve apostles. This was primarily done to establish precedence in terms of the leadership of the church. Furthermore, based on this premise, the Father designed the church to be apostolic. In support of this, recall that 1 Corinthians 12:28 says, "God hath set some in the church, first apostles." Hence, as it relates to rank, the Father positioned the apostles to have a primary function in the church. In addition, Ephesians 2:20 states the church is built upon the foundation of the apostles and prophets with Jesus Christ being the chief cornerstone. Therefore, just as a foundation provides strength and stability to a building, so too do apostles (and prophets) to the church. However, in this function, they must be aligned with Christ who is the chief cornerstone. This is to ensure that the building or the church is stable and in the right position.

In essence, Ephesians 2:20 identifies apostles and prophets as the principal leaders of the church. They are responsible for establishing the foundational doctrine concerning Jesus Christ and making sure the church is in alignment with it. Hence, there is a tremendous accountability factor associated with this responsibility. Moreover, in emphasizing their primary function, Ephesians 3:5 says that the mystery of Christ, which was once hidden, was revealed by the Father unto His holy apostles and prophets by the Holy Spirit. Therefore, as His premier agents, God first entrusted them with this revelation. In fact, the majority of the Bible was written either by an apostle or a prophet. Hence, we see the consistency of these offices relative to the church.

In addition, as it pertains to doctrine, Acts 2:42 says the church continued in *the apostles' doctrine, which we have determined* is the message of the kingdom of God. This means that they were the ones who established the doctrine of the church. This also signifies that there was a singleness of doctrine, and all the apostles subscribed to the same tenet. They were unified in their message.

B) THEY ARE PLANTERS AND WISE MASTER BUILDERS

Not only do apostles have a foundational purpose in relation to the church, but as 1 Corinthians Chapter 3 emphasizes, they are also planters and wise master builders. As it pertains to the doctrine of the church, 1 Corinthians 3:11 says, "For other foundation can no man lay than that is laid, which is Jesus Christ." As the context of the chapter relates to doctrine, Christ therefore represents the principle on which the doctrine of the church is established. Hence, in relation to doctrine and his function as an apostle, Paul provides two analogies in 1 Corinthians Chapter 3. In the first example, he uses an agricultural model comparing the church to a vineyard and likens his role to that of planting. He says in 1 Corinthians 3:6, "I have planted, Apollos watered; but God gave the increase." In this instance, the process of planting and that which is planted (the seed) represents the initial activity. This includes the primary work of ministry and teaching the principles of the Word of God. As the example details, another worker (in this case Apollos) comes after the seed is planted and provides water. This essential action facilitates the germination and nourishment of the seed but based on the example, the apostle's role is clearly defined. However, regardless of the function, Paul is quick to point out that the emphasis is not on the one who plants or waters but on God who provides the increase. Furthermore, in the example, the message of unity among ministers is clearly underscored. Therefore, despite the different responsibilities, ministers share a single and united purpose. Despite the varying roles, there was still the unity of the Spirit. Additionally, regardless of the efforts of ministers, God causes growth and development in the lives of believers.

In reinforcing his position as an apostle, Paul provides a second illustration by comparing the church to a building. Accordingly, he compares his fundamental work and teaching to that of laying a foundation as in the process of construction. As we have discussed, with any building, the principal work involves laying the foundation. Notice specifically, Paul says in 1 Corinthians 3:10, "As a wise master builder I have laid the foundation and another buildeth thereon. But let every man take heed how he buildeth thereupon." In this instance, he is speaking of his teaching and that of other ministers. Furthermore, he affirms in 1 Corinthians 3:11 that the foundation he lays is

Jesus Christ. This encompasses who He is, His teaching, and His purpose for humanity. Hence, as an apostle, the foundation laid or the doctrine he provides is a representation of the message Christ promoted. Therefore, if someone promotes any message other than the kingdom of God and the mystery of godliness the foundation is not Jesus Christ.

Similar to the first illustration of watering, others will come behind and build on the foundation; however, the role of the apostle is once again clearly described. Additionally, despite the significance of laying the foundation, building on the foundation is an important responsibility. Even though the foundation serves as a fixed and stabilizing force, what is built on it also has tremendous importance with the overall soundness of the building. In terms of doctrine, the passage provides two distinct categories of materials used in the construction of the lives of believers. Note that the materials figuratively represent teachings or doctrines. The first category of doctrine consists of wood, hay, and stubble, while the second group includes gold, silver, and precious stones. In his caveat, Paul admonishes other ministers to take heed of the material or doctrine used in building on the foundation. Notice that wood, hay, and stubble are all flammable materials that are consumed by fire. On the other hand, gold, silver, and precious stones are refined by fire or intense heat. What does this signify? 1 Corinthians 3:13 says, "Every man's work shall be made manifest: for the day shall declare it, because it shall be revealed by fire; and the fire shall try every man's work of what sort it is." Fire exposes the type of doctrine or the material used in building the lives of God's people. In a figurative sense, Scripture uses fire to represent trials (1 Peter 4:12) and the hardships of life. Therefore, as ministers, the substance of the material used in building the sons of God will be revealed on the day of test and tribulation. Hence, it is imperative that proper doctrine or materials are being used upon the foundation that has been laid. This will be further examined in Chapter 12.

In this example of the church and the materials involved in its construction, Paul refers to himself as a "wise master builder" to demonstrate his position and function as an apostle. Unlike a regular mason worker, a master builder is a chief contractor and an architect. Not only do master builders carefully oversee the construction of the building, but as those who have been given the design by the Father, they follow the blueprint meticulously with no deviation. Wise master builders follow the pattern. They ensure that the correct material is being used for the construction of the building and those working on it are indeed skilled laborers.

The challenge with the church is there are many masons and a few skilled laborers but not many wise master builders. A person's ability to build a wall does not mean he or she is a qualified master builder. Master builders must have the ability to understand the entire blueprint, not just a section of the building. It requires a holistic perspective concerning the building or the church.

C) THEY ESTABLISH ORDER AND STRUCTURE, WHICH FOSTERS GROWTH

This is a government responsibility. In simple terms, the word "government" means, administration, or management of an organization or institution. A basic principle of good leadership is that it institutes order and structure, which serves to the benefit of those involved. This entails the arrangement or organization of a situation so it functions properly. To emphasize this, we will revisit two points presented in Chapter 6. As discussed during the conversation on the importance of structure, Exodus Chapter 18 outlines that in the initial phase of Moses' leadership of Israel, he assumed sole responsibility for judging all the matters they brought to him. Obviously, this was an enormous responsibility, especially for one person.

After observing that this judiciary undertaking lasted from morning to evening, Jethro, Moses' father-in-law offered him some advice. Jethro not only pointed out the inadequacy of the system that was in place, but he also highlighted the advantages of the organizational change. As we concluded earlier, Jethro's advice provided several things for all those involved. First, it brought structure and organization to the judiciary process of Israel. Also, the appointment of the legislators to preside over the various groups of people created more leaders in the nation. In essence, this transfer of responsibility resulted in the reproduction of leadership, which should be the objective of any leader. Moreover, it removed a tremendous burden from Moses thereby eliminating frustration and weariness for him and the people. As a result, the Israelites were able to have their matters resolved in a timely manner. In this example of Moses and Jethro, the beneficial impact of order and structure is clearly visible. Equally so, this principle of leadership can also be seen relative to the apostles in the early days of the church.

Recall that when Jesus appointed the twelve apostles in Luke Chapter 6, the general concept of organization and structure was involved in the decision. Therefore, apart from the specific tasks of apostles and the other ministry gifts detailed in Ephesians Chapter 4, one of their primary duties is to establish order and structure. They provide the appropriate framework for the church to experience an increase. Involved in this process is ensuring that responsibilities and functions are clearly delegated in the church, which then fosters harmony and growth. For example, in the early days of their stewardship, just like Moses, the apostles overextended themselves concerning the aspects of ministry. They were involved in everything.

Acts 4:34-35 details that whenever the people sold their possessions, they brought the money and laid it at the apostles' feet. Hence, in addition to their primary responsibilities, they also had oversight of the distribution of goods to the poor. However, as the church grew, the enormity of the task also increased; consequently, the distribution became inconsistent. As a result, frustrations mounted, and the Greek believers complained their widows were being neglected. Obviously, the system that was in place had some deficiencies. Just as we did in the exchange on the importance of structure in Chapter 6, let us revisit the account in Acts 6:1-7

1. And in those days, when the number of the disciples was multiplied, there arose a murmuring of the Grecians against the Hebrews, because their widows were neglected in the daily ministration.
2. Then the twelve called the multitude of the disciples unto them, and said, it is not reason that we should leave the word of God, and serve tables. (Acts 6:1-2)

To be clear, the apostles were not implying the task of serving tables was beneath them, for they had the disposition of servants. However, the challenge was that the responsibility had become so great their purpose was now obscure. They were preoccupied with performing a task that was not their principal function. Unfortunately, whenever this occurs, it is a disservice to all those involved. Therefore, to remedy the situation, the apostles gathered the disciples together to implement organization and structure to the distribution process. However, it should be noted that even though this example is specific to the distribution of goods, the apostles were setting a premise for all matters regarding the functioning of the church. First, they stated it was not proper they should leave the Word of God and serve tables. In other words, they were identifying that their primary purpose and focus was the preaching of the gospel. Hence, purpose and responsibility have to be known and clearly defined for order to be established. With that said, they asked the disciples to select seven qualified men to oversee the distribution of goods to the poor, thereby relieving them of the task. Through divesting themselves of this excess responsibility, they would then have more time for prayer and the ministry of the Word of God.

3. Wherefore, brethren, look ye out among you seven men of honest report, full of the Holy Ghost and wisdom, whom we may appoint over this business.
4. But we will give ourselves continually to prayer, and to the ministry of the word.
5. And the saying pleased the whole multitude: and they chose Stephen, a man full of faith and of the Holy Ghost, and Philip, and Prochorus, and Nicanor, and Timon, and Parmenas, and Nicolas a proselyte of Antioch:
6. Whom they set before the apostles: and when they had prayed, they laid their hands on them. (Acts 6:3-6)

After the disciples made their selections, they brought them before the apostles, and they laid their hands upon them. This was an indication that the apostles had given them the authority or commission to perform the responsibility. Like the example of Moses, changing the structure had several advantages. First, it allowed the apostles to be realigned with their primary purpose. When leaders are not functioning in the capacity to which they have been called, then disorder prevails and growth cannot be experienced. In addition, where there was once neglect and frustration due to an improper distribution system, the needs of the poor were now being adequately met. Furthermore, through the appointment of the seven men, leadership roles were being created. In the aggregate, when order and structure are established, the church experiences growth and the Word of God increases. Growth is therefore a product of proper organization. Acts 6:7 says, "And the word of God increased; and the number of the disciples multiplied in Jerusalem greatly; and a great company of the priests were obedient to the faith." However, when proper organization absent, the opposite is also true.

Once individuals are aligned with the tasks God has assigned them, success follows. Notice that in both examples, order and structure translate to a favorable outcome, not only for the leaders but for the people they serve as well. This, therefore, is a primary function of the apostles.

D) THEY ORDAIN CHURCH LEADERSHIP BASED ON ESTABLISHED REQUIREMENTS

While on the subject of leadership, another function of an apostle is that of ordination. In the book of Acts, several examples serve as templates for apostolic order. Again, I reiterate that in terms of structure, the church is apostolic in nature. However, by no means does this infer that the other gifts of Christ are less important. On the contrary, this simply conveys the organizational structure that the Father has instituted for the church. In accordance with Scripture, apostles are responsible for the appointment of elders or pastors, as well as general church oversight. Recall that Acts 14:23 in reference to Paul and Barnabas says "And when they had ordained them elders in every church, and had prayed with fasting, they commended them to the Lord, on whom they believed."

As apostles, Paul and Barnabas (Acts 14:14) were charged with the responsibility of ordaining pastors or overseeing their appointment by the members of the church. The process is similar to what was discussed during the appointment of Matthias in Acts Chapter 1 and the seven ministers in Acts Chapter 6. Based on the context of the passage, the word "ordain" means the following:

- To vote by stretching out the hand
- To elect or designate to an office
- To create or appoint by vote: one to have charge of some office or duty.

In simple terms, the word "ordain" means to appoint or to set one over a thing. The two epistles to Timothy along with the one to Titus are commonly referred to as Pastoral Epistles due to their concentration on aspects of church leadership. However, these three books, along with all the other New Testament epistles are actually apostolic in nature, for they all reveal apostolic responsibility concerning the church. Nevertheless, these epistles stand out in that they provide more insight into church leadership and show a particular relationship between an apostle and the church.

Embedded in the context of these books are specific instructions regarding church administration and doctrine to maintain structure in the church. In particular, the signature statement that best describes the objective of 1 Timothy is reflected in 1 Timothy 3:14-15. Paul, in addressing Timothy says, "These things write I unto thee, hoping to come to you shortly: But if I tarry long that thou mayest know how though oughtest to behave thyself in the house of God, which is the church of the living God, the pillar and ground of the truth." As an apostle, Paul left Timothy in Ephesus and sent him correspondence anticipating he would come there in person. However, as Paul indicated, the epistle served as a directive on church governance in the event of his delay. Consequently, one of these guidelines he gave Timothy pertained to church leadership; the charge was to appoint bishops and deacons based on specific qualifications. Just as had Paul ordained Timothy, he now had the responsibility to appoint church leadership in accordance with certain criteria. In this regard, 1 Timothy Chapter 3 provides detailed requirements for both bishops and deacons. We will discuss those in detail in chapter 10 of this book.

Just as Paul left Timothy in Ephesus in his capacity as an apostle, he also left Titus in Crete with similar instructions. In Titus 1:5, Paul provides a synopsis of the purpose of the letter. He says to him, "For this cause left I thee in Crete, that thou shouldest set in order the things that are wanting, and ordain elders in every city, as I had appointed thee." Paul ordained Timothy to carry out a specific responsibility, and he similarly assigned Titus to ordain elders based on certain qualifications. To be clear, ordination is simply the process of an individual being appointed to an office based on the recognition of the gift that already exists. Ephesians 4:11 is abundantly clear that Christ is the one who gives the gifts to individuals. Therefore, the act of ordination by itself does not create a gift if it is nonexistent. It is essentially a confirmation of the gift that has been recognized by leadership. To put it simply, *a gift is not conferred by ordination; it is confirmed by ordination.*

As a point of emphasis, I reiterate Paul's statement to the church at Ephesus in his letter to the Ephesians. He says in Ephesians 3:7, "Whereof I was made a minister, according to the gift of the grace of God given unto me by the effectual working of his power." In accordance with Ephesians 4:11, he affirms that the capacity in which he was functioning was based on the gift of the grace of God. God made him a minister. Furthermore, Paul adds in Galatians Chapter 2 that the gift, which is by God's grace, was evident or visible to others. "And when James, Cephas, and John, who seemed to be pillars, *perceived the grace that was given unto me, they gave to me and Barnabas the right hands of fellowship*; that we should go unto the heathen, and they unto the circumcision" (Galatians 2:9).

When the other apostles recognized the grace given to Paul, they gave both him and Barnabas the right hand of fellowship. The gift of apostleship was therefore evident in them and as a result, they were acknowledged as fellow apostles.

According to 1 Timothy 4:14, the presbytery or the body of elders serve to confirm the gift that already exists in an individual. Again, they do not confer the gift, but ordination is based on the recognition of the gift given by God. Therefore, based on the parameters outlined in Scripture, elders or pastors are identified by the members of the church. The apostles through the laying on of hands provide their approval and blessing. Throughout Scripture and even now, laying on of hands is a common method of imparting a blessing or setting aside an individual for office (Matthew 19:15, Acts 6:6, Acts 13:3). A similar reference is provided in 1 Timothy 4:14 and 2 Timothy 1:6

"Neglect not the gift that is in thee, which was given thee by prophecy, with the laying on of the hands of the presbytery" (1 Timothy 4:14).

"Wherefore I put thee in remembrance that thou stir up the gift of God, which is in thee by the putting on of my hands" (2 Timothy 1:6).

This entire exercise is also an example of spiritual parenting in which fathers raise up sons. Apostles appoint others in the ministry and consequently reproduce themselves. In a spiritual sense, both Timothy and Titus were sons of Paul, which provides a perfect avenue to the next function of an apostle.

E) THEY ARE FATHERS, NOT JUST TEACHERS

To accentuate his function as an apostle, Paul provides an example that embodies the essence of the ministry gift of an apostle. To highlight his office, he creates a comparison between the responsibilities of a father to that of a teacher or instructor.

15. For though ye have ten thousand instructors in Christ, yet have ye not many fathers: for in Christ Jesus I have begotten you through the gospel.
16. Wherefore I beseech you, be ye followers of me.
17. For this cause have I sent unto you Timotheus, who is my beloved son, and faithful in the Lord, who shall bring you into remembrance of my ways which be in Christ, as I teach everywhere in every church. (1 Corinthians 4:15-17)

To have an appreciation for the distinction between a father and a teacher, the attributes of each must be taken into consideration. The word "teacher" in this context is a tutor, instructor, or somewhat of a supervisor who provides instructions for guidance. Hence, the main attribute of teachers is that they impart knowledge. Additionally, the passage also suggests that due to the distinction that exists, teachers seem to be more plentiful than fathers. In respect to the example, while instructors are important and necessary, when contrasted to the qualities of a father, the difference is remarkable.

First, a teacher conveys a teacher-student relationship; whereas, a father represents a father-son relationship. Obviously, in terms of intimacy and care, the function of a father outweighs that of a teacher. Also, while a teacher's role may be limited and occasional, a father is more methodical and dependable. Therefore, the example is a contrast of relationships. To further emphasize the qualities of the example and parallel them to that of an apostle, let us look at some of the attributes of a father.

- A father is one who imparts life and is committed to the development of the child.
- A father not only begets but also labors until Christ is formed in his children (Galatians 4:19).
- A father teaches, nurtures, trains, and disciplines his children.
- A father is a mentor.
- A father enriches the lives of his children.
- A father provides for and protects his children.
- A father leads by example.
- A father is one who has an intimate connection and relationship with his children.

Therefore, in consideration of the above qualities, Paul says while you can have an abundance of teachers, I am a father to you. In the context of the passage, the paternal example of a father provides insight into the responsibilities of an apostle in relation to children begotten by the gospel. Romans 1:20 is a foundational principle for understanding spiritual things. It says we understand spiritual things by examining natural things or the things which are made or available in creation. Hence, the compelling qualities of a natural father can certainly provide us with a better appreciation of the function or responsibilities of an apostle compared to that of the other ministry gifts. In that vein, there is definitely a heightened degree of responsibility associated with that gift.

One of the roles of a father and by extension an apostle is reproduction, and this occurs in two spheres. In the first instance, an apostle gives birth in the initial sense. In 1 Corinthians 4:15, Paul speaks of begetting the Corinthian church through the gospel. This means that through his preaching of the gospel of Christ, he has fathered them and considers them his children. In the second instance, reproduction goes beyond procreation and involves the duplication of an original. On this note, in Galatians 4:19 Paul says, "My little children, of whom I travail in birth again until Christ be formed in you." This speaks of coming into the measure of the fulness of Christ.

To qualify the magnitude of work and effort involved in manifesting the character of Christ, Paul uses the word "travail." This word points to the pain a mother experiences while in childbirth. Therefore, in taking hold of the analogy, Paul says I labor again until you are a reflection of Christ's image or character. Moreover, with the usage of the word "again," Paul is stating that as a father involved in the reproduction process, there are multiple instances where he travailed in birth. The first was in begetting them through the gospel, which on a fatherly level is elementary. However, his responsibilities as a father did not end there because birth was not the end of his assignment. As a father, he also worked strenuously to reproduce the image of Christ in them, and they had him as an example. Hence, Paul says in 1 Corinthians 4:16, "Wherefore I beseech you, be ye followers of me."

In the epistles to Timothy and Titus, Paul specifically uses the words, "my own son" and "my dearly beloved son" in his greetings to them. These salutations are an acknowledgment of the father-son relationship that existed between them, which surpasses the relationship of a teacher. Therefore, to further emphasize the distinction between a father and a teacher, Paul says something of significance in 1 Corinthians 4:17. He says, "For this cause have I sent unto you Timothy, who is my beloved son, and faithful in the Lord, who shall bring you into remembrance of my ways which be in Christ, as I teach everywhere in every church."

After admonishing the Corinthian believers to be followers of him, Paul says, "In my absence, I am sending a representative who is a product of a father-son relationship. In other words, he is "exhibit A" of what I am referring to. He is not just coming to teach you, but as a son, he is a reflection of me. For that reason, when he comes, he will bring you into remembrance of my ways in Christ. When you see him, he will remind you of me." Recall that one of the attributes of a son is that he is an extension and representation of the father. This is one of the reasons Jesus said in John 14:9, "He that hath seen me hath seen the Father." Hence, when Paul sent Timothy to the church at Corinth, he went as his representative, reflecting the image he had witnessed with his father. Paul had reproduced himself in Timothy to such a degree that he could comfortably say, "He will remind you of my ways in Christ."

F) THEY FUNCTION AS NURSES

Oftentimes, whenever we think of a nurse, the image of someone who is caring, understanding, and empathetic comes to mind. Therefore, in another example of his duty as an apostle, Paul uses the illustration of how a nurse shows tender care for her children.

5. For neither at any time used we flattering words, as ye know, nor a cloke of covetousness; God is witness:
6. Nor of men sought we glory, neither of you, nor yet of others, when we might have been burdensome, as the apostles of Christ.
7. But we were gentle among you, even as a nurse cherisheth her children:
8. So being affectionately desirous of you, we were willing to have imparted unto you, not the gospel of God only, but also our own souls, because ye were dear unto us. (1 Thessalonians 2:5-8)

Again, this natural example, which portrays empathy and a caring nature, provides an awareness of the mantle of an apostle. As with the attributes of the father, the reference of a nurse points to that of a nourisher. It speaks of cherishing children with tender love or fostering them with gentle care. Furthermore, as with the previous example, the responsibility goes beyond simply imparting the Word (as a teacher does) but also the inclination of laying down their lives due to the affection that exists. Therefore, by the two examples of a father and nurse, we have a comprehensive illustration of the heart of an apostle.

G) THEY RECONCILE DOCTRINE AND THEREBY MAINTAIN UNITY

By consensus, it is the responsibility of apostles to provide reconciliation concerning doctrine and establish the church's position on certain topics. From our previous discussion regarding the circumcision of Gentile believers, Acts Chapter 15 reveals that the function of an apostle (in collaboration with elders) is to provide clarity concerning church doctrine and practice. Apostles maintain unity and protect against divisions in the church. Notice that as a matter of principle, whenever there was a doctrinal query, the apostles (along with elders) provided the decisive answer in resolving the matter. They were not a disjointed body but operated in unison. Let us revisit the example that was presented during the discussion of the importance of structure in Chapter 6.

1. And certain men which came down from Judaea taught the brethren, and said, Except ye be circumcised after the manner of Moses, ye cannot be saved.
2. When therefore Paul and Barnabas had no small dissension and disputation with them, they determined that Paul and Barnabas, and certain other of them, should go up to Jerusalem unto the apostles and elders about this question. (Acts 15:1-2)

And the apostles and elders came together for to consider of this matter. (Acts 15:6)

Based on the uncertainty that surrounded the practice of circumcision, it was determined Paul, Barnabas, and others would present the matter before the apostles and elders to reconcile the matter. As mentioned, they conducted what can be considered an *apostolic council*. Hence, after the contributions of Peter, Paul, Barnabas, and James, it was collectively agreed that circumcision was not required. Therefore, based on this pattern from Scripture, the apostles serve as the body to resolve doctrine and related practices pertaining to the things of God. Notice that in reconciling the subject they used both Scripture, as well as the testimony of the apostles. Moreover, after the determination had been made concerning circumcision, the apostles sent correspondence to churches of the Gentiles. They cemented their conclusion in writing so everyone would be informed. In the letter, they made it abundantly clear that circumcision was not required but rather highlighted the things which were necessary.

22. Then pleased it the apostles and elders, with the whole church, to send chosen men of their own company to Antioch with Paul and Barnabas; namely, Judas surnamed Barsabas, and Silas, chief men among the brethren:
23. And they wrote letters by them after this manner; The apostles and elders and brethren send greeting unto the brethren which are of the Gentiles in Antioch and Syria and Cilicia:
24. Forasmuch as we have heard, that certain which went out from us have troubled you with words, subverting your souls, saying, Ye must be circumcised, and keep the law: to whom we gave no such commandment:
25. It seemed good unto us, being assembled with one accord, to send chosen men unto you with our beloved Barnabas and Paul,
26. Men that have hazarded their lives for the name of our Lord Jesus Christ.
27. We have sent therefore Judas and Silas, who shall also tell you the same things by mouth.
28. For it seemed good to the Holy Ghost, and to us, to lay upon you no greater burden than these necessary things;
29. That ye abstain from meats offered to idols, and from blood (Acts 15:22-29)

Based on this premise, when Paul and Silas went to Debre and Lystra, they delivered the mandate of the apostles and elders. In this regard, we have another example of apostolic order. Consequently, Acts 16:4 says, "And so were the churches established in the faith, and increased in number daily." This is identical to the outcome we saw in Acts Chapter 6 regarding the apostles establishing order in the church. Similarly, once there is clarity concerning church doctrine and practice, which contributes to divine order, the result is a fortified church and growth.

In this particular scenario, the matter pertained specifically to circumcision; nevertheless, the model should be the same when it comes to the reconciliation of all church doctrine. This is also a great example of how the unity of the Spirit is maintained in the bond of peace. Unfortunately, this type of reconciliation often occurs in the confines of denominational walls as opposed to the entire body. However, the principle of apostolic reconciliation is to foster unity in the body and promote the unity of the faith. This also guards against false doctrine and errors.

Furthermore, we see a level of accountability with the apostles and Jesus during His ministry. For example, based on what Jesus instructed them, Mark 6:30 says, "And the apostles gathered themselves together unto Jesus, and told him all things, both what they had done, and what they had taught." After sending them out in Mark 6:7-12 to preach the gospel of the kingdom, cast out demons, and heal the sick, they returned to Him and gave a report, because they were accountable unto Him.

H) THEY SET THE PARAMETERS FOR SOUND DOCTRINE

In addition to their instructions regarding leadership appointments in the church, the letters to Timothy and Titus also focus on the importance of sound doctrine. As an apostle, Paul in his communication to both Timothy and Titus is persistent in the promotion of sound doctrine, as well as guarding against false teachings. In this regard, he says in 1 Timothy 1:3, "Teach no other doctrine." In other words, based on the teachings you have received from me, do not deviate from them to teach another doctrine. Again, we see where apostles set the parameters for doctrinal truth. However, Paul made this statement, not primarily on his apostolic authority but because he was persuaded by the certainty of his message. To support this, he says in Galatians 1:8, "But though we, or an angel from heaven, preach any other gospel unto you than that which we have preached unto you, let him be accursed." Hence, there was no doubt in his mind that what he was preaching came directly from the Father. Nevertheless, in the religious environment in which the church exists today, I am convinced some are likewise persuaded. However, for a doctrinal position to be accepted, it has to stand the test of all Scripture. This is referred to as the whole of Scripture context.

From an educational perspective, when Paul instructed Timothy to teach no other doctrine, he was saying, stick to the syllabus I have provided. As the apostle, he provided the doctrine that was to be taught to the church. Recall that during the early days of the church, Acts 2:42 says the people continued in the apostles' doctrine. They were the ones who established doctrine and the church was steadfast in their instructions.

To ensure the continuance of the doctrine that was established, Paul adds in 2 Timothy 1:13, "The things that thou hast heard of me among many witnesses, the same commit thou to faithful men, who shall be able to teach others also." This is how the continuance of sound doctrine persists from generation to generation.

Apostles also foster an environment of sound doctrine for those who follow. Moreover, in his letter to Titus, Paul says in Titus 2:1, "But speak thou the things which become sound doctrine," thereby echoing the same sentiments conveyed to Timothy. As a premise, sound doctrine is based on the tenets of the mystery of godliness. For more on the mystery of godliness, please refer to my book, *Faith: Who Hath Bewitched You?*

Attached to the qualification of a bishop, which also encompasses elders and pastors, is the skillfulness of teaching. This includes not just the ability to "teach" but the proficiency to teach the apostles' doctrine. Finally, Paul drives the message regarding sound doctrine with the importance of study. 2 Timothy 2:15 says, "Study to shew thyself approved unto God, a workman that needeth not to be ashamed, rightly dividing the word of truth."

I) THEY ARE CONTENDERS FOR THE FAITH

In addition to being purveyors of sound doctrine, apostles are also contenders for the faith. Indeed, all believers are charged with this responsibility, but apostles stand at the forefront in this regard. In principle, this is accomplished with the combination of furnishing sound teaching, as well as being gatekeepers against false teachers. Concerning sound doctrine, Jude 1:3 says, "Beloved, when I gave all diligence to write unto you of the common salvation, it was needful for me to write unto you, and exhort you that ye should *earnestly contend for the faith which was once delivered unto the saints."*

The word "contend" means to engage in a campaign to win or achieve something. Therefore, as it pertains to doctrine, the admonishment of Jude illustrates a battle against those who seek to pervert the gospel of Christ (Galatians 1:7). These are the same grievous wolves mentioned in Acts 20:29-30 who do not spare the flock. This also includes those within the ranks of the church who speak perverse things to draw disciples after themselves. Furthermore, Peter also speaks of false prophets or false teachers who bring in damnable heresies.

1. But there were false prophets also among the people, even as there shall be false teachers among you, who privily shall bring in damnable heresies, even denying the Lord that bought them, and bring upon themselves swift destruction.
2. And many shall follow their pernicious ways; by reason of whom the way of truth shall be evil spoken of.
3. And through covetousness shall they with feigned words make merchandise of you: whose judgment now of a long time lingereth not, and their damnation slumbereth not. (2 Peter 2:1-3)

When Jude uses the term, "the faith," it is to be understood this refers to the singularity of the gospel of Christ. It is God's "why." 1 Timothy 6:3 classifies it as wholesome words, even the words of our Lord Jesus Christ and the doctrine according to godliness. Therefore, contending for the faith means to campaign or launch an offensive against any doctrine contrary to the gospel of the kingdom of God and the mystery of godliness.

J) THEY ELIMINATE DIVISIONS AND PROMOTE UNITY IN THE BODY OF CHRIST

In simple terms, apostles are unifiers; they do not create or promote walls of division in the body of Christ. In the book of 1 Corinthians, based on details received from members of the house of Chloe, Paul was informed that there were contentions in the church of Corinth. These contentions resulted in divisions. At face value, we are inclined to think that the divisions simply depicted the preferences of ministers. However, at its core, it was more far-reaching and represented divisions in the church similar to the denominational schisms that exist today.

Based on the account, some of the people indicated they were of Paul; others said they were of Apollos. Another group placed their allegiance to Cephas or Peter and finally, some disregarded the human options and said they were of Christ. As a point of reference, because this group said they followed Christ, it doesn't mean they were correct in their position because it was still a divided disposition. Therefore, the main point being addressed in the passage is that there are no divisions in Christ.

To foster the position of unity in the body, the question is asked, "Is Christ divided?" In other words, is Christ separated or split into fractions. Today, we live in a fractured Christian environment consisting of many denominations, each claiming to be the purveyors of the gospel of Christ. However, Scripture points out that the fuel for such divisions is envy and strife, which is born from carnal behavior (1 Corinthians 3:3).

As it relates to the body of Christ, the concept of unity involves two things: the position of unity and the message of unity. First, with the position of unity, there is the understanding that regardless of the role, ministers of the gospel are one and laborers together with God. In his position as an apostle and addressing the subject of division in the church, Paul injects himself and Apollo into the equation. In 1 Corinthians Chapter 3, he uses the illustration of one planting and the other watering to demonstrate the unified work of ministers. In fact, he concludes that they are one. Hence, the adoption of this premise serves to eliminate the divisive notion of people being loyal to particular groups.

Second, with the message of unity, 1 Corinthians 3:11 identifies the foundational directive of the body of Christ as the doctrine of Jesus Christ. As stated, this is the message of the kingdom of God according to godliness. Therefore, as an apostle, the responsibility is to cultivate and maintain an environment of unity in the body. Ephesians 4:13 pinpoints the unity of the faith as the specific mandate of those who have been bestowed the gift of Christ.

K) THEY OVERSEE CHURCHES AND MINISTRIES

Of all the responsibilities of an apostle, this one seems to be the most pronounced and practiced in the church today. In fact, some are of the opinion that once they have met this qualifier, they then can assume the mantle of the apostle. However, by itself, this function is not an automatic criterion for the position. As a reminder, apostleship is based on the gift of Christ regardless of the extent of one's oversight. In using the book of Acts as a premise, the apostles, while operating in their gift, established churches. However, they did not become apostles as a result of establishing churches. In other words, the gift of apostleship was already present before churches were established. For example, in Acts Chapter 13, when the Lord set apart Barnabas and Saul (Paul) for the work He had called them to do, they were already apostles.

1. Now there were in the church that was at Antioch certain prophets and teachers; as Barnabas, and Simeon that was called Niger, and Lucius of Cyrene, and Manaen, which had been brought up with Herod the tetrarch, and Saul.
2. As they ministered to the Lord, and fasted, the Holy Ghost said, Separate me Barnabas and Saul for the work whereunto I have called them.
3. And when they had fasted and prayed, and laid their hands on them, they sent them away. (Acts 13:1-3)

Moreover, early in their ministry, both Barnabas and Paul were clearly identified as apostles (Acts 14:4, 14). Therefore, the main point being emphasized is that they were not apostles because of what they did. Rather, they did what they did because they were apostles.

The book of Acts provides several examples of an apostle's oversight and the involvement of the church. For instance:

- Barnabas and Paul in their capacity of apostles preached the gospel and established churches (Accts 13, 14; 1 Corinthians 4:15)
- They also revisited the churches they established, strengthening them, supporting them, and exhorting them to continue in the faith (Acts 14:21-22).
- They ordained bishops or elders to oversee the churches they established (Acts 14:23).
- In particular, Paul not only wrote letters to the churches he established providing them with doctrine and instructions in righteousness, but he also engaged in dialogue (written) with them (1 Corinthians 7:1). They had questions, which needed to be answered, and he used the correspondence of 1 Corinthians to address their queries.
- Paul sent representatives to the churches to set things in order (1 Timothy 1:3, Titus 1:5).

In essence, all these functions encapsulate the responsibilities of an apostle mentioned in this section. Now that we have adequately discussed the responsibilities of an apostle, we can discuss what is meant by proof of apostleship.

PROOF OF APOSTLESHIP

In the introduction of several of the epistles written by Paul, he specifically points out that as an apostle, he was appointed by Jesus Christ. However, in the introduction of his letter to the Galatians, he deliberately emphasizes that his appointment was not by man.

1. Paul, an apostle, (not of men, neither by man, but by Jesus Christ, and God the Father, who raised him from the dead;)
2. And all the brethren which are with me, unto the churches of Galatia. (Galatians 1:1-2)

The source of his appointment is specifically mentioned in this epistle because Paul wanted to make the distinction that while some appointments are indeed made by men, his was by God. Additionally, in defending the authenticity and authority of his office, he makes several noteworthy statements in the book of 1 Corinthians. For example, in 1 Corinthians 9:1-2, he affirms that the seal or proof of his apostleship was the Corinthian church:

1. Am I not an apostle? am I not free? have I not seen Jesus Christ our Lord? are not ye my work in the Lord?
2. If I be not an apostle unto others, yet doubtless I am to you: for the seal of mine apostleship are ye in the Lord.

As in many circumstances, there is always a fruit or a manifestation of a gift or calling. In this instance, Paul declares that the lives impacted by his ministry were a reflection of the legitimacy of his apostleship. Similarly, in 2 Corinthians 3:1-2, he stated that in his position as an apostle, he neither needed letters of commendation to the church nor did he require letters of commendation from the church. In this case, the word "commendation" refers to an official letter of recommendation. Whereas others were providing letters introducing themselves to validate their position, Paul emphasized that the believers themselves were his letters of recommendation, known and read by all men. Hence, as opposed to actual letters, he insisted that if they wanted a tangible, official recommendation of his office, they should look at those who are products of my ministry. They were the token of his apostleship. To be clear, Paul is not talking about numbers, for this is not the measure of the office. Rather, he is saying the character of Christ is manifested in the lives of the people, so much so, they are the epistles or letters of Christ. They were living epistles, or the Word made flesh. Furthermore, in 2 Corinthians 12:11-12, Paul points out that the signs of an apostle were performed by him:

11. I am become a fool in glorying; ye have compelled me: for I ought to have been commended of you: for in nothing am I behind the very chiefest apostles, though I be nothing.
12. Truly the signs of an apostle were wrought among you in all patience, in signs, and wonders, and mighty deeds.

APOSTOLIC RELATIONSHIP WITH THE CHURCH

In addition to what we have discussed, Scripture provides other examples of the relationship that should exist between an apostle and the church. Interestingly enough, based on the examples from Scripture, the churches did not have an independent relationship in terms of apostolic oversight. In our modern spiritual environment, the proliferation of independent churches with no oversight or accountability is a contributing factor to the disunity that currently exists in the body of Christ. However, when the proper structure is adhered to and the apostolic relationship is functional, it not only fosters unity, but it also safeguards the members of the church. For example, in Acts Chapter 20, while in Miletus, Paul sends for the elders of the church at Ephesus to give them specific instructions, as well as to warn them about what would occur once he left.

> 17. And from Miletus he sent to Ephesus, and called the elders of the church.
> 18. And when they were come to him, he said unto them. (Acts 20:17-18)

> 28. Take heed therefore unto yourselves, and to all the flock, over the which the Holy Ghost hath made you overseers, to feed the church of God, which he hath purchased with his own blood.
> 29. For I know this, that after my departing shall grievous wolves enter in among you, not sparing the flock.
> 30. Also of your own selves shall men arise, speaking perverse things, to draw away disciples after them.
> 31. Therefore watch, and remember, that by the space of three years I ceased not to warn every one night and day with tears. (Acts 20:28-31)

In his capacity as an apostle, Paul called an assembly of all the Ephesian elders/pastors and said several things to them:

- Take heed of yourselves.
- Take heed to the flock or the church over which the Holy Ghost has made you overseers.
- Feed the church of God.

- Grievous wolves from without and within shall come with false doctrines and damnable heresies to draw disciples after them.
- Be vigilant and pray.

These specific points will be discussed in greater detail in Chapter ten as a part of the responsibilities of a pastor. However, their inclusion at this point is to provide a glimpse of Paul's function as an apostle, and his relationship with the church. As an apostle, this was his collective message to the church at Ephesus, thereby not only making them aware of what was to come but also putting them in the position to be vigilant against such attacks. Furthermore, based on what was tabled during the meeting, Paul also put additional measures in place to safeguard the church. In this regard, he left Timothy at Ephesus with oversight over the church along with specific responsibilities.

1. Paul, an apostle of Jesus Christ by the commandment of God our Saviour, and Lord Jesus Christ, which is our hope;
2. Unto Timothy, my own son in the faith: Grace, mercy, and peace, from God our Father and Jesus Christ our Lord.
3. As I besought thee to abide still at Ephesus, when I went into Macedonia, that thou mightest charge some that they teach no other doctrine. (1 Timothy 1:1-3)

This is a perfect illustration of what an apostolic relationship looks like. Knowing that those with false doctrines would come as wolves and attack the church, Paul, in addition to meeting with the Ephesian elders, also asked Timothy to stay at Ephesus. Hence, he left his apostolic representative there and gave him a specific mandate. His charge to him was that the church only teaches the doctrine that he gave them. Recall that during our discussion on the responsibilities of an apostle, one of the functions is that they set the parameters for sound doctrine. In other words, they establish the curriculum for what is to be taught. Therefore, this type of training makes it easier to recognize false doctrine and the promoters of it. When we examine the content of Paul's letters to Timothy, the underlying theme is guarding against false teaching, the qualifications for leadership, and the guidelines for church behavior. Hence, the context of the letters was directed toward a specific purpose for the church. Thus, as a direct correlation, these letters add additional support to the conditions that would arise at Ephesus. Taken together, in this example we see the comprehensive elements of the apostolic relationship with the church. Not only did Paul meet with the church leaders and leave his representative there to support them, but he also furnished Timothy with specific instructions and guidelines to assist them. In addition to this reference, Paul also left Titus in Crete and gave him similar responsibilities and instructions. Wherefore, the circumstances surrounding the letter to Titus also serves as an example of apostolic responsibility in the church.

1. Paul, a servant of God, and an apostle of Jesus Christ, according to the faith of God's elect, and the acknowledging of the truth which is after godliness;
2. In hope of eternal life, which God, that cannot lie, promised before the world began;
3. But hath in due times manifested his word through preaching, which is committed unto me according to the commandment of God our Saviour;
4. To Titus, mine own son after the common faith: Grace, mercy, and peace, from God the Father and the Lord Jesus Christ our Saviour.
5. For this cause left I thee in Crete, that thou shouldest set in order the things that are wanting, and ordain elders in every city, as I had appointed thee (Titus 1:1-5)

In unison, these two examples offer a good perspective on the apostolic relationship and are consistent with the responsibilities of an apostle discussed earlier. Being his sons in the faith, both Timothy and Titus were Paul's representatives who were given an apostolic mandate to function in his stead. Therefore, despite being absent from the church at Ephesus and Crete, Paul gave them both authority and responsibility to act on his behalf. Overall, when we take into account all the letters written to all the churches, in combination, they provide a wonderful perspective of an apostolic relationship.

They were not generic letters. In fact, they were specifically written to convey a precise message based on God's purpose and the circumstances that were present in the church. For instance, 1 Corinthians in its entirety represents somewhat of a dialogue between Paul and the Corinthian church. At the beginning of the letter, Paul spends the first six chapters addressing matters that were brought to his attention by members of the house of Chloe (1 Corinthians 1:11). After tabling these concerns, he then turns his attention to answer the questions the church wrote to him. In 1 Corinthians 7:1, he says, "Now concerning the things whereof ye wrote unto me." Apparently, the church had several doctrinal queries, and they needed answers. Therefore, throughout the book, we see Paul engaging with the church providing insight based on the letter they wrote to him. Hence, this entire epistle is a declaration of the apostolic relationship between him and the church at Corinth.

FALSE APOSTLES

As with many genuine things, there also exists the counterfeit or the imitation. Just as there are apostles who are defined by the criteria covered in this chapter and are true, others carry the title but are false apostles and deceitful workers. For this reason, in 2 Corinthians Chapter 11, the apostle Paul addresses the matter of false apostles. The term "false apostle" is the Greek word *pseudapostolos,* which is the combination of two words *pseudes* meaning false and *apostolos* meaning apostle. Moreover, the Greek word *pseudes* comes from the root word *pseudomai,* which means to speak deliberate falsehoods or to utter an untruth to deceive by falsehood.

Before discussing false apostles, it should be noted that because an individual is not a genuine apostle, this does not mean that he or she is a false apostle. Obviously, this statement requires qualification. Notice the definition indicates that false apostles speak deliberate falsehoods for the purpose of deception. Hence, their purpose or objective is to deceive. However, a person can be a genuine believer with an incorrect title. Through ignorance or pride, he or she holds a self-appointed office without being called. On the other hand, a false apostle is one who deliberately misrepresents the truth, and subtly operates in deception. Generally speaking, they are the antithesis of everything we have discussed in this chapter.

Before explicitly mentioning the term "false apostle" later in the chapter, 2 Corinthians 11:3 directs its attention to the operation of false prophets. For it is based on the scriptural definition that we will have a better understanding of the operation of a false apostle.

> But I fear, lest by any means, as the serpent beguiled Eve through his subtilty, so your minds should be corrupted from the simplicity that is in Christ. (2 Corinthians 11:3)

To explain the operation of false apostles, the passage uses a familiar example. It states that just how the serpent beguiled Eve in Genesis Chapter 3, false apostles can corrupt the minds of believers from the simplicity of Christ. Like the serpent, notice the mechanism used by false apostles is the art of subtlety, which means they operate in a cunning or deceptive manner. Furthermore, because the operation is subtle, only those who are mature and whose senses have been trained can discern the difference between good and evil (Hebrews 5:11). However, the result of such deception is a change in the condition of the heart, which then leads to defilement. According to the passage, defilement occurs when the heart abandons the simplicity of Christ. The word "simplicity" means purity or singleness. It is not mixed with anything else. When you take something pure or of a single substance and combine it with other ingredients, the product inevitably loses its purity or simplicity. Similarly, because of deception and defilement, the heart or mind is no longer single. In His teachings, Jesus says when the eye (mind) is single, the whole body is full of light (Matthew 6:22). In other words, it is pure. He goes on to say that a single mind is one that does not serve two masters: God and mammon (Matthew 6:23). Mammon is a comprehensive word that includes all types of possessions, earnings, and gains. It is a designation used to describe material value. Therefore, Jesus creates a contrast between being a servant of God and a servant of the material world. Additionally, in the statement, He is dealing with the concept of having divided loyalty indicating that you cannot be faithful to two masters. Thus, if the heart is divided between the things of God and the things of the world, it is no longer single and has therefore moved from the simplicity of Christ.

A single heart or mind is one that is wholly dedicated to the Father. Hence, any teaching or doctrine, which causes the heart to divert its attention or focus from the Father to pursue the things of this life, is a tool of false apostles and teachers. These teachings turn the hearts of the people from God and make them servants of the world, which also includes pursuing their own interests. This is how false apostles operate. Moreover, what makes their doctrine so subtle is that it contains a mixture of the Spirit and the flesh. The result of such a mixture is a doctrine that is not pure. In fact, in Galatians 1:7, Paul refers to this fusion as perverting or corrupting the gospel of Christ. An example of this is seen in Galatians 3:2, where Paul asks the question, "Having begun in the Spirit, are ye now made perfect by the flesh?"

The challenge with the Galatian church was that they wanted to have an amalgamation of the things of the Spirit and the things of the flesh. It was a doctrine of convenience, which allowed them to claim a spiritual position, while still enjoying the pleasures and operations of the flesh. This is why Paul opened Chapter 3 with the question, "Who has bewitched or tricked you?" One of the reasons Paul used the word "bewitched" is because the promoters of the doctrine used the art of subtly. This makes it difficult to distinguish. A direct example of a doctrine that corrupts the heart from the simplicity of Christ is the faith and prosperity doctrine. This teaching has created wantonness in the hearts of believers influencing them to pursue the material things of this world. As a result, many have become servants of it and therefore are not servants of the kingdom of God.

Furthermore, Paul continues the discussion on the subtle nature of false apostles by characterizing them as deceitful workers. They are imposters who pretend to be genuine apostles but are not. Just as Satan has transformed himself into an angel of light, false apostles, through pretense, also transform themselves into the apostles of Christ. They may have the form or appearance of righteousness, but there is no power of godliness (2 Timothy 3:5). Armed with subtly and a mixed doctrine of Spirit and flesh they are in truth, deceitful workers. Notice that the passage uses the word "transformed," which in this context is the Greek word *metaschmatizo*. It is a combination of two Greek words *meta* meaning after and *schema* meaning fashion, mold, or external conditions. Hence, unlike being transformed into the image of Christ, which is a transformation of righteous character, this is simply a transformation of the external appearance. It is an external conversion with no inward power. Therefore, it looks the part. It seems to say the right things, but it is only camouflage. Thus, with most things of a counterfeit nature, it is often difficult to distinguish the difference. This is especially true about those who are untrained or unskilled in the word of righteousness.

> 13. For such are false apostles, deceitful workers, transforming themselves into the apostles of Christ.
> 14. And no marvel; for Satan himself is transformed into an angel of light.
> 15. Therefore it is no great thing if his ministers also be transformed as the ministers of righteousness; whose end shall be according to their works. (2 Corinthians 11:13-15)

Just how true apostles are ambassadors sent by the Father with a specific message and mandate, false apostles are representatives of Satan with an alternative message and mandate. True apostles are the promoters of the kingdom of God, but false apostles are sent with the message of the kingdom of darkness and are advocates of the things of the flesh.

As an ambassador, an apostle acts on the behalf of the Father and serves a fundamental role in relation to the church. Therefore, based on what we have discussed in this chapter, it should be apparent why Scripture places significant emphasis on the office. Certainly, with the weight and responsibility of the gift, it is not one to be taken lightly but with a consciousness of God's purpose. It is a foundational gift that sets the framework and agenda for the entire body of Christ. It is designed by the Father to create order in the body, to be the gatekeepers of the truth, and to reproduce the image of Christ on the earth.

CHAPTER 8

THE GIFT OF CHRIST EXPLAINED: PROPHET

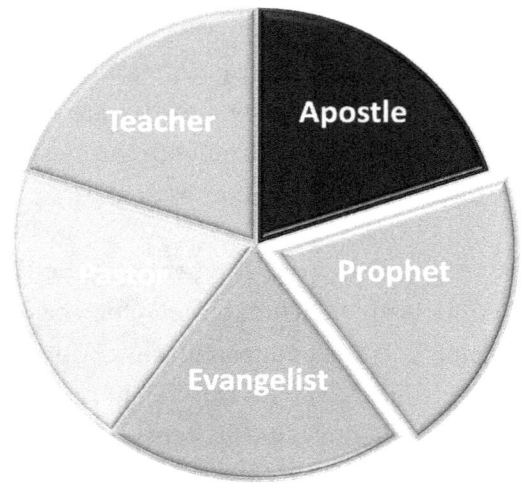

*And he gave some, apostles; and some, **prophets**; and some, evangelists; and some, pastors and teachers. (Ephesians 4:11)*

Having addressed the role of the apostle in the previous chapter, our attention will now be directed toward the gift of the prophet. However, in doing so, we will first reexamine the correlation that exists between these two gifts. Recall that Ephesians 2:20 says the house of God is built upon the foundation of the apostles and prophets with Jesus Christ being the chief cornerstone. Therefore, in addition to the apostles, prophets also serve a foundational role in the body of Christ. Accordingly, just as apostles, they represent the strength and integrity of the church. They play a pivotal role in relation to building God's house. Furthermore, as it pertains to the revelation of the mystery of Christ, recall that Ephesians 3:5 says what was once hidden, was now being made known unto God's holy apostles and prophets by the Holy Spirit. Hence, along with the apostles, God also chose them to channel His revelation.

I reiterate 2 Corinthians 12:28 which says, "And God hath set some in the church, first apostles, secondarily prophets, thirdly teachers, after that miracles, then gifts of healings, helps, governments, diversities of tongues." From the discussion on the importance of structure, it is clear that apostles have precedence in the church. Additionally, the position of the prophet was identified as second in rank or "the other of two." Therefore, based on the connection that these gifts share, they are designed to operate in tandem. Undoubtedly, the office of the prophet has tremendous significance in the church and requires a detailed explanation.

Hebrews 1:1 provides the premise that it was through the prophets that God spoke to His people in time past. As we will discover, the usage of the word "prophet" in this context carries with it a broad application meaning they simply spoke on God's behalf. They were His representatives and it was through them that He communicated His will and purpose. They were not just foretellers or predictors of the future but also preachers and teachers. For example, 2 Peter 2:5 refers to Noah as a preacher of righteousness, and Ezra, who was also a scribe, had the responsibility of teaching the statutes of the Law to the Israelites (Ezra 7:10). Therefore, in general, prophets spoke for God. They were responsible for measuring the behavior of the people, reminding them of God's covenant, and warning of His judgment. In several instances, prophets provided advanced notice of impending events allowing the people to act. For example, Acts 11:27-30 says,

27. And in these days came prophets from Jerusalem unto Antioch.
28. And there stood up one of them named Agabus, and signified by the spirit that there should be great dearth throughout all the world: which came to pass in the days of Claudius Caesar.
29. Then the disciples, every man according to his ability, determined to send relief unto the brethren which dwelt in Judaea:

30. Which also they did, and sent it to the elders by the hands of Barnabas and Saul.

Before we immerse ourselves in the gift of the prophet, let us consider the context of this passage concerning prophecy. Certainly, this has bearing on what often occurs in the church today when it comes to prophecy of this nature. In Acts 2:28, the Lord revealed to the prophet Agabus that there was going to be a famine in the days of Claudius Caesar. Therefore, as a precedence, the purpose of the prophecy was to provide advance notice in order to take action or assist those who would need it. Hence, based on what was prophesied, they put a plan in motion to help the brethren in Judaea. Having said that, it is futile that after events occur, many recall what a prophet revealed concerning the matter, but no action was taken. Unfortunately, despite no action being taken, many use the opportunity to validate the gift of prophecy in the individual. However, the purpose of prophecy in this respect is never to say, "I told you so" once the event has occurred. On the contrary, whenever the Father reveals something it is for a specific purpose.

Throughout Scripture, when God revealed a future event, it was to deliver His people, for correction, judgment, for them to act, or simply to reveal His purpose concerning a matter. Consistent with this discussion, when a prophecy is given, there should also be an awareness of what action is to be taken. In other instances, when a prophecy is given, it is just to bring awareness with no action to be taken. For example, on another occasion, the same prophet (Agabus) in Acts 21:11 took Paul's girdle and bound his own feet and hands. Upon doing this, he said, "Thus saith the Holy Ghost, So shall the Jews at Jerusalem bind the man that owneth this girdle, and shall deliver him into the hands of the Gentiles." Despite many persuading Paul not to go to Jerusalem, he was still determined to go saying, "The will of the Lord be done." In this instance, the purpose of the prophecy was not to take action but simply to provide an awareness of what would transpire. It was basically to reveal the will of God.

In today's environment, there seems to be tremendous ambiguity and misunderstanding concerning the function and responsibilities of a prophet. However, based on what we have already discussed along with the parameters offered in Ephesians Chapter 4, the overall purpose of the prophet as with the other gifts is clearly defined. It is unfortunate that in some cases, the perspective of prophets has been reduced to personal fortunetellers who seem to be aligned with the faith and prosperity doctrine. Along these lines, a good portion of what is communicated pertains to the procurement of material possessions or the attainment of earthly benefits. Certainly, this cannot be the measure of the enormous responsibility Scripture outlines for a prophet that gives them foundational credence.

As we progress through this chapter, we will examine the distinction between what it means to be a prophet, what is the gift of prophecy, and in general terms what it means to prophesy. Therefore, to add more substance to this discussion, let us take a closer look at the words "prophet," "prophecy," and "prophesying."

PROPHET DEFINED

The word "prophet" is the Greek word *prophetes*, which means the following:

- One who speaks openly before anyone (in a general sense) or one who speaks for another
- An interpreter of the oracle of a divine message or hidden things
- One to whom and through whom God speaks and reveals His purpose
- One who, moved by the Spirit of God and as His spokesperson solemnly declares to men what he has received by inspiration

Based on the definition of "one who speaks for another," Exodus 7:1-2 provides us with a practical illustration of what it means to be a prophet. When the Lord commanded Moses to go to Pharaoh, his response in Exodus 6:30 was that he was not a skillful speaker. Consequently, in Exodus 7:1, the Lord appointed Aaron as Moses' prophet or one who would speak on his behalf. Therefore, God spoke to Moses revealing His will. In turn, Moses communicated to Aaron what was to be said to Pharaoh. As Moses was the Lord's prophet (Deuteronomy 18:15), Aaron, in the matter pertaining to Pharaoh was Moses' prophet. Thus, from a general perspective, a prophet's role is to speak on behalf of another, expressing the person's heart or mind. Notice that in this example (and the definitions), the function of a prophet is not premised solely on the foretelling of future events but rather conveying another's message. Certainly, predicting events is involved in the operation of a prophet, but the office is not predicated on it. In fact, what is communicated and subsequently spoken by the prophet can involve either past, current, or future events. The main point is that a prophet is essentially one who speaks what he or she has received by inspiration. Therefore, as it pertains to the Father, a prophet is one who speaks on His behalf with the message being consistent with His Word and character. Simply put, a prophet is God's spokesperson.

In the New Testament, when the word "prophet" is used, it is specifically referring to the office of the prophet based on the gift of Christ mentioned in Ephesians 4:11. It is an official designation and appointment by the Father to speak on His behalf. As mentioned, in terms of church significance, it is second in rank and authority to that of the apostle. Therefore, with such weight attached to the office, there needs to be a clear understanding of the office and its function. One of the initial acceptances regarding the office is that *not everyone who prophesies is a prophet; however, every prophet will prophesy.* Even in the Old Testament, 1 Samuel Chapter 10 provides the account that while in the company of prophets, the Spirit of the Lord came upon Saul, and he began to prophesy among them. Saul prophesied, but that did not make him a prophet. Hence, the saying, "Is Saul also among the prophets?" Therefore, the ability to prophesy does not necessarily make someone a prophet. To have a clearer perspective of prophecy, let us look at the definitions of prophecy and prophesying.

PROPHECY AND PROPHESYING DEFINED

The word "prophecy" is the Greek word *propheteia*, which means the following:

- To speak by divine inspiration, declaring the purposes of God whether by reproving and admonishing the wicked, comforting the afflicted, or revealing things hidden, especially by foretelling future events.

The word "prophesying" is the Greek word *propheteuo*, which means the following:

- To predict or foretell future events, especially pertaining to the kingdom of God
- To declare truths by the inspiration of God's Holy Spirit, whether by prediction or not
- To declare a thing, which can only be known by divine revelation

Based on a consensus of the definitions, it should be apparent that prophecy, contrary to what is commonly believed, is not limited to the foretelling of future events. In fact, it is comprehensive and includes teaching, declaring God's purpose, and revealing what is unknown, all by the inspiration of the Holy Spirit. In short, prophecy is simply declaring the heart and mind of the Father. In relation to this general concept of prophecy, as it pertains to believers, Joel 2:28-29 provides significant insight. It reveals that prophecy is an inherent endowment to *all believers* by the Holy Spirit. *Every believer has been called to prophesy.*

28. And it shall come to pass afterward, that I will pour out my spirit upon all flesh; *and your sons and your daughters shall prophesy,* your old men shall dream dreams, your young men shall see visions:
29. And also upon the servants and upon the handmaids in those days will I pour out my spirit. (Joel 2:28-29)

Based on the Lord pouring out His Holy Spirit, Joel declares that both men and women shall prophesy. Does this mean that every believer is a prophet? Of course not. What is this specifically referring to? As we have discussed, prophecy in this instance is a general term and it simply means to speak by divine inspiration. This is evident by the account of Acts Chapter 2, which provides the details of the fulfillment of Joel's prophecy.

1. And when the day of Pentecost was fully come, they were all with one accord in one place.
2. And suddenly there came a sound from heaven as of a rushing mighty wind, and it filled all the house where they were sitting.

3. And there appeared unto them cloven tongues like as of fire, and it sat upon each of them.
4. And they were all filled with the Holy Ghost, and began to speak with other tongues, as the Spirit gave them utterance.
5. And there were dwelling at Jerusalem Jews, devout men, out of every nation under heaven.
6. Now when this was noised abroad, the multitude came together, and were confounded, because that every man heard them speak in his own language.
7. And they were all amazed and marvelled, saying one to another, Behold, are not all these which speak Galilaeans?
8. And how hear we every man in our own tongue, wherein we were born?
9. Parthians, and Medes, and Elamites, and the dwellers in Mesopotamia, and in Judaea, and Cappadocia, in Pontus, and Asia,
10. Phrygia, and Pamphylia, in Egypt, and in the parts of Libya about Cyrene, and strangers of Rome, Jews and proselytes,
11. Cretes and Arabians, we do hear them speak in our tongues the wonderful works of God.
12. And they were all amazed, and were in doubt, saying one to another, What meaneth this?
13. Others mocking said, These men are full of new wine.
14. But Peter, standing up with the eleven, lifted up his voice, and said unto them, Ye men of Judaea, and all ye that dwell at Jerusalem, be this known unto you, and hearken to my words:
15. For these are not drunken, as ye suppose, seeing it is but the third hour of the day.
16. But this is that which was spoken by the prophet Joel;
17. And it shall come to pass in the last days, saith God, I will pour out of my Spirit upon all flesh: and your sons and your daughters shall prophesy, and your young men shall see visions, and your old men shall dream dreams:
18. And on my servants and on my handmaidens I will pour out in those days of my Spirit; and they shall prophesy. (Acts 2:1-18)

After receiving the Holy Spirit on the Day of Pentecost, the one hundred and twenty believers began to speak in other tongues as the Spirit gave them utterance. To be clear, this is not unknown tongues as mentioned in 1 Corinthians 14:2. Rather, these were identifiable known languages. As there were people from many countries present at Jerusalem for the Feast of Pentecost, the Holy Spirit inspired them, enabling them to speak in the languages of the people from the various countries. They spoke in the language of the Parthians, Medes, Elamites, etc. What precisely were they saying in these different languages? Acts 2:11 says they were speaking the wonderful works of God, which Joel refers to as prophecy. In other words, they were simply speaking by the inspiration of the Holy Spirit. Furthermore, after Peter confirmed that what they were doing was based on Joel's prophecy, he began to preach and as a result, three thousand souls were added to the church. Therefore, this strengthens the conclusion that to prophesy in general terms simply means to speak by inspiration and includes teaching/preaching. As a general endowment, the Holy Spirit has granted this ability of prophecy to every believer. He has endowed each believer to speak on His behalf. Having examined prophecy in a broad sense, let us look at the distinction between what it means to be a prophet or the office of a prophet and the gift of prophecy.

THE GIFT OF PROPHECY VERSUS THE OFFICE OF THE PROPHET

Depending on the particular church that you attend or visit, you may witness what many might regard as a prophetic demonstration. For example, someone may stand up and begin their declaration with, "Thus saith the Lord" followed by a specific decree. When this occurs, the normal assessment is that the individual giving the prophecy is a prophet. In fact, if this happens a few times to the same individual, many may regard this person as a prophet and the title may even be conferred upon him or her. However, operating in the gift of prophecy does not necessarily make someone a prophet. Hence, there is a distinction between the gift of Christ, which makes someone a prophet, and the gift of prophecy by which someone is able to prophesy. Again, I reiterate, every prophet can prophesy but not everyone who prophesies is a prophet.

After highlighting the gifts of Christ in Ephesians Chapter 4, 1 Corinthians Chapter 12, on the other hand, details the gifts of the Spirit. Therefore, as a premise, there is a distinction between the gifts of Christ and the gifts of the Spirit. Along these lines, here is another principle: the fact that an individual operates in the gifts of the Spirit does not mean he or she has been bestowed the gifts of Christ. However, those who have been given the gifts of Christ will function in the gifts of the Spirit.

1. Now concerning spiritual gifts, brethren, I would not have you ignorant.
2. Ye know that ye were Gentiles, carried away unto these dumb idols, even as ye were led.
3. Wherefore I give you to understand, that no man speaking by the Spirit of God calleth Jesus accursed: and that no man can say that Jesus is the Lord, but by the Holy Ghost.
4. Now there are diversities of gifts, but the same Spirit.
5. And there are differences of administrations, but the same Lord.
6. And there are diversities of operations, but it is the same God which worketh all in all.
7. But the manifestation of the Spirit is given to every man to profit withal.
8. For to one is given by the Spirit the word of wisdom; to another the word of knowledge by the same Spirit;
9. To another faith by the same Spirit; to another the gifts of healing by the same Spirit;
10. To another the working of miracles; to another prophecy; to another discerning of spirits; to another divers kinds of tongues; to another the interpretation of tongues:
11. But all these worketh that one and the selfsame Spirit, dividing to every man severally as he will. (1 Corinthians 12:1-11)

To have a better appreciation for the book of 1 Corinthians, it is necessary to understand its overall format. As previously mentioned, the epistle is divided into two sections. In the first portion of the letter (chapters one to six), Paul, as the apostle of the church at Corinth is addressing a report provided by members of Chloe's house (1 Corinthians 1:11). After responding to the items listed in the report, he turns his focus to the letter that the church wrote to him. Hence, the second part of 1 Corinthians (essentially the remainder of the epistle) represents a written dialogue between Paul and the Corinthian church. In this segment, he is systematically responding to matters of concern that the church wrote to him (1 Corinthians 7:1). One of the subjects they wanted clarity on pertained to spiritual gifts, and he begins to address this issue in 1 Corinthians Chapter 12. However, it is important to understand that Paul's entire conversation on spiritual gifts also includes chapters thirteen and fourteen. According to the principles of rightly dividing the Word of God, these three chapters comprise what is referred to as *a passage context*. In short, a passage context states that one or two verses of a particular chapter must not be isolated and handled alone or separated from that chapter or passage. Furthermore, a passage relating to a specific topic can be made up of more than one chapter. This means that a passage context (as in this instance) can be based on several chapters.

To have a comprehensive understanding of the gifts of the Spirit, which includes the gift of prophecy, we have to carefully examine these three chapters in detail. Even though the gifts are listed in Chapter 12, the discussion progresses through chapters thirteen and fourteen. Hence, one of the reasons there is a misunderstanding of spiritual gifts is because the entire passage context is not considered.

In 1 Corinthians 12:1, Paul begins the discussion concerning spiritual gifts by saying, "I do not want you to be ignorant or unaware." In other words, l will explain what they are and how they function. According to 1 Corinthians Chapter 12, there are nine spiritual gifts, one of which is *the gift of prophecy*. To be clear, the gift of prophecy, though distinct from the general endowment of prophecy, still falls under the umbrella of general prophecy mentioned in Joel Chapter 2. The baptism of the Holy Spirit provides every believer with the ability to prophesy or speak by inspiration of the Holy Spirit. Therefore, prophecy is a general term and is an umbrella ability, which encompasses several of the gifts of the Holy Spirit that are vocal in nature. This includes the word of wisdom, the word of knowledge, the gift of prophecy, divers kinds of tongues, and the interpretation of tongues. Hence, when Joel says that believers will be able to speak by the inspiration of the Holy Spirit or prophesy these are all included (see diagram). However, the Holy Spirit within the general realm of the ability to prophesy bestows specific vocal gifts to individuals as He wills.

EXHIBIT 7

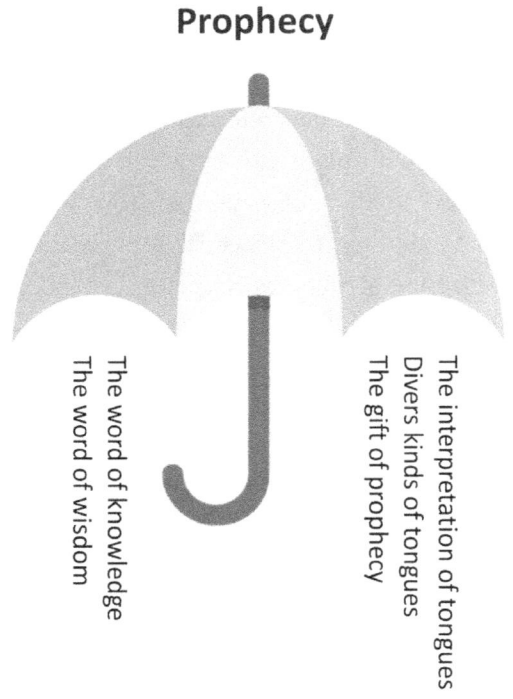

Prophecy
- The word of wisdom
- The word of knowledge
- The gift of prophecy
- Divers kinds of tongues
- The interpretation of tongues

As a precursor to its discussion on spiritual gifts, 1 Corinthians 12:4 first establishes an important foundation regarding them. First, it says even though there are different gifts, it is the same Spirit who grants them. Furthermore, 1 Corinthians 12:5 adds that even though there are variations of how they are administered or served, it is the same Lord who administrates them. Finally, 1 Corinthians 12:6 says regardless of the differences in how they operate, the same God effectually works them all. Therefore, the core message is that despite being many, there is still unity and harmony. Hence, even though there are variations, it is the Holy Spirit who dispenses, orchestrates, and coordinates the gifts. Additionally, 1 Corinthians 12:7 says in their entirety, the gifts of the Spirit are bestowed to be of benefit to everyone.

After listing the gifts, 1 Corinthians 12:11 states that the Holy Spirit divides them to every man severally as He will. The word "severally" in the passage refers to the fact that the gifts inherently belong to the Holy Spirit. Therefore, He allocates them according to His purpose. Every believer can have one or more of the gifts operating in him or her as God determines. Hence, the Spirit distributes them as He wills, and the gifts operate based on the need at that particular time. This also means that the gifts cannot be activated by our own volition. Additionally, as the gifts are manifested from time to time, they are not permanent or continuous assignments. Hence, the functioning of the gifts of the Spirit, in this instance, the gift of prophecy, is temporary in the believer. On the other hand, the gifts of Christ, in this instance, the designation or the office of the prophet is permanent and functions for the life of the prophet.

To be abundantly clear, an individual is designated as a prophet because of the gift of Christ whereas the gift of prophecy is a gift of the Spirit. Hence, there is a distinction between the two, and understanding the difference is important. As Ephesians 4:8 outlines, when Christ ascended on high, He gave gifts to humanity one of which is being a prophet. This endowment therefore creates the office of the prophet. However, 1 Corinthians 12:10 speaks of the gift of prophecy as a function, not an office. To this end, even though the manifestation of the gift of the Spirit may operate in an individual, *he or she is not identified by the gift*. Again, in using the example of prophecy, despite the gift of prophecy being expressed through an individual, this does not mean the person is a prophet. On the other hand, when the gift of Christ, in particular, being a prophet, is bestowed on an individual, the person is identified by the gift. Hence, functioning in the spiritual gift does not constitute an office or calling, but the gift of Christ does. Moreover, since being a prophet is a gift of Christ, it carries a different degree of responsibility and authority. The chart below encapsulates the distinctions between being a prophet and the gift of prophecy.

TABLE 1

PROPHET	GIFT OF PROPHECY
• Ephesians 4:11	• 1 Corinthians 12:10
• Gift of Christ	• Gift of the Spirit
• Office	• Function
• Foundational	• Non-foundational
• For the perfecting of the saints • For the work of the ministry • For the edifying of the body of Christ	• Edification • Exhortation • Comfort
• Permanent	• Temporary
• Some	• Dividing to every man as the Lord wills
• Identified by the gift	• Identifies the operation of the Spirit in an individual
• Leadership role	• Non-leadership role

UNDERSTANDING SPIRITUAL GIFTS

To fully appreciate the dynamics of prophecy, a better understanding of spiritual gifts is required. As explained, 1 Corinthians Chapters 12 to 14 represent a passage context, and the subject of prophecy is discussed multiple times throughout the chapters. With that said, let us take a look at the passage context in detail.

One of the underlying principles for understanding spiritual gifts is despite the diversity that exists, unity is being emphasized. This is evident in the statement in 1 Corinthians 12:4, which says, "Now there are diversities of gifts, but the same Spirit." In other words, "there are many gifts, yet one Spirit." Thus, the prevailing message regarding spiritual gifts is that despite the differences and various functions of the gifts, there is still unity and harmony. What is interesting is that even though 1 Corinthians Chapter 12 seems to pivot from its discussion on spiritual gifts to address the subject of members of the body, the principle of unity and harmony is still being expressed. Therefore, in emphasizing this message, 1 Corinthians 12:12-27 provides the illustration of the human body. In this regard, Corinthians 12: 12 says, "For as the body is one, and hath many members, and all the members of that one body, being many, are one body: so also is Christ." In essence, the passage is simply saying, "There are many members, yet, one body." Hence, even in this example, the message of unity and harmony is still consistent.

Based on the analogy of the human body, the Father fashioned it in such a way as to create unity and harmony. Hence, each member makes a specific meaningful contribution to the proper functioning of the body. Furthermore, based on the Father's design, He molded it in this manner so there should be no divisions in the body. To support this, 1 Corinthians 12:24 says that He "tempered the body together," which means to assimilate or unite one thing to another. Therefore, just as the parts of the human body are interdependent, so too are the members of the body of Christ. The Lord created the body to function in harmony and to create a balanced dependency. Thus, as 1 Corinthians 12:17 states, if the whole body were an eye, it would not have the capacity to hear.

After ensuring that its communication of unity and harmony was reinforced with the example of the human body, which depicts the church, the passage once again embraces the discussion of spiritual gifts. However, this time, it introduces order and structure to the body of Christ and to the orchestration of the gifts. Therefore, the passage is communicating that for unity and harmony to prevail, there must be order. This was the emphasis during the discussion on the importance of structure.

> 28. And God hath set some in the church, first apostles, secondarily prophets, thirdly teachers, after that miracles, then gifts of healings, helps, governments, diversities of tongues.

29. Are all apostles? Are all prophets? Are all teachers? Are all workers of miracles?
30. Have all the gifts of healing? Do all speak with tongues? Do all interpret?
31. But covet earnestly the best gifts: and yet shew I unto you a more excellent way. (1 Corinthians 12:28-31)

The passage establishes the fact that, yes, there is unity and harmony with the gifts, as well as with the body of Christ. However, in the midst of this, there is still an order of things. Indeed, all the members are one and there is interdependence, but there is still organization. Hence, the earnest discussion of order in the body of Christ begins before 1 Corinthians 14:40 says, "Let all things be done decently and in order." 1 Corinthians Chapter 12 invests a considerable amount of time emphasizing the message of unity and harmony because order facilitates these two components. Therefore, without established order, unity and harmony cannot exist. For this reason, 1 Corinthians 12:28 states what that order is.

It says the order is first apostles, second prophets, thirdly teachers, then miracles, and so on. Unfortunately, this important principle of church structure is predominately absent in the body of Christ today. Notice in the scheme of things, God's divine order begins with His established leadership and then it progressively embraces the gifts of the Spirit. Therefore, from God's perspective, His model for leadership in terms of priority has precedence over the functioning of the gifts of the Spirit. In fact, it is in an environment of order and structure that the gifts function effectively. Thus, leadership is critical and serves as the foundation for the proper functioning of the gifts of the Spirit.

Again, in emphasizing the point, the church is not established on pastoral order but rather, apostolic order. Unity and harmony in the body of Christ are deficient because the appropriate structure is missing. However, as Ephesians 2:21 highlights, once the proper foundation is established, growth or increase follows. Hence, for the church to experience development and maturity, it must reacquaint itself with the structure or order outlined in Scripture.

SPIRITUAL GIFTS AND CHARITY

After highlighting spiritual gifts earlier in the chapter, 1 Corinthians 12:31 revisits the gifts and admonishes believers to burn with zeal for the best ones. Therefore, there is strong encouragement to desire spiritual gifts but with specific instructions to pursue those that are more advantageous. This then creates a distinction among spiritual gifts. In harmony with this perspective, the reasonable question is what then are the best gifts? From early in my studies, it was constantly communicated to me that the Bible interprets itself or simply put, Scripture interprets Scripture and, in this instance, this principle is consistent. However, before communicating what the best gifts are, Scripture uses 1 Corinthians Chapter 13 as a platform to outline the more excellent way to be zealous for the gifts. Thus, the focal point of 1 Corinthians 12:31 is that there is a pre-eminent way to pursue the gifts. Hence, the purpose and operation of the gifts are best realized within a particular parameter, which 1 Corinthians Chapter 13 says is love.

For the most part, when 1 Corinthians Chapter 13 is read, it is done in isolation, without considering what was said in Chapter 12 or in respect to its contextual setting. Indeed, the chapter offers an outstanding description of what charity or love is, but the perspective is within the context of the operation of spiritual gifts. Recall that the communication of the passage context, which includes 1 Corinthians Chapters 12-14, is the operation of spiritual gifts. Therefore, 1 Corinthians Chapter 13 is describing how to function in spiritual gifts following the more excellent way. It is saying that for the gifts to be meaningful, they must include love. Keep in mind that the principal intent of spiritual gifts to benefit humanity. They are not for the purpose of recognition or acclaim. With this in mind, 1 Corinthians Chapter 13 is related to the intent of the heart while operating in the gifts. Hence, while functioning in spiritual gifts, if my objective is not for the benefit of humanity but rather self-serving, then it is unprofitable. It is saying, no matter how proficient I am in the operation of spiritual gifts or in my leadership position in the body, if I do not have love, it is of no benefit to anyone.

1. Though I speak with the tongues of men and of angels, and have not charity, I am become as sounding brass, or a tinkling cymbal.

2. And though I have the gift of prophecy, and understand all mysteries, and all knowledge; and though I have all faith, so that I could remove mountains, and have not charity, I am nothing.
3. And though I bestow all my goods to feed the poor, and though I give my body to be burned, and have not charity, it profiteth me nothing. (1 Corinthians 13:1-3)

Admittedly, we all love good speeches. We are mesmerized by the skillful manner in which someone speaks, for great orators fascinate us. However, regardless of the language people speak or how eloquent they sound, without love, words resemble one of two things. They are either hollow, empty sounds that reverberate or constant loud clashing of cymbals that irritate. In both cases, their words simply sound like noise.

Love is the most important ingredient in any speech and outweighs eloquence. Furthermore, despite how proficient we are in prophecy, regardless of our vast knowledge and understanding, and irrespective of our tremendous faith, if we do not have love, we are nothing. Notice that in this instance, the scripture makes the conclusion personal. It says, "We are nothing" or of no significance. Indeed, operating in the gifts may create the appearance and illusion we are important; however, without love, Scripture offers a different opinion. In other words, we are not identified by the manifestation of the gifts but rather, the demonstration of love, which defines us.

The emphasis is not on how fluent we are in the spiritual gifts but our proficiency in showing love. Moreover, 1 Corinthians 13:3 adds that no matter how generous we are to those in need or even if we are martyrs, without love, it is no benefit to us. In combination, 1 Corinthians 13:1-3 says, without love, we are nobodies who make noise with no benefit. Hence, the greatest display of the spiritual gifts and the gifts of Christ is manifested through love. Therefore, the major focus should not be on the exhibition of the gift but the demonstration of love. In this regard, the chapter goes on to qualify what love is.

4. Charity suffereth long, and is kind; charity envieth not; charity vaunteth not itself, is not puffed up,

5. Doth not behave itself unseemly, seeketh not her own, is not easily provoked, thinketh no evil;
6. Rejoiceth not in iniquity, but rejoiceth in the truth;
7. Beareth all things, believeth all things, hopeth all things, endureth all things. (1 Corinthians 13:4-7)

Notice that in describing love, its attributes have nothing to do with emotions or feelings. Rather, based on the passage, it is actually righteous character being manifested. In short, love is the character of God. For this reason, 1 John 4:8 says that God is love; He is the very essence and expression of it. God does not simply love; it is His very nature. Furthermore, the demonstration of love is not based on the action or response of someone; it is an act of the will regardless of what the other person does. For example, Romans 5:8 says, "But God commendeth (or exhibited) His love toward us, in that, while we were yet sinners, Christ died for us." Therefore, love has no reciprocal circumstances attached to it; it is unconditional.

The word "charity" or "love" in this passage is the Greek word *agape*. This is distinct from other Greek words for love such as *eros*, which is romantic love and *philia*, which involves friendship. Unlike these types of love, agape is not sensory. It is not based on what I see, hear, or feel. What is interesting is that the Bible does not really define what love is; rather, it describes what love looks like, how it behaves, and how it responds to or treats others. For instance, 1 John 3:1 says, "Behold, what manner of love the Father hath bestowed upon us, that we should be called the sons of God." Furthermore, John 15:13 says, "Greater love hath no man than this, that a man lay down his life for his friends." In both instances, Scripture demonstrates the nature of love; it is concerned about the welfare and benefit of others.

In harmony with 1 Corinthians Chapter 13, the true expression of ministry is not in how well we can teach/preach, how inspiring we are when we sing, or how well we flow in the gift of prophecy. Undoubtedly, these have their significance. However, they are only meaningful when they are demonstrated from a position of love or a pure heart. The gifts are beneficial when they are the products of gentleness, kindness, self-control, etc. Indeed, this is "the more excellent way" 1 Corinthians 12:31 refers to. *Therefore, to be effective in the gifts of the Spirit and the gifts of Christ, we must operate in love, which is the fruit of the Spirit.*

It is important to understand there is no separation between the gifts and the fruit of the Spirit. In fact, as the passage reveals, it is the fruit that makes the gifts effective and beneficial to humanity. Furthermore, without love, the gifts are merely self-serving, self-promoting, and therefore have no value. Unfortunately, the church seems to be more concerned about the operation of the gifts than the fruit. Hence, they often use them as the basis for appointments and ordinations. However, based on Scripture, this should not be the case. A good example of this can be seen in Acts Chapter 6 when the seven were chosen to oversee the distribution of goods to the poor. Notice the criteria for the selection was not based on whether they could prophesy, work miracles, or speak in tongues. Rather, Acts 6:3 says, "Wherefore, brethren, look ye out among you seven men of honest report, full of the Holy Ghost and wisdom, whom we may appoint over this business." Hence, their appointment was premised on their characters. However, if the fruit of the Spirit serves as your foundation, the gifts would be an automatic consequence. Along these lines, Acts Chapter 7 reveals that Stephen, being one of the seven who was chosen, was, in fact, well-versed in Scripture. However, this was not the predominant reason for his selection.

Moreover, Jesus was very effective because He functioned in the gifts of the Spirit, as well as the fruit of the Spirit. The barometer of who we are and our effectiveness in ministry should not be how proficient we are in the manifestation of the gifts but in our demonstration of the fruit. As believers, the gifts do not define who we are. Love or the fruit of the Spirit does. As we have seen in 1 Corinthians Chapter 13, it is possible to have tremendous success in the gifts but be bankrupt in righteous character, thereby making the gift fruitless (literally).

Furthermore, when we compare the qualities of love mentioned in 1 Corinthians 13:4-7 to the fruit of the Spirit in Galatians 5:22-23, it is evident they share tremendous similarities. **To be clear, love is the fruit of the Spirit**, and the other characteristics are attributes or expressions of love. Hence, all the qualities of love are depicted by the fruit of the Spirit. See the comparison chart on "Love and the Fruit of the Spirit" for the parallels. Also, notice that in highlighting the fruit of the Spirit, Galatians 5:22 does not say that the fruit of the Spirit "are." It says the fruit of the Spirit "is," making it a single product. Hence, without love, there can be no joy, peace, longsuffering, gentleness, goodness, faith, meekness, and temperance.

TABLE 2

LOVE: THE FRUIT OF THE SPIRIT

LOVE	FRUIT OF THE SPIRIT
• Suffereth long (to be longsuffering or patient in bearing offences) **Patience**	• Love
• Kind (Mild) **Gentleness**	• Joy (Gladness)
• Envieth not (is not jealous, does not covet) **Goodness**	• Peace (Tranquility)
• Vaunteth not itself (is not boastful). **Meekness**	• Longsuffering (Patience)
• Is not puffed up (is not proud or arrogant) **Meekness**	• Gentleness (Kindness or integrity)
• Does not behave itself unseemly (improper behavior or rude) **Temperance**	• Goodness (Uprightness of heart and life)
• Seeketh not her own (is not self-serving)	• Faith (the character of one who can be relied on)
• **Goodness and Meekness**	• Faith (the character of one who can be relied on)
• Not easily provoked (is not easily angered) **Temperance**	• Meekness (Mildness and humility)
• Thinketh no evil (It does not take into account or make a record of the wrong suffered.) **Peace**	• Temperance (Self-control – the virtue of one who masters his desires and passions especially sensual appetites.)

• Rejoiceth not in iniquity (It is not joyful in injustice or acts of unrighteousness.) **Joy**	
• Rejoiceth in truth (It is joyful in righteousness.) **Joy**	
• Beareth all things (It protects or keeps by covering.) **Faith**	
• Believeth all things (It thinks something to be true.) **Faith**	
• Hopeth all things (It is unwavering.) **Faith**	
• Endureth all things (It perseveres or has fortitude.) **Faith**	
• Never fails (It is steadfast.) **Faith**	

THE PURPOSE OF PROPHECY

After addressing the connection between love and spiritual gifts in Chapters 12 and 13, 1 Corinthians Chapter 14 takes the baton and continues the conversation. However, in doing so, it combines the two previous chapters and adds practical application to the discussion. To accomplish this, it opens with the statement, "Follow after charity, and desire spiritual gifts, but rather that ye may prophesy." In the context of the passage, the word "follow" means to run swiftly to reach a goal or to acquire something. Therefore, based on priority, it says love is what we must eagerly pursue. As a point of emphasis, it does not say we are to follow after spiritual gifts and desire love, but rather, the opposite. Hence, while in pursuit of love, we are also to strive after spiritual gifts. Again, Scripture reinforces that as it pertains to love and spiritual gifts, love is the principal thing.

In reiterating the message of the passage context, let us do a quick recap. 1 Corinthians Chapter 12 introduced us to the conversation of spiritual gifts or gifts of the Spirit. However, because the gifts by themselves are meaningless, 1 Corinthians Chapter 13 presented the fruit of the Spirit or love. It says if we operate in the gifts of the Spirit without the character of love, it is worthless.

Again, there is no separating the gifts of the Spirit from the fruit of the Spirit. Consequently, after having a better appreciation for the combination of love and the gifts, 1 Corinthians 14:1 says, follow after love and desire spiritual gifts. Hence, seeking spiritual gifts without first running after love is a futile pursuit.

Notice specifically, that 1 Corinthians 14:1 says to desire spiritual gifts, but it places emphasis on prophecy. Why does Scripture place greater concentration on prophecy as opposed to the other gifts? Earlier in this segment, we touched on 1 Corinthians 12:31, which says, "Covet earnestly the best gifts." In addressing the question of which ones are the best gifts, the principle was submitted that Scripture interprets Scripture and sure enough, the Bible provides the answer. Why is prophecy therefore highlighted as one of the best gifts? In answering this question, the passage offers a comparison between speaking in an unknown tongue or dialect and prophesying.

2. For he that speaketh in an unknown tongue speaketh not unto men, but unto God: for no man understandeth him; howbeit in the spirit he speaketh mysteries.
3. But he that prophesieth speaketh unto men to edification, and exhortation, and comfort. (1 Corinthians 14:2-3)

In comparison to unknown tongues with which we speak unto God, when we prophesy, we speak unto men or humanity. For the sake of clarity, an unknown tongue is a heavenly language or dialect not understood by men. Moreover, even the person speaking in unknown tongues is unaware of what is being said because he or she is speaking mysteries. Therefore, it is a communication in the Spirit directed to the Father. While those speaking in unknown tongues only edify themselves, prophecy, on the other hand, edifies the church. Prophecy in the context of this passage is consistent with the general definition of speaking by divine inspiration. On this note, 1 Corinthians 14:3 says that prophecy serves a three-fold purpose. It is for edification, exhortation, and comfort. In short, prophecy serves to promote growth, encourage, and comfort the church. Therefore, the distinction between unknown tongues and prophecy is that one gift benefits only one person; whereas, the other benefits everyone.

In this regard, Scripture serves as a witness that the best gifts are the ones that aid the interest of others.

Categorically, they are for the benefit of the body of Christ and are not self-serving. For this reason, 1 Corinthians 14:5 adds, "I would that ye all spake with tongues, but rather that ye prophesied: for greater is he that prophesieth than he that speaketh with tongues, except he interpret, that the church may receive edifying." Hence, while speaking in unknown tongues has value, the passage emphasizes that prophesying has greater value because it edifies others. Moreover, 1 Corinthians 14:19 adds, "Yet in the church, I had rather speak five words with my understanding, that by my voice I might teach others also, than ten thousand words in an unknown tongue."

In reiterating its position on spiritual gifts, 1 Corinthians 14:12 provides a wonderful summation of this discussion. It says, "Even so ye, forasmuch as ye are zealous of spiritual gifts, seek that ye may excel to the edifying of the church." Recall that the general purpose of the gifts is to benefit everyone. Therefore, the best gifts are the ones that benefit or edify the church. In the final comparison of this discussion, 1 Corinthians 14:22 points out that tongues serve as a sign to those who do not believe, whereas prophecy is a token for those who are believers. The chart below provides a snapshot of the comparison between unknown tongues and prophecy.

TABLE 3

UNKNOWN TONGUES	PROPHECY
• Speaks unto God	• Speaks unto men (humanity).
• No person understands what is being said. Even the understanding of the speaker is unfruitful—in the Spirit they speak mysteries.	• People understand what is being said. It is for edification, exhortation, and comfort.
• Edifies themselves (has value)	• Edifies the church (has greater value)
• Benefits one person	• Benefits others
• A sign for them that do not believe	• A sign for them that believe

After reconciling the benefits of speaking in unknown tongues compared to that of general prophecy, 1 Corinthians 14:29-33 pivots to address prophets in particular. In the context of dealing with order in the church and the contributions of members, the matter of prophets is subsequently tabled.

29. Let the prophets speak two or three, and let the other judge.
30. If any thing be revealed to another that sitteth by, let the first hold his peace.
31. For ye may all prophesy one by one, that all may learn, and all may be comforted.
32. And the spirits of the prophets are subject to the prophets.
33. For God is not the author of confusion, but of peace, as in all churches of the saints. (I Corinthians 14:29-33)

In this instance, Scripture is speaking specifically to those in the office of the prophet and not the general concept of prophesying. Whenever the New Testament explicitly uses the word "prophet," it is in direct reference to the office and not the gift of prophecy. Once again, as mentioned throughout this chapter, it is important to understand the difference between the two. Additionally, the reference to prophets speaking in this passage is unrelated to the concept of "sermons" in the church today. In the interest of establishing order and ensuring that things were done properly, guidelines were put in place. Therefore, as it pertains to prophets and maintaining order in the church, the instructions are that two or three prophets speak while the other prophet weighs what is said. Furthermore, to reinforce that order is indeed possible, 1 Corinthians 14:31 provides a cautionary note and states that the spirit of the prophet is subject to the prophet.

Additionally, prophecy and the gift of prophecy are both associated with the word of wisdom and the word of knowledge. The word of wisdom is when God gives you a revelation about a future event that has not yet occurred. It is predictive. In some cases, when this occurs, its purpose is for warning to provide an opportunity for change through intercession. The word of knowledge is when God gives a revelation about a past or current event. Jesus' encounter with the Samaritan woman in John Chapter 4 is an example of the word of knowledge. When a person functions in a word of wisdom or a word of knowledge, this does not make him or her a prophet; however, a prophet will function in both.

FALSE PROPHETS

Because our perspective of a prophet or prophecy is often short-sighted, our conclusions of what it means to be a false prophet are also often incorrect. In normal church culture, when we hear the term "false prophet," the notion of an individual missing the mark in terms of predictions is what comes to mind. However, as we have discussed, this is based on the reduced understanding that prophecy is limited solely to the foretelling of future events. However, just as the word "prophecy" has a broad definition, the designation of a false prophet does as well. From the beginning, the tactic of the devil has been two-fold.

First, his objective has always been to imitate the Father. Recall Ezekiel 14:14 where his ambition was to be like the Most High or present himself as if he is God. Even though the actual attempt failed, he has successfully created an image that closely resembles the Father. Hence, 1 Corinthians 11:14 says, "For Satan himself is transformed into an angel of light." Therefore, despite it being a false representation or a counterfeit, only those whose senses are exercised can discern between good and evil (Hebrews 5:14). Additionally, the second tactic the devil employs is an alternative message. He distorts the message of the Father or the Word of God so it appeals to flesh or human interests. A good example of this operation can be seen in Genesis Chapter 3 where what the Father said was perverted to create deception. Interestingly, both strategies of the devil are false representations of the Father and are promoted by false prophets.

Generally speaking, the Bible refers to false prophets as those who come in sheep's clothing but inwardly, they are ravening wolves (Matthew 7:15). Just as these animals are contrasting in nature, so is the distinction between how they appear and their intentions. Despite their meek façade, their primary objective is to devour. Outwardly, they seem to have righteous character or a form of godliness; however, on the inside, they have a totally different agenda.

The Five-Fold Ministry Gifts

While true prophets speak on behalf of the Father and promote His agenda, false prophets are oracles of the devil carrying out his program. Through disguise, they purport to be who they are not using deceit as their major mechanism. How do they accomplish this? According to Scripture, false prophets use the vehicle of false teaching. Let us look at a few scriptures, which speak of the association between false prophets and false teachers.

1. But there were false prophets also among the people, even as there shall be false teachers among you, who privily shall bring in damnable heresies, even denying the Lord that bought them, and bring upon themselves swift destruction. (2 Peter 2:1)

3. For the time will come when they will not endure sound doctrine; but after their own lusts shall they heap to themselves teachers, having itching ears;
4. And they shall turn away their ears from the truth, and shall be turned unto fables. (2 Timothy 4:3-4)

29. For I know this, that after my departing shall grievous wolves enter in among you, not sparing the flock.
30. Also of your own selves shall men arise, speaking perverse things, to draw away disciples after them. (Acts 20:29-30)

1. Beloved, believe not every spirit, but try the spirits whether they are of God: because many false prophets are gone out into the world.
2. Hereby know ye the Spirit of God: Every spirit that confesseth that Jesus Christ is come in the flesh is of God:
3. And every spirit that confesseth not that Jesus Christ is come in the flesh is not of God: and this is that spirit of antichrist, whereof ye have heard that it should come; and even now already is it in the world. 1 John 4:1-3)

Notice that in all the above passages, the recurring theme regarding false prophets surrounds false teaching or false doctrine. Therefore, as previously stated, it has very little to do with incorrectly foretelling future events. In fact, as 2 Peter 2:1 points out, false prophets are the promoters of destructive heresies whose primary objective is to create an atmosphere of disunity within the body of Christ. For more on what qualifies a teaching to be classified as heresy, please refer to my book, *Faith: Who Hath Bewitched You?*

The term "false prophet" is the Greek word *pseudoprophetes*. Just as we saw with the term "false apostles," the expression false prophet is also a combination of two words *pseudes* and *prophetes*. Again, based on the root word for false, *pseudomai*, it means to deliberately or intentionally speak lies or falsehoods. Therefore, a false prophet is a counterfeit, one who pretends to speak on behalf of the Father but actually speaks deceptive words. In plain language, if a false prophet is a false teacher, then this further certifies that a prophet of God also teaches. Deuteronomy 13:1-5 provides an excellent example of what a false prophet is.

1. If there arise among you a prophet, or a dreamer of dreams, and giveth thee a sign or a wonder,
2. And the sign or the wonder come to pass, whereof he spake unto thee, saying, Let us go after other gods, which thou hast not known, and let us serve them;
3. Thou shalt not hearken unto the words of that prophet, or that dreamer of dreams: for the LORD your God proveth you, to know whether ye love the LORD your God with all your heart and with all your soul.
4. Ye shall walk after the LORD your God, and fear him, and keep his commandments, and obey his voice, and ye shall serve him, and cleave unto him.
5. And that prophet, or that dreamer of dreams, shall be put to death; because he hath spoken to turn you away from the LORD your God, which brought you out of the land of Egypt, and redeemed you out of the house of bondage, to thrust thee out of the way which the LORD thy God commanded thee to walk in. So shalt thou put the evil away from the midst of thee.

Note the passage begins with the premise that what the prophet predicts actually comes to pass. This is significant because oftentimes, we are so enthralled with manifestations that we neglect doctrine. In the example, the weight of whether the prophet is true or false is not associated with a sign or wonder but their doctrines and intentions. In fact, they use signs and wonders as an opportunity to deceive. Therefore, any prophet who promulgates a teaching or doctrine that causes humanity to turn away from God, regardless of his or her accuracy in determining events or ability to work miracles is a false prophet. Furthermore, Mark 13:22 adds to this dialogue and says that false Christs and false prophets shall rise and show signs and wonders to seduce, if it were possible, the elect. Therefore, the ability to perform signs does not provide validation as being true. To this end, 2 Peter Chapter 2 outlines the many characteristics associated with false prophets. For example,

- They are pernicious or lascivious.
- They are the vehicles through which the truth is blasphemed.
- They are covetous.
- They make merchandise of people or use them for gain.
- They walk after the flesh in the lusts of uncleanliness.
- They despise authority.
- They are bold, arrogant, and speak evil of those worthy of honour and glory.
- They are as animals destitute of reason.
- They speak evil of the things they do not understand.
- They consider it a delight to indulge in immorality and femininity even in the daytime.
- They are moral blemishes who live in luxury while they feast with you.
- They have eyes (minds) full of uncleanness and unfaithfulness that cannot cease from sin.
- They entice unstable souls.
- They have minds trained in covetous practices and a greedy desire to have more.
- They are cursed children.
- They have forsaken the righteous way and gone astray.
- Their model is Balaam and just like him, they also love the wages of unrighteousness.
- They are wells without water. They are empty and disappointing.
- They are clouds carried with a tempest. Again, they are empty.
- They speak with extravagant words of perverseness and have no truth. They use this tactic to entice those who were almost free through the lusts of the flesh.

- They promise liberty, but they themselves are servants of depravity.

Notice that as it pertains to false prophets, there is a consistent thread embedded in the list as it relates to character. False prophets are therefore not only identified by trafficking in false doctrine and heresies but also by the works of the flesh. In other words, they are recognized not just by their words but also their fruits. Hence, despite how they may appear on the outside or how persuasive their words may be, it is by their fruits or character that they are defined.

THE MORE SURE WORD OF PROPHECY

For our final discussion regarding prophecy, it is important to understand that all facets of prophecy must align with the sure word of prophecy or Scripture.

16. For we have not followed cunningly devised fables, when we made known unto you the power and coming of our Lord Jesus Christ, but were eyewitnesses of his majesty.
17. For he received from God the Father honour and glory, when there came such a voice to him from the excellent glory, This is my beloved Son, in whom I am well pleased.
18. And this voice which came from heaven we heard, when we were with him in the holy mount.
19. We have also a more sure word of prophecy; whereunto ye do well that ye take heed, as unto a light that shineth in a dark place, until the day dawn, and the day star arise in your hearts:
20. Knowing this first, that no prophecy of the scripture is of any private interpretation.
21. For the prophecy came not in old time by the will of man: but holy men of God spake as they were moved by the Holy Ghost. (2 Peter 1:16-21)

To accentuate the sureness of Scripture, Peter uses the comparison of having heard the Father speak versus the written Word of God. They both represented the authentic Word of God, but according to the passage, one holds precedence over the other. In the passage, Peter recounts his experience recorded in Matthew Chapter 17. He says when they were in the holy mountain during Jesus' transfiguration, they heard God speak. The Father said, "This is my beloved Son, in whom I am well pleased." Not only did they receive this word of prophecy, but they were also eyewitnesses of Christ's majesty. However, despite this wonderful encounter and the sure word of prophecy they received, Peter states that the written Word of God represents *the more sure word of prophecy*. Hence, what is written or Scripture, carries greater weight than what is heard or seen. Furthermore, as a principle, what is heard must be within the parameters of what is written to be valid.

I believe the Lord allowed this illustration to be included for two reasons. First, based on the authenticity of Scripture, we are to place greater credence in the written Word of God over what we hear. Second, the utterance of a spoken word does not replace what is written. Often, those who speak on behalf of the Father preface their statements with "Thus says the Lord, or God told me to tell you." However, the veracity of what they say does not replace the Word of God. It should also not be held in higher regard than what is written. The *more sure* Word of God or Scripture holds precedence over the words of any prophet.

Notice that 1 Peter 1:20-21 says that no prophecy of Scripture is of any private interpretation, but the prophets spoke as they were moved by the Holy Spirit. What exactly does this mean? First, the statement "No prophecy of Scripture is of any private interpretation" means that when the prophets spoke, they were not operating based on their own will. They did not say what they wanted to say or inject their will or opinion into the equation. They spoke as they were moved by the Holy Ghost or as God inspired them. Therefore, this establishes the premise that there is no prophetic movement if God is not moving. It is similar to a ship with a sail whose direction and movement is totally dependent upon the wind. When the wind of God's Spirit moves, the prophets are directed what to say; they follow the direction of the wind. To accomplish this, prophets are required to spend time in the presence of God so that when He has something to say to His people, they are in a position to hear.

CHRIST AS A PROPHET

As discussed, a prophet, in the basic sense, is one who speaks on behalf of another. In essence, this represented the ministry of Jesus Christ in its entirety. Therefore, when Jesus said "Repent: For the kingdom of heaven is at hand," He was serving as the Father's spokesperson. He is the One to whom and through whom God spoke and revealed His purpose.

1. God, who at sundry times and in divers manners spake in time past unto the fathers by the prophets,
2. Hath in these last days spoken unto us by his Son, whom he hath appointed heir of all things, by whom also he made the worlds, (Hebrews 1:1-2)

When Hebrews Chapter 1 uses the term "the prophets," it is specifically and collectively referring to those of the Old Testament. Hence, at various times and in many parts, they were the ones who spoke on God's behalf. However, under the new covenant, the Father spoke through His Son, Jesus Christ. Therefore, He is also the Father's prophet. Furthermore, just as Moses was God's prophet in matters related to Israel, he prophesied in Deuteronomy 18:15 that the Lord will raise another prophet similar to himself. In this regard, Moses' function pointed to the work that Christ would do. Thus, as a prophet, He was the One charged with communicating the Father's purpose in matters related to all humanity.

Consistent in both the Old and New Testaments, prophets spoke on behalf of the Father. They served in an official capacity as His representatives. Notice that Hebrews 1:2 says Christ was the *official* spokesperson through whom the Father spoke. When He came to earth, He came as God's prophet with a specific message. What message did He convey from the Father? In Matthew 4:17, when He began His ministry, He said, "Repent: for the kingdom of heaven is at hand." As we have determined, this involved the restoration of humanity to the kingdom of God and the family of God. He came as a representative proclaiming God's "why." Therefore, when He gives of Himself and bestows the gift of the prophet, He is conferring the official capacity to speak on behalf of the Father. Hence, for those who operate in His stead, in the office of the prophet, the message is the same.

Additionally, when it says the Father spoke through His Son, it is also to be understood that Christ represents the personification of the Father. He is the Word made flesh. He is the mystery that was hidden from ages and from generations, which is Christ in us, the hope of glory (Colossians 1:27). He represents the fullness of God's purpose to humanity. All that the Father predetermined from before the foundation of the world has its fulfillment in Christ. Therefore, just like the apostles, the prophets of God are responsible for declaring the spiritual blessings, which are in Christ. Thus, even though an aspect of their ministry involves revealing what is yet to come, what is revealed still has to be consistent with the Father's overall purpose.

CHAPTER 9

THE GIFT OF CHRIST EXPLAINED: EVANGELIST

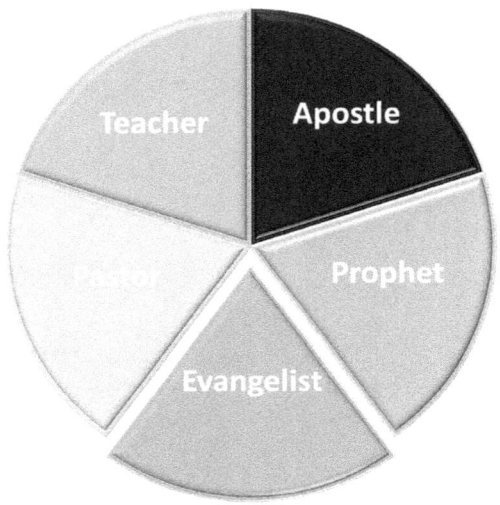

And he gave some, apostles; and some, prophets; and some, **evangelists**; *and some, pastors and teachers. (Ephesians 4:11)*

As a child, my memory of the evangelist consisted of a group of middle-aged women in white dresses and adorned with white hats. Based on their attire, this certainly made them quite distinct from everyone else. Furthermore, the group to which they belonged was referred to as the Missionary Circle and there was even a president. On occasion, they would go on street corners or visit different islands in the Bahamas preaching the gospel of Christ and the message of repentance. Needless to say, I was always impressed by them. Having no alternative persuasion, this image of the evangelist persisted until I saw Billy Graham on television. It was through watching and listening to him that my understanding and outlook regarding the work of the evangelist drastically evolved.

For the first time, I saw the evangelist, a male at that, on a grand stage preaching the message of repentance. This was certainly in stark contrast to what I was exposed to as a child. For some reason, the church seems comfortable in resigning itself to the notion that most of the gifts of Christ are more suitable for men, whereas the evangelist is more appropriate for women. In this vein, the argument is often made that a woman cannot be an apostle or a pastor. However, these conclusions are usually abandoned when it comes to the office of the evangelist. Perhaps, this is because compared to the other gifts of Christ, the evangelist in the opinion of some is more relegated. Nevertheless, as these perspectives are not supported by Scripture, it is the purpose of this chapter to reveal the significance and far-reaching effects of this office. Furthermore, it should also be noted that none of the gifts of Christ are gender-specific. As a premise, Galatians 3:28 affirms that in Christ, there is neither male nor female, for we are all one in Him. Again, I refer you to my book, *Freedom: The True Perspective about Women in Ministry*.

Of all the gifts of Christ, the evangelist is perhaps the most misunderstood and at times, it seems the most underrated. In this age of titles and appointments, it does not appear to have the same grandeur attached to it as the other four gifts. However, regardless of this shortsighted perspective, Scripture assigns the evangelist the same measure of importance as the other gifts. In fact, I am of the opinion this office is fundamental in that the others are reliant upon it. Therefore, to change the current perception of an evangelist requires an awareness of the responsibilities and functions of the office. Let us begin our journey by defining what an evangelist is.

EVANGELIST DEFINED

The word "evangelist" is from the root word "evangel," which means the gospel or the good tidings of the redemption of the world through Jesus Christ. Therefore, the evangelist is a herald or an official charged with proclaiming salvation through Christ. Based on the definition, the good news carried by the evangelist is the message of humanity's restoration to the Father's house and His kingdom through Christ's redemptive work. Notice the message is the same for all the gifts; however, each one has a different administration in executing that message. Even though Jesus functioned in all five of the gifts, He still had one consistent message. Despite having a singular message, how He administered it was different depending on the gift He was functioning in. With redemption being the central focus of the evangelist, let us revisit the definition of the word "redeem." Recall that the word "redeem" means:

- To deliver, buy back, or ransom
- To restore to honour, worth, or reputation
- To recover possession or ownership by payment of a price
- To recover from captivity, especially by a money payment

As previously discussed, when Adam sinned, all of humanity was subjected to another dominion and as a result, we needed to be ransomed. Therefore, in reference to salvation, redemption involves delivering humanity from the dominion of sin and consequently restoring us to the Father. However, as the definition indicates, ransom or the redemptive process has a price associated with it. From the examples provided in several movies, in order to reclaim an individual who has been abducted or captured, the assailant normally dictates the terms of the ransom, which is often a monetary value. Hence, once the terms of the ransom have been met, the captive is usually set free. However, as it pertains to the redemption of humanity, the circumstances were different. In this instance, the Father, who is the Liberator, established the terms for our ransom. To accomplish this, He subjected Himself to a particular principle. Hence, the standard associated with redemption is outlined in Hebrews 9:22 that says, "Without shedding of blood is no remission."

In support of this rule, 1 Peter 1:18-19 says that the price for our redemption was not corruptible things such as gold and silver, but rather, the precious blood of Christ. Consequently, through Christ's sacrifice, He has paid the price for the redemption of humanity or satisfied the terms of the ransom. Thus, the evangelist, as an advocate of God's grace and mercy, is charged with proclaiming the good news of this salvation. As a point of reference, salvation is not about dying and going to heaven; it is about being restored to the Father.

Therefore, evangelism operates from the perspective of restoring sons to the Father's house or family.

As mentioned in Chapter 1, the illustration Jesus gave in Luke Chapter 15 of the Prodigal Son encapsulates the message of evangelism. The account speaks of a son who as a member of his father's house enjoyed the full benefits of a son. However, he left his father's house and consequently lost the inheritance given to him by his father. Nevertheless, with a repentant heart, he acknowledged that the conditions of his father's house were far better than those he had subjected himself to. Additionally, because of his transgression, his disposition changed. He determined that he was no longer worthy to be called a son but instead, would advocate for the position of a servant. It is amazing that sin often causes us to settle for less than our inherent position. However, based on the compassion and affection of his father, he was fully restored to his position of a son as if he had never left. This also included the reinstatement of his inheritance. This example truly expresses the heart of the Father and His commitment to the restoration of humanity to His house.

THE WORK OF AN EVANGELIST FROM A SCRIPTURAL PERSPECTIVE

Of all the passages associated with evangelism, Romans 10:4-17 is perhaps one of the most popular. Undoubtedly, it provides tremendous insight regarding the purpose and the work of the evangelist.

4. For Christ is the end of the law for righteousness to everyone that believeth.
5. For Moses describeth the righteousness which is of the law, That the man which doeth those things shall live by them.
6. But the righteousness which is of faith speaketh on this wise, Say not in thine heart, Who shall ascend into heaven? (that is, to bring Christ down from above:)
7. Or, Who shall descend into the deep? (that is, to bring up Christ again from the dead.)

8. But what saith it? The word is nigh thee, even in thy mouth, and in thy heart: that is, the word of faith, which we preach;
9. That if thou shalt confess with thy mouth the Lord Jesus, and shalt believe in thine heart that God hath raised him from the dead, thou shalt be saved.
10. For with the heart man believeth unto righteousness; and with the mouth confession is made unto salvation.
11. For the scripture saith, Whosoever believeth on him shall not be ashamed.
12. For there is no difference between the Jew and the Greek: for the same Lord over all is rich unto all that call upon him.
13. For whosoever shall call upon the name of the Lord shall be saved.
14. <u>How then shall they call on him in whom they have not believed? and how shall they believe in him of whom they have not heard? and how shall they hear without a preacher?</u>
15. And how shall they preach, except they be sent? as it is written, How beautiful are the feet of them that preach the gospel of peace, and bring glad tidings of good things!
16. But they have not all obeyed the gospel. For Esaias saith, Lord, who hath believed our report?
17. So then faith cometh by hearing, and hearing by the word of God. (Romans 10:4-17)

In communicating the message of salvation, the passage begins the conversation by laying a foundation. It creates a distinction between the righteousness of the Law compared to righteousness by faith. As a principle, it asserts that righteousness by the Law was based on works, whereas righteousness by faith is based on belief. Furthermore, it concludes that righteousness by the Law was made obsolete through Christ's death, which then implemented righteousness by faith. Therefore, as it pertains to the discussion of righteousness, one was obtained by merit and the other by grace. For this reason, Ephesians 2:8-9 says, "For by grace are ye saved through faith; and that not of yourselves: it is the gift of God: Not of works, lest any man should boast." This is such a beautiful passage, for it expresses that salvation is not based on our own works or anything we can do, but it is simply believing in Christ. Based on this premise, the passage submits that what is necessary for righteousness is not a difficult undertaking; it simply requires belief. This is why the role of the evangelist is so important. Romans 10:8 says, through the preaching of the gospel, they provide the words required for salvation. Hence, Romans 10:17 says faith or belief comes by hearing the Word of God. When the evangelist preaches the Word of God or the message of salvation, this produces faith or belief.

Also, as it pertains to the message of salvation, the passage refers to a specific message that was being preached. According to Romans 10:9, they were preaching, "That if thou shalt confess with thy mouth the Lord Jesus, and shalt believe in thine heart that God hath raised him from the dead, thou shalt be saved." What is the significance of this statement? First, the word "confess" in this context means to say the same thing as another or to agree with. Hence, to confess with our mouths the Lord Jesus means we not only acknowledge who He is, but that we are also in agreement or harmony with what He has declared. Therefore, confession is not based on lip service or repeating empty words. Rather, it is being aligned with Christ's principles and what He says. Additionally, it is an audible recognition and acceptance that Jesus is Lord. Furthermore, salvation also requires we believe in our hearts that God raised Jesus from the dead. The reason this is so important is that the resurrection of Jesus Christ is fundamental to the hope of every believer.

1 Corinthians 15:12-19 points out that if Christ is not risen then our preaching has no purpose, and our faith is empty. Moreover, it adds that if there is no resurrection then we are false witnesses of God and still in our sins. Additionally, with no resurrection, those who die in Christ have perished. Plus, of all men, those who believe in God would be the most miserable. For these reasons, believing that God raised Jesus from the dead is the cornerstone of salvation. In essence, the passage simply says that the message of salvation can be summarized as "Jesus Christ and Him crucified." We will discuss this in the next section.

After discussing the process of salvation in the first portion of Romans Chapter 10, the purpose of the evangelist takes center stage. Therefore, to emphasize the importance of the office, Romans 10:14-15 presents a series of questions, which highlight the work of an evangelist.

- How then shall they call on Him in whom they have not believed?
- How shall they believe in Him of whom they have not heard?
- How shall they hear without a preacher?
- How shall they preach except they are sent?

Based on the substance of the questions and the context of Romans Chapter 10, we are furnished with a scriptural description of the evangelist. However, this depiction is also consistent with the definition provided at the beginning of this chapter and what has been discussed to this point. Hence, based on consensus, the evangelist is one gifted and sent by God to preach Jesus Christ and the gospel of salvation particularly, to those who do not believe. They are charged with the responsibility of persuading humanity to acknowledge the Lord Jesus Christ by making an audible profession of their acceptance of Him and what He declares through His Word. They accomplish this through the preaching of the gospel and the demonstration of the power of God. Specifically, they are categorized as preachers even though they have the capability of teaching. The distinct difference between preaching and teaching will be explained in Chapter 11 of this book.

Additionally, even though evangelists have a function outside of the body, they also have a responsibility to the body. Ephesians 4:12 specifies that evangelists have a part to play in the perfecting of the saints, in the work of the ministry, and in the edifying of the body of Christ. Therefore, this erases the narrow perspective concerning the work of evangelists, for they also work in concert with the other gifts of Christ to bring the body of Christ into maturity.

JESUS CHRIST AND HIM CRUCIFIED

In recounting the memories from my youth, when I heard Billy Graham speak, his messages were simple but yet extremely profound. Interestingly enough, regardless of what story he told, his core message was always "Jesus Christ and Him crucified." In harmony with Paul's position in 1 Corinthians 2:2, this phrase was the foundation for everything Billy Graham said.

1. And I, brethren, when I came to you, came not with excellency of speech or of wisdom, declaring unto you the testimony of God.
2. For I determined not to know anything among you, save Jesus Christ, and him crucified. (1 Corinthians 2:1-2)

In rejecting rhetoric that appeals to the flesh, Paul makes a pointed statement regarding his manner of preaching the gospel. He says that when he came declaring who God is, he did not do so with eloquent words or an arsenal of humanity's wisdom. Based on his credentials, he was certainly qualified to engage in such a dissertation. However, in his communication to the church, he made it abundantly clear that his singular focus and priority was "Jesus Christ and Him crucified." Many times, messages are so shrouded in needless oration that the core communication is obscure. Additionally, to appeal to human intellect or display their range of intelligence, ministers sometimes engage in what can be termed as verbal gymnastics. However, Paul made it perfectly plain that "Christ and Him crucified" was his primary conveyance.

What was the significance of this message that would warrant such a staunch declaration? First, let me say that this statement serves as the central message, not only of the evangelist but also for all the other gifts of Christ and every believer. In this regard, the phrase embodies the essence of Scripture in its entirety, as well as the manifold wisdom of God. In one pronouncement, Paul embraces all that the Father had purposed from before the foundation of the world. This was the concentrated focus of all Paul's teachings and ministry because it was through Christ and the cross that humanity was restored to the Father. In its entirety, it is therefore the pivotal message of reconciliation. When we analyze all the messages of Scripture, this expression stands at the forefront of God's purpose for humanity. Hence, this statement is also a testimony of God's "why."

Notice that although it is a single statement, there are two components to it. The first portion reflects on the person of Christ and who He is, while the second part speaks of Christ crucified or the message of the cross. Of note, the message of the cross is comprehensive in that it also embraces the resurrection of Jesus Christ. This is the same message discussed in Romans Chapter 10 regarding confessing the Lord Jesus and believing that God raised Him from the dead. Thus, these two passages embrace both the person of Jesus Christ and His purpose.

In terms of His personage, Christ is the one charged with orchestrating the eternal purpose of the Father. As a Son, He came as an extension of His Father to fulfill His purpose. Moreover, all the spiritual blessings, which the Father predetermined for humanity before the foundation of the world, are realized in Christ. Therefore, every promise, blessing, and covenant recorded in Scripture has its foundation in Christ. As it pertains to the cross, it is the ultimate demonstration of the grace of God and His love. Romans 5:8 says that God demonstrated His love toward us in that while we were yet sinners Christ died for us. Hence, Jesus' sacrifice provided the means for humanity's restoration to the Father's kingdom and His house. Not only did the cross provide an acquittal from sin, but it also released humanity from the dominion or power of sin (Romans 6:1-14). The cross both forgave and reconciled.

The statement, "Jesus Christ and Him crucified," encapsulates both the message of the kingdom of God and the restoration of humanity to the Father's house and His kingdom. Recall that in Chapter 1 of this book, it was affirmed that God's purpose from the beginning was to establish His kingdom on Earth. Consequently, He created man (humanity) and gave him dominion over the earth (Genesis 1:26). This created a kingdom environment on Earth. In addition, man was also created in the capacity of a son (Luke 3:38), which also produced a family environment. Thus, in addition to establishing His kingdom on Earth, incorporated with His purpose was also having a family. Therefore, humanity belonged both to the kingdom of God, as well as to the house of God. However, after humanity's disobedience recorded in Genesis Chapter 3, we were separated or estranged from both the Father's kingdom and His house. Hence, when Christ came, His primary message was repent, for the kingdom of heaven is at hand (Matthew 4:17). Essentially, this was a message of restoration to both the kingdom of God and the house or family of God. However, to restore humanity, Christ had to offer Himself as an atonement for our sins (Hebrews 9:11-14). Therefore, the cross of Christ is at the center of God's purpose. This is in harmony with the principle established by God that without the shedding of blood, there is no remission (Hebrews 9:22).

The word "remission" means to restore to a former status or condition. With humanity's former status being sons of both the kingdom of God and the family of God, restoration was provided through Christ's sacrifice. Thus, when Paul said the only thing he was interested in was "Jesus Christ and Him crucified," this is what he was referring to. His comment was in alignment with the Father's original purpose for humanity. However, prior to making this statement in 1 Corinthians Chapter 2, Paul provides a prelude in 1 Corinthians Chapter 1 to support his position.

18. For the preaching of the cross is to them that perish foolishness; but unto us which are saved it is the power of God.
19. For it is written, I will destroy the wisdom of the wise, and will bring to nothing the understanding of the prudent.
20. Where is the wise? where is the scribe? where is the disputer of this world? hath not God made foolish the wisdom of this world?
21. For after that in the wisdom of God the world by wisdom knew not God, it pleased God by the foolishness of preaching to save them that believe.
22. For the Jews require a sign, and the Greeks seek after wisdom:
23. But we preach Christ crucified, unto the Jews a stumblingblock, and unto the Greeks foolishness;
24. But unto them which are called, both Jews and Greeks, Christ the power of God, and the wisdom of God. (1 Corinthians 1:18-24)

CHRIST: THE POWER OF GOD

Associated with the statement of, "Jesus Christ and Him crucified," is also the message of "Christ the power of God and the wisdom of God." As we have acknowledged, the preaching of the cross is essentially the message of humanity's restoration to our original status. It is the means by which we are reconciled to the Father. As stated earlier, Ephesians 1:7, in highlighting spiritual blessings, speaks of redemption through Christ's blood and the forgiveness of sins according to the riches of God's grace. Furthermore, in qualifying the type of redemption, Hebrews 9:12 says that through Christ's sacrifice, He accomplished eternal redemption. This means that it is once and for all (Hebrews 10:10).

First, Christ being the power of God means He is the strength and might of the Father. When it comes to the restoration of humanity, how does the preaching of the cross show that Christ is the strength of God? As a matter of principle, humanity's opinion of strength and God's perspective of strength are diametrically opposed to each other. To support this, 1 Corinthians 1:25 states, "The foolishness of God is wiser than men; *and the weakness of God is stronger than men.*" Furthermore, 1 Corinthians 1:27 confirms that God uses the weak things of the world to confound the mighty. Therefore, the strength of God is demonstrated in ways that are foreign to humanity. Thus, humanity's concept of what portrays strength is actually weakness to the Father. For example, in Isaiah 53:1, the question is asked, "Who hath believed our report? And to whom is the arm of the Lord revealed?" What report is Isaiah referring to?

Let me begin by dispelling the erroneous notion that these questions are related to an unfavorable doctor's report or any unwelcomed feedback from a financial institution or related organization. Additionally, even though there are popular songs and sermons associated with this verse, it is still being used out of context. With the context of the book of Isaiah being the Messiah and the salvation of humanity, the questions are directly related to this subject. Based on Isaiah's vision of the Messiah and the events associated with Him, His immediate question was, "Who is going to believe this report?" In other words, the image I am seeing does not portray strength, so who is going to believe this announcement?

In determining the context of what is being said, let us examine the substance of Isaiah Chapter 53. First, the word "arm" in Isaiah 53:1 is symbolic of strength or might. Furthermore, with the usage of the personal pronoun "He," Isaiah 53:2 personifies the arm of the Lord indicating that it is a person. Therefore, with the subject of the chapter being Jesus Christ, He undoubtedly represents the strength of the Lord. Hence, based on the image of Jesus Christ presented to Isaiah, he asked the question, "Who shall believe our report concerning the arm or strength of the Lord?" To support the question, the chapter describes the Messiah as one who is despised and rejected. As opposed to the grandeur and magnificence expected by the people, He comes in a manner that no one would desire Him. There is no glory or splendor; therefore, He was overlooked.

In essence, contrary to man's opinion of strength, the illustration of Jesus presented in Isaiah Chapter 53 appears to be one of weakness. Nevertheless, despite His appearance and His subsequent rejection, as the arm of the Lord, He accomplished His purpose. To this end, Isaiah 53:5 says, "He was wounded for our transgressions. He was bruised for our iniquities. The chastisement of our peace was upon Him, and with His stripes, we are healed." In context with the chapter, the healing spoken of here is in reference to being pardoned from sin resulting in remission and restoration to our original position. Therefore, contrary to Christ's portrayal in the chapter, the outcome is still the reconciliation and restoration of humanity. Because Christ did not come in the manner of what strength normally looks like, Isaiah asked the question, "Who shall believe our report?" Who is going to believe that the strength of God is represented by what seems weak and uncomely? Moreover, not only was Jesus dishonoured, but He was also put to death in the most disgraceful manner.

The cross is a symbol of suffering and death and was reserved for the vilest of criminals. Therefore, Christ and Him crucified based on man's perception of strength actually gave the impression of weakness. However, from the perspective of the Father, it represents strength. Furthermore, in a parallel example, when the world determines that as believers we are weak, in reality, the strength of God is on display. The salvation of humanity was accomplished through someone perceived as weak but in truth, it was a demonstration of the power of God.

CHRIST: THE WISDOM OF GOD

In addition to Christ being the strength of God, He is also the wisdom of God. Generally speaking, the word "wisdom" means intelligence or skillfulness in the management of affairs. Hence, this speaks of the proficiency by which the Father executed His purpose. Therefore, as it pertains to the management of

God's affairs, Christ is the personification of His wisdom. Furthermore, just as there is a contrast between what humanity deems as strength compared to God's idea of strength, the same distinction exists concerning the perspectives of wisdom. In fact, the wisdom of God and the wisdom of man are the antitheses of each other. This is evident in 1 Corinthians 1:18-31, where the passage offers a comparison between the two. In accordance with man's wisdom, selections are often based on might, appearance, pedigree, knowledge, and other fleshly attributes. On the other hand, the wisdom of God uses quite different criteria. Along these lines, 1 Corinthians 1:26 says, "For ye see your calling, brethren, how that not many wise men after the flesh, not many mighty, not many noble, are called."

Contrary to man, God chooses those who have no reputation, those who are least esteemed, and those who are common to accomplish His purpose. As the wisdom of God, Christ came as the benchmark of these principles. Therefore, Christ was rejected and despised because He did not "check the boxes" according to man's wisdom. Based on their calculations and expectations, He did not fit the mold. He had no splendor or majesty, and His appearance was undesirable. As a principle, appointments made by the wisdom of man result in the glory of the flesh, whereas those made by the wisdom of God are designed for the glory of God.

In continuing the conversation, 1 Corinthians 1:27 offers a dynamic perspective. It says God uses the foolish things of the world to confuse the wise. To manifest His wisdom, the Father uses the things the world categorizes as foolish. Consequently, by focusing on the things that are aligned with the wisdom of the world, humanity will continue to miss what the Father is doing. As it pertains to the salvation of humanity, the Father chose a method that when viewed through the eyes of humanity seemed foolish. In this regard, 1 Corinthians 1:18 says, "For the preaching of the cross is to them that perish foolishness; but unto us which are saved it is the power of God."

According to the wisdom of man, the cross represents weakness and defeat but based on the wisdom of God, it is an illustration of His power. In reference to man's wisdom, the cross is associated with someone who is despised; therefore, it is difficult to comprehend how it can be related to the salvation of humanity.

Hence, when Isaiah saw the suffering Messiah, he asked the question, who is going to believe this report? It was contrary to humanity's opinion of wisdom.

As noted earlier, before the foundation of the world, the Father predestinated humanity unto the adoption of children by Jesus Christ to Himself (Ephesians 1:5). Hence, the purpose of the Father was always to have a family of sons in a kingdom environment who share His very nature. To summarize His intent, the Father simply wanted to reproduce Himself. Thus, when He created man, He made us in His image and after His likeness (Genesis 1:26). This was the visible manifestation of His purpose, which He determined in Himself before the foundation of the world. However, because of Adam's transgression, humanity became estranged from both the family of God and the kingdom of God.

Scripture serves as a written account of God's plan to realign humanity to His original purpose. For this reason, the entire Bible is a message of reconciliation and restoration. It is the message of evangelism. However, in conveying this message through Scripture, the Father adopted a progressive approach in His plan to restore us to His family and kingdom. In addition to His plan being progressive, "the management of His affairs" was also conducted in a hidden manner, or simply put, it was a mystery. The Father was both tactful and masterful in the coordination and execution of His plan throughout the ages. His plan included types, shadows, symbols, and covenants along with a veiled approach to guarantee the salvation of humanity. For example, even the arrangement of the tabernacle in the wilderness, its furniture, and the sacrifices all represented Christ and the work He would do. This is why Hebrews 10:7 in reference to Jesus says He came in the volume of the book, for it is written of Him. Hence, Christ came in the fullness of what Scripture pointed to, for it represents the complete package of the Father's purpose. Therefore, when we search the Scripture and take note of the manner in which the Father organized His plan through Christ, we are beholding God's wisdom. Isn't it ironic that the Father used what is repudiated by humanity as the emblems of His strength and wisdom? Both the strength of God and His wisdom are demonstrated in the cross of Christ. When we take into account the Father's brilliance and the intricacies involved in discharging His plan, we can identify with Romans 11:33 which says, "O the depth of the riches both of the wisdom and knowledge of God! How unsearchable are his judgments, and his ways past finding out!"

With the eternal purpose of the Father orchestrated through Jesus Christ, He is the agent responsible for the fulfillment of the Father's purpose. It is through Him and the things pertaining to Him that we witness the wisdom of God. Furthermore, by using the foolish things to confound the wise, the Father was able to veil what He was doing, thereby making it a mystery. To this end, 1 Corinthians 2:6-8 says,

6. Howbeit we speak wisdom among them that are perfect: yet not the wisdom of this world, nor of the princes of this world, that come to nought
7. But we speak the wisdom of God in a mystery, even the hidden wisdom, which God ordained before the world unto our glory:
8. Which none of the princes of this world knew: for had they known it, they would not have crucified the Lord of glory.

From before the foundation of the world, the Father ordained that humanity would be glorified. The word "glory" encapsulates the essence of Ephesians Chapter 1, which speaks of partaking of the Father's nature, being members of His family, and the complete message of reconciliation and restoration. However, as we have affirmed and Scripture has testified, God made our glorification a hidden wisdom or a mystery. He kept it a secret for the benefit of humanity. If Christ had come in the fashion of man's wisdom, the rulers of this world would have known what the Father was doing, and consequently, they would not have crucified the Lord of glory. Thus, as the wisdom of God, Christ represents the mystery the Father hid in Himself, which was designed to bring us unto glory. Therefore, in the cross of Jesus Christ, we see both the manifestation of God's power, as well as His wisdom. The Father instituted operations that were contrary to man's wisdom to conceal His intent. Based on the realization of His purpose, the church is now charged with the responsibility of declaring the manifold wisdom of God unto the principalities and powers in heavenly places.

CHRIST AS AN EVANGELIST

When we search the Gospels, many accounts reveal Jesus functioned as an apostle, prophet, teacher, and pastor. However, based on the Father's purpose, His core ministry pertained to the work of an evangelist. To support this principle, 2 Corinthians 5:19 provides us with a summary of Jesus' purpose. It says, "God was in Christ reconciling the world unto himself." Hence, Jesus came to reconcile the world or humanity to the Father. First, the prefix "re" means again and indicates a backward motion to a previous state or position. Furthermore, the word "conciliate" is from the Latin word *conciliare* meaning to unite. Therefore, the word "reconcile" means to bring back to a former state of unity or to make one again. It also means to reestablish a close relationship between opposing parties. As a result of Adam's transgression, we were separated from the Father. Where unity once existed, there was now dissension. Therefore, when Christ came, He came with a unifying purpose.

The word "reconciliation" also means atonement, which is the condition of being "at one." Hence, to reconcile humanity, Christ had to make the exchange of equivalent value. In other words, life for life. Consequently, He died that we may live. Romans 5:10 says, "For if, when we were enemies, we were reconciled to God by the death of his Son, much more, being reconciled, we shall be saved by his life." Through reconciliation, we are once again united with the Father, citizens of His kingdom, and members of His house. Not only did the Father eliminate the variance between Himself and humanity but also He simultaneously eliminated the division between humanity in general, for we are all one in Christ (Galatians 3:28). Therefore, the gospel of Jesus Christ is truly a uniting message. It is a message of unity.

With the reconciliation of humanity being His main focus, everything He did, including the miracles and everything He said was to accomplish the objective of reconciliation. From the onset, when He said the words, "Repent: for the kingdom of heaven is at hand," this was a statement of reconciliation and restoration. With His mandate of repentance, He called on the people to change their way of thinking because a different governing influence or administration was present. The kingdom of God or the Father's original idea was being reintroduced to humanity. When we consider all the spiritual blessings mentioned in Ephesians Chapter 1, in totality, they represent the message of the kingdom of God. Therefore, Jesus was saying, repent for all the blessings the Father predetermined for humanity are available.

Notice the blessings were ordained before the world began; however, to access them, the requirement is repentance. Repentance is therefore the key to unlocking what the Father has already prescribed for us. With the reintroduction of the kingdom of God, this meant the opportunity was being provided for humanity to once again be members of God's kingdom and His house. Therefore, the message of the evangelist is designed to reposition humanity to the original purpose of the Father. Evangelism was Jesus' primary function, and it should be the same for the entire body of Christ. When we set aside all the things on the periphery, the reconciliation of humanity is the number one objective of the church. This is the foundation, for everything else is predicated on this happening.

Throughout the Synoptic Gospels, there are several passages where Jesus was clearly functioning as an evangelist. Let us look at a few of the passages.

> And Jesus went about all Galilee, teaching in their synagogues, and *preaching the gospel of the kingdom*, and healing all manner of sickness and all manner of disease among the people. (Matthew 4:23)

> 14. Now after that John was put in prison, *Jesus came into Galilee, preaching the gospel of the kingdom of God,*
> 15. And saying, *The time is fulfilled, and the kingdom of God is at hand: repent ye, and believe the gospel.* (Mark 1:14-15)

> And he said unto them, *I must preach the kingdom of God* to other cities also: for therefore am I sent. (Luke 4:43)

> And it came to pass afterward, that he went throughout every city and village, *preaching and shewing the glad tidings of the kingdom of God*: and the twelve were with him. (Luke 8:1)

In His capacity as an evangelist, note the particular manner in which Jesus was conveying His message. It says specifically that He was *preaching* the gospel of the kingdom. The word "preach" is the Greek word *euaggelizo*. Furthermore, this is also the root word for *euaggelistes*, which in the Greek means evangelist. Therefore, an evangelist is inherently a preacher or one who proclaims the gospel. Again, this is contrasted with the activity of a teacher. Recall that one of the definitions of an evangelist is a herald or one tasked with announcing important news. Moreover, evangelists are official messengers who represent a monarch. Hence, Jesus, in His official capacity as a herald and representing the Father, was charged with announcing the message of the kingdom. By design, heralds are not quiet; yet, for some reason, we have the perception that Jesus was tranquil while preaching the gospel of the kingdom. In simple terms, to preach means to declare with conviction or to diligently persuade. Thus, in preaching the kingdom of God, He was vocal.

Additionally, as an evangelist, Jesus also operated in the power of God, healing those who were sick. Hence, this anointing serves as the persuasive power of God to support the work of the evangelist. According to John 20:30-31, Jesus performed miracles to persuade the people that He was indeed the Christ, the Son of God. Additionally, the passage also says that by believing, they might have life through His name. Therefore, the purpose of miracles is not for performances but to persuade people to salvation.

When we consider the series of questions that are put forth in Romans Chapter 10, the preacher or the herald who is sent by God is tasked with persuading people to call upon the Lord. For that reason, God works miracles through His preachers to accompany the preaching of the gospel. This was also evident in Acts Chapter 3 where Peter, after healing the lame man at the temple, used that as an opportunity to preach the gospel. Consequently, Acts 4:4 says those that heard the Word believed, and the number was five thousand men. After seeing the miracle followed by Peter's preaching, they were persuaded.

Furthermore, in Luke 4:18, during the early days of Jesus' ministry, as was customary, He went into the synagogue in Nazareth. While there, He stood up to read and was given the book of Isaiah. Subsequently, he turned to Isaiah 61:1 and said, "The Spirit of the Lord is upon me, because he hath anointed me to preach the gospel to the poor; he hath sent me to heal the brokenhearted, to preach deliverance to the captives, and recovering of sight to the blind, to set at liberty them that are bruised." After reading the passage, He closed the book and said, "This day is this scripture fulfilled in your ears." With this pronouncement, He set the agenda for His ministry, particularly that of an evangelist. When we carefully examine the components of what Jesus said, these are all certainly the responsibilities of those engaged in evangelism.

JESUS AND NICODEMUS

In continuing with our narrative of Jesus as an evangelist, the gospel of John provides several accounts of Him functioning in this capacity. In particular, His interaction with Nicodemus in John Chapter 3, and His conversation with the Samaritan woman in John Chapter 4 are wonderful examples. However, for the sake of conciseness, we will only examine the exchange between Jesus and Nicodemus.

1. There was a man of the Pharisees, named Nicodemus, a ruler of the Jews:
2. The same came to Jesus by night, and said unto him, Rabbi, we know that thou art a teacher come from God: for no man can do these miracles that thou doest, except God be with him.
3. Jesus answered and said unto him, Verily, verily, I say unto thee, Except a man be born again, he cannot see the kingdom of God.
4. Nicodemus saith unto him, How can a man be born when he is old? can he enter the second time into his mother's womb, and be born?
5. Jesus answered, Verily, verily, I say unto thee, Except a man be born of water and of the Spirit, he cannot enter into the kingdom of God.
6. That which is born of the flesh is flesh; and that which is born of the Spirit is spirit.
7. Marvel not that I said unto thee, Ye must be born again.
8. The wind bloweth where it listeth, and thou hearest the sound thereof, but canst not tell whence it cometh, and whither it goeth: so is every one that is born of the Spirit. (John 3:1-8)

In framing the conversation, John Chapter 3 opens with two noteworthy details concerning Nicodemus. It states that he was a Pharisee, as well as a ruler of the Jews. As a Pharisee, he along with the other religious groups represented the religious establishment of Jesus' day. Additionally, he was also a member of the Sanhedrin. The Sanhedrin, which is also referred to as the council of elders, was a ruling body of twenty-one members with the high priest as the chief officer (Luke 26:66). Under Roman rule, its functions included religious, political, and judicial responsibilities. Therefore, based on these credentials, the chapter presents Nicodemus as someone of significance, particularly from a religious and leadership perspective. Hence, when he came to Jesus and said, "Rabbi, we know that thou art a teacher come from God: for no man can do these miracles that thou doest, except God be with him," this was a considerable admission.

Notice specifically that he says, "We know," which means there were others of his circle who held the same persuasion regarding Jesus. I find it interesting that despite the opposition to Jesus and His teaching, they were still persuaded of who He was. Notice that the basis of his belief was not only the recognition of Jesus as Rabbi but also the miracles that Jesus did. Thus, this reinforces the purpose of miracles discussed earlier. Additionally, although people sometimes reject things, they will always bear witness to what is true. Throughout the Gospels, the scribes, Pharisees, and Sadducees had many contentious public encounters with Jesus. However, in private, they could not deny that God was with Him. Hence, their public opposition was partly because He challenged their position of authority over the people and the substance of their doctrine. Furthermore, in addressing Jesus, notice that Nicodemus specifically uses the title of Rabbi or teacher, which was a designation of great honour and authority. Hence, it was significant that a Pharisee made such recognition.

Nevertheless, despite Nicodemus' flowery endorsement, the response Jesus gave was a true testament of His office as an evangelist. Therefore, in unbroken stride, He replied and said, "Except a man be born again, he cannot see the kingdom of God." As ministers, we are often exposed to similar compliments and sometimes we allow them to overshadow our core purpose. However, in showing little regard for flattery, Jesus redirects the conversation to something more meaningful and His purpose. In harmony with His general message and platform regarding the kingdom of God, Jesus said to see or understand the kingdom, you must be born again.

Notice that to explain the process of entering the kingdom of God, Jesus specifically uses the term "born again." In response, Nicodemus applies a natural concept to what Jesus said. He speaks of entering his mother's womb and being born a second time. However, as a principle, Jesus was simply employing a natural example to explain a spiritual operation (Romans 1:20). Natural birth signifies a new birth or the emergence of a new creature; being born again also indicates the same. Hence, 2 Corinthians 5:17 says, "If any man be in Christ, he is a new creature: old things are passed away; behold, all things are become new."

The qualitative difference is that natural birth is associated with being born after the flesh, while being born again expresses being born by the Spirit of God. For this reason, Jesus says, "That which is born of the flesh is flesh; and that which is born of the Spirit is spirit." From a spiritual perspective, our natural birth made us citizens of the kingdom of darkness. In this regard, Psalm 51:5 states that we were born in sin and shaped in iniquity. On the contrary, our spiritual birth made us citizens of the kingdom of God and members of His house. Being born again is how we are realigned to the Father's original purpose. Therefore, to be granted entrance into the kingdom of God, Scripture is abundantly clear that we *must* be born again.

In continuing His conversation with Nicodemus, Jesus offers a wonderful summation to the discussion of being born again. For some reason, when reading John 3:16, it is read in isolation not considering the context of the dialogue Jesus was having with Nicodemus.

16. For God so loved the world, that he gave his only begotten Son, that whosoever believeth in him should not perish, but have everlasting life.
17. For God sent not his Son into the world to condemn the world; but that the world through him might be saved. (John 3:16-17)

In harmony with 2 Corinthians 5:19, these verses state why Jesus came; therefore, they are the epitome of God's why. Indeed, the passage expresses the message of reconciliation, but it says the reason for it is because of the Father's immense love for humanity. When John 3:16 says that God "gave" His only begotten son, this signifies that of His own accord, He bestowed Christ as a gift to humanity. Therefore, those who believe in Him will inherit the gift He imparts, which is eternal life. Of note, the Father did not send Christ into the world to condemn the world or to pronounce judgment because through sin, we were already condemned. Hence, He came as God's agent to reconcile humanity and thereby acquit us.

JESUS AND HIS DISCIPLES

Not only did Jesus function as an evangelist but in selecting the Twelve, He also gave them the same mandate of evangelism. As a point of reference, the Twelve, who would eventually be appointed as apostles, first functioned as evangelists. Because this was His primary purpose when He called them, He classified their function as fishers of men.

18. And Jesus, walking by the sea of Galilee, saw two brethren, Simon called Peter, and Andrew his brother, casting a net into the sea: for they were fishers.
19. And he saith unto them, *Follow me, and I will make you fishers of men.* (Matthew 4:18-19)

This passage supports the premise established at the beginning of this chapter concerning the fundamental role of the evangelist. As stated, while many ministers appear to be concerned with seemingly more "grander titles," evangelism is a foundational responsibility for every believer. Hence, the significance of the evangelist is evident when we take into consideration Jesus' purpose regarding His twelve disciples. Immediately after launching His ministry and establishing its platform of the kingdom of God, Jesus' pitch to those He identified as leaders was, "Follow me, and I will make you fishers of men." Using their natural vocation to illustrate a spiritual calling, the statement captures the essential purpose on which their ministry would be built.

As fishermen by trade, they were able to identify with the concept of becoming "fishers of men." Jesus did not say, "Follow me, and I will make you apostles, prophets or pastors," but rather, He identified the principal reason for their calling. With humanity's restoration to the Father's kingdom and His house at the forefront of Jesus' mind, His task to His leaders involved the same concept. Furthermore, even though they were eventually appointed as apostles, they still continued to function as evangelists because this is their principal responsibility.

14. And he ordained twelve, that they should be with him, and that he might send them forth to preach,
15. And to have power to heal sicknesses, and to cast out devils. (Mark 3:14-15)

1. Then he called his twelve disciples together, and gave them power and authority over all devils, and to cure diseases.
2. And he sent them to preach the kingdom of God, and to heal the sick. (Luke 9:1-2)

THE EVANGELIST VERSUS EVANGELISM

THE EVANGELIST

Similar to the statement that was made regarding prophecy, the same principle applies to evangelism. Recall that in Chapter 8, it was said every believer can prophesy but not every believer is a prophet. In the same vein, every believer is called to evangelize, but not every believer is an evangelist. Therefore, as there is a distinction between the two, let us first look at the specific office of the evangelist.

Based on Ephesians 4:11, the evangelist, just as the apostle and prophet, is a distinct office established on the gift of Christ. For example, Scripture specifically identifies Philip as an evangelist.

> And the next day we that were of Paul's company departed, and came unto Caesarea: and we entered into the house of

> Philip the evangelist, which was one of the seven; and abode with him. (Acts 21:8)

During our discussion on the gift of the apostle, Philip was identified as one of the seven who was appointed to assist with the daily ministration. According to Acts Chapter 6, their responsibility was to ensure that what was provided for believers in need was adequately distributed. Therefore, the office of the evangelist was not his initial designation. This is an important principle because it highlights the significance of faithfulness and being a good steward in the things of God. Hence, over the course of time and based on the manifestation of the gift of Christ, Philip was identified as an evangelist. However, when we study the book of Acts and follow the life of Philip, it becomes evident that he was an evangelist prior to his official recognition in Acts 21:8. Thus, the acknowledgment of the office or the gift occurs as a result of the evidence of the gift. As mentioned previously, the presbytery through the laying on of hands do not confer a gift, they simply acknowledge its existence based on the activities of the individual.

After the stoning of Stephen in Acts Chapter 8, there was a great persecution against the church at Jerusalem. Consequently, the believers who were scattered went throughout the regions of Judaea and Samaria preaching the Word of God. Therefore, Philip went to the city of Samaria and preached Christ unto them. Acts 8:6 says, "And the people with one accord gave heed unto those things which Philip spake, hearing and seeing the miracles which he did." Again, even before Scripture specifically mentions him as an evangelist, he was already functioning in the capacity of one. Furthermore, in doing the work of an evangelist, not only was he preaching the gospel, but his preaching was accompanied by the working of miracles. This reinforces the statement that was made earlier concerning the combination of preaching and miracles relative to the work of an evangelist.

Additionally, the latter part of Acts Chapter 8 offers another account regarding Philip's work as an evangelist. This example speaks of his encounter with an Ethiopian eunuch.

26. And the angel of the Lord spake unto Philip, saying, Arise, and go toward the south unto the way that goeth down from Jerusalem unto Gaza, which is desert.
27. And he arose and went: and, behold, a man of Ethiopia, an eunuch of great authority under Candace queen of the Ethiopians, who had the charge of all her treasure, and had come to Jerusalem for to worship,
28. Was returning, and sitting in his chariot read Esaias the prophet.
29. Then the Spirit said unto Philip, Go near, and join thyself to this chariot.
30. And Philip ran thither to him, and heard him read the prophet Esaias, and said, Understandest thou what thou readest?
31. And he said, How can I, except some man should guide me? And he desired Philip that he would come up and sit with him.
32. The place of the scripture which he read was this, He was led as a sheep to the slaughter; and like a lamb dumb before his shearer, so opened he not his mouth:
33. In his humiliation his judgment was taken away: and who shall declare his generation? for his life is taken from the earth.
34. And the eunuch answered Philip, and said, I pray thee, of whom speaketh the prophet this? of himself, or of some other man?
35. Then Philip opened his mouth, and began at the same scripture, and preached unto him Jesus.
36. And as they went on their way, they came unto a certain water: and the eunuch said, See, here is water; what doth hinder me to be baptized?
37. And Philip said, If thou believest with all thine heart, thou mayest. And he answered and said, I believe that Jesus Christ is the Son of God.
38. And he commanded the chariot to stand still: and they went down both into the water, both Philip and the eunuch; and he baptized him.
39. And when they were come up out of the water, the Spirit of the Lord caught away Philip, that the eunuch saw him no more: and he went on his way rejoicing.
40. But Philip was found at Azotus: and passing through he preached in all the cities, till he came to Caesarea. (Acts 8:26-40)

As a point of consideration, it is necessary to state that even though Scripture appropriately identifies Philip as an evangelist, he was also able to teach as evident in the passage. Having said that, notice the passage is specific in its emphasis that Philip preached Jesus. Therefore, I reiterate that the primary focus of the evangelist is always Jesus Christ and Him crucified. In acknowledgement of Philip as an evangelist, Scripture provides ample validation of his office based on the work he did. Hence, the recognition that he was an evangelist was simply a confirmation in light of the work in which he was constantly engaged. It was not a mere title; he was functional in the role. Additionally, in Paul's second letter to Timothy, he admonishes him to do the work of an evangelist. He encourages him to function in the capacity of the office, for he understood the significance of the gift. Moreover, in doing the work, Paul also exhorts him to make full proof of his ministry. The term "make full proof" means to cause a thing to be shown or to fulfill the ministry in every part. Therefore, based on Paul's mandate to Timothy, he is also identified as an evangelist.

> But watch thou in all things, endure afflictions, do the work of an evangelist, make full proof of thy ministry. (2 Timothy 4:5)

EVANGELISM: THE MINISTRY OF RECONCILIATION

In addition to the specific office of the evangelist, Christ has also given every believer the work of evangelism. 2 Corinthians 5:18 states that every single believer has been given a ministry, which is the ministry of reconciliation. Hence, every believer has been given the mandate of fulfilling the Father's "why."

> 18. And all things are of God, who hath reconciled us to himself by Jesus Christ, and hath given to us the ministry of reconciliation.
> 19. To wit, that God was in Christ, reconciling the world unto himself, not imputing their trespasses unto them; and hath committed unto us the word of reconciliation. (2 Corinthians 5:18-19)

As we have discussed, 2 Corinthians 5:19 summarizes the purpose of Christ as that of reconciliation. Hence, just as God was in Christ reconciling the world to Himself, He is also in us accomplishing the same purpose. As His ambassadors, He has given us the same ministry. Thus, every believer, regardless of title or position has the same ministry. In this regard, the ministry of reconciliation, which involves evangelism, is the foundation on which every other ministry is built. Therefore, it stands to reason that before anyone is an apostle, prophet, pastor, or teacher, his or her principal ministry is reconciliation. In a general sense, no believer should question whether he or she has a ministry. Again, so much focus is placed on titles and establishing individual ministries that the primary calling and ministry, which the Lord has bestowed on every believer have been neglected.

In everything that we say and do, we are reconcilers. Therefore, as believers with the responsibility of evangelism, our messages and actions serve to foster unity with the Father and each other. Furthermore, to accompany the ministry of reconciliation, the Father has also committed unto us the word of reconciliation. Simply put, this is the gospel of Jesus Christ.

MAKING DISCIPLES

The objective of evangelism is not limited to salvation alone, but it also involves creating disciples.

> 18. And Jesus came and spake unto them, saying, All power is given unto me in heaven and in earth.
> 19. Go ye therefore, and teach all nations, baptizing them in the name of the Father, and of the Son, and of the Holy Ghost:
> 20. Teaching them to observe all things whatsoever I have commanded you: and, lo, I am with you alway, even unto the end of the world. Amen. (Matthew 28:18-20)

The word "teach" in Matthew 20:19 means to make a disciple. Simply put, a disciple is a follower or one who believes and helps spread the doctrine of another. Therefore, the true manifestation of evangelism is not only embracing the message of reconciliation but also being a promoter of the same message and exhibiting the message.

Based on what we have covered in this chapter, the significance of the evangelist can certainly be better appreciated. This gift serves a fundamental role as a catalyst for church growth and the other gifts. As we have discussed throughout this chapter, the main purpose of evangelism is the reconciliation of humanity based on the love of God. It is a message of unity that makes us one with the Father. As a specific office, Christ has conferred the gift of an evangelist to certain individuals; however, the mandate of evangelism has been entrusted to every believer. In this vein, the Father has committed unto us all the word of reconciliation or the gospel of the kingdom of God. Contained within this message are the spiritual blessings, which the Father predetermined for humanity before the foundation of the world. However, these blessings are only realized through Jesus Christ. Therefore, the evangelist's core message is Jesus Christ and Him crucified. For it is only through the cross of Christ that we are reconciled with the Father and consequently reinstated as members of His kingdom and His house.

THE GIFT OF CHRIST EXPLAINED: PASTOR

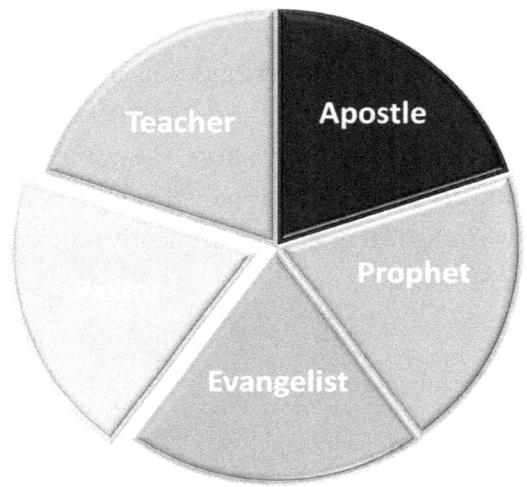

And he gave some, apostles; and some, prophets; and some, evangelists; and some, **pastors** *and teachers. (Ephesians 4:11)*

THE INCEPTION OF THE CHURCH

In examining the gift of the pastor, let us begin by discussing the inception of the church as outlined in the book of Acts. This will allow us to establish a foundation concerning the local church and revisit some of the principles relative to the structure of the church. In doing so, we will have a better perspective of the role and responsibilities of the pastor in relation to the other ministry gifts.

In earnest, the beginning of the church is associated with the Day of Pentecost mentioned in Acts Chapter 2. In accordance with the purpose of the Father, this day was not random, for it was both prophetic, as well as strategic. First, it was prophetic based on what the Feast of Pentecost or the Feast of Weeks represented. The Feast was implemented in Leviticus Chapter 23 and was a time of thanksgiving for the firstfruits of the wheat harvest. This celebration was to express thanks to God for the blessing of the harvest.

In Matthew 9:37, Jesus, while speaking concerning the multitude, figuratively referred to the people as harvest. He said, "The harvest truly is plenteous, but the laborers are few." Hence, on the Day of Pentecost and in harmony with the precepts of the feast, there was truly a celebration of the harvest as three thousand souls were added to the church. Thus, as a type, the feast foreshadowed the harvest of souls as a result of the outpouring of the Holy Spirit. Additionally, the day was also strategic because on the Day of Pentecost, Jews from many nations came to Jerusalem to celebrate. Hence, with a convergence of Jews from several countries in one place, the Lord used this as an opportunity to preach the gospel to the diaspora. When the apostles and disciples were baptized in the Holy Spirit, they were inspired to speak in the different languages of the Jews who were present.

6. Now when this was noised abroad, the multitude came together, and were confounded, because that every man heard them speak in his own language.
7. And they were all amazed and marvelled, saying one to another, Behold, are not all these which speak Galilaeans?
8. And how hear we every man in our own tongue, wherein we were born?
9. Parthians, and Medes, and Elamites, and the dwellers in Mesopotamia, and in Judaea, and Cappadocia, in Pontus, and Asia,
10. Phrygia, and Pamphylia, in Egypt, and in the parts of Libya about Cyrene, and strangers of Rome, Jews and proselytes,
11. Cretes and Arabians, we do hear them speak in our tongues the wonderful works of God. (Acts 2:6-11)

On the Day of Pentecost, the baptism of the Holy Spirit followed by speaking in *known tongues* or identifiable languages was deliberate based on the diversity of the audience. Furthermore, with the new converts being from various places, this meant when they returned to their respective countries, they took the experience and message of the gospel with them. Hence, God's strategy was for them to also become the instruments for spreading the gospel to their home countries. What an ingenious plan for the furtherance of the gospel! Moreover, when they returned home, they also needed an environment where they could be discipled. Consequently, this eventually fostered the establishment of local churches in the regions they came from. Thus, through one event, we not only have the institution of the church, but also its eventual expansion.

Additionally, in terms of doctrine, Acts 2:42 says that the church continued faithfully in the apostles' doctrine. As we have established, this is the same teaching the apostles received from Christ, which is the message pertaining to the kingdom of God. The apostles did not have a separate agenda from what Christ instructed them. Hence, in accordance with their mandate, they made disciples based on the principles of the kingdom of God. This foundation created an atmosphere in the church where there was unity of the faith. Furthermore, it engendered an environment where there was unity among the members of the church, for they had all things in common. Thus, once the foundation is correct, an atmosphere of unity is produced. Unfortunately, the opposite is also true, for when the foundation is false, this gives rise to division and a fertile ground for hirelings or those who are self-seeking.

Based on the events from the Day of Pentecost, the church continued to grow, and people were added daily. In fact, after healing the lame man at the temple gate, Peter and John preached the gospel, and five thousand men (not including women) were added to the church (Acts 4:4). Up to this point, Scripture speaks only concerning the church in Jerusalem. However, that was about to change. After the persecution that arose as a result of Stephen's death, believers were scattered to different countries and they preached the gospel wherever they went (Acts 8:4, Acts 11:19-20). What is interesting is that some of them went to the same countries as the Jews who were in Jerusalem on the Day of Pentecost. Therefore, the Lord allowed the persecution to serve as a catalyst, not only to promote the gospel in these regions but also to expand the church beyond Jerusalem.

In the first instance, Philip (the evangelist—Acts 21:8) went to Samaria and preached the gospel. Consequently, when the apostles at Jerusalem heard that Samaria had received the Word of God, they sent Peter and John there to support the work and establish the church. Furthermore, as mentioned previously, to promote the expansion of the church, the apostles at Jerusalem also sent Barnabas to Antioch. With Paul, he was instrumental in establishing the church there. In fact, it is at Antioch that the believers were first referred to as Christians. Additionally, with the churches being established in various countries, Paul and Barnabas ordained elders or pastors in every church. Moreover, based on Acts 14:23, we get the impression of the plurality of elders or pastors as opposed to the notion of an individual having oversight of a church.

While this may be the case, the emphasis at this point is to focus on the responsibility and role of the local church. Notice that during the entire expansion of the church, the apostles were directly involved, and there was unity in the process. Furthermore, in his capacity as an apostle, Paul wrote letters to the churches he established, thereby providing them with doctrine, reproof, correction, and instruction in righteousness. Similarly, the apostle Peter and the other apostles also wrote letters to the church for the same purpose. Thus, from the inception of the church, Scripture provides several examples of the apostolic relationship between apostles and the church. Based on this principle, the structure of the church was well defined.

THE CONCEPT OF TITLES

As stated in the previous chapter, the church seems to exist in an environment fixated on the attainment of various ecclesiastical titles. Moreover, in certain circles, the adoption of titles such as apostle and bishop appears to be gaining momentum. With the exclusion of those who have truly been bestowed the gift of Christ, this disposition of title recognition is nothing new. In fact, it is similar to the characteristic of the religious establishment in Jesus' day. Jesus noted in Matthew 23:7 that they loved greetings in the markets and to be called of men, Rabbi, Rabbi. Similarly, today's religious leaders revel in being addressed by their ecclesial title no matter the setting. However, according to Scripture, titles were simply used to describe the function or the gift in which an individual operated. In other words, the gift was not a replacement for their actual names. Hence, they did not walk around addressing each other by the gift that was bestowed upon them. For example, even in the official correspondence or letters that Paul sent to the churches, the salutation was always, Paul followed by his function. Hence, the greeting was "Paul an apostle of Jesus Christ." Similarly, Acts 21:8 in referring to the function of Philip says, "Philip the evangelist." The point is that they still maintained their identity and the titles were simply used to describe their functions. To be clear, this has nothing to do with giving honour to whom honour is due but simply a matter of following the blueprint provided in Scripture. The gift was not a substitute for their name or how they were always addressed. I am not suggesting the complete elimination of titles. I accept that at times they are warranted. However, it is the disposition similar to what Jesus addressed in Matthew 23:7 to which I refer.

While on the subject of titles, I would also like to address the designation of "Reverend," which is popularly used in the church. Despite many church leaders adopting this title, based on the context of Scripture, it should only be ascribed to the Father. Additionally, certain denominations further compound the misapplication of this title with the use of superlatives such as "The Most Reverend" or "The Very Reverend." These distinctions are made to create a hierarchy among those who adorn the title. In Scripture, the word "reverend" is mentioned on one occasion, in Psalm 111:9. The passage says, "He sent redemption unto His people: He hath commanded His covenant forever: holy and reverend is His name."

According to the context of the entire passage, the subject being discussed is the holiness, awesomeness, and graciousness of the Lord. Therefore, the chapter has a single focus directed toward a single subject: God. Thus, after highlighting what the Lord has done and who He is, David then says, "Holy and reverend is His name." However, for some reason, the church either through ignorance or the pursuit of lofty designations has taken that which exclusively belongs to the Creator and assigned it to the creation. Whereas the passage is attributing honour to the name of the Lord, many have taken it and assigned honour to their own name.

Similarly, in recent times, the titles of "His Grace" or "His Eminence" appear to be gaining popularity among certain church leaders. Let me say unequivocally, such identifications should only be ascribed to one person, Jesus Christ. Specifically, in reference to the title of "His Grace," Ephesians 2:8-10 says that as believers, we are all recipients of God's grace. However, we are not grace personified. It is by the Father's grace that we are saved, not by our own merit. Therefore, the allocation or adoption of such titles contributes to vain worship, which can result in idolatry. Throughout the Gospels, Jesus rebuked the religious establishments because they operated in vainglory and functioned as lords over God's heritage.

Furthermore, even among the titles that are ordained by the Father, false designations are still applied. For example, among those who wear the mantle of an apostle, a few have elevated themselves to the position of the chief apostle in order to create a distinction between themselves and others. However, as previously discussed, there is only one chief apostle and that is Jesus Christ. Hebrews 3:1 says, "Wherefore, holy brethren, partakers of the heavenly calling, consider the Apostle and High Priest of our profession, Christ Jesus."

In Chapter 6, it was highlighted that the definite article "the" before "Apostle" means that the noun, Christ Jesus, is the only one in that context. Hence, when compared to all the other apostles, He is the preeminent or chief apostle among all others. Likewise, the same principle can be applied to the title of "Master Prophet." Again, there seems to be a constant campaign to create a hierarchical structure as it pertains to titles in the church. However, these have no foundation in Scripture. While there were prophets who were greatly used by the Lord throughout the Bible, none of them were classified as master prophets. Based on the seventeen "prophetic books" of the Old Testament, five have been designated as major prophets, and twelve are regarded as minor prophets. However, this identification by theologians was simply to make a distinction based on the volume of their writings, not their significance. Furthermore, not all prophets were inspired by the Lord to write; hence, we cannot use this as a barometer of their levels. For instance, even though the Lord used Elijah and Elisha significantly, they did not write books. While I agree that there are prophets who are masterful in their function, the title itself has no foundation in Scripture.

Personally, I think that many of these titles have been adopted in ignorance and are based on the environment in which the church exists. However, to be effective ministers of God, we truly have to strip ourselves of such vanities, for they only cater to the flesh and the promotion of self. Additionally, I also felt that it was important to include this perspective on titles as a preface to our discussion on the office of the pastor. There seems to be tremendous ambiguity regarding the titles of bishop, pastor, and elder.

BISHOP, PASTOR, AND ELDER

Within the church, the titles of bishop, pastor, and elder seem to operate with varying degrees of authority and responsibility. Moreover, I find it interesting that depending on who you ask or the denomination to which an individual is aligned, the perspectives of these designations are different. For the most part, a bishop is seen as having prominence over a pastor and a pastor is determined to have prevalence over an elder. Furthermore, the transition from an elder, to a pastor, and then to a bishop is often viewed as a promotion from one position to the next. Therefore, within the church, a leadership hierarchy has been created concerning these three positions. However, this is contrary to the organizational structure outlined in Scripture and the premise of rightly dividing the Word.

Despite the uncertainty that exists with these titles, our conclusions must always be based on what Scripture says and not subjective reasoning. In this vein, Scripture is resolute that these three offices are identical with no distinctions between them. In truth, these titles simply provide a different picture of the same function; they offer a different perspective of the same office. Hence, before we can have an earnest discussion concerning the office of the pastor, there must first be a settlement of the three functions.

PASTOR

First, based on Scripture, the gift of Christ is distinctly referred to as a pastor. Ephesians 4:11 says, "And he gave some, apostles; and some, prophets; and some, evangelists; and some, pastors and teachers." Notice particularly that bishop and elder are not specifically identified as gifts of Christ; yet, in many churches, they function on a similar plateau. Therefore, the purpose of this discussion is not only to reconcile the three titles but also to conclude they are indeed equal. The word "pastor" is the Greek word *poimen,* which means the following:

- A shepherd (of people as a flock)
- To guard or care for; to look after
- To nourish or to feed

To guard, care for, and nourish His people, Christ gave shepherds to the church. Compared to the other gifts of Christ, the office of the pastor offers a greater degree of intimacy as we will soon discuss. Although Ephesians 4:11 includes "pastor" in the gifts of Christ, the origin of the office has its roots in the Old Testament, and just like the New Testament reference, it is associated with leadership. In the Old Testament, the Lord uses the general title of "Pastor" in reference to the leaders of Israel.

> And I will give you pastors according to mine heart, which shall feed you with knowledge and understanding. (Jeremiah 3:15)

1. Woe be unto the pastors that destroy and scatter the sheep of my pasture! Saith the LORD.
2. Therefore thus saith the LORD God of Israel against the pastors that feed my people; Ye have scattered my flock, and driven them away, and have not visited them. (Jeremiah 23:1-2)

Although the usage of the word "pastor" in the above passages carries a negative connotation, they offer insight into the function of the office. In conjunction with the definition, a pastor is defined as a shepherd, one who cares for, protects, feeds, and looks after the sheep. Therefore, even though we cross the threshold into the New Testament, the responsibilities of a pastor are the same.

ELDER

As a gift of Christ, the word "pastor(s)" is specifically used just once throughout the entire New Testament (Ephesians 4:11). Why do you suppose this is? In the above section, we concluded that as a shepherd, a pastor's general responsibility is to care for and feed the flock or the people of God. Hence, the office is defined by its responsibilities. Therefore, as a matter of scriptural reconciliation, it behooves us to determine which New Testament office has similar responsibilities and functions to that of a pastor.

1. The elders which are among you I exhort, who am also an elder, and a witness of the sufferings of Christ, and also a partaker of the glory that shall be revealed:
2. Feed the flock of God which is among you, taking the oversight thereof, not by constraint, but willingly; not for filthy lucre, but of a ready mind;
3. Neither as being lords over God's heritage, but being ensamples to the flock.
4. And when the chief Shepherd shall appear, ye shall receive a crown of glory that fadeth not away. (2 Peter 5:1-4)

First, in identifying the role of an elder as a leadership position, the apostle Peter also refers to himself as an elder. Furthermore, notice that similar to the pastors, elders are charged with feeding the flock of God. Additionally, as a part of their responsibilities, they are also called upon to take oversight of the flock. The word "oversight" is the Greek word *episkopeo*. It is a combination of two Greek words *epi* meaning over or upon and *skopeo* meaning to fix one's eyes upon or to direct one's attention to. Hence, the word refers to taking management of the flock of God by looking diligently after them.

Interestingly, the same Greek words from which we get the word "oversight," are the same root words for "bishop," which we will discuss in the next section. Thus, the apostle Peter is indicating that elders have been given the same responsibility assigned to bishops. Moreover, in their leadership capacity, they are also admonished to be examples to the flock or worthy of imitation. Like pastors, the passage also identifies elders as shepherds with Jesus Christ being referred to as the Chief Shepherd. Therefore, based on the responsibilities and functions of an elder outlined in 1 Peter Chapter 5, this serves as a witness that the office of the pastor and elder are identical.

Recall from the previous chapter that Acts 14:23 says, "And when they (Paul and Barnabas) *had ordained them elders in every church*, and had prayed with fasting, they commended them to the Lord, on whom they believed." Moreover, Acts 20:17-38 provides the account that while in Miletus, *Paul called the elders of the church* together to give them instructions and specific warnings. Notice that in both instances, the titles of pastor or bishop are not specifically used. Rather, the responsibility of the local church came under the purview of the elder. Hence, contrary to what is widely accepted and believed, the office and function of a pastor and elder are the same in relation to the church. Nevertheless, in many churches, their structure places the pastor above the position of elder with a clear distinction between the two.

In Paul's epistle to Titus, he informs him that the reason he left him in Crete was to complete the things he had left undone. Additionally, Paul also instructs him to ordain or appoint elders in every city. Again, in this example, the designation of "elder" is used as opposed to that of "pastor." Therefore, the directive given to Titus was to set elders over the churches of Crete, and consequently, the apostle Paul provided him with the qualifications for the office. However, based on the determinations we have made, we can also conclude that the listed qualifications also pertain to the office of a pastor.

5. For this cause left I thee in Crete, that thou shouldest set in order the things that are wanting, and ordain elders in every city, as I had appointed thee:
6. If any be blameless, the husband of one wife, having faithful children not accused of riot or unruly.
7. For a bishop must be blameless, as the steward of God; not selfwilled, not soon angry, not given to wine, no striker, not given to filthy lucre;

8. But a lover of hospitality, a lover of good men, sober, just, holy, temperate;
9. Holding fast the faithful word as he hath been taught, that he may be able by sound doctrine both to exhort and to convince the gainsayers. (Titus 1:5-9)

It is indeed interesting that while presenting the criteria for an elder, the passage makes a seamless transition in providing the qualifications for a bishop. The passage uses the titles elder and bishop interchangeably as they are in reference to the same office. However, we will delve into this in more detail during our discussion on bishops once we have concluded our review on the office of elder. Let us look at the definition of an elder.

The word "elder" is the Greek word *presbyteros,* which means the following:

- Advanced in life
- A term of rank or office
- Those who preside over assemblies or churches

Just like pastors, elders also have their origin in the Old Testament. The word is derived from the fact that in early times, the rulers of the people were selected from elderly men. Therefore, throughout Scripture, an elder has been associated with a position of leadership and authority (Numbers 11:16, Leviticus 9:1, Joshua 24:1, Matthew 27:1). Hence, when the church was established, it was a familiar title to define leadership responsibility in the church (Acts 15:2, Acts 15:23, Acts 16:4). This was evident in Acts Chapter 15 during the "apostolic council," when while referring to the leaders, the phrase "the apostles and elders" was used multiple times throughout the chapter. Let us look at several other passages regarding the position of the elder as it relates to the church.

17. Let the elders that rule well be counted worthy of double honour, especially they who labour in the word and doctrine.
18. For the scripture saith, Thou shalt not muzzle the ox that treadeth out the corn. And, The labourer is worthy of his reward.
19. Against an elder receive not an accusation, but before two or three witnesses.

20. Them that sin rebuke before all, that others also may fear. (1 Timothy 5:17-20)

Is any sick among you? Let him call for the elders of the church; and let them pray over him, anointing him with oil in the name of the Lord (James 5:14)

This review dismisses the notion that the role of the pastor is higher than that of an elder. In this vein, an elder should not be a position appointed by a pastor, which is the common practice in the church, for they are the same. However, because the entire organizational structure of the church is out of alignment such practices persist.

BISHOP

As indicated, the title of "Bishop" is often viewed as having prevalence over the office of pastor or elder. Even though some denominations have instituted this structure, as it has been determined, this has no foundation in Scripture. Furthermore, this concept has also influenced several independent churches with the notion that the title represents an advancement from the office of pastor. In fact, while speaking to a pastor some time ago, he indicated that instead of "Pastor," he was going to change his title to "Bishop." However, after pointing out to him that both titles were the same, his response was that the Lord told him to do it. While this response is often a default statement by many believers, one thing is certain: what God says is always within the parameters of what is written. Therefore, what we perceive He said will never be in contravention of His written Word. In fact, based on the principle offered in 2 Peter 1:16-21, what is written represents a "more sure" word than what is spoken. However, in the church, there seems to be a reversal regarding this principle.

Needless to say, after the conversation, he adopted the title of "Bishop-elect," which indicated the title was perceived as a promotion over his former role. After carrying this title for about three months, he then assumed the title of bishop. In several settings, this title has been adopted to represent a transition to the office of bishop. However, when someone is already a pastor, there is no such designation as "Bishop-elect." Such a classification is simply conformity to religious posturing. Along these lines, some have even taken on the title of "Apostle-elect" for a specified period with the notion that it also represents a transition to that office. For the record, with the positions of a pastor, elder, and bishop being identical, alternating between them is not the concern. The challenge lies in the notion that one title is superior to the other and therefore is seen as a promotion.

The Father ordained a particular structure for the church, and Scripture offers a clear blueprint of what that structure looks like. Furthermore, many pastors also chose the title of "Bishop" to create a noticeable distinction between them and the other pastors within the same assembly. In this regard, "Senior Pastor" is sufficient.

Similar to Titus who was left in Crete, Paul also left Timothy in Ephesus with the same instructions regarding the appointment of leaders and the promotion of sound doctrine. Just as Paul gave Titus the qualifications about an elder, he gave Timothy those related to a bishop and deacon. In providing him with the qualifications of what constitutes a position of leadership in the church, Paul was also giving them instructions on how to conduct themselves in the house of God.

14. These things write I unto thee, hoping to come unto thee shortly:
15. But if I tarry long, that thou mayest know how thou oughtest to behave thyself in the house of God, which is the church of the living God, the pillar and ground of the truth. (1 Timothy 3:14-15)

Within the qualifications for the position is also the requirement for conduct in the house of God. Hence, when the standards for leadership are maintained or diminished, this is reflected in the character and behavior of the church. Thus, in the words of Dr. John C. Maxwell, "Everything rises and falls on leadership." Similar to the word "pastor," the word "bishop(s)" is also used sparingly in the New Testament. In fact, it only appears in the New Testament on three occasions. One reference is Titus 1:7, which we have already discussed. The second one is found in Philippians 1:1 where in the salutation of the letter, Paul makes mention of the bishops and deacons. Finally, the third one is found in 1 Timothy Chapter 3. Let us therefore look at this passage.

1. This is a true saying, If a man desire the office of a bishop, he desireth a good work.
2. A bishop then must be blameless, the husband of one wife, vigilant, sober, of good behaviour, given to hospitality, apt to teach;
3. Not given to wine, no striker, not greedy of filthy lucre; but patient, not a brawler, not covetous;
4. One that ruleth well his own house, having his children in subjection with all gravity;
5. (For if a man know not how to rule his own house, how shall he take care of the church of God?)
6. Not a novice, lest being lifted up with pride he fall into the condemnation of the devil.
7. Moreover he must have a good report of them which are without; lest he fall into reproach and the snare of the devil. (1 Timothy 3:1-7)

Notice that when we create a parallel between the criteria for an elder listed in Titus Chapter 1 and those of a bishop highlighted in 1 Timothy Chapter 3, the qualifications are identical. Furthermore, as indicated earlier, while stating the qualifications for the office, Titus uses the titles of elder and bishop interchangeably. Therefore, when we reconcile all the passages regarding these titles, there is tremendous evidence that all three offices are truly the same. Let us now define the word "bishop."

The word "bishop" is the Greek word *episkope,* which means the following:

- Overseer
- Presiding officers of a Christian church
- One who looks upon and inspects
- The office of an elder

During Paul's farewell address to the elders of the Ephesian church, he said in Acts 20:28, "Take heed therefore unto yourselves, and to all the flock, over the which the Holy Ghost hath made you overseers, to feed the church of God, which he hath purchased with his own blood." Notice that in relation to the flock or the church, the elders were appointed as overseers. This is the same responsibility that we spoke of earlier regarding the elders in 1 Peter

5:2 where they were given oversight. In this regard, the word "overseers" in the passage is the Greek word *episkopos*, which is from the same root words *epi* and *skopos* for the word "oversight." The only distinction is that the word "oversight" in 1 Peter 5:2 is a verb, and the word "overseer" in Acts 20:28 is a noun. One speaks of the function, whereas the other speaks of the office. Therefore, the function of a pastor or an elder is to be an overseer or bishop of the church. Hence, it is not a position that is distinct from that of a pastor or elder but simply describes their responsibility.

Again, throughout Scripture, the office of pastor, elder, and bishop is used interchangeably, but they all represent the same function. However, the misunderstanding concerning the office of bishop comes into play by those who misinterpret the function of an overseer. By taking great liberty with the term "overseer," many are of the opinion that a bishop presides over or has oversight over other pastors or ministries. Hence, the popularity of the title "Presiding Bishop." While it is possible that a bishop may preside over several churches, based on Scripture, this is not the qualifier for the office of bishop. Furthermore, as it pertains to church structure, the office, which offers a more fitting description regarding this type of oversight, is actually that of an apostle.

Recall that as it pertains to the church, apostles are the first in rank, position, and authority. They are followed by prophets (1 Corinthians 12:28). Moreover, in accordance with Scripture, apostles appoint bishops, pastors, or elders. Therefore, the current perspective of the office of a bishop is contrary to the structure ordained by the Father. Now that we have reconciled the functions of elders, pastors, and bishops, we can have an earnest discussion about the office of the pastor. Nevertheless, in support of what Scripture says, the three terms will be used synonymously throughout this discussion.

QUALIFICATIONS OF A PASTOR, ELDER, OR BISHOP

What makes an individual a pastor? Is it attending a theological seminary? Is it because their parent(s) are pastors and they are supposedly "next in line?" Is it based on how well an individual can preach? Is being ordained by the presbytery the qualification for the office? Regardless of these conditions, Scripture reveals that becoming a pastor is solely based on receiving the gift of Christ to function in this capacity. Let me say emphatically, it does not matter who your parents are, how charismatic an individual sounds, or if he or she has a degree in theology. Along these lines, I reiterate what the apostle Paul said in Ephesians 3:7, "Whereof I was *made* a minister, according to the gift of the grace of God given unto me by the effectual working of his power." Paul attributes his calling and position as a minister to the gift of God's grace bestowed upon him by the Holy Ghost. Therefore, pastors and ministers in general, are only appointed by Jesus Christ. In this regard, He is the ultimate qualifier for the office. On the note of children being the successors of their parents who are pastors, I am not suggesting that this is impossible; however, it is not an automatic assignment, for God makes ministers.

In addressing the office of the bishop, 1 Timothy Chapter 3 says, "If a man desire the office of a bishop, he desireth a good work." First, even though the passage uses the word "man" the office of a bishop is certainly not male or gender-specific. In fact, in Christ, gender (male/female), ethnicity, and social status do not exist, for we are all one (Galatians 3:28). Moreover, our identity is not based on the attributes associated with the flesh. Nevertheless, in order to stay on point, again I refer you to my book, *Freedom: The True Perspective about Women in Ministry*.

1 Timothy 3:1 says that the office of a bishop is a good work and a position of honour; it is a suitable office to desire. Therefore, being a pastor is an essential function and great honour, for they are the ones who shepherd the flock of God. Based on the consolidation of the qualifications of an elder and bishop outlined in 1 Timothy 3:1-7 and Titus 1:5-9, outlined below are the credentials for the position.

TABLE 4

CHARACTER	ABILITY
• A bishop must be blameless (as the steward of God). As the manager of God's household and its affairs, his or her conduct must be beyond reproach. He or she must have a character that cannot be called into account.	• A bishop must be apt or able to teach. He or she must be skillful in teaching.
• A bishop must be the husband of one wife. Let me say without reservation that the apostle Paul is not saying that one of the requirements for the office is marriage. On the contrary, this statement is based on the condition that the elder, pastor, or bishop is already married. For a proper context of what is being said, we need the reconciliation of Scripture. For example, in 1 Corinthians 7, Paul offers a perspective concerning marriage and doing the work of the Lord. 1 Corinthians 7:32-33 says, "He that is married cares for the things of the world, how he may please his wife; however, he that is unmarried cares for the things of the Lord, how he may please the Lord." Hence, being unmarried would allow believers to attend to the work of the Lord without distraction. With this in mind, Paul says in 1 Corinthians 7:7, that he wishes all men were unmarried like him, but not everyone has the gift of celibacy. Therefore, in his letters to	• A bishop must be able to hold fast the faithful Word as he hath been taught. He or she must be firm in the truth of the gospel so that through sound doctrine/teaching he or she may persuade those who oppose the truth.

Timothy and Titus, this premise does not change. Hence, the main point being emphasized is that if a bishop is married, he should be monogamous and consequently faithful to his wife.	
• A bishop must be vigilant. This refers to being sober-minded or temperate. He or she must be conscious and attentive to his or her behavior.	
• A bishop must be sober. He or she must be discreet and of sound mind. A bishop must exercise self-control with proper restraints on his or her passions and desires. It is a person who limits his or her own freedom and ability with proper thinking.	
• A bishop must be of good behavior. He or she must be modest and mannerly.	
• A bishop must be given to or a lover of hospitality. He or she must be hospitable, sociable, and friendly.	
• A bishop must not be given to wine. He or she must not have a habit of drinking or be accustomed to sitting with those who indulge in wine. In fact, it is advisable to avoid it altogether.	
• A bishop must not be a striker. He or she must not be a quarrelsome person, contentious, or combative.	
• A bishop must not be given to filthy lucre. He or she must not be greedy for money or despicable gain.	
• A bishop must be patient. He or she must be gentle and modest.	

• A bishop must not be a brawler. He or she must not be inclined to fight.	
• A bishop must not be covetous. He or she must not be a lover of money. This is in addition to not being greedy for filthy lucre.	
• A bishop must be one who rules his/her own house well, having his/her children in subjection with all gravity. That is having faithful children not accused of riot or being unruly. Again, this statement is based on the condition that the elder, pastor, or bishop is married, has children, and therefore has his/her own household. Therefore, as the steward of God or the manager of God's household, the requirement of the office would be for the person to properly govern his/her own house. 1 Timothy 3:5 says plainly, "For if a man know not how to rule his own house, how shall he take care of the church of God?" For the sake of clarity, the reference to children in this passage does not apply to adult children but rather, to underage children. Therefore, the children must not be disobedient to authority, disorderly, or lawless. Hence, in governing his/her house, the children of that house must be in submission and he/she should exercise seriousness in this regard.	
• A bishop must not be a novice. He or she should not be a new convert or a newcomer to the faith.	

• A bishop must have a good report of them which are without. He or she must have a good reputation even among those who are not believers. A bishop's character must be one of integrity, not just to those of the household of faith but to everyone.	
• A bishop must not be self-willed – He or she must not be self-pleasing or arrogant.	
• A bishop must not be soon angry. He or she must not be prone to anger or be touchy or irritable.	
• A bishop must be a lover of good men. He or she must love and promote that which is good.	
• A bishop must be just. He or she must exercise righteousness and be upright in all dealings.	
• A bishop must be holy. He or she must be righteous in character. This is toward both God and man.	
• A bishop must be holy. He or she must be righteous in character. This is toward both God and man.	

Notice that of all the qualifications for an elder, pastor, or bishop only two of them pertain to the ability to teach or have a firm command of the Word of God. Oftentimes, our endorsement of what makes someone a "good" pastor is his or her ability to preach a provocative sermon. The words they use and their voice modulations provide emotional chills and an exciting atmosphere. While there is certainly nothing wrong with this, this is not how we determine or appoint someone to the bishopric. Note that according to the chart, the qualifications for the office are predominately character related. In fact, throughout Scripture, this standard has always been consistent. However, as a body, we seem to be more interested in style or performance rather than substance or character. Therefore, in revisiting the question of what makes an individual a pastor, Scripture is clear that righteous character is a significant component. Additionally, these righteous qualifications also apply to everyone who operates in any of the gifts of Christ.

RESPONSIBILITIES OF A PASTOR

Now that we have highlighted the qualifications of a pastor, let us look at the responsibilities or duties of the office from the perspective of Scripture. Depending on who you ask, the functions of a pastor are greatly varied and seem to differ from church to church. Moreover, this statement is also true depending on the denomination to which one is associated. On the periphery, the responsibilities of the office include performing wedding ceremonies, conducting baby christenings, visiting the sick, performing funeral services and conducting counselling sessions, etc. While these are all necessary functions that need to be performed, they do not represent the predominant responsibilities of a pastor according to Scripture. In this vein, the duties of the office are best understood in why the office was instituted in the first place, not primarily what it has evolved into. In terms of core responsibilities, Scripture is clear on what are the duties of the calling. For example, while addressing the elders of the church at Ephesus in Acts 20:28, Paul gives them specific instructions in relation to their responsibilities. Even though this was in light of the pending attacks on the church, it still provides an awareness of the general responsibilities of the office. He says to them:

- **<u>Take heed unto yourselves</u>**

    Interestingly, the first responsibility the apostle Paul mentioned was directed at leadership. In focusing on the elders or bishops, the first thing he said was to give careful consideration to yourselves. Because of what leaders represent, this was the first instruction. In essence, he was saying to them, despite what is on the horizon, make sure you are fortified and in position.

Knowing that grievous wolves or false teachers would come in and not spare the flock, they were admonished to be on guard. In addition to this attack from without, Paul also warned them that some from within the church will distort the truth. Therefore, because leaders represent the first line of defense against all forms of attacks, they have to be equipped. Furthermore, the advice to take heed also pertains to leaders being in righteous standing. For example, Paul in 1 Corinthians 9:27 says, "But I keep under my body, and bring it into subjection: lest that by any means, when I have preached to others, I myself should be a castaway." Hence, in addition to edifying others, leaders also have a responsibility to themselves. This means it's not just about teaching, but they have to ensure that they themselves are walking in righteousness. Moreover, being in a leadership position can sometimes be draining and the person you neglect the most is often yourself.

In light of this, Luke 5:12-16 gives us the example that on occasion, even Jesus withdrew himself and prayed in solitude. Therefore, taking time to recharge with the Father in prayer is necessary. Based on the nature of the attacks mentioned in the passage, taking heed also includes being purveyors of sound doctrine. Thus, to defend against wolves, leaders have to study. In this regard, 2 Timothy 2:15 speaks of studying the Scriptures in order to be approved by God. Taken together, the principle is that if leaders are vigilant concerning themselves, they will also be vigilant in relation to the flock.

- **<u>Take heed to all the flock</u>**

The statement, "Take heed unto yourself," is all-encompassing concerning the role of leadership. Therefore, the implication is the same as the statement, "Take heed to all the flock," for it pertains to everything in relation to the people of God. First, by comparing God's people to sheep, this puts the leaders in the position of shepherds. Hence, if the shepherds do not take heed to themselves, it is easy to scatter the sheep. Additionally, by using the analogy of sheep to characterize the people of God, this also reveals the type of care that pastors should have for the church. Notice that the passage says, "all the flock," which means the same care should be directed to every member, not a selected few. Furthermore, with believers being referred to as sheep, it is necessary to understand the characteristic of sheep. Not only will this assist us in defining the duties of a pastor, but it will also help in determining the specific care to be administered. In truth, as it pertains to the church, Scripture offers a shepherd-sheep relationship. With that said, there is a direct correlation between the type of animal being looked after and the responsibilities placed upon the caretaker.

Characteristics of Sheep

- They cannot defend themselves and are therefore vulnerable.
- They are dependent creatures. They are totally reliant on the shepherd.
- They are the only domestic animal that cannot exist without man. They need care and protection.
- They follow the voice of the shepherd; instinctively they are followers and need guidance.
- They have no sense of direction; they get lost easily and therefore must be directed.
- They are easily led astray.
- They are easily disturbed.

Based on these characteristics, we can better define the statement "Take heed to all the flock." From the preceding list, it is apparent that sheep require constant care, guidance, and protection. Therefore, the responsibilities of the office are best understood by understanding the nature of the people in your care. For the sake of discussion, the church is not compared to a flock of birds or a pride of lions because then the duties of the caretaker would drastically change. Additionally, from a business perspective, once you know the idiosyncrasies of your customer, this defines your strategies and shapes the business model. Therefore, Scripture uses the natural proclivities of sheep to explain the leadership responsibilities of pastors. Furthermore, a wonderful illustration of the relationship between the shepherd and sheep is provided in Psalm 23. Knowing therefore the disposition of sheep, a pastor must be vigilant in his or her care for them. This includes the duties of feeding, guarding, and guiding the flock.

- **They are overseers**

    Included in the mandate of "taking heed to all the flock" is the notion of oversight. Notice specifically that Acts 20:28 reinforces the principle that it is the Holy Ghost who appoints elders or overseers. It says, "Take heed therefore unto yourselves, and to all the flock, over the which the Holy Ghost hath made you overseers, to feed the church of God, which he hath purchased with his own blood." This is a reverberation of what was stated earlier in that it is the Lord who makes or appoints ministers. With the people of God being referred to as sheep, then pastors or shepherds are overseers. They are charged with oversight of the flock or function as bishops. According to the *Free Dictionary* by Farlex, an overseer is a supervisor or a person who oversees others. Hence, they are the ones who exercise watchful care of the flock, who serve as guardians, and inspect everything.

    Having oversight is a management responsibility and it means that bishops, with the ability to see, are charged with discerning the operations of good and evil in the lives of God's people and others. Therefore, based on this ability to see, they can implement measures for the safety and protection of the flock.

    However, there is a stark contrast between being an overseer and having the disposition of being lords over God's people. In the capacity as overseers, 1 Peter 5:3 admonishes elders to not act as lords over God's heritage but rather, be examples to the flock. Anytime authority is conveyed, there is also the possibility of the abuse of power. In this regard, Scripture is keen to remind us that the flock belongs to the Father, for they are His acquisition. In this regard, leaders are stewards or caretakers, not lords. The word "lords" in this passage speaks of being masters or having others under one's power. Therefore, even though leaders have been placed in positions of authority over the flock, they are not the masters over God's people.

The concept of lording over God's people can be conducted overtly or subtly. In terms of what is easily recognizable, the people of God through a sense of obligation and will-worship can be made the servants of pastors or leaders. In many instances, leaders are even treated like celebrities. However, this is the same spirit of prominence and recognition that Jesus addressed in Matthew Chapter 20 in relation to James and John. This spirit is also evident in the adoption of such titles as "His Grace, " "His Eminence," or other titles that are chosen to communicate positions of importance. Thus, by the assignment of such titles, leaders sometimes position themselves as lords over God's people, and because of the nature of sheep, there is a sense of obligation. In truth, some leaders exalt themselves above what the Lord intended for the position. Unfortunately, the motive behind such an operation is the pride of life.

Regarding subtle ways, in Matthew Chapter 15, Jesus gave the example of the teaching of the scribes and Pharisees. To benefit themselves financially, they implemented their own doctrinal principles in contradiction to Scripture. Instead of allowing the people to fulfill their financial obligations to their parents, the money was redirected to them in the form of a gift. Therefore, by means of doctrine, the people were manipulated into withholding financial assistance to their parents and redirecting it to the religious leaders as gifts. Acting as lords or masters over God's heritage is when leaders think that the people exist for their own benefit.

- **<u>Feed the Church of God</u>**

The word "feed" in this context is not limited to offering teaching and instructions; it also embodies the entire function of the shepherd. It encompasses everything pertaining to the wellbeing of the sheep. This includes guarding, guiding, nourishing, governing, and protecting the flock. Psalm 23 provides a comprehensive illustration of what it means to "feed" the sheep.

In sticking with the sheep and shepherd analogy, recall Paul said in Acts 20:29-30, that after his departure, grievous wolves shall enter among the believers not sparing the flock. As noted, the passage uses wolves to figuratively depict false teachers who are intent on devouring and scattering the sheep. The entire purpose of this is to disrupt the unity of the faith. Additionally, he also emphasizes that not only will false teachers come from outside the church, but they will also come from within. Significantly, Paul instructs pastors to be vigilant because wolves do not always come looking like wolves. Matthew 7:15 says, "Beware of false prophets which come to you in sheep's clothing but inwardly they are ravening wolves." These are the same false apostles, false prophets, and false teachers who have transformed themselves into the ministers of Christ. However, once the leaders take heed to themselves and all the flock, they can effectively guard against such attacks. Moreover, the shepherd has a rod and staff for his/her benefit; these are for correction and protection. They guide, protect, and correct the sheep.

ADDITIONAL RESPONSIBILITIES OF A PASTOR

As I said before, while chiding the shepherds of Israel in Ezekiel Chapter 34, the Lord was simultaneously providing the responsibilities of a true shepherd. Hence, often when we are highlighting unacceptable behavior, there is an underlying message of what is expected. Some of these responsibilities were mentioned in the previous section; however, Ezekiel 34:1-6 adds to the list.

1. And the word of the LORD came unto me, saying,
2. Son of man, prophesy against the shepherds of Israel, prophesy, and say unto them, Thus saith the Lord GOD unto the shepherds; Woe be to the shepherds of Israel that do feed themselves! Should not the shepherds feed the flocks?

3. Ye eat the fat, and ye clothe you with the wool, ye kill them that are fed: but ye feed not the flock.
4. The diseased have ye not strengthened, neither have ye healed that which was sick, neither have ye bound up that which was broken, neither have ye brought again that which was driven away, neither have ye sought that which was lost; but with force and with cruelty have ye ruled them.
5. And they were scattered, because there is no shepherd: and they became meat to all the beasts of the field, when they were scattered.
6. My sheep wandered through all the mountains, and upon every high hill: yea, my flock was scattered upon all the face of the earth, and none did search or seek after them.

As discussed, shepherds in this context refer to the general function of leadership. Therefore, the responsibilities of a shepherd are also included in the list.

- **Feed the flock**. This responsibility was detailed in the previous section; however, based on Ezekiel Chapter 34, we also have the perspective of clothing the flock. As stated, the word "feed" encompasses a myriad of responsibilities relative to the wellbeing of the sheep. Additionally, in this rebuke, it is evident that the shepherds were of the mindset that the sheep exist for their benefit. It paints the picture of leaders living in comfort and luxury while the sheep were neglected. Unfortunately, this is just as true today as it was then.

- **They are to strengthen the flock**. The word "diseased" refers to being wounded, weak, sick, grieved, and in pain. These conditions require urgent attention. The sheep must be strengthened to survive; this involves encouragement, restoration, and making sure they are established. Fostering their growth and development is essential.

- **They are to heal the flock**. It is also the shepherd's responsibility to heal the flock. This is particularly specified in James 5:14-15, which says,

14. Is any sick among you? Let him call for the elders of the church; and let them pray over him, anointing him with oil in the name of the Lord:
15. And the prayer of faith shall save the sick, and the Lord shall raise him up; and if he have committed sins, they shall be forgiven him.

- **They are to bind up those that are broken**. This involves ministering to those who have suffered tragedy or who are broken. In Luke 4:18, Jesus referred to this as healing the brokenhearted.

- **Recover those who were driven away and seek those that are lost**. This is obviously a two-fold responsibility. Sometimes sheep are scattered and have to be retrieved. Other times, they wander and get lost. In both instances, it is the responsibility of the shepherd to seek them. To support this point, in Luke Chapter 15, Jesus provided the example of a shepherd who left his ninety-nine sheep in order to retrieve his one sheep that was lost. Upon retrieving the sheep, he rejoiced, which emphasizes that it was not about numbers but rather the significance of every sheep. This responsibility pertains to deliverance and restoration.

Now that we have examined the responsibilities of a shepherd from several examples in Scripture, let us look at Jesus in His capacity of a shepherd. As a staple throughout this discussion, it was emphasized that for all the gifts of Christ, Jesus is indeed the benchmark.

JESUS AS A PASTOR (THE GOOD SHEPHERD)

In John 10:11 Jesus said, "I am the Good Shepherd." By using the qualifier "good" to describe His role as a Shepherd, Jesus was in fact contrasting Himself to other shepherds." In the account of Jeremiah 23:1-2, along with the example of Ezekiel 34:1-6, we have illustrations of what constitutes a bad pastor or shepherd. Moreover, with the statement, Jesus was doing two things. First, He was establishing the benchmark of what a good shepherd looks like. Additionally, He was also highlighting the characteristics of what made someone a "bad shepherd or pastor." Hence, the passage offers a complete picture of leadership, both good and bad. However, before getting into the specifics of what Jesus meant and His role as a Shepherd, we must first establish the context of why He made this statement.

In John Chapter 9, Jesus healed a man who was blind from birth. Therefore, when the Pharisees heard it, they contended with the man and questioned him on how he received his sight. After a lengthy debate with them concerning the matter, the Pharisees were displeased with him and consequently put him out of the synagogue. In other words, he was excommunicated. However, when Jesus found him, He said to him, "For judgment I am come into this world, that they which see not might see; and they that see might be made blind" (John 9:39). Upon hearing this, the Pharisees that were with the man asked, "Are we blind also?" Jesus responded and said to the Pharisees, "If you were blind, ye should have no sin: but now ye say, 'We see'; therefore your sin remaineth."

Based on the principle established in Scripture, the Pharisees along with other members of the religious establishment were regarded as the shepherds of Israel. Therefore, when Jesus engaged the Pharisees in John Chapter 9, He was addressing them from the perspective of shepherds. Hence, in John Chapter 10, the conversation continues, and He uses the opportunity to create a contrast between His leadership and theirs. By identifying Himself as the Good Shepherd, He was, by comparison, calling their oversight as shepherds into question. In conveying His message, Jesus compares the people of God to sheep and offers the illustration of a shepherd and a sheepfold.

1. Verily, verily, I say unto you, He that entereth not by the door into the sheepfold, but climbeth up some other way, the same is a thief and a robber.
2. But he that entereth in by the door is the shepherd of the sheep.
3. To him the porter openeth; and the sheep hear his voice: and he calleth his own sheep by name, and leadeth them out.
4. And when he putteth forth his own sheep, he goeth before them, and the sheep follow him: for they know his voice.

5. And a stranger will they not follow, but will flee from him: for they know not the voice of strangers. (John 10:1-5)

To understand the analogy, it is necessary to define what a sheepfold is. A sheepfold is a stone enclosure where the sheep are kept at night for their protection. In the day, they would graze in the field, and at night, the shepherd would place them in the sheepfold from thieves and predators. It only had one entrance and either the shepherd or a porter (gate warden) would sit at the door or opening and guard the sheep during the night. See Exhibit 8.

EXHIBIT 8

In continuing with the example of the sheepfold, Jesus says to the Pharisees, "He that entereth not by the door of the sheepfold, but climbeth up some other way, the same is a thief and a robber." On the other hand, He says, "He that enters in by the door of the sheepfold is the shepherd of the sheep." The passage therefore presents two methods of having access to the sheep and two distinct categories of leaders. There are those who climb over the wall of the sheepfold and those who enter by the door. The ones who climb over the wall are regarded as thieves and robbers, whereas the shepherd is the one who enters through the gate.

In John 10:7, Jesus says plainly to the Pharisees that He is the door of the sheep. In other words, He was saying, "I am the access to the sheep. Those that want access to the sheep but do not come through Me and what I represent are thieves and robbers." Again, I reiterate, that God referred to the leaders of Israel as pastors or shepherds. Ezekiel 34:1-3 says,

1. And the word of the LORD came unto me, saying,
2. Son of man, prophesy against the shepherds of Israel, prophesy, and say unto them, Thus saith the Lord GOD unto the shepherds; Woe be to the shepherds of Israel that do feed themselves! Should not the shepherds feed the flocks?
3. Ye eat the fat, and ye clothe you with the wool, ye kill them that are fed: but ye feed not the flock.

Even though the Lord referred to the leaders as shepherds, they were not genuine shepherds. They were shepherds in name only, not in function. With this perspective in mind, Jesus said (in the context of the passage) all those who came before Him (and were supposedly shepherds) were actually thieves and robbers. As the Pharisees along with the Sadducees and scribes represented the shepherds of Israel at the time, He was specifically referring to them. However, Jesus being the door says that proper access to the sheep is only through Him. Hence, shepherds who want access to the sheep and circumvent Christ and all that He represents are simply thieves and robbers. Because they have a different agenda, the message is not the same. They are not representations of who Christ is.

These are the same people Peter spoke about in 1 Peter 2:1. "But there were false prophets also among the people, even as there shall be false teachers among you, who privily shall bring in damnable heresies, even denying the Lord that bought them, and bring upon themselves swift destruction." Furthermore, Jesus also adds that as the door, "By me if any man enter in, he shall be saved, and shall go in and out and find pasture." In His depiction of being the door, He is saying that not only does He represent access to the sheep but salvation in general. He represents the comprehensive package, which for all sheep includes protection, as well as having all your needs supplied.

Furthermore, in John 10:10, Jesus continues the conversation about thieves and robbers and says, "The thief cometh not, but for to steal, and to kill, and to destroy: I am come that they might have life, and that they might have it more abundantly." In sticking with the context of the passage, the thief, based on what we have established, refers to leaders who want access to the sheep for their own purposes. Also, their intent is to create a following without going through Christ (the door). Therefore, He is using the word "thief" to describe the character of the Pharisees and the religious leaders.

Ezekiel Chapter 34 provides a vivid illustration of the attributes of a thief or a "bad shepherd." It says that instead of feeding the sheep, they feed themselves. Instead of guarding and protecting the sheep, they prioritize their own wellbeing. In addition, they do not have the disposition of serving the sheep but are persuaded that the sheep exist to cater to their needs. They eat the fat. They clothe themselves with the wool from the sheep and kill the sheep that are fed. The sole purpose of their position is to have access to the sheep for their own pleasure. Therefore, Jesus categorized their actions and said their objective is to steal, kill, and destroy. However, in contrast to this, Jesus said in John 10:10, "I am come that they might have life, and that they might have it more abundantly." To be clear, when Jesus says that the thief comes to steal, kill, and destroy, He is not directly referring to the devil. While it is his influence that motivates these types of leaders, the passage specifically identifies the thief as shepherds who use the sheep for their own advantage. Hence, to distinguish Himself from "bad shepherds" whose purpose is to devour the sheep, Jesus says in John 10:11, "I am the Good Shepherd" who gives His life for the sheep.

> 11. I am the good shepherd: the good shepherd giveth his life for the sheep.

12. But he that is an hireling, and not the shepherd, whose own the sheep are not, seeth the wolf coming, and leaveth the sheep, and fleeth: and the wolf catcheth them, and scattereth the sheep.
13. The hireling fleeth, because he is an hireling, and careth not for the sheep (John 10:11-13)

GOOD SHEPHERD VERSUS HIRELING

Just as there are false apostles, false prophets, and false teachers, a hireling is the antithesis of a good shepherd. Hence, a hireling can be classified as a false pastor. After creating a contrast with the Pharisees, who pretended to be shepherds, Jesus furthers the distinction between Himself and them by characterizing them as hirelings. Therefore, "bad shepherds" are not only thieves and robbers, but they are also hirelings. In simple terms, hirelings are those who do a job solely for money. Their motivation is completely self-serving and for earthly or material gain. Again, from the example of Ezekiel Chapter 34, hirelings feed themselves and have no regard for the interest of the sheep.

Hirelings are not concerned about the safety of the sheep. John 10:12 says when they see the wolf coming, they run away and leave them defenseless. Consequently, with the sheep being abandoned, the wolf can scatter and catch them. Notice that having a hireling instead of a shepherd results in the sheep being scattered. This shows that good shepherds promote unity, whereas hirelings give rise to divisions. Additionally, when a shepherd is not fortified with sound doctrine, it is much easier for the wolves or false teachers to scatter and devour the flock.

Through the example of Jesus Christ, we are furnished with the benchmark of what it means to be a good shepherd. Good shepherds give their lives for the sheep. Their highest priority is the safety and wellbeing of the sheep, even at the expense of their own lives. As noted, Jesus said in John 10:11, "I am the good shepherd: the good shepherd giveth his life for the sheep." Additionally, a good shepherd has a relationship with the sheep. Jesus said in John 10:14, "I am the good shepherd, and know my sheep and am known of mine." He signifies a personal and intimate relationship between the shepherd and the sheep. The shepherd knows the characteristics and tendencies of the sheep and the sheep know the shepherd and his voice. Jesus also provides additional insight into the characteristics of hirelings.

Just as Ezekiel 34:1-6 highlighted the qualities of a good shepherd, it also speaks of the characteristics of hirelings or bad shepherds. They are as follows:

- They feed themselves, not the sheep.
- They clothe themselves and neglect the flock.
- They do not strengthen the sheep.
- They do not heal the sick.
- They do not bind up those who are broken.
- They do not retrieve the sheep that are scattered or those who are lost.

It is unfortunate that even today, many of these characteristics are prevalent in several people who purport to be shepherds. Because they serve their own interest, they are constantly engaged in activities that make merchandise of God's people. As a result of covetousness, they are the masters of feigned words. With a hireling's purpose being self-serving, how they shepherd the flock and the substance of their messages reflect that objective. For example, the faith and prosperity doctrine constitutes a hireling teaching because it serves to benefit the hireling.

Fundamentally, this doctrine emphasizes that gain is godliness, and there is a direct correlation between our earthly possessions and God's favor in our lives. However, Scripture teaches us that godliness with contentment is great gain (1 Timothy 6:5-6). Because they are in it for the money, their messages are designed to foster a steady flow of cash. To this end, they also invent schemes and gimmicks behind spiritual silhouettes to fleece money from the sheep. Scripture also refers to this as making merchandise of God's people (2 Peter 2:3).

To be clear, Scripture supports pastors or those in ministry benefiting from their work. Specifically, Paul in 1 Corinthians 9:7 says, "Who goeth a warfare any time at his own charges? Who planteth a vineyard, and eateth not of the fruit thereof? Or who feedeth a flock, and eateth not of the milk of the flock?"

Furthermore, in 1 Corinthians 9:11, he adds, "If we have sown unto you spiritual things, is it a great thing if we shall reap your carnal things?" "Carnal things" refer to earthy rewards, which also include money. Additionally, 1 Timothy 5:17-18 says,

17. Let the elders that rule well be counted worthy of double honour, especially they who labour in the word and doctrine.
18. For the scripture saith, Thou shalt not muzzle the ox that treadeth out the corn. And, the labourer is worthy of his reward.

Based on these examples, Scripture makes provision for shepherds to benefit from the sheep. However, the difference is that hirelings do it solely on the basis of money or for their own advantage. They serve themselves.

Based on the premise of Ezekiel Chapter 34, the shepherds were enjoying a substantially better life than that of the sheep. They ate the finest and wore the best, while the sheep were impoverished. Hence, even the accepted model we have today and the wealth disparity between leaders and followers are based on the standard of a hireling. Without any reservation, this design is established on the proclivity of thieves and robbers. Moreover, hirelings will never correct the sheep because they only see them as their livelihood. They are afraid that through correction, the sheep would become offended and leave the fold, thereby impacting their standard of living. This also includes avoiding teachings on chastisement, which are designed to produce mature sons and manifest the fruit of righteousness (Hebrews 12:5-11). A hireling's decision and methods are not based on producing righteous character but simply to make money.

For clarity, the sheepfold mentioned in John 10:1 explicitly represented the children of Israel. While in conversation with the Canaanite woman who pleaded with Jesus to deliver her daughter who was vexed with a devil, He said unto her in Matthew 15:24, "I am not sent but unto the lost sheep of the house of Israel." Therefore, in His initial conversation with the Pharisees, he was speaking specifically concerning Israel. However, Jesus added in John 10:16, "And other sheep I have which are not of this fold; them also I must bring, and they shall hear my voice; and there shall be one fold and one shepherd."

The Five-Fold Ministry Gifts

By this statement, He was referencing the inclusion of the Gentiles as it was a foreshadow of making Jews and Gentiles one. Hence, it was a statement of unity, for in the kingdom of God, there is only one sheepfold or one family.

"THE" SHEPHERD

In defining Christ's position as the Shepherd, Scripture not only uses the adjective "good," but it also uses other distinguishing qualifiers such as *great* and *chief*. For example, Hebrews 13:20 says, "Now the God of peace, that brought again from the dead our Lord Jesus, *that great shepherd of the sheep*, through the blood of the everlasting covenant." Additionally, 1 Peter 5:4 says, "And when *the chief Shepherd* shall appear, ye shall receive a crown of glory that fadeth not away." With the inclusion of these two adjectives, it is apparent that in comparison to those who have been appointed as shepherds, Christ has the preeminence. Just as Christ is the chief Shepherd or pastor, He is also the chief Apostle. In fact, in describing Christ as the Shepherd, 1 Peter 2:25 applies the definite article "the" to Shepherd as an indication that He is the only one in the context.

> *For ye were as sheep going astray; but are now returned unto the Shepherd and Bishop of your souls. (1 Peter 2:25)*

Therefore, with Christ being distinguished as the great or chief Shepherd, pastors are appropriately classified as under-shepherds. On a broader scope, the acknowledgement of Christ as "the Shepherd" also conveys several other messages. First, it expresses that all sheep inherently belong to the Father; consequently, there is one sheepfold. Psalm 100:3 says, "We are His people, and the sheep of His pasture." Moreover, as the passage indicates, there is only one pasture or flock. Hence, the recognition of Christ's position should foster an atmosphere of unity in the body of Christ. Particularly, when shepherds embrace the premise that in truth, there is indeed one Shepherd and one flock, then divisions would be eliminated.

MISLEADING CONCEPTS OF PASTORS AND THE CHURCH

- A pastor is not like a sole proprietor who is unanswerable or unaccountable to anyone. Based on the structure the Father has implemented for the church, pastors are appointed by apostles. Therefore, they do not operate with absolute autonomy but in harmony with apostles and others who have been bestowed the gift of Christ. They are not one-man bands.

- The position of pastor is not hereditary and the church is not a family enterprise. The position of pastor is solely based on the gift of Christ, not family affiliation. Therefore, Christ is the one who makes ministers and appoints pastors. A family business can be passed on to children, but the church or the position of pastor does not operate on these principles. I am not suggesting that a son or daughter be prevented from succeeding a parent who is a pastor. I am simply saying that children's affiliations do not guarantee them these positions. It is based on Christ bestowing the gift.

- Being able to preach does not make someone a pastor. The qualifications are predominately based on being bestowed the gift of Christ and righteous character.

- Pastors are not mediators or arbitrators between God and man. There is one mediator between God and man—Jesus Christ (1 Timothy 2:5).

ARE PASTORS A COVERING?

Quite often, particularly among believers, the question is asked, "Who is your covering?" Based on the question, the idea of "spiritual covering" pertains to submitting to the authority of a spiritual leader. Therefore, what they are really asking is, "Whose spiritual authority are you under?" More often than not, the response given refers to a pastor or bishop as the head of a local church. Moreover, the question is also premised on the notion that for a believer to function in ministry or to be seen as legitimate, he or she must be in submission to a specific person. Hence, those who are not under such a "covering" are seen as rebellious or not operating under authority.

Under this framework, believers are required to consult their leaders when performing ministry duties at other assemblies or when it comes to making significant personal decisions. In fact, a leader once insisted that his opinion should be solicited in relation to making major decisions. In principle, leaders who operate under this form of accountability have established themselves as lords over God's heritage. With the perspective of covering being so prevalent, does Scripture support this notion? Is this based on God's design for the church?

Generally speaking, the Bible supports the principle of submission. Along these lines, Romans 13:1 instructs us to be in subjection to those in authority in a comprehensive sense. This includes leaders in government and at work. Ephesians 5:21 also speaks of mutually submitting ourselves to each other. For the most part, the concept of covering is derived from several references namely, 1 Corinthians 11:3 and 1 Thessalonians 5:12-13. 1 Corinthians 11:3 says, "But I would have you know, that the head of every man is Christ; and the head of the woman is the man; and the head of Christ is God." The passage then goes on to discuss the concept of spiritual covering. Based on the context of this scripture, three spiritual coverings are being discussed.

- The head of every man or every individual is Christ. Christ serves as the covering for everyone. This speaks of his responsibility in our lives. Moreover, if a woman is not married, Christ is also her covering.
- The head of the woman (wife) is her husband. This is his responsibility concerning his wife.
- The head of Christ is God. This speaks of the dynamics of the Father-Son relationship.

In these three examples, headship speaks of submission to authority but within the confines of the function and responsibility of each relationship. For instance, in a family relationship, the husband is the covering or head of the wife. This is his function and responsibility as it pertains to his wife. While it is agreed that leaders in general, inclusive of pastors, have been placed in positions of authority in relation to the flock, it is not the same as the covering mentioned here. On the contrary, the passage is explicit in defining the true perspective of spiritual covering. The second passage that serves as a reference for covering is 1 Thessalonians 5:12-13:

> 12. And we beseech you, brethren, to know them which labour among you, and are over you in the Lord, and admonish you;
> 13. And to esteem them very highly in love for their work's sake. And be at peace among yourselves.

First, let us consider the phrase "over you in the Lord." Without understanding what is being conveyed, misappropriations occur. The phrase refers to those who have been placed or established over the flock. More specifically it means the following:

- To superintend over
- To preside over
- To be a protector or guardian
- To care for or to give attention to

Based on our course of study, we see that this responsibility is in alignment with the function of an elder, pastor, or bishop. However, it is not exclusive to them alone but rather, to all those in spiritual authority. Therefore, the passage is simply reiterating the duty of an overseer. Unfortunately, the phrase "over you in the Lord" has been taken to mean "spiritual covering," whereas it simply refers to having the responsibility of oversight of the flock. Recall that the duty of an overseer is predominately to exercise watchful care of the flock, ensuring their wellbeing. This also includes guarding and protecting the flock. Furthermore, based on their labour, 1 Thessalonians 5:13 says that all spiritual leaders should be esteemed very highly in love for their work's sake. In simple terms, this means to cherish and respect them. Before concluding this discussion, there are two other scriptures we need to consider to settle this topic of spiritual covering. They are Hebrews 13:7 and Hebrews 13:17.

Remember them which have the rule over you, who have spoken unto you the word of God: whose faith follow, considering the end of their conversation. (Hebrews 13:7)

Obey them that have the rule over you, and submit yourselves: for they watch for your souls, as they that must give account, that they may do it with joy, and not with grief: for that is unprofitable for you. (Hebrews 13:17)

In most instances, when we hear the word "obey," we often think of following someone's commands or instructions with unquestionable loyalty. While this may be the prevailing idea, obey in Hebrews 13:7 has a different connotation. It refers to having confidence in or being persuaded by those that rule over us. Furthermore, just like the word "obey," the word "rule" is also often misrepresented. The word "rule" in both passages speaks of leaders whom the Lord has appointed in positions of authority to guide us to a particular destination. It is leadership with purpose. Hence, because they have been appointed by the Father to fulfill His purpose in our lives, believers are admonished to trust them and submit to them.

The passages are calling on believers to have confidence in their leadership because of the mandate they have been given. Moreover, we are to submit to their authority because the Lord has appointed them as overseers or bishops who watch for our souls. Thus, as stewards of God, they are answerable to God for their stewardship.

According to what we have discussed, this concept of "spiritual covering" practiced in the church is not supported by Scripture. Indeed, leaders have been given oversight of the people of God, and based on their work, they are to be esteemed. However, this does not include the notion of spiritual covering where an individual serves as an authority figure to validate someone's spiritual walk. As a matter of fact, this concept is more consistent with being lords over God's heritage mentioned in 1 Peter 5:3. The proliferation of independent churches and a misunderstanding of Scripture have caused the entire concept of authority to be abused. Nevertheless, as leaders, those who have been bestowed the gift of Christ, the responsibility is tremendous and the accountability significant.

DEACONS

In addition to the appointment of pastors or bishops, Timothy was also given the qualifications of a deacon. The role of the deacon is to support elders or pastors in the local church which, in turn, frees them to focus more on oversight. This is similar to the example provided in Acts Chapter 6, where the seven were appointed so the apostles could give themselves to prayer and the teaching of the Word of God. The word "deacon" is the Greek word *diakoneo*, which generally means a minister. However, more specifically, it refers to rendering assistance to pastors and helping with the physical needs of the church.

8. Likewise must the deacons be grave, not doubletongued, not given to much wine, not greedy of filthy lucre;
9. Holding the mystery of the faith in a pure conscience.
10. And let these also first be proved; then let them use the office of a deacon, being found blameless.
11. Even so must their wives be grave, not slanderers, sober, faithful in all things.
12. Let the deacons be the husbands of one wife, ruling their children and their own houses well.
13. For they that have used the office of a deacon well purchase to themselves a good degree, and great boldness in the faith which is in Christ Jesus. (1 Timothy 3:8-13)

Notice in 1 Timothy 3:8-13 that the qualifications for a deacon are basically the same as the bishop, pastor, or elder with minor exceptions. Therefore, regardless of whatever the office is, God's requirements are the same. In fact, the righteous requirements outlined in Scripture are for every believer whether in office or not. However, for some reason, when it comes to righteous behavior, we seem to hold those in leadership to a higher standard when the same standard exists for everyone.

THE PURPOSE OF THE LOCAL CHURCH

Similar to the perspectives related to the qualifications of a pastor, the responses regarding the purpose of the local church are also varied. Nevertheless, in addressing this subject, we will once again follow the benchmark provided by Scripture. From the principle provided in Acts 2:42 when the believers assembled, they were engaged in the following:

- Teaching or instruction
- Fellowship
- Breaking of bread
- Prayer

Based on this premise, we can conclude that the purpose of the local church is to have a common environment for the expression of these activities. Additionally, from its inception, the church has also been committed to facilitating the needs of the less fortunate. That still serves as a pattern today. Moreover, based on the activities occurring in the Corinthian church, we can add the singing of psalms to the list as this introduces the concept of corporate worship (1 Corinthians 14:26). Therefore, even though the church may be engaged in a myriad of activities, these are its most identifiable core objectives. However, it should be noted that at this point in the church's existence, (when the letters were written) a distinct public structure did not exist. Therefore, the assemblies were conducted in the private dwellings of individuals. For example, Colossians 4:15 says, "Salute the brethren which are in Laodicea, and Nymphas, and the church which is in his house." Additionally, Romans 16:3-5 speaks of the church that was in the house of Aquilla and Priscilla.

Even though today there are elaborate houses and edifices for public worship, the core activities of the church remain the same. Taken together, based on a survey of the scriptures, the purpose of the church serves as an atmosphere that fosters the growth and development of the sons of God. It is a place where believers can encourage and support each other.

After Jesus' resurrection, He met with His apostles privately and gave them a specific mandate. In Matthew 28:19-20, He took His leaders aside and said, "Go ye therefore, and teach all nations, baptizing them in the name of the Father, and of the Son, and of the Holy Ghost: Teaching them to observe all things whatsoever I have commanded you." In truth, this directive represented the blueprint for both the activity and message of the church. The word "teach" in the passage means to make disciples or followers. Therefore, the activities or the purpose of the local church are all designed to make disciples. However, included in the notion of discipleship is also the principle of transformation. Disciples, therefore, are not just those who believe and promote the doctrines of another but who also transform into the image of whom they promote. In other words, disciples manifest the character of the one they follow. To this end, 2 Corinthians 3:18 says, "But we all, with open face beholding as in a glass the glory of the Lord, are changed into the same image from glory to glory, even as by the Spirit of the Lord." Therefore, it is not enough for the church to simply amass great numbers under the banner of having disciples, but there must also be a transformation.

The church is charged with the responsibility of developing the people of God and reproducing the image of Christ in the earth. With the local church being an environment for instruction, its doctrines and teachings truly matter. In order to manifest the image of Christ, the teaching has to be based on the principles, which support being conformed to Christ's image. It must be the message of true discipleship. In understanding the entire spectrum involved in teaching, it includes doctrine, reproof, correction, and instruction in righteousness. Hence, when all of these elements operate in succession, the result is sons of God who are mature and thoroughly furnished unto all good works (2 Timothy 3:16).

Furthermore, Acts 2:42 is very specific regarding the nature of the doctrine that was being taught. When the believers assembled, they were taught the apostles' doctrine. There was singleness of doctrine in the church. Again, based on the responsibilities of an apostle, they are the ones who establish the doctrine of the church. As we have concluded on several occasions, this doctrine is the same one Jesus taught: the message of the kingdom of God. Therefore, the concept of true discipleship can only be based on this teaching. On the other hand, if disciples are created on any other premise, the purpose is self-serving and caters to the glory of man. Recall that the principles of the kingdom of God represent the embodiment of the promises the Father predetermined for humanity before the foundation of the world. Hence, they express the pillars of the doctrine that should be taught in the local church. Furthermore, this teaching is also the basis of the unity of the faith; thus, it is the doctrine that fosters unity amongst believers. Wherefore, it is the doctrine of the kingdom of God that creates unity in the church.

Because the doctrine of the kingdom promotes unity, this then creates fellowship among believers. Fellowship is defined as a community of people who share common interests. Therefore, the local church serves as a place where believers can convene and thereby create a community effect. With the church being a family, this gathering is one of communion, intimacy, and social bonding. The local church is instrumental in making disciples; thus, commitment to a local church is a necessity. This is why Hebrews 10:25 says, "Not forsaking the assembling of ourselves together, as the manner of some is; but exhorting one another: and so much the more, as ye see the day approaching."

It is within this community that believers can exhort or encourage each other. On this note, when people say they do not need to go to church to be Christians, they are correct. However, to grow and strengthen others, it requires a community; the assembly provides that environment. Additionally, it offers a sense of belonging where believers can interact and care for each other.

Within the confines of the fellowship and community that existed, Acts 2:42 says that believers also got together to break bread. This provides another perspective of the social aspect of believers assembling. For the sake of this discussion, the concept of breaking bread is literal and figurative. From a figurative point of view, breaking bread speaks of sharing a sense of brotherhood or having a meaningful connection over a meal. Moreover, from a literal point of view, it precisely refers to the partaking of food. However, regardless of the vantage point, the act of breaking bread or having a meal fosters a connection with others. Based on the community-based relationship that existed, everyone had the perspective that all things were common or generally owned. Therefore, they went from house to house breaking bread, eating their meat with gladness and singleness of heart. Additionally, they also sold their possessions and distributed the proceeds to other members based on their needs.

Another activity that Acts 2:42 mentions concerning the gathering of believers is that of prayer. Though not exclusively reserved for the confines of the assembly, the church serves as an environment set aside or suited for the offering of prayer. Additionally, it is also a place for corporate worship. In all, the local church serves an essential role in the fulfillment of God's purpose. It is a place where what the Father has purposed for us can be expressed among those who are partakers of His blessings.

For the local church to be effective and accomplish God's objective, the appropriate structure based on God's design has to be in place. Hence, the responsibility of creating disciples is not the sole function of the pastor. Recall that for perfecting the saints, the Lord gave apostles, prophets, evangelists, pastors, and teachers. However, many pastors have been turned into lone rangers and the five-fold ministry gifts have been seemingly reduced to a one-fold operation. Obviously, based on this structure, the church is being shortchanged and therefore not perfected to the measure that it should be. However, when all of the gifts function in unity, the body experiences growth and increase. Furthermore, when we take into consideration the characteristics of sheep and the role of the shepherd, this gives us a great perspective of the purpose of the local church.

Whether the person charged with the oversight of God's people goes by the titles of elder, pastor, or bishop is irrelevant. What is important is the function. As an overseer, the shepherd's primary responsibilities include feeding, strengthening, healing, delivering, and restoring the sheep. Pastors play a pivotal role in relation to the wellbeing and development of the sons of God. They do so by managing an environment of discipleship consisting of teaching, fellowship, social interaction, and prayer. Just like the other gifts of Christ, the mandate of the pastor is also to promote the message of the kingdom of God. However, their administration involves more of a community focus in relaying this message.

CHAPTER 11

THE GIFT OF CHRIST EXPLAINED: TEACHER

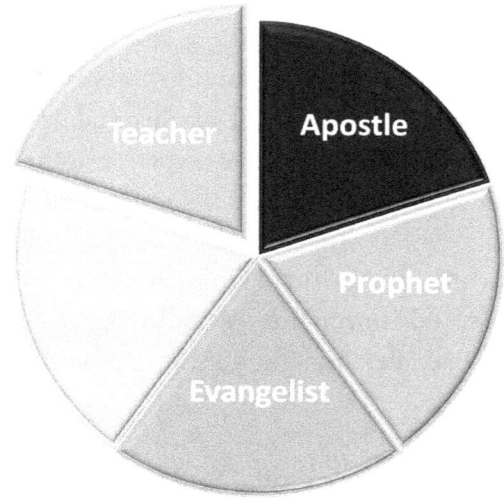

And he gave some, apostles; and some, prophets; and some, evangelists; and some, pastors and **teachers.** *(Ephesians 4:11)*

TEACHER: THE DISTINCTION

Having already discussed the offices of the apostle, prophet, evangelist, and pastor, the focus of this chapter is the office of the teacher. Just as the other four offices are distinct and have a specific function in relation to the body, so too does the teacher. While there may be some who combine the office of a pastor and teacher into a solitary office of "pastor-teacher," this is not the communication of Scripture. Interestingly, those who take this position hang their hats solely on the grounds that the word "some" precedes all the other gifts except for the teacher. However, this conclusion is based on not understanding the scope and responsibility of the gift of the teacher. Also, this conclusion is void of what is referred to as "the whole of Scripture context." This simply means that to have the proper perspective concerning a subject, all of the scriptures related to that topic must be considered. Just as Christ functioned distinctly in both the capacities of pastor and teacher, when He gives of Himself and bestows the gifts to humanity, the endowments are also specific. Furthermore, while one of the qualifications of a pastor is the ability to teach (1 Timothy 3:2), not all teachers are necessarily gifted as pastors or all pastors gifted as teachers. However, based on the premise of the plurality of elders/pastors overseeing a church, perhaps this challenge can be mitigated. Nevertheless, it is the purpose of this chapter to bring enlightenment concerning the gift of the teacher and its specific relevance to the body of Christ. In this vein, there are several scriptures where the role of a teacher is specified as a distinct function. For example,

Now there were in the church that was at Antioch certain prophets and teachers; as Barnabas, and Simeon that was called Niger, and Lucius of Cyrene, and Manaen, which had been brought up with Herod the tetrarch, and Saul. (Acts 13:1)

Additionally, 2 Timothy 2:11 reveals that Paul functioned in both the capacity of an apostle and a teacher.

> Whereunto I am appointed a preacher, and an apostle, and a teacher of the Gentiles. (2 Timothy 2:11)

As a general requirement, all those who have been bestowed the gift of Christ, as well as believers in general, should be able to teach. 2 Timothy 2:24 says, "And the servant of the Lord must not strive; but be gentle unto all men, apt to teach (or skillful in teaching)." Furthermore, recall that in the qualifications for a bishop or elder, one of the consistent competencies is the ability to teach or to hold firmly the faithful word (1 Timothy 3:2, Titus 1:9). Therefore, the ability to teach is not exclusively reserved for those in leadership. However, just as there is a distinction between the ability to prophesy and being a prophet, there is also a difference between being able to teach and being a teacher.

Concerning God's established order, recall that 1 Corinthians 12:28 says, "And God hath set some in the church, first apostles, secondarily prophets, thirdly teachers, after that miracles, then gifts of healings, helps, governments, diversities of tongues." Remember that the context of this verse says that even though there is unity in the body, there is still a specific order of things. Therefore, according to Scripture, after apostles and prophets, teachers are third in terms of rank and position. However, it should be noted that "teacher" in this context, also includes the offices and functions of both pastor and evangelist. Hence, the passage is simply highlighting the importance of teaching/preaching relative to the operations that are listed thereafter.

As mentioned on several occasions, the church is built on the foundation of the apostles and prophets with Jesus Christ being the chief cornerstone (Ephesians 2:20). Hence, the communication of the passage says that the proper foundation of leadership, followed by teaching, takes precedence over the other functions that are listed. Therefore, in terms of priority in the church, the emphasis is on proper structure and teaching above miracles, healings, helps, governments, and tongues. Conversely, when this priority is reversed in the church, and the others hold precedence, then there is neither order nor substance. Consequently, there is no growth.

TEACHER DEFINED

The word "teacher" is the Greek word *didaskolas,* which means the following:

- One that explains and expounds on a thing
- Someone who holds discourse with others in order to instruct them.
- One that instills doctrine into another
- It was a name of respect that was given to Jewish scribes.
- Instructor, master, or doctor
- Teacher implies authority based on qualification.

To express the significance of a teacher, Scripture often substitutes it with the word "master." It is not just a title, but it also conveys the relationship between one who instructs and one who learns. Furthermore, it does not just refer to that which is taught but it emphasizes the authority of the one who instructs. In martial arts, the title of "Sensei" also means teacher or master. However, from a broader perspective, the title is also used to show respect to someone who has achieved a certain level of mastery in other endeavors. Hence, just as with Scripture, the title teacher recognizes the authority of someone who is skilled, experienced, and knowledgeable. With this context as a backdrop, Jesus in His capacity of Teacher was often referred to as Master (Matthew 9:11, Mark 4:38, Luke 18:18, and John 13:13). In fact, as it relates to Him, the words "teacher" and "master" were often used interchangeably. Additionally, the disciples also referred to Jesus as Rabbi, which is an official title of honour used to address teachers. However, it is also translated as master.

In Luke 2:46, when Jesus' parents were looking for Him during the Passover, they found Him in the temple sitting with doctors both hearing them and asking them questions. Interestingly, the word "doctor" used in Luke 2:46 is the same Greek word *didaskolas* for teacher or master. Therefore, the word "doctor" was used to express their degree of proficiency regarding the interpretation of the Law. Moreover, in reference to the term "doctors of the law" mentioned in Luke 5:17, the Greek word is *nomodidaskolas*, which is a combination of *nomos* meaning law and *didaskolas* meaning master or teacher. The same title was also attributed to Gamaliel in Acts 5:34, who as a master was the one who instructed Paul in the Law (Acts 22:3). Hence, with the words "master" and "doctor" used equally with "teacher," this conveys the message that a teacher is not just someone who instructs but an individual who is skilled in the interpretation of Scripture. They are masterful teachers or scholars. When Ephesians 4:11 says Jesus gives teachers to the body of Christ, this is the gift He confers.

To shed additional light on the perspective of a teacher, a parallel can be drawn to the functions of a scribe in the Bible. The religious establishment of Jesus' day consisted of the Pharisees, Sadducees, and scribes. Collectively, they were the ones who sat in Moses' seat or exercised authority concerning the interpretation of the Law, its execution, and judgment (Matthew 23:2). In particular, the scribes were highly skilled in the interpretation of the Law and were the ones entrusted with its teaching and application. They were scholars of the Old Testament Law. The word "scribe" is the Greek word *grammateus* and it means the following:

- One who writes—they were responsible for making copies of official or legal documents.
- A learned man in the Mosaic Law
- An interpreter and teacher

One of the more notable scribes in Scripture was Ezra. He was responsible for teaching the Law to Israel when they returned from Babylonian captivity.

> This Ezra went up from Babylon; and he was a ready scribe in the law of Moses, which the LORD God of Israel had given: and the king granted him all his request, according to the hand of the LORD his God upon him. (Ezra 7:6)

> For Ezra had prepared his heart to seek the law of the LORD, and to do it, and to teach in Israel statutes and judgments. (Ezra 7:10)

As a scribe, Ezra was ready or skilled concerning the Law of Moses. However, in Jesus' day, the scribes, along with the Pharisees and Sadducees, made the Word of God ineffective because of the traditions of men (Mark 7:13). In other words, they added man-made practices to the Law and made substitutions to what God said. Consequently, these traditions were then considered more important than the Law itself. This was especially evident when their distorted interpretation of the Law served to their own benefit (Mark 7:9-12). Therefore, they opposed Jesus because their interpretation and application of the Law were different from what He was teaching. As those skilled in the interpretation of Scripture, the contrast between Jesus and the scribes was indisputable. Mark 1:21-22 says, "And they went into Capernaum; and straightway on the sabbath day he (Jesus) entered into the synagogue, and taught. And they were astonished at his doctrine: for he taught them as one that had authority, and not as the scribes."

Even though the scribes were regarded as being skillful in the interpretation of Scripture, there was a distinction between the manner of their teaching and that of Jesus. The difference is that He taught the people as one who had authority. The word "authority" is the Greek word *exousia,* which means the power of rule or government. It also means jurisdiction or delegated influence. Therefore, as the representative of the kingdom of God and acting in the official capacity as a teacher, He taught as one having official power or legal authority. He had the power of influence and the people recognized the difference. Therefore, the distinction will always be made between teachers who speak the truth and those who promote their own agendas. Even the religious leaders were astonished by Jesus and wondered how He attained His wisdom and performed mighty works (Matthew 13:54).

Based on the definition of a teacher, along with the principle of Scripture, a teacher is one who is skillful in the interpretation of Scripture and has the authority to instruct. Teachers are skilled, experienced, and knowledgeable in the Word of God. By building on the foundation established by apostles and prophets, they systematically teach the doctrine of the kingdom of God. The word "systematically" is characterized by order and planning. Therefore, a teacher uses an established curriculum to teach the Word of God in a structured and progressive manner. By all accounts, they are considered doctors of the scriptures, but this obviously takes time to develop.

AQUILA AND PRISCILLA

A practical example of the function of a teacher can be found in Acts Chapter 18, which speaks of the exchange between Aquila and Priscilla and Apollos.

24. And a certain Jew named Apollos, born at Alexandria, an eloquent man, and mighty in the scriptures, came to Ephesus.
25. This man was instructed in the way of the Lord; and being fervent in the spirit, he spake and taught diligently the things of the Lord, knowing only the baptism of John.

26. And he began to speak boldly in the synagogue: whom when Aquila and Priscilla had heard, they took him unto them, and expounded unto him the way of God more perfectly. (Acts 18:24-26)

Notice that despite the qualifications attributed to Apollos, he still had a limited perspective regarding the various types of baptisms. He was only familiar with water baptism, but he was ignorant about the baptism of the Holy Spirit. However, when Aquila and Priscilla heard him speak, they befriended him and expounded unto him the Word of God more perfectly. They explained to him or taught him the way of God more precisely. As teachers skilled in the Scriptures, Aquila and Priscilla not only recognized where the deficiency was, but with a spirit of meekness, they were also able to instruct Apollos in what was lacking.

QUALIFICATIONS AND RESPONSIBILITIES OF A TEACHER

- **As with the other gifts of Christ, being a teacher is based on receiving the gift of Christ.**
  As noted earlier, every believer, particularly those in church leadership, should be able to teach (2 Timothy 2:24, 1 Timothy 3:2). However, a teacher is someone distinctly different. As a result of receiving the gift of Christ and based on the spirit of wisdom and revelation, a teacher is a master of the scriptures who with authority articulates God's purpose through Scripture. Teachers do not simply read Scripture and offer a commentary on it. They are also not solely the products of seminaries or Bible colleges. Indeed, there are institutions designed to nurture or develop the gifts, but mere attendance at such schools does not produce the gift. Being a teacher is based on an endowment from the Father.

- **The primary responsibility of a teacher is to study.**
  As with any gift, the gift of teaching has to be nurtured. From the example of Jesus Christ, after sitting with the doctors of the law, Luke 2:52 says, "And Jesus increased in wisdom and stature and in

favor with God and man." The word "increased" signifies process and development. Somehow, we get the impression that Jesus did not have to study, but this conclusion is incorrect. Notice that in the exchange with the doctors, He was both listening to them, as well as asking them questions. Certainly, these two attributes are the hallmarks of any good student.

Furthermore, in many of His discourses, Jesus would preface His response with the phrase, "It is written," followed by the relevant scripture. This was an indication that He not only knew Scripture but also the proper context of Scripture based on the particular situation. As a principle for all believers, Timothy 2:15 says, "Study to shew thyself approved unto God, a workman that needeth not to be ashamed, rightly dividing the word of truth." As with any discipline or calling, there are rules to follow in the attainment of excellence or to be skillful. Even in giving the example of athletes, 1 Corinthians 9:25 says those who strive for the mastery must adhere to certain laws or principles. Similarly, to be approved, acceptable, and exemplary as God's worker, the requirement is to study by rightly dividing the Word of Truth. To accomplish this, the principles associated with rightly dividing the Word of God must be known and utilized. There must be an understanding of covenants, dispensations, Bible language, Bible layout, etc. Furthermore, in-depth study takes time, dedication, and effort. There must be an innate desire or a hunger to study God's Word. This desire is driven not only by the need to understand the Father's purpose, but also to communicate it to His people for their development. The objective of studying is also to guard against false doctrine and those who try to pervert the gospel of Christ (Galatians 1:7).

- **Teachers are not appointed based on human intellect or wisdom.** Being a teacher is not based primarily on intelligence or the fact that someone is smart. To support this, 1 Corinthians 1:20 offers the principle that the wisdom of this world is foolishness with God. Furthermore, 1 Corinthians 1:26-27 says,

26. For ye see your calling, brethren, how that not many wise men after the flesh, not many mighty, not many noble, are called:

27. But God hath chosen the foolish things of the world to confound the wise; and God hath chosen the weak things of the world to confound the things which are mighty

The point is that an individual's knowledge based on the wisdom of this world does not automatically mean he or she is called as a teacher in the body of Christ. If this were the criteria, an abundance of revelation would come from those with an extensive academic background. Unfortunately, in some instances, believers are appointed as teachers in the church based on this premise.

Additionally, the hallmark of a good teacher is not associated with eloquent speech. In addressing the church at Corinth, Paul says in 2 Corinthians 2:1, "And I, brethren, when I came to you, came not with excellency of speech or of wisdom, declaring unto you the testimony of God." Hence, as it pertains to the things of God, these two qualities are not automatic endorsements for the office. Having said that, it should also be stated that being intelligent and possessing good elocution are also not disqualifiers for the office of a teacher. One thing is certain: the Father always provides a good balance. Notice that 1 Corinthians 1:26 is careful to use the term "not many" in referring to God's selection of those who are wise or intelligent. Primarily this is done so that no flesh should glory in His presence (1 Corinthians 1:29).

In using the example of Paul, by all accounts, he was a well-educated man who sat at the feet of Gamaliel, a notable doctor of the law. However, after the Lord called him, notice what he says in Galatians 1:11-12:

11. But I certify you, brethren, that the gospel which was preached of me is not after man.

12. For I neither received it of man, neither was I taught it, but by the revelation of Jesus Christ.

Therefore, despite his privileged education and knowledge of the Scriptures, as a Pharisee, he concluded that what he was preaching was a result of revelation from Jesus Christ. Certainly, his educational background was useful to him in ministry, but it was not the basis of his revelation.

- **Teachers depend on guidance from the Holy Spirit.**
A teacher does not rely on his or her understanding for scriptural interpretation. Additionally, the truth of Scripture is not solely derived from an understanding of Hebrew and Greek words. While this resource is indeed beneficial as I can attest, it is certainly not the basis of revelation knowledge. As a premise, Ephesians 1:17 says that it is through the spirit of wisdom and the spirit of revelation that the Father provides enlightenment and knowledge.

During my early years of studying the Word of God (before the internet), I was adequately armed with a huge concordance, a Hebrew/Greek dictionary, an expository dictionary of Bible words, and many other helpful reference books. I would literally spend hours every day combing through these resources to have a better understanding of the scriptures. While I still rely on these references today, there is indeed a significant difference in terms of dependency. Because of the development of the gift of a teacher in my life, there is now a greater reliance on the Holy Spirit. Needless to say, the Lord used that foundation to transition me to where I am now and develop the gift in me.

With that said, while studying the Word of God, oftentimes the Lord supernaturally imparts information into my spirit. In many instances, I had limited or no knowledge regarding the subject I was writing about. This is based on the principle of Job 32:8 which says, "But there is a spirit in man: and the inspiration of the Almighty giveth them understanding." Therefore, what is bestowed is often beyond my intellect and human understanding so much so that while I am writing, the Father is literally teaching me at the same time. Thus, I am not writing out of the abundance of my own knowledge or based on someone else's. I am by no means suggesting that I sit there without engaging in the study; however, it is through study and not simply relying on word definitions and intellect that the Lord brings His Word to light. Additionally, this also requires having a pure heart and being in constant prayer.

However, there is an interesting twist to this discussion. On several occasions, as a result of teaching, I was referred to as intelligent or smart. Without question, I would dare say that when God gives you a gift to function on His behalf, along with it comes a measure of intelligence. While I do not consider myself to be smart, through the study of God's Word and development of the gift He has given me, it may appear that way at times. But this is simply the wisdom and grace of God on display. Furthermore, because of the distinction that exists between teaching and preaching, many seem to associate teaching with intellectual ability. However, this is a misunderstanding of the dynamics of the gift or its purpose.

- **Teachers exhibit righteous character.**
  Similar to the qualifications of a bishop, pastor, or elder, the requirements for a teacher or any office, pertain more to righteous character than the ability to teach or preach. Based on the premise offered in 1 Corinthians Chapter 13, possessing gifts but not having love or the fruit of the Spirit is meaningless. Furthermore, as an admonition, James 3:1 says, "My brethren, be not many masters, knowing that we shall receive the greater condemnation." As discussed previously, the word "masters" in this passage is the same Greek word for teacher. Therefore, the communication of this verse goes beyond the responsibility of proper doctrine. It also pertains to the righteous examples of those who are teachers.

Jesus, in His rebuke of the Pharisees and scribes, said in Matthew 23:3, "All therefore whatsoever they bid you observe, that observe and do; but do not ye after their works: for they say, and do not." The Pharisees and scribes in their positions as teachers said one thing, but their actions were contrary to their words. Therefore, for integrity to be in place, words and actions must be in harmony.

- **Teachers produce other teachers.**
  The responsibility of a teacher exceeds being able to elucidate the Word of God. Teachers are also charged with producing other teachers. In fact, this is also a principle of good leadership. For example, in his communication to Timothy, Paul says in 1 Timothy 2:2, "And the things that thou hast heard of me among many witnesses, the same commit thou to faithful men, who shall be able to teach others also." In other words, you are a product of my stewardship, therefore produce other teachers who, in turn, will teach others. The responsibility of leadership is to reproduce itself. Along these lines, Timothy was also required to operate within an established framework. Inherent in this principle are several things.

  First, there is the concept of systematic teaching. According to the relationship that existed between Paul and Timothy, Paul charged him with reproducing that pattern. In other words, "Develop a teacher-student relationship with those who are faithful and deposit in them what I taught you." He was mandated to teach the established doctrine or curriculum.

  The word "faithful" speaks of those who are worthy of trust and can be relied upon. Hence, Timothy was charged with identifying and selecting those who fit certain criteria. Because of the significance of the task, the responsibility was to choose those who were worthy. This was necessary because they would also be tasked with teaching others, thereby duplicating the relationship once again. This is the template of how leaders are developed from one generation to the next. On the other hand, when this principle is ignored through selfishness or neglect, the body of Christ suffers, and development does not occur.

- **Teachers are gatekeepers and protectors of the truth.**
  Again, in Paul's letters to Timothy, a central theme of both epistles is to guard against false doctrine. In fact, from the onset of his first epistle

to Timothy, Paul sets the parameter and instructs Timothy to charge some in the church that they teach no other doctrine (1 Timothy 1:4). Furthermore, the same sentiment is echoed in 2 Timothy 1:13 where Paul says to Timothy, "Hold fast the form of sound words, which thou hast heard of me, in faith and love which is in Christ Jesus." Therefore, as an apostle, he established the framework for what teachers should teach. Hence, based on this premise, throughout the epistles, there is constant warning against false teachers and false doctrines. Teachers are essential because they are on the frontline with those who are earnestly contending for the faith. However, when true teachers neglect the responsibilities of their office, then false teachers can bring in damnable heresies.

FALSE TEACHERS

Similar to false apostles, false prophets, and hirelings who we can classify as false pastors, there are also false teachers. Just as there are teachers who are authentic and appointed by the Father, there are also those who represent the counterfeit. The term "false teacher" is the Greek word *pseudodidaskalos*. Again, just as we saw with the others, this term is a combination of two words *pseudes* meaning false and *didaskalos* meaning teacher. The word "false" means to deceive by a lie or to speak deliberate falsehoods. Given this is an intentional act, we need to qualify the term "false teacher." Based on the definition, we can conclude that if people are preaching a doctrine in ignorance, they cannot necessarily be regarded as false teachers. However, if the proper perspective of Scripture is revealed to them and they bear witness that it is true, yet continue preaching the same message, they can be classified as false teachers. They are now deliberate in preaching a message contrary to sound doctrine. In this instance, they have rejected the truth to promote their own ideals and a separate agenda. Additionally, because of lust and no desire for the truth, people will seek false teachers who will say what they want to hear. This is the same operation spoken of in 2 Timothy 4:3-4:

3. For the time will come when they will not endure sound doctrine; but after their own lusts shall they heap to themselves teachers, having itching ears;
4. And they shall turn away their ears from the truth, and shall be turned unto fables.

From the beginning, it has always been the plan and purpose of the devil to offer an alternative to what God says and does. In Genesis 3:17, the Lord said, "But of the tree of the knowledge of good and evil, thou shalt not eat of it: for in the day that thou eatest thereof thou shalt surely die." However, the devil offered an alternative message and outcome that appealed to the flesh and human desire. This is the operation and trademark of false teachers. They always reverse what God says and establish a different principle in its place. False teachings will always appeal to the flesh, cater to human desires, and overall, be in contravention to what God says.

This substitute is always presented in a subtle manner making it difficult to distinguish the counterfeit from the genuine. For example, at face value, a fraudulent work of art can appear to be authentic to those who are unskilled. However, to the trained eye or someone who is a master, the forgery is more apparent. As a point of emphasis, the term "false teacher" is an all-inclusive application for all those who promote false doctrine and heresy regardless of the office. Hence, a false teacher can also be an apostle, a prophet, an evangelist, or a pastor. 2 Peter 2:1-3 offers additional insight regarding them.

1. But there were false prophets also among the people, even as there shall be false teachers among you, who privily shall bring in damnable heresies, even denying the Lord that bought them, and bring upon themselves swift destruction.
2. And many shall follow their pernicious ways; by reason of whom the way of truth shall be evil spoken of.
3. And through covetousness shall they with feigned words make merchandise of you: whose judgment now of a long time lingereth not, and their damnation slumbereth not.

This passage reveals with great clarity how false teachers operate and reinforces what we have already discussed. However, notice that false teachers are not just identified by what they teach but also by their characters. For it is their characters and the condition of their hearts that drive the doctrines they promote. Truly, out of the abundance of the heart, the mouth speaks (Matthew 12:34). Not only are their messages fraudulent but so are they. Motivated by greed and lust, they craft deceitful messages in order to use people for their gain. Unfortunately, this practice is extremely prevalent in the body of Christ today. These men and women are just like shepherds who use the sheep for their own benefit and do not care for their wellbeing. False teachers operate just like hirelings whose objective is to kill, to steal, and destroy.

Note that according to the passage, the message of false teachers is categorized as damnable heresies. What exactly does this mean? First, the word "heresy," refers to an opinion or doctrine that represents a departure from the truth of Scripture. More specifically, it is a doctrine that appeals to human desires and is designed to cause disunion or dissension in the body of Christ. Based on the works of the flesh mentioned in Galatians 5:19-21, heresy is one of its attributes. Therefore, heresies are manifestations of the deeds of the flesh.

If you want to determine whether a teaching or doctrine is heresy, look for the operation of the flesh or if it caters to fleshly desires. Furthermore, to describe the type of heresy being promoted, the passage uses the word "damnable" or destructive. However, the word is also used to describe the effect that it has on those who adhere to such teachings. Based on 2 Peter 2:1-3, an example of a damnable heresy promoted by false teachers is the doctrine that denies Jesus Christ and His redemptive work.

On one occasion, someone told me that humanity did not have a sin problem but rather, our thinking was corrupt. He added that Christ did not have to die for our sins, we just have to change the way we think. However, this type of teaching promotes self-efficacy, appeals to the human intellect, and in reality, is a humanistic doctrine. While Romans 12:2 does say that as believers we are transformed by the renewing of our minds, this is only possible because of a change in nature. As a result of Christ's sacrifice, Romans 6:6 says that our old man or our old nature was crucified with Christ. Consequently, this freed us from the dominion of sin or from being servants of sin. It is this freedom that makes the renewal of the mind achievable. Furthermore, as a result of Christ's resurrection, this made it possible for us to walk in the newness of life. Therefore, without the redemptive work of Christ, none of this is attainable.

Additionally, because heresy appeals to the flesh, it is also void of true righteousness. Even though it may appear to have elements of righteousness in it, the objective of false teaching is to eliminate or reduce God's standard of righteousness. In terms of reducing God's standard of righteousness, the intent is to make the teaching more acceptable. This is why 2 Peter 2:1 says that false teachers shall privily or subtly introduce damnable heresies. The teaching is designed to be palatable to those who want to walk after the flesh but also desire to hear aspects of the truth. It is teaching with a combination of both flesh and Spirit. This type of doctrine represents a form of godliness, but it lacks the power of transformation. Therefore, those who seek a righteous façade but do not want to give up the pleasures of the flesh gather to themselves false teachers. These are people with itching ears who do not want to hear the truth; therefore, they find false teachers who tell them what they want to hear. They desire to hear something pleasant that reduces their righteous obligation. Unfortunately, many shall follow the destructive ways of false teachers whose overall purpose is to discredit the truth. For more on this operation, please see my book *Faith Who Hath Bewitched You?*

JESUS AS A TEACHER

While on Earth, Jesus functioned in the capacity of a teacher. This was distinct from Him operating as an apostle, prophet, evangelist, or pastor. Furthermore, as indicated earlier, in recognition of Him as a teacher, He was often acknowledged as Master or Rabbi. Recall that in John Chapter 3, Nicodemus who was a Pharisee, as well as a teacher, addressed Jesus as both Rabbi and Teacher.

1. There was a man of the Pharisees, named Nicodemus, a ruler of the Jews:

2. The same came to Jesus by night, and said unto him, Rabbi, we know that thou art a teacher come from God: for no man can do these miracles that thou doest, except God be with him. (John 3:1-2)

There were many instances throughout the Gospels where Jesus was actively engaged in teaching the people. In fact, immediately after establishing His platform of the kingdom of God, Matthew 5:1-2 says, "And seeing the multitudes, he went up into a mountain: and when he was set, his disciples came unto him: And he opened his mouth, and taught them, saying"

The "Sermon on the Mount," represents a wonderful example of the functions and responsibilities of a teacher. In its entirety, the message is presented in a progressive and systematic format. Keep in mind that the teaching begins in Matthew Chapter 5 and does not conclude until Matthew Chapter 7. Therefore, even though it addresses a myriad of topics, they are all related to the principles of the kingdom of heaven. Hence, in an organized manner, Jesus first establishes a foundation and highlights the disposition of the citizens of the kingdom. He says, "Blessed are the poor in spirit: for theirs is the kingdom of heaven" (Matthew 5:3). After listing several other attitudes associated with the kingdom of God, He then goes on to speak about two general characteristics of those of the kingdom. Thus, He refers to the people as the salt of the earth and light of the world. In other words, He is telling them what their purpose is. At this point in His teaching, Jesus then outlines His purpose and qualifies His message. Therefore, being fully aware of His audience, He establishes a premise and says in Matthew 5:17, "Think not that I am come to destroy the law, or the prophets: I am not come to destroy, but to fulfil." Furthermore, based on His teaching, He creates a higher standard of righteousness than what they were accustomed to. In this regard, He says to enter the kingdom of heaven the righteousness required must exceed that of the scribes and Pharisees. In essence, He was also creating a distinction between what the scribes and Pharisees were promoting and what He was teaching. Moreover, to illustrate what this higher standard of righteousness looks like, He dedicates the remainder of the teaching to explain the righteous principles of the kingdom of God. In many of the examples, He first outlines what was previously taught, and then He offers an alternative perspective. This is evident by the statement, "You have heard," followed by the contrasting point of view, "But I say unto you." With this exercise, He was methodically changing the way they thought, which would impact their behavior.

Additionally, throughout the Gospels, other instances reveal Jesus was consistently engaged in teaching the people.

> And when he was come into his own country, he taught them in their synagogue, insomuch that they were astonished, and said, Whence hath this man this wisdom, and these mighty works? (Matthew 13:54)

> And they went into Capernaum; and straightway on the sabbath day he entered into the synagogue, and taught. (Mark 1:21)

> And he taught daily in the temple. But the chief priests and the scribes and the chief of the people sought to destroy him. (Luke 19:47)

> And early in the morning he came again into the temple, and all the people came unto him; and he sat down, and taught them. (John 8:2)

PREACHING VERSUS TEACHING

In the church, there is often a debate about preaching and teaching. Many are of the opinion that teaching is quiet and even-toned, whereas preaching involves shouting and is more expressive. Furthermore, some believe that preaching is based on revelation, while teaching is premised on information. Moreover, some are persuaded that preaching is directed at the heart, while teaching focuses on the head. As Scripture does not validate these positions, it is necessary to examine both perspectives based on Scripture. First, the word "preach" is the Greek word *kerysso*, which means to be a herald or to proclaim openly. However, the word "teach" is the Greek word *didasko*, which means to hold discourse with others in order to instruct them. It also means to impart doctrine to someone or to explain or expound a thing.

Once again, in using the example of Jesus, we can adequately validate the difference between preaching and teaching. Matthew 4:17 says, "From that time Jesus began to *preach*, and to say, Repent: for the kingdom of heaven is at hand." When Jesus started His ministry, He made a proclamation and announced that the kingdom of God was at hand. He was heralding that something was available and that was the kingdom. However, after making this declaration, He needed to explain what the kingdom of God is. He had to teach the principles of the kingdom of God. As we discussed in the previous section, Matthew 5:1-2 says, "And seeing the multitudes, he went up into a mountain: and when he was set, his disciples came unto him: And he opened his mouth, and taught them, saying." Hence, after proclaiming or preaching that the kingdom of God was at hand, He also had to explain or teach what the kingdom of God is. Therefore, none can be discredited or preferred over the other, for they both serve a distinct purpose.

Furthermore, again using 2 Timothy 2:15 as a foundation, teaching involves the utilization of principles to a greater degree than preaching does. In an environment of false teachings and preparing others to be teachers, Paul reminds Timothy to, "Study to shew thyself approved unto God, a workman that needeth not to be ashamed, rightly dividing the word of truth." In order to be established by authority or given God's authoritative approval, the requirement is study. In fact, anyone who strives for the mastery in any endeavor has to be temperate in all things or exercise discipline. Therefore, to receive God's approval as one of authority or be regarded as a masterful teacher, the discipline is study.

Even though reading is necessary for study, reading itself is not studying. Study involves a detailed inspection of the subject and giving attentive consideration to it. Study also involves the application of principles; these fundamentals are based on the tenets of rightly dividing the Word of Truth. The term "rightly dividing the word" speaks to dissecting the Word and ensuring that it is taught correctly. Therefore, when we study the Word of God, we make incisions, but at the same time, we maintain a straight course. However, to keep on the right path, certain principles must be adhered to. For example, there must be an understanding of Bible language, covenants, dispensations, types, etc.

Hence, to avoid being ashamed as God's workman, the theses principles must be known and implemented when studying and dissecting the Word of God.

The chart below offers a comparative example of the differences between preaching and teaching.

TABLE 5

PREACHING	TEACHING
• Proclamation: to herald or announce something that has been done	• Explanation: to explain things about Scripture that people do not understand
• Motivation (It stirs you)	• Education (It instructs you.)
• Foundational and more random	• Progressive and systematic
• Driven more by illustrations	• Driven more by principles

A teacher has the responsibility for providing progressive and systematic instructions regarding God's purpose for humanity. While all believers are called to teach, teachers are specifically skilled in the interpretation of the Scriptures. Based on the gift of Christ, they have been given authority to teach. In using the educational system as a parallel, teachers are responsible for providing instructions according to the established curriculum. They are also tasked with guarding against false teachers whose purpose is to create disunity in the body. Hence, when it comes to the unity of the faith, teachers play a crucial role. Moreover, not only are they charged with teaching the body but also developing other teachers. Through inspiration from the Father and study, they are masterful in providing insight and understanding regarding God's Word.

CHAPTER 12

THE COLLECTIVE PURPOSE OF THE GIFTS OF CHRIST

At the beginning of this book, the fundamental question was asked: what is the purpose of the five-fold ministry gifts? In other words, as it pertains to the church, why does the Father give apostles, prophets, evangelists, pastors, and teachers? First, in answering this question, we discussed God's purpose for humanity which He predetermined before the foundation of the world. Therefore, before God created anything, He made a determination in Himself and established His purpose for us. Hence, when He created humanity, He did so with a distinct and specific purpose. Furthermore, in accordance with His purpose for us, Ephesians Chapter 1 offers a detailed outline of the components of the Father's purpose. These are referred to as spiritual blessings in Christ Jesus. Therefore, based on the components of the blessings mentioned in the chapter, we can surmise the following regarding God's purpose for humanity:

1. The Father chose us to be His sons who would share His very nature or be just like Him.
2. As members of His family, He prescribed an inheritance for us.
3. He gave us His Holy Spirit as a guarantee of our eternal inheritance until the redemption of our bodies.

In short, the Father's purpose was simply to have a family born of His nature with whom He could bestow an eternal inheritance.

Recall that when the Father established His purpose, it was for all humanity. This means it was not subjected to ethnicity, gender, social status, denominations, or any factors that serve to divide us. Therefore, His purpose is also one of unity. This is why the book of Ephesians is deliberate in its communication of God's purpose and the message of unity prior to the pronouncement of the gifts. *For it is in this atmosphere that the gifts exist.* Hence, to understand and function in the gifts of Christ, these two principles must serve as a foundation. If I purport to function in the gifts and my message creates a wall of partition between humanity or if I believe that the Father's purpose is only limited to a special group of people, then the true purpose of the gifts has evaded me. Notice that right on the threshold of listing the gifts of Christ, Ephesians 4:3-6 makes a clarion call regarding the message of unity.

3. Endeavouring to keep the unity of the Spirit in the bond of peace.
4. There is one body, and one Spirit, even as ye are called in one hope of your calling;
5. One Lord, one faith, one baptism,
6. One God and Father of all, who is above all, and through all, and in you all.

Undoubtedly, the passage echoes the message of God's singular purpose in the atmosphere of unity. Thus, after setting the prerequisite, the chapter then proceeds to discuss the direct purpose of the gifts in a meaningful way.

Significantly, not only do the gifts have a footing in unity, but they also function in a united manner. Over the last several chapters, we conducted a comprehensive review of the gifts of Christ highlighting the specific function of each one. Therefore, in continuation, the focus of this chapter is to discuss their collective responsibility relative to God's purpose for His people. When referring to the gifts of Christ and their responsibilities, they are often spoken of in isolation. Unfortunately, this perspective has contributed to the disunity, which is present in the body of Christ. However, based on God's purpose and the witness of Scripture, the gifts are given to function as a whole. They have an interdependent relationship as opposed to an independent one. The purpose of the individual gift is also better understood based on its relationship to the whole, not individually. With that said, let us once again look at Ephesians 4:11-15

11. And he gave some, apostles; and some, prophets; and some, evangelists; and some, pastors and teachers;

12. For the perfecting of the saints, for the work of the ministry, for the edifying of the body of Christ: Till we all come in the unity of the faith, and of the knowledge of the Son of God, unto a perfect man, unto the measure of the stature of the fulness of Christ:
13. That we henceforth be no more children, tossed to and fro, and carried about with every wind of doctrine, by the sleight of men, and cunning craftiness, whereby they lie in wait to deceive;
14. But speaking the truth in love, may grow up into him in all things, which is the head, even Christ:
15. From whom the whole body fitly joined together and compacted by that which every joint supplieth, according to the effectual working in the measure of every part, maketh increase of the body unto the edifying of itself in love.

When we examine Ephesians 4:11-15, the passage distinctly outlines the collective purpose of all the gifts as it pertains to the church. Hence, they are given for the following purpose:

In very plain language, the Bible outlines the purpose and mandate of the gifts of Christ. Apostles, prophets, evangelists, pastors, and teachers are given to perfect the saints, to function in the ministry, and to foster growth in the body of Christ. Please note that these three tasks are related, for it is through the perfecting of the saints that the church is edified. Simultaneously, the work of the ministry is being performed. By this point, it should be apparent that the gifts are not mere titles, even though they are distinct offices. When we consider the big picture, they all have an equally shared responsibility. Despite each gift having a specific function, they all exist and contribute to the same purpose.

God gave the ministry gifts to foster unity in the entire body and to bring His people into maturity. Therefore, if a leader's platform does not promote these principles, then his or her objective has to be called into question.

1. FOR THE PERFECTING OF THE SAINTS

In addressing the "why" from the beginning of this study, we did not take the traditional straight-lined approach. Instead, we spent a significant amount of time understanding the original purpose of the Father. Accordingly, Ephesians Chapter 1 revealed that before the foundation of the world, the Father determined humanity, in the capacity of sons, would be just like Him and possess His very nature and character. Essentially, He simply wanted to duplicate Himself through humanity. However, despite being born again and possessing His divine nature, development and training are still required to manifest the character of Christ. The principle offered in Genesis 1:11 is that every seed produces after its own kind. Therefore, when the first Adam sinned, his seed became corruptible. Consequently, when he reproduced, all humanity became products of that seed and this was reflected in our nature and character. However, through the sacrifice of the last Adam, Jesus Christ, those who believe in Him are born again of an incorruptible seed (1 Peter 1:23). Hence, we inherited the nature of the Father and are now capable of reflecting His character of righteousness and holiness. To accomplish this, nurturing is necessary; this is the responsibility of those to whom Christ bestows His gifts.

The Bible uses the term "born again" primarily to indicate the new birth. However, contained in this concept is the notion of the initial stage of being babes in Christ. Therefore, despite having the nature of the Father, just like babes in the natural require nurturing to transition into adulthood, the same process applies to spiritual babes. The nature that we have inherited from the Father, gives us the ability to be transformed into the image of Jesus Christ. Hence, 2 Corinthians 3:18 says, "But we all, with open face beholding as in a glass the glory of the Lord, are changed into the same image from glory to glory, even as by the Spirit of the Lord."

The term "glory to glory" indicates a progressive journey by which we transition from being babes in Christ to maturity. This also encompasses the transformation from being carnal to becoming spiritual and exhibiting the character of Christ. However, to assist in accomplishing this objective, the Father has instituted what we will call "perfecters." Naturally, babies are not left to fend for themselves. Likewise, they should not be deserted spiritually. Similar to parents or guardians who are responsible for nurturing babies to maturity, the Father has given apostles, prophets, evangelists, pastors, and teachers to perform the same task. This is what Ephesians 4:13 refers to as, "the perfecting of the saints."

To be clear, the perfecting of the saints requires a collaborative effort of all the gifts and is not the responsibility of just one gift. Therefore, perfecting the saints is not the sole function of the pastor as each of the gifts has a part to play in ensuring believers are developed and come into maturity. Based on the identifiable roles we discussed for the gifts of Christ, they each adequately contribute to the perfecting of the saints. This also includes training and developing others who have been bestowed the gifts. Hence, they also assist in activating the gifts in other believers.

The word "perfecting" in the passage is the Greek word *katartismos*, which means the following:

- To make complete
- To strengthen
- To completely furnish or equip
- To make someone what he or she ought to be

First, the word "perfecting" is a present participle, which means that the verb is continuous. Therefore, the perfecting of the saints refers to a continuous action and responsibility. As long as those who have been bestowed the gift of Christ function in the ministry, they are responsible for perfecting the saints. Additionally, not only is the task continuous, but the word "perfecting" is also used to signify that there is a process involved, as we will soon discuss.

Based on the above definitions, apostles, prophets, evangelists, pastors, and teachers are appointed to completely furnish the church, so it becomes what the Father has ordained it to be. In essence, they are also spiritual mentors charged with the development and maturity of the sons of God so that they manifest His character. In placing emphasis on the definition "to completely furnish or equip," let us look at a practical example. On this note, Romans 1:20 provides the principle that we understand the invisible or spiritual things by examining natural or earthly things.

To understand what it means to completely furnish believers, let us look at a natural example of outfitting a house. When a home is new, at first, it contains no furniture. Perhaps the first item added is the bed, followed by a stove, then a refrigerator or a television. After the essentials are put in place, then maybe more cosmetic items are added such as a vase, an area rug, or a piano. Through this exercise, elements are strategically added over the course of time until the house is completely furnished. Similarly, those conferred with the gifts of Christ are charged with furnishing believers to ensure they are complete. Have you ever visited a house that has existed for a while, yet, a substantial amount of furniture is absent? Admittedly, you get the feeling that something is missing or that the house is lacking essential elements. Certainly, the paint is well-coordinated, and it looks good; the tiles have a brilliant shine and the light fixtures are true attention grabbers. However, without furniture, the feeling of emptiness still exists. Therefore, based on the analogy, the "perfecters" are tasked with providing believers with the necessary furniture in order to be complete. This is the same as being mature.

To describe the different stages of our development, Scripture uses words such as "babes" and those who are mature or of full age. Again, through figurative language, we are presented with a natural illustration to explain a spiritual operation. Therefore, similar to the natural development involved in transitioning from being a baby to coming into maturity, this experience pertains to the development of believers. For example, 1 Peter 2:2 says, "As newborn babes, desire the sincere milk of the word that ye may grow thereby." In this instance, new converts are referred to as babes because they have similar characteristics and tendencies to that of babies. On the other hand, Hebrews 5:13 says, "But strong meat belongeth to them that are of full age, even those who by reason of use have their senses exercised to discern both good and evil." In contrast to babes, some believers are of full age or mature.

Therefore, just as adults in the natural have a different disposition from babies, those who are mature spiritually, also have different characteristics and tendencies from babes in Christ.

The development of the sons of God is the responsibility of those who have been bestowed the gift of Christ. Hence, the perfecting of the saints means that as leaders, they aid believers in the transitioning from being babies to coming into maturity. They are therefore not babysitters but rather developers. This is obviously a tremendous responsibility and requires enormous effort. As mentioned, not only is this task continuous but it is also a process. In this vein, the diagram below illustrates that process.

EXHIBIT 9

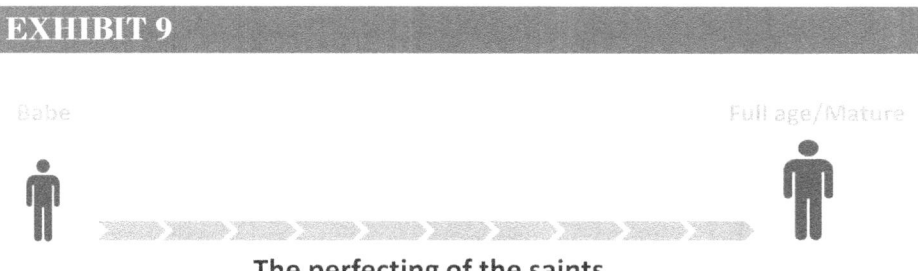

The perfecting of the saints

Leaders are responsible for furnishing the saints and ensuring they are complete, but exactly how is this accomplished? Notice in both 1 Peter 2:2 and Hebrews 5:13, the Word of God is the consistent tool used in the development of believers. In this regard 2 Timothy 3:16-17 says,

> 16. All Scripture is given by inspiration of God, and is profitable for doctrine, for reproof, for correction, for instruction in righteousness:
> 17. That the man of God may be perfect, thoroughly furnished unto all good works.

The instrument for the development of the sons of God is the Word of God. As a whole, the Word of God is beneficial for doctrine, reproof, correction, and instruction in righteousness. When these four constituents of the Word of God are used effectively, it results in having believers who are perfect, thoroughly furnished unto all good works. In other words, they are complete and equipped, which also speaks of being mature or of full age. To understand the operation involved, let us first look at the definition of each component of the Word of God. After discussing the definitions, we will then examine how they are interrelated. See the diagram below.

a) **Doctrine**: *Merriam-Webster's Dictionary* defines doctrine as a principle or position. It is a body of principles in a branch of knowledge or a set of beliefs. Moreover, it is a system of teachings related to a particular subject. As it pertains to the Word of God, it is the basis for righteous instruction. Hence, doctrine serves as a foundation for the other three constituents of the Word of God.

b) **Reproof**: In simple terms, the word "reproof" means conviction or rebuke. In our daily lives, the Word of God or established doctrine is the standard by which we measure our behavior. Therefore, righteous doctrine is used to portray the image or character of Jesus Christ. Consequently, when I hear the Word and see the character of Christ, the Word then convicts or reproves me based on the shortcomings in my life. It is the same as looking into a mirror. However, if the doctrine is a mixture of flesh and Spirit and makes allowances for carnal behavior then the impact of the reproof is minimal or non-existent. This is why it is essential to have the correct doctrine.

c) **Correction**: According to *Merriam-Webster's Dictionary*, correction is defined as the act of making something (such as an error or a bad condition) accurate or better. Correction may involve rebuke or punishment, but its main purpose is the improvement of life or character. It is not enough for the Word of God to simply reveal our faults but there has to be the ability to improve our state and consequently set things right in our lives.

d) **Instruction in Righteousness**: This pertains to teaching that intends to increase virtue in believers. It involves chastisement or nurturing, which is designed to produce the fruit of righteousness (Hebrews 12:11).

EXHIBIT 10: ALL SCRIPTURE

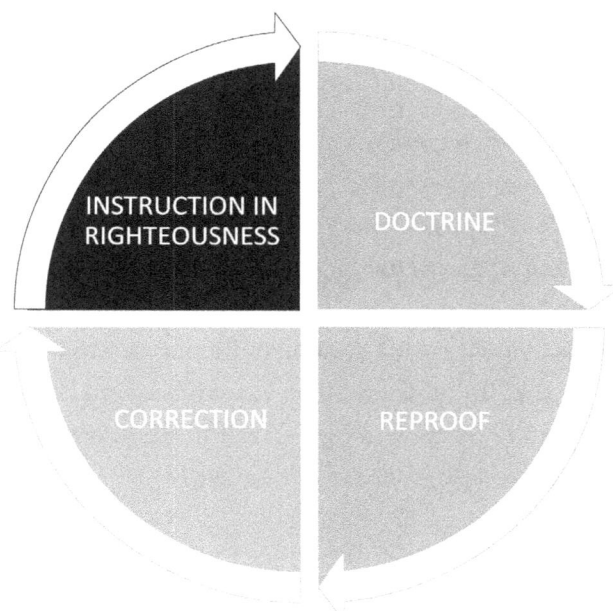

Any teaching designed to bring maturity to the sons of God must include all four of these components. Furthermore, based on the definitions, it should be apparent that these four constituents of the Word of God are interrelated and represent a continuous flow in the development of believers. Each contributes to the next one and the result is believers who through submission to the Word are thoroughly furnished and complete. Again, I reiterate the importance of sound doctrine as this represents the foundation or the starting point. It is the principle that forms the basis of what is taught and believed. Therefore, if the doctrine is incorrect or flawed, the other three components are subsequently ineffective. Hence, one of the reasons so many believers are not completely furnished or mature is because of erroneous doctrine. For example, based on a misinterpretation of Romans Chapter 7, the doctrine of the dual nature is prevalent in the church. In short, this doctrine advocates that despite being born again, the sin nature still exists in believers. Thus, it promotes that in addition to having the nature of God, sons of God still have the nature of sin. However, based on the principles of rightly dividing the Word of God and the proper perspective of Scripture, we know this doctrine to be incorrect. Nevertheless, when this is taught, instead of being reproved when we sin, excuses are made such as, "All have sinned and come short of the glory of God" or "There is none righteous, no not one." Of note, both these scriptures are often quoted out of context and have nothing to do with our present condition as believers.

Unfortunately, this doctrine makes allowances for sin; therefore, rather than reproof, a cloak for sin is provided instead. For an accurate perspective on Romans Chapter 7 and these verses, please refer to my book, *The Volume of the Book: Insights into Rightly Dividing the Word of Truth*. In short, in Romans Chapter 7, Paul provides an account of his life *prior to salvation*. How do we know this? This is evident by the statement he makes in Romans 7:14, "I am carnal, sold under sin." To be clear, a believer can be carnal but not sold under sin. The word "carnal" refers to living after the flesh; however, "sold under sin" speaks of being in captivity to sin or a slave to sin.

Recall that redemption refers to the price paid to ransom humanity from the power that held us captive. Therefore, through Christ's death, He paid the price to redeem us from the captivity of sin. Furthermore, to reinforce this position, Romans 6:14 says that sin shall not have dominion over us. Wherefore, even though we may engage in carnal behavior, a believer cannot be sold under sin or be under the dominion of sin. Moreover, based on the context of the chapter, the reference points specifically to the Law (Romans 7:14). Hence, the experience spoken of in Romans Chapter 7 reveals Paul's dependency on the Law as an instrument of righteousness. In this regard, seeing that the Law could not produce righteousness, there was constant frustration and a feeling of wretchedness.

Now that we have a proper understanding of the context of the chapter, the doctrine changes. Additionally, excuses for not submitting to the righteousness of God are eliminated. Furthermore, this is why those charged with the responsibility of perfecting the saints must be the purveyors of sound doctrine. For without it, there can be no true development of the sons of God. Through the redemption of Christ, the Father took care of the nature problem. However, we still have a nurture problem; that's why He gave "perfecters." One of the main issues in the body is that we are confusing nature with nurture; however, we will discuss this in the next chapter.

When sound doctrine based on the righteousness of God is promoted by leaders, reproof is possible. In support of the definition offered earlier, reproof can be further defined as an inward working in the heart that occurs when I am made aware of God's righteous standards. Consequently, based on the circumstances of my life, which are not in harmony with God's Word, the Holy Spirit convicts me. The conviction is based on the fact that I have not attained the mark that I am capable of achieving or what righteousness demands.

In short, reproof is a product of hearing the righteousness of God's Word and having a pure heart with a desire to be transformed into the image of Christ. It is a driving force, which propels you to fulfill your righteous purpose and manifest the character of Christ. According to the image that is presented before me, I see my potential and press toward that mark. Based on the image of Christ illustrated by the Word of God as if looking into a mirror, I am convinced I can conform to the very image (2 Corinthians 3:18). On the contrary, if the doctrine I receive persuades me that the righteous standard is unattainable, then there is little to no conviction. This is what 1 Corinthians 12:3 refers to as the mind being corrupted from the simplicity of Christ. Consequently, my true potential is diminished, and I replace it with excuses of why I cannot be transformed into the character of Christ. In essence, I develop a comfort zone. Therefore, having proper doctrine and understanding how maturity occurs is essential. If the doctrine taught caters to the flesh, there is no conviction and by extension, no correction.

In practical terms, though it may seem ambiguous at times, the objective of the penal system has a corrective function. Indeed, punishment is a component of correction, but the predominant intent is the improvement of character and behavior. For the most part, when an individual is convicted of wrongdoing, the primary purpose of the conviction is to bring correction to the behavior. For example, the law of the land creates an image of what is expected from its citizens. It produces a model of conformity. However, when the standard is disregarded or violated, correction is warranted.

If I am persuaded I did nothing wrong or I could never attain the standard outlined in the law, then correction is a moot point. Similarly, in accordance with the doctrine or the Word that I receive, if the image of Christ is perceived as unattainable, then there is no conviction to correct my behavior. Simply put, if I am persuaded that my very nature prohibits me from waking in righteousness, there is no need for correction. When the Holy Spirit convicts us, it is to correct our behavior. When this occurs, we have a decision to make. Do we want to hold on to this behavior because it pleases our flesh, or do we submit to the righteousness of God? This is obviously a difficult process involving pain and a myriad of emotions. However, if we have a heart after God, we will submit to Him, knowing that this process is designed to make us completely furnished. As a point of reference, this entire operation is outlined in Hebrews 12:5-11 and is described as the chastening of the Lord. Chastening involves correction and discipline designed to amend behaviour, thereby producing the peaceable fruit of righteousness in the sons of God.

> 5. And ye have forgotten the exhortation which speaketh unto you as unto children, My son, despise not thou the chastening of the Lord, nor faint when thou art rebuked of him:
> 6. For whom the Lord loveth he chasteneth, and scourgeth every son whom he receiveth.
> 7. If ye endure chastening, God dealeth with you as with sons; for what son is he whom the father chasteneth not?
> 8. But if ye be without chastisement, whereof all are partakers, then are ye bastards, and not sons.
> 9. Furthermore we have had fathers of our flesh which corrected us, and we gave them reverence: shall we not much rather be in subjection unto the Father of spirits, and live?
> 10. For they verily for a few days chastened us after their own pleasure; but he for our profit, that we might be partakers of his holiness.
> 11. Now no chastening for the present seemeth to be joyous, but grievous: nevertheless afterward it yieldeth the peaceable fruit of righteousness unto them which are exercised thereby. (Hebrews 12:5-11)

According to Hebrews Chapter 12, the Lord uses chastening as a tool to bring His sons into maturity or manifest the character of Christ. As a Father, it is a manifestation of His love toward us; therefore, it is not something to be despised or regarded lightly. Notice that the absence or the rejection of chastisement results in an individual being classified as a bastard, not a son.

In today's society, the word "bastard" certainly has a negative connotation; however, Scripture uses it to create a contrast to a son. Therefore, a bastard is an antithesis of what a son represents. In short, a bastard is defined as someone who is illegitimate and consequently does not share in the Father's inheritance. Furthermore, based on the analogy of Isaac and Ishmael offered in Galatians Chapter four, bastards are also categorized as being associated with the flesh. Hence, being a bastard also refers to one who lives after the flesh. Therefore, if I reject the correction or chastisement of the Lord, choosing rather the works of the flesh, then I have taken on the mantle of a bastard, even though I am born again.

As apostles, prophets, evangelists, pastors, and teachers charged with the responsibility of perfecting the saints, the doctrine that is taught must be in accordance with this objective. It must be of a perfecting nature. However, many leaders seem to be more occupied with doctrines that appeal to the flesh and the attainment of earthly possessions. This is why the faith and prosperity doctrine is one of the more destructive messages allowed to enter the church. With this teaching, the priority is no longer the perfection of the saints but the pursuit of material things. This has resulted in a generation of bastards consumed with the lust of the eyes, the lust of the flesh, and the pride of life. Simple and plain, doctrine matters!

Additionally, it is not good enough just to have teaching void of error, but the doctrine must also be of the right substance. Keep in mind that the mantle placed on the five-fold ministry is the perfection of the saints; therefore, the doctrine has to contain ingredients that foster or promote growth. Similar to natural foods that are essential for growth and development at the various stages of our lives, there are also spiritual foods designed for the same purpose. For example, in characterizing the development substance of various doctrines, the Bible figuratively uses terms such as milk, meat, and strong meat. To be clear, the differences between these three food groups are not depicted by so-called "levels of revelation" but by their developmental properties. Let us look at these three categories in detail and how they impact growth in believers. These are the three classifications of the Word of God used in the perfecting of the saints.

A. MILK

Recall that 1 Peter 2:1 says, "As newborn babes, desire the sincere milk of the word, that ye may grow thereby." Hence, the primary purpose of milk is that it facilitates growth. Just as it is intended for the development of babies in the natural, milk doctrine accomplishes the same objective in spiritual babies. From a natural perspective, milk is fundamental because it contains calcium, fat, and vitamins essential for building strong bones and teeth. Therefore, based on these qualities, it is vital for human growth and development. Furthermore, with milk being in liquid form, it is easier to digest and absorb compared to more solid foods. Thus, it is easy to consume, and it does not put tremendous demands on the body while still facilitating growth. Consequently, in a parallel concept, the sincere or pure milk of the Word accomplishes the same thing in spiritual babies. It is basic, easy to absorb, and not that demanding.

In the church, sometimes there is a debate concerning which doctrines qualify as milk. Along these lines, the church often confuses the delivery of the Word with its substance. For if I preach a milk message with great excitement, this does not change the content that was presented. On the other hand, if I teach a meat doctrine without much fanfare, by comparison, the perspective may be different. While both methods and message have their appropriate place, we have to be able to distinguish the difference. Nevertheless, as a principle, *Scripture always interprets Scripture*; therefore, the Bible states plainly what is considered to be milk doctrine. In its effort to explain elementary doctrine, Hebrews 5:12 uses the phrase, "first principles of the oracles of God" as a substitute for milk doctrine. Similarly, in emphasizing the same concept, Hebrews 6:1-3 uses the term "principles of the doctrine of Christ." However, Hebrews Chapter 6 takes the discussion a step further and explains the six specific teachings that qualify as milk doctrine.

1. Therefore leaving the principles of the doctrine of Christ, let us go on unto perfection; not laying again the foundation of repentance from dead works, and of faith toward God,
2. Of the doctrine of baptisms, and of laying on of hands, and of resurrection of the dead, and of eternal judgment.
3. And this will we do, if God permit. (Hebrews 6:1-3)

Based on the scriptural definition, the milk doctrine includes the following six tenets. They are the primary and fundamental principles of the Word of God.

- Repentance from dead works
- Faith toward God
- The doctrine of baptisms
- The laying on of hands
- The resurrection of the dead
- Eternal judgment

As the beginning principles of the oracles of God, these teachings are indeed foundational and extremely beneficial. However, they are the equivalent of elementary or primary level education. Notice that Hebrews 5:13 says, "For every one that useth milk is unskilful in the word of righteousness: for he is a babe." Therefore, even though milk facilitates growth, those that use it are unskillful or have no experience in the Word of righteousness. In other words, they have not been trained to discern the operation of both good and evil in their lives or the lives of others. They are not masters when it comes to the application of righteousness. Hence, Hebrews 6:1 says that to go onto perfection or maturity, it is necessary to leave these teachings because they represent the beginning stage. However, because they cannot be abandoned altogether, Hebrews 6:3 says we can revisit these teachings if God permits. To set the record straight, Hebrews Chapter 6 uses such strong language because the conversation was not addressed to babies. On the contrary, it was directed to those who should have been mature, but they wanted to hold onto milk and remain babes. As we will discover during our discussion of the meat doctrine, believers choose to hold onto milk because meat demands growth and maturity. Whereas milk provides a comfort zone for carnal behavior, meat demands transformation.

In the aggregate, it is unfortunate that these six tenets represent the predominant message of many churches today. In particular, many ministries have been established on the doctrine of faith toward God and the laying on of hands. This means not only is there a steady flow of the milk doctrine in the body of Christ but also a good number of glorified babysitters who think they are perfecting God's people. Again, I reiterate that even though milk is essential, it does not have the nutrients to create adults. Furthermore, it is impossible to use the milk of the Word to develop masters who are skillful in the Word of God.

B. MEAT

In continuing with our natural illustration, just how a baby is eventually weaned off milk by introducing more solid foods into their diets, so it is with spiritual development. However, this process is more of a transition from milk to other foods, as opposed to the sudden abandonment of milk. For example, in a baby's diet, complementary foods such as fruits and vegetables are introduced in addition to milk for a period of time. Therefore, during this transition period, it makes more solid foods easier to accept. Furthermore, as time progresses, for further development to occur, more substantial food like meat is eventually inserted into the diet. Based on its natural properties, meat is a good source of protein, zinc, potassium, magnesium, iron, fatty acids, vitamin A and B-Complex, etc. Hence, with these characteristics, meat is essential for accomplishing the ideal growth and development of our bodies. This statement is not only true from a natural perspective but also a spiritual one. Recall in Paul's rebuke of the Corinthian church, he said he fed them with milk and not meat because they were not able to bear it. Let us look at 1 Corinthians 3:1-4:

1. And I, brethren, could not speak unto you as unto spiritual, but as unto carnal, even as unto babes in Christ.
2. I have fed you with milk, and not with meat: for hitherto ye were not able to bear it, neither yet now are ye able.
3. For ye are yet carnal: for whereas there is among you envying, and strife, and divisions, are ye not carnal, and walk as men?
4. For while one saith, I am of Paul; and another, I am of Apollos; are ye not carnal?

First, Paul fed the church milk instead of meat because of where they were collectively in their development stage. Very plainly, he identified them as carnal. Moreover, because they lived according to the flesh, they resembled babes in Christ. Additionally, the passage also says that he gave them milk because they were not able to bear the meat doctrine. This means they could not endure or stomach it. Just as a baby cannot bear meat, neither could they. Meat is designed not only for those that are spiritual or mature, but it is also used to transition to maturity. In short, Paul is saying with an air of disappointment that he wanted to move them forward, but their disposition and behavior forced him to address them as babies.

The passage also creates a contrast between what it means to be spiritual compared to carnal conduct. Notice that the church was engaged in carnal behavior. Hence, based on the condition of their hearts, the substance of his doctrine was according to their spiritual location. According to 1 Corinthians 1:3, they were engaged in envy, strife, and division that created walls and disunity in the church. I reiterate that Paul gave them milk instead of meat because they could not bear it. Furthermore, they could not bear the meat of the Word because they were carnal. What is it about the meat of the Word and its impact on carnal behavior?

In contrast to the milk of the Word, the meat of the Word is defined as teaching, which addresses carnal behavior to develop righteous character. Just as meat with its nutritional characteristics is used to develop us naturally, the meat of the Word has the nutrients necessary for spiritual maturity. Paul as an apostle with the responsibility of the perfecting of the saints, despite chiding the church, was still concerned about their development. Therefore, after he highlighted their state, he also offered teaching to deliver them from their carnal behavior. In referring to one of the components of the Word of God, he then reproved or rebuked them. This was designed to convict them of their behavior. Paul did not leave them in the same state they were in. In following the format discussed earlier, after rebuking them, the next step was to correct them in order to change their carnal behavior.

To change their carnal perspective, Paul provided two examples that demonstrate the principles of ministry. With the church engaged in division as a result of envy and strife, the teachings were designed to convey the message of unity and ministerial responsibility. Moreover, by promoting the message of unity in the body, he was also eliminating the concept of division.

In addressing the matter, Paul starts with the question, "Who then is Paul, and who is Apollos but ministers by whom ye believed?" In today's religious environment of titles and names, this question is as fitting now as it was then. Oftentimes, too much emphasis is placed on ministers to the point that the Lord Himself is overshadowed. However, by asking such a fundamental question, he was taking the focus off Apollos and himself and directing it to the Father where it rightly belongs. Furthermore, contained within the two illustrations was also an example of the meat of the Word.

In the first analogy, Paul uses the agricultural example of a vineyard to describe the work of the ministry. He says in this vineyard, "I have planted, Apollos watered; but God gave the increase." By this statement, he was identifying several things. First, he was figuratively explaining the roles of both he and Apollos as it pertains to their ministry functions. With the statement, "I have planted," he was indicating that he did the initial work. Moreover, with the phrase, "Apollos watered," this means that Apollos came behind and contributed to the work. However, regardless of their efforts, Paul states plainly that "God gave the increase." In other words, despite their activities, it is the Father who is ultimately responsible for the development of His people.

The word "increase" is the Greek word *auxano*, which means to cause to grow and to become greater. Not only does the example demonstrate the harmony and unity of those who labor in the gospel, but it also identifies the Father as the One who produces growth and maturity in His sons. Therefore, no matter how effective we think we are when it comes to the perfecting of God's people, He is the One who is truly responsible. Furthermore, in addressing their carnal disposition and the concept of division in the church, Paul says plainly in 1 Corinthians 3:8, "Now he that planteth and he that watereth are one."

In the second illustration, Paul offers a construction example and compares the church to a building. Therefore, as an apostle, and in accordance with the analogy, he appropriately describes himself as a wise master builder. This means that ministers of the gospel involved in the perfecting of the saints are also regarded as builders. Just as an actual building has a foundation, Paul indicates that through his preaching, the foundation he laid was Jesus Christ. In other words, he did the fundamental work. Subsequently, others like

Apollos came behind and built on the foundation that was laid. His caution, however, was for them to take heed of how they built on the foundation.

With ministers having the mantle of builders, Paul is actually saying to be careful of the materials used in building the lives of God's people. Hence, the material used in the construction of believers must be of a certain substance. Along these lines, the passage then offers two categories of building materials. The first group consists of gold, silver, and precious stones while the second one includes wood, hay, and stubble. Noticeably, there is a contrast between the two categories of building materials.

In determining the nature of the materials used, the passage says that the type of work will be revealed by fire. Therefore, the building materials used by ministers in the construction or the perfecting of believers will be manifested by fire. In Scripture, fire is often used figuratively to depict the trials that come to try us (1 Peter 4:12) in order to manifest the character of Christ. Hence, fire or the trials we face are God's mechanism to perfect us. By comparison, fire refines gold, silver, and precious stone but consumes wood, hay, and stubble. Therefore, as ministers responsible for perfecting God's people, it is imperative to use materials that will stand during the fiery trials of our lives. Doctrine must be of the right substance to deal with the many issues of life. This is a perfect illustration of the effect of the meat doctrine. Furthermore, in his continuance of offering the meat doctrine, the apostle Paul in the subsequent chapters addresses behaviors in the church such as pride (1 Corinthians 4), fornication in the church (1 Corinthians 5) and believers taking each other to court (1 Corinthians 6).

C. STRONG MEAT

First, we discussed the milk of the Word, which was then followed by the meat of the Word. Our focus now turns to the third category of spiritual food mentioned in Scripture which is strong meat. Specifically, the term "strong meat" is mentioned in Hebrews 5:12-14.

12. For when for the time ye ought to be teachers, ye have need that one teach you again which be the first principles of the oracles of God; and are become such as have need of milk, and not of strong meat.
13. For every one that useth milk is unskilful in the word of righteousness: for he is a babe.
14. But strong meat belongeth to them that are of full age, even those who by reason of use have their senses exercised to discern both good and evil.

In describing the specific type of meat, the above passage explicitly uses the adjective "strong," which makes it different from the meat of the Word mentioned in 1 Corinthians Chapter 3. The word "strong" is the Greek word *stereos*, which means sure, firm, and immovable. Based on the context of the passage, it signifies doctrine for those that are already mature. Whereas the meat of the Word is intended to facilitate our growth and development, the strong meat of the Word is designed for those who are considered spiritual adults or mature. However, in discussing the subject thoroughly, let us consider the context of the entire passage.

Hebrews 5:12 begins with the phrase, "For when for the time ye ought to be teachers." Consistent with its usage throughout this book, the word "teacher" is the Greek word *didaskolas*, which as we have discovered speaks of someone who is a master or has authority based on his or her qualification. It also refers to someone who is a scholar and skilled in the interpretation of Scripture. Therefore, it does not point to novices but those who are mature and seasoned in the things of God. In this vein, Hebrews 5:12 offers a rebuke to those who were expected to be mature believers because of their time in the church but were not. Even though there is no specific timeframe in which an individual transitions spiritually from being a baby to maturity, there are still appropriate expectations. These same projections apply to natural development, for after a prescribed number of years, maturity is also expected. Hence, Hebrews 5:12 is addressing those who, based on a reasonable period of time, should have been masters. Yet, they needed to once again be taught the first principles of the oracles of God. Notice that the passage says they need to be taught "again" the first principles of the oracles of God. This indicates that they were already

The Five-Fold Ministry Gifts

taught the milk of the Word. However, instead of progressing, they regressed. Rather than a diet of strong meat, they once again required milk.

In making the distinction between milk and the strong meat of the Word, the passage says that everyone who uses milk is unskillful in the Word of righteousness. The word "unskillful" speaks to the fact that babes have no experience when it comes to the Word of God. This goes beyond just having information; it extends to learning by experience or action. Therefore, someone becomes skillful in the Word of Righteousness by the application and manifestation of the Word of God in their lives. This comes about through testing. Hence, as a result of enduring temptation, the Word becomes flesh and people behold our glory, which is the glory of the Father. This position of being a babe and having no experience in the Word of Righteousness is in stark contrast to a teacher who is a scholar and skillful in the scriptures. Of note, this skillfulness also transcends simply having an abundance of knowledge or information regarding the scriptures. Instead, it refers to those who are mature or full-grown and through using the strong meat of the Word have exercised their senses to discern both good and evil. As mentioned previously, this means those who are mature have been trained to discern the operation of both good and evil, not only in their lives but also in the lives of others. Strong meat causes us to be proficient in understanding the circumstances and situations in our lives. Hence, this creates those who are masters in the application of the Word of Righteousness in their lives. The chart below illustrates the three scriptural food substances and their impact.

EXHIBIT 11

The perfecting of the saints

As a noteworthy point, those who have responsibility for the perfecting of the saints must be well-versed in all facets of the Word of God. This means they should be skilled in the milk of the Word, the meat of the Word, and also the strong meat of the Word. If leaders are only proficient in the milk of the Word, there will be a deficiency in the effectiveness of their ministries. Furthermore, this shortcoming will be reflected in the lives of the people they have been given the responsibility to develop. Therefore, as a result of only being accomplished providers of milk, not only have they relegated themselves to the position of babysitters, but they also hinder the development of those who should have been perfected. On the other hand, if they only concentrate on the meat or strong meat of the Word, this means they have no regard for the proper development process. Can you imagine giving an infant calculus instead of the fundamental building blocks of simple math? This is not practical in the natural or spiritual.

Moreover, being well-rounded in all aspects of the Word of God is essential because not everyone is at the same location on this spiritual journey. According to the principles of Scripture, you can tell where people are based on the activities they engage in or their behaviors. Recall that Paul, in addressing the Corinthian church, said in 1 Corinthians Chapter 3 that he gave them milk because they were not able to bear meat. Therefore, based on discernment and identification of behavior, the appropriate substance can be fashioned to address God's people. Hence, leaders must know which food source is appropriate for the audience they are addressing. In reiterating the point expressed earlier, certainly, you do not want to sit in front of babies and offer them meat, for they will not be able to bear it and may take offence. Similarly, you do not feed milk to a group of adults because it is not designed for them.

2. FOR THE WORK OF THE MINISTRY

Apostles, prophets, evangelists, pastors, and teachers are also given for the work of the ministry. However, before we can earnestly discuss the work of the ministry, we must first have a proper perspective on what the ministry is. First, with the definite article "the" in front of the word "ministry," this points to a specific single entity. Hence, Ephesians 4:13 is referring distinctly to the ministry of Jesus Christ. In this regard, those who have been bestowed the gift of Christ, are all under single employment and purpose. With that said, there is only **one** ministry. Indeed, some use their names to headline what the Lord has called them to, but there is still only one ministry. Therefore, in the context of this particular responsibility, when Scripture uses the term "the ministry," it points to the collective and unified work the Lord has called the church to do. Let us look at several other scriptures, which speak to the one ministry concept.

> Giving no offence in anything, that *the ministry* be not blamed. (1 Corinthians 6:3)
>
> And say to Archippus, Take heed to *the ministry* which thou hast received in the Lord, that thou fulfil it. (Colossians 4:17)
>
> And I thank Christ Jesus our Lord, who hath enabled me, for that he counted me faithful, putting me into *the ministry*. (1 Timothy 1:12)

In light of this perspective, whenever the word "ministry" is used in this book, the position is always the ministry of Jesus Christ. The word "ministry" is the Greek word *diakonia,* which means the service of those who execute the commands of others. Therefore, the service or the work of those chosen is connected to a particular purpose. They are selected to perform a specific responsibility, which is determined by the one who sends them. Hence, embedded in this definition is also the notion of a servant. As servants of God, the primary objective of those in the ministry is to fulfill the purpose or the will of the Father. Recall that Jesus said, in John 6:38, "For I came down from heaven, not to do mine own will, but the will of him that sent me." Hence, to be effective servants, we must have a full understanding of why we are sent by God. Despite the distinct function of each gift, they all serve a collective purpose: the administration of executing the Father's purpose. Additionally, contrary to popular perspectives, ministry is not just about speaking but about service.

As it pertains to the ministry of Jesus Christ, recall that Ephesians 3:11 says the eternal purpose of the Father is orchestrated through Him. In essence,

God gave Christ a ministry. Therefore, Christ's ministry, or *the ministry*, is the execution of God's purpose, which He predetermined for humanity before the world began. In His capacity as a Son, He came as an extension of the Father to execute His commands or fulfill His purpose. Furthermore, in carrying out the Father's purpose, Christ's only message was the kingdom of heaven or the kingdom of God. This is why from the onset, when He began His ministry, He established His platform with the words, "Repent: For the kingdom of heaven is at hand." Hence, this message was aligned with the restoration of humanity to both the kingdom of God and His house. Similarly, just as the Father sent Christ and gave Him a ministry, He subsequently sent His disciples and gave them a ministry. He said to His disciples in John 20:21, "Peace be unto you: as my Father hath sent me, even so send I you."

As sons of the Father who have been bestowed the gift of Christ, we also have the same mandate. Moreover, seeing that there is one purpose, then there is only one message that conveys that purpose. Just like Christ, the focus of the gifts is the kingdom of God, for this is the message of the ministry. When Christ bestows His gifts, the recipients become extensions of His ministry. The gifts, therefore, are to fulfil His ministry. Again, this addresses the question that was presented at the beginning of this book, "Why did the Father give apostles, prophets, evangelists, pastors, and teachers?" Without an understanding of why they are appointed in the first place, the scope of ministry cannot be fully appreciated. The ministry therefore serves as an encapsulation of the Father's purpose for humanity, which He determined before the foundation of the world. It is the vehicle to accomplish the Father's purpose.

The term "the ministry" represents a single entity; thus, it also conveys the message of unity. Hence, the work of the ministry encompasses not only the message regarding the Father's purpose but also a unified effort in conveying that message. In 1 Corinthians 1:13, Paul asks the question, is Christ divided? In truth, he was really asking, is His ministry not one? With the ministry of Christ being a single purpose, then those who are extensions of His ministry should also be unified in fulfilling that purpose. The focus of this responsibility transcends denominational agendas.

In this age of divisions, many leaders have a myopic approach to their responsibilities as ministers. While many of these leaders may place emphasis on a particular assembly, the gift is intended to serve the entire body. Hence, if they have the perspective that there is truly only <u>one</u> ministry, many of the challenges faced in the body of Christ would be eliminated. In the previous section, we discussed the operation of division that existed in the church at Corinth. Even though there was a consistent and single message, there were still divisions because the concept of a single ministry was missing. Let us revisit the account.

In 1 Corinthians Chapter 1, Paul revealed he had received a report from members of the house of Chloe. Based on this account, there were contentions or arguments in the Corinthian church, which arose due to divisions among the people.

> 10. Now I beseech you, brethren, by the name of our Lord Jesus Christ, that ye all speak the same thing, and that there be no divisions among you; but that ye be perfectly joined together in the same mind and in the same judgment.
> 11. For it hath been declared unto me of you, my brethren, by them which are of the house of Chloe, that there are contentions among you.
> 12. Now this I say, that every one of you saith, I am of Paul; and I of Apollos; and I of Cephas; and I of Christ.
> 13. Is Christ divided? was Paul crucified for you? or were ye baptized in the name of Paul? (1 Corinthians 1:10-13)

Within the church at Corinth, there were those who attached their spiritual loyalties to certain ministers; this created fractions in the body. Although Paul uses specific names in the passage to highlight the divisions, they could easily be substituted for the various denominations that are prevalent today. In fact, in certain circles, it is argued that the names were figuratively used to simply emphasize the point. Nevertheless, the principle of division is what is being communicated in the passage. In this regard, some said they were of Paul; others said they were of Apollos; a sect identified with Cephas (Peter), and the remainder indicated they were of Christ.

It is important to note that this division exceeded the common notion of preferences of ministers. The church was actually divided because they were subscribing to the individuals and "their ministries." They did not see the whole but the part. In essence, this represented the seeds of denominationalism and provides insight into how it occurs. Therefore, while chiding the church for the fractions that existed, Paul asked three rhetorical questions, which were designed to challenge their disposition. "Is Christ divided? Was Paul crucified for you? Or were ye baptized in the name of Paul?"

Earlier, we addressed the question concerning whether Christ was divided. The questions were framed in such a manner that the underlying intent was to provoke the message of unity. In asking these questions, not only was Paul rebuking the church, but he was also calling their fealty into question. In particular, the last two questions were designed to take the emphasis off ministers as they are not the ones to whom the church owes its allegiance. This provides insight that one of the reasons for fractions in the body of Christ is that too much regard is attributed to individual ministers. Again, with titles such as "His Grace," "His Eminence," and other similar designations, the implication is the same.

In the church today, we have created a culture where ministers are treated as celebrities and not the servants they are. However, Ephesians 4:11-16 provides the correct model and emphasizes the true purpose of ministry. The same questions Paul asked also apply to the devotion many have on a denominational level. Oftentimes, followers of the various denominations are so nearsighted their dedication to the denomination is greater than it is to the entire body of Christ.

Additionally, Paul includes that the concept of divisions is due to being carnal and a byproduct of being babes in Christ (1 Corinthians Chapter 3). Hence, in plain language, it can be concluded that division (which arises from envy and strife) is the consequence of carnal behavior and being a babe. On the other hand, unity is the expression of those who are spiritual and mature. When I speak of divisions in the body, it is in reference to the macro, as well as micro level. This encompasses divisions evident by the many denominations in Christianity and the schisms that are visible in individual churches. However, regardless of the scope, they all germinate from the seed of carnal behavior and being babes in Christ.

In consideration of the religious environment that exists today, the circumstances in Corinth seem more relevant today than they were back then. For with so many denominations within the body of Christ, there are more fractions now than ever before. One of the ways to eliminate divisions and simultaneously promote the message of unity is to offer the proper perspective regarding the roles of ministers. To this end, Paul shows in 1 Corinthians Chapter 3 that ministers are not only united in their responsibility, but they are also one. Recall that in reference to Apollos and himself, Paul says in 1 Corinthians 3:8, "Now he that planteth and he that watereth are one." Therefore, despite the various functions performed by ministers, there is an interdependent relationship as they are united in their efforts. There is truly only one cause.

Furthermore, according to 1 Corinthians Chapter 3, the enablers of divisions are fed on doctrine classified as milk, whereas those who promote unity are on a diet consisting of meat and strong meat. With that said, many denominations and fractions exist in the body of Christ today because the predominant diet is milk. As said before, this is an indicator that many leaders of the church are primarily babysitters. I know at times this language may seem hard, but it is precisely what the passage is saying. Therefore, for there to be a difference, the diet has to be changed from milk to meat and strong meat. This will produce adults in the body, thereby eliminating the concept of division; it will create a unified body.

Another reason there is so much division in the church today is that there is no adherence to the divine order outlined in Scripture. Therefore, to effectively do the work of the ministry, the structure of the church from a biblical perspective has to be adhered to. From our discussion on the importance of structure, we addressed the framework that provides clarity concerning specific functions and responsibilities. It is a tool used to promote harmony and order in any organization. Unfortunately, the opposite is also true as the absence of proper structure results in disorder, and unity is often the casualty. From our examination of the five-fold ministry gifts, it was determined that the church is apostolic as opposed to pastoral. Hence, for the church to function in unity, there must be an alignment with the ordained structure. The book of Acts provides many examples that as a result of proper structure, the Word of God increased, and the church experienced tremendous growth. Additionally, a proper organizational structure also ensures the reconciliation of doctrine contributing to the unity of the faith. This particular point will be further detailed in the next chapter during the discussion on "The Unity of the Faith."

Now that we have a better understanding of what *the ministry* is and that it conveys the message of unity, we have a more enlightened perspective of *the work of the ministry*. As we have indicated throughout this section, the work of the ministry is simply an extension and continuation of what Jesus began to do and teach. Hence, the gifts are given to accomplish that purpose. When we consider all the responsibilities of an apostle, prophet, evangelist, pastor, and teacher, we are presented with a complete picture of the work of the ministry. Again, the communication here is one of unity because, for the ministry of Jesus Christ to be effective, all the gifts must operate in a cohesive manner.

When we are deprived of any one of these gifts then as it pertains to the fullness of the ministry, the church is being shortchanged. This then results in saints who are not fully perfected, and the body of Christ is not completely edified. When Christ functioned in ministry, He was the embodiment of all the gifts. He was effective because all the gifts were in operation. Therefore, to fulfill His ministry and be effective, all the gifts must be represented in the body. When each of the gifts performs its specific task, then we have a complete picture of what the work of the ministry looks like. As indicated, the work of the ministry involves the execution of the Father's purpose, which He predetermined from before the foundation of the world.

3. FOR THE EDIFYING OF THE BODY OF CHRIST

According to Ephesians 4:12, the third responsibility Christ assigns to apostles, prophets, evangelists, pastors, and teachers is the edifying of the body of

Christ. The word "edifying" is the Greek word *oikodome,* which means the following:

- To build or the act of building up
- To promote another's growth
- To establish

As with the perfecting of the saints and the work of the ministry, this task is also the collective responsibility of those who have been bestowed the gifts of Christ. For the body of Christ to be properly edified, each of the gifts must adequately function in the body. In this regard, if any of the gifts are neglected then the edification of the church is compromised. Based on the above definitions, this assignment surpasses the basic notion of encouragement. It speaks to something of greater significance. Hence, the edifying of the body of Christ involves the operation of building and establishing the lives of God's people. Similar to the perfecting of the saints, this mandate also includes promoting the growth and development of the sons of God. Furthermore, when this occurs on an individual level, it contributes to the overall result of building and establishing the entire body of Christ. This is what Ephesians 4:16 refers to when it says "according to the effectual working in every member." This helps with the growth and maturity of the entire body.

Just like the word "perfecting," the word "edifying" is also a present participle, which means it denotes a continuous action. Additionally, it speaks of a process. What does this process entail? One of the definitions of the word "edify" is to build; given that, the concept of edifying the body of Christ is similar to the process undertaken in the construction of an actual building. In fact, in relation to the church, Paul supports this position and says in 1 Corinthians 3:9, "Ye are God's building." Moreover, as the church is described as the building of God, Paul provides a practical illustration in 1 Corinthians 3:10-11:

> 10. According to the grace of God which is given unto me, as a wise masterbuilder, I have laid the foundation, and another buildeth thereon. But let every man take heed how he buildeth thereupon.

> 11. For other foundation can no man lay than that is laid, which is Jesus Christ.

Comparing the edification of the church with the process involved in the construction of a physical building is another illustration of Scripture using a natural example to explain a spiritual operation. Therefore, just as a building has a contractor, Paul, in his capacity as an apostle, refers to himself as a wise master builder. Unlike a mason, a master builder is a chief contractor and an architect qualified in all aspects of the building's construction. Being proficient in the art of building, they also ensure that quality construction takes place. Furthermore, Paul not only emphasizes that he is a master builder but a wise master builder indicating that he is skilled or an expert when it comes to his craft.

As it pertains to the work of the ministry, wise master builders supervise the construction of God's people meticulously following the blueprint provided by the Father. In other words, they precisely follow the pattern of Scripture. This also includes ensuring that the appropriate materials are used for the edifying or building of God's people. As a point of emphasis, notice Paul says that his function as a wise master builder was based on the grace of God that was given to him. This means that wise master builders are exclusively appointed by the Father. They are not self-appointed. This is similar to what Paul said in Ephesians 3:7: "Whereof I was made a minister, according to the gift of the grace of God given unto me by the effectual working of his power."

In restating a principle mentioned earlier, "Ministers are made by God." Not everyone has been called to be a wise master builder, for it is an endowment based on God's grace. With that said, many ministers purport to be master builders in the body of Christ, but resemble masons. It is not that their contributions are insignificant; the challenge is there is a limited understanding of the scope of the work required for the construction of the entire building.

In speaking directly to the Corinthian church, Paul, in his capacity as a wise master builder, states that he is the one who laid the foundation. As it is with natural buildings, the foundation is the most important part of the structure and serves as a fixed and stabilizing force for the entire building. Moreover, the strength of the building lies in its foundation, and it keeps the edifice upright. Therefore, if the foundation is faulty, then the entire building will be compromised. Not only is the foundation of the building the most important part of the structure, but establishing it is also the most important responsibility. For this reason, this task is specifically assigned to master builders or those who have been bestowed the gift of Christ.

In his analogy of laying the foundation, Paul unequivocally states that as it pertains to the church, there is no other foundation than Jesus Christ. To be clear, the reference here to "foundation" is different from Ephesians 2:20, which says the church is built on the foundation of the apostles and prophets with Jesus Christ being the chief cornerstone. As we already have determined, this speaks of the foundational role in terms of doctrine and leadership responsibility entrusted to them concerning the church. Hence, it speaks of the responsibility bestowed on apostles and prophets and not their actual personage. Additionally, they are still subjected to the standard of the chief cornerstone and must be in alignment with Him. On the other hand, Jesus Christ, the foundation of the church, is all-encompassing and speaks to who He is.

Based on the characteristics of a natural foundation, Christ provides the same important function when it comes to the church. In Matthew 16:13, Jesus asked His disciples, "Whom do men say that I the Son of man am?" After a few responses, Peter said in Matthew 16:16, "Thou art the Christ, the Son of the living God." Upon hearing this, Jesus responded and said in Matthew 16:18, "That thou art Peter, and upon this rock I will build my church; and the gates of hell shall not prevail against it." A rock is something solid and, in most cases, stable or immovable. Obviously, the rock was not in reference to Peter himself but the solid principle of what he said. Hence, the church is built or established on Jesus being the Christ and the Son of God. What exactly does this involve?

First, the designation of Christ identifies Jesus as the long-awaited Messiah who based on the Davidic covenant would establish His kingdom and throne forever (1 Samuel 7:11-17). This points to a kingdom concept of the kingdom of God or the kingdom of heaven. Additionally, Peter also identified Jesus as the Son of God, which speaks of a Father-Son relationship and a family environment. Moreover, included in the Davidic covenant is the Lord's promise to build David a house or a family. In particular, 2 Samuel 7:16 says, "And thine house and thy kingdom shall be established for ever before thee: thy throne shall be established forever." Therefore, in Peter's statement, we have both the kingdom of God, as well as the family of God. Consequently, Jesus responded and said it is upon this solid principle (rock) that He will build His church. This is the foundation on which the church is built, and it depicts who Christ is and His purpose.

The church is built upon a kingdom and family concept, which is the agenda Jesus came to fulfill. Of note, this also represents the Father's purpose from before the foundation of the world. Therefore, the aspects of Christ's foundational role in relation to the church include who He is, His purpose, and His principal teaching. When Paul went to Corinth and laid the foundation of Jesus Christ, this is what he preached. It was the doctrine of being members of both the kingdom of God and the family of God.

In continuing the construction analogy, what is built on the foundation is also important in relation to the overall soundness of the building. Hence, as it pertains to doctrine, Paul said other builders or contractors will come behind and build on the foundation he laid. To this end, he says in 1 Corinthians 3:12-13:

> 12. Now if any man build upon this foundation gold, silver, precious stones, wood, hay, stubble;
> 13. Every man's work shall be made manifest: for the day shall declare it, because it shall be revealed by fire; and the fire shall try every man's work of what sort it is.

In keeping with the context of building the lives of God's people, Paul says the quality of the materials used by the contractor will always be revealed. In discussing this point, we will reiterate some of the details previously addressed in our exchange on the perfecting of the saints. Just as the quality of a natural building can be determined based on the type of materials used, the condition of the church can be assessed. In accordance with this, ministers in their capacity of edifying or building the church can use gold, silver, and precious stones or wood, hay, and stubble. As a builder, how do you evaluate the type of materials you are using? How do you determine the type of material used in the construction of God's people? 1 Corinthians 3:13 says it shall be revealed by fire because the purpose of fire is to prove every man's work to determine what quality it is.

As stated previously, in some instances, fire figuratively speaks of the trials that come to prove us (1 Peter 4:12). Therefore, the quality of a minister's work in building God's people is not determined by how well they can preach. It is possible to preach an animated message but the material may still be wood, hay, and stubble. In this instance, despite the excitement, the saints are only being equipped with flammable materials. Hence, the value is in the substance of the message. Based on this, the true evaluation of the doctrine is how it stands up in the times of trial and temptation.

According to the chapter, a good example of wood, hay, and stubble doctrine is teaching based on the wisdom of this world. It is a doctrine that promotes humanistic teaching and the focus is the glory of man. On the other hand, there is also doctrine which consists of gold, silver, and precious stones. Not only are these materials difficult to burn but specifically gold and silver are refined by fire. In other words, fire removes the impurities contained in them resulting in excellence. Therefore, this type of teaching involves chastening and transformation, which are designed for the perfecting or maturity of the saints. Doctrine of this quality was addressed during the discussion on the meat and strong meat of the Word. As a builder or an edifier of lives, ask yourself the all-important question, have the saints been built with the appropriate materials to withstand the fire when it comes?

After presenting the analogy of the builders and the material used in the construction of God's people, the apostle Paul then asks the church a very important question in 1 Corinthians 3:16. Keep in mind that the context of the chapter is still the work of the ministry and the materials or doctrine used in building the lives of God's people. For some reason, many believe that when this question is asked, the context of the conversation changes, but it does not.

16. Know ye not that ye are the temple of God, and that the Spirit of God dwelleth in you?
17. If any man defile the temple of God, him shall God destroy; for the temple of God is holy, which temple ye are. (1 Corinthians 3:16-17)

Based on the entire discussion and the context of the chapter, the question is asked, "Know ye not that ye are the temple of God?" This is equivalent to the phrase mentioned in 1 Corinthians 3:9, "Ye are God's building." In other words, even though the analogy of a building is being used to describe the people of God, the word "temple" is used to signify that the building is sacred and holy. Thus, the building being built is actually God's temple. Therefore, as the building is the dwelling place of God, it is no ordinary edifice and should be treated as such. Hence, by understanding the significance of a temple, the measure of the responsibility of those charged with building it increases. In the book of Exodus, those charged with building the tabernacle, which was a precursor to the temple, were specifically chosen by the Lord. In particular, the Lord said in Exodus 31:3 concerning Bazaleel, "And I have filled him with the spirit of God, in wisdom, and in understanding, and in knowledge, and in all manner of workmanship." The Lord did this because the tabernacle had to be constructed according to the pattern He showed Moses on the mountain (Exodus 25:40). In other words, the blueprint had to be followed precisely with no deviation. Similarly, with the church being God's building or temple, those charged with building the lives of His people have to be called by Him and skillful in edifying the body of Christ. Moreover, they have to precisely follow the blueprint of Scripture.

The work of the ministry is sacred. To this end, 1 Corinthians 3:17 says if any person by means of the doctrine they teach defile or pollute God's people, God shall severely punish him or her. Just as a temple can be defiled, believers can also be defiled with doctrine according to the wisdom of this world. Evidently, ministry is a huge responsibility as there are serious consequences attached to it. This is why James 3:1 says, "My brethren, be not many masters, knowing that we shall receive the greater condemnation." As we have determined, the word "master" in this context refers to those who function as teachers. Hence, those that teach shall give a stricter account because of the responsibility that comes with the office.

At the beginning of 1 Corinthians Chapter 3, Paul was faced with an atmosphere of division in relation to the work of the ministry. Therefore, the purpose of the chapter was not only to emphasize unity as it pertains to the workers of the ministry but also to highlight the measure of their responsibility in building the house of God or edifying the body of Christ. After thoroughly addressing the matter, he offers a wonderful conclusion, which is a hallmark of unity.

21. Therefore let no man glory in men. For all things are yours;
22. Whether Paul, or Apollos, or Cephas, or the world, or life, or death, or things present, or things to come; all are yours;
23. And ye are Christ's; and Christ is God's. (1 Corinthians 3:21-23)

Despite the individual functions of those who have been bestowed the gifts of Christ, their collective responsibilities are far more important. In the words of Aristotle, "The whole is greater than the sum of its parts." Therefore, when the individual gifts work together and in unison, then the purpose of the Father can be realized. Based on Ephesians 4:12, the gifts are given for the perfecting of the saints, the work of the ministry, and the edifying of the body of Christ. This involves bringing the sons of God into maturity, in unity continuing the work that Jesus started, and building the lives of God's people.

Being restored to the Father's house and His kingdom is only the initial step. Even though restoration is significant, that is not the end of the journey for the sons of God. Now that we are sons of His house and citizens of His kingdom, we have to be perfected or brought into maturity. Being a son is not something we are accustomed to; in fact, it is foreign to us. Therefore, training and development are necessary to manifest the character of our Father. Fortunately, He gave us His Son so we could bear witness of His character and also see how sons ought to behave. By the same token, Jesus also serves as the image to which we should transform.

CHAPTER 13

THE UNITY OF THE FAITH AND MATURITY BASED ON THE STANDARD OF CHRIST'S FULLNESS

Whenever assignments or job responsibilities are given out, objectives are often attached to them. However, to know if the objectives are being met, they have to be quantified or be measurable. For example, if you are appointed as a sales manager for an organization and the mandate is to increase sales, there have to be specific targets in order to evaluate your success. Similarly, in bestowing the gifts of Christ, the Lord not only stated the objectives, but He also attached the specific measurements to define the goal.

> 11. And he gave some, apostles; and some, prophets; and some, evangelists; and some, pastors and teachers;
> 12. For the perfecting of the saints, for the work of the ministry, for the edifying of the body of Christ:
> 13. Till we all come in the unity of the faith, and of the knowledge of the Son of God, unto a perfect man, unto the measure of the stature of the fulness of Christ (Ephesians 4:11-13)

When we closely examine the above passage, it is evident that the Lord is systematic in His intent for bestowing the gifts. In fact, the passage reveals a progressive and organized format concerning their purpose. First, in assigning apostles, prophets, evangelists, pastors, and teachers to the church, the Lord gives each a specific function. However, regardless of the precise function that each gift has, they all share three collective objectives. As stated in the previous chapter, they are for:

- The perfecting of the saints
- The work of the ministry
- The edifying of the body of Christ

Furthermore, both the gifts and these three objectives are all relevant until two particular targets or goals have been achieved. They serve as established indicators to determine if the objectives have been met. They are:

- Until the body of Christ comes into the unity of the faith
- Until a level of maturity measuring that of Jesus Christ's fullness is attained

The Amplified Bible provides a wonderful rendition of the two goals.

Until we all reach oneness in the faith and in the knowledge of the Son of God, [growing spiritually] to become a mature believer, reaching to the measure of the fullness of Christ [manifesting His spiritual completeness and exercising our spiritual gifts in unity]. (Ephesians 4:13)

Based on the two goals, it is evident a focused perspective surrounds the purpose of the gifts. The diagram below illustrates the progression.

EXHIBIT 12

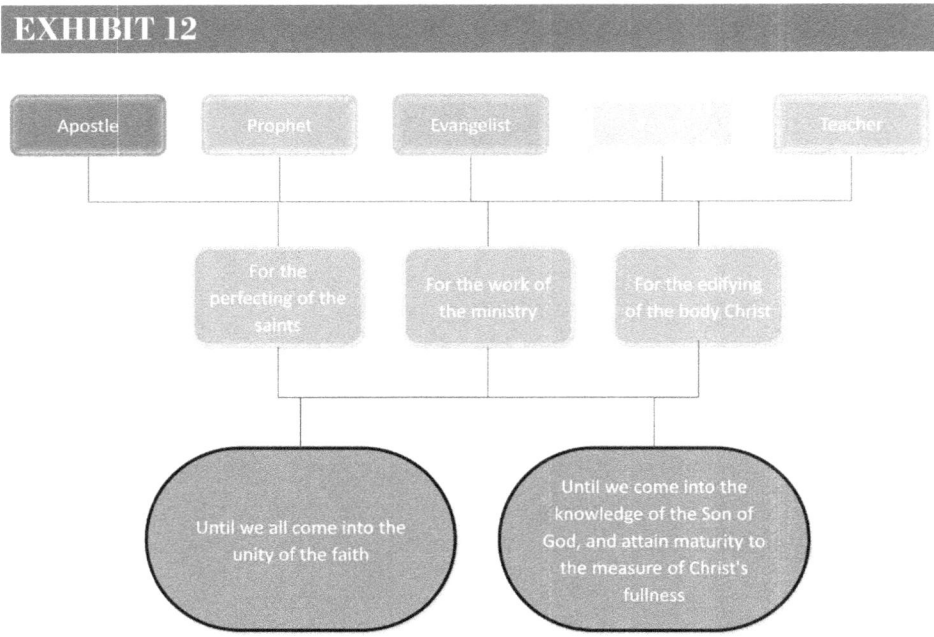

In many circles, the role of the apostle and to a certain extent, that of the prophet, are considered obsolete. They are of the opinion that these gifts no longer exist. However, based on the principle applied throughout this study, the Bible is the final authority on any subject matter. Hence, for any persuasion to be valid, it must be able to stand the test of all Scripture. In part, this diminished perspective is due to a lack of truly understanding the fundamental roles of the offices in relation to the body of Christ. Indeed, apostles and prophets were responsible for writing the scriptures; however, that was not their only function. Having discussed their responsibilities in detail earlier in this book, hopefully, that opinion has been modified.

Notice the passage says specifically that all the gifts are given until two targets have been realized. Therefore, the only way we can conclude that the functions of the apostle and prophet are discontinued is by determining that the goals have already been met. If this is the case, then there should be great excitement. However, based on the current climate of the church, we know this is not true. With all the denominations that exist and the plethora of contrasting doctrines, certainly, the unity of the faith has not been achieved. In fact, the church seems more divided now than at any point in its history. Moreover, with the prevailing state of the church being that of babes, a level of maturity measuring that of Christ's fullness is a standard we have not yet attained.

In an interrelated way, it is impossible to achieve maturity in an environment of division. In other words, if there is no unity of the faith, there cannot be maturity. Unity, therefore, is a prerequisite to achieving the full stature of Christ. From the example of the Corinthian church, we see they were babes in Christ because of division, and simultaneously, there was division because they were babes. This means that there is a direct connection between babes, division, unity, and maturity. This reinforces the principle that for true growth to occur in the church, we must first have unity. From the examples provided throughout the book of Acts, once unity was fostered, growth always ensued.

Recall that when the matter of circumcision threatened to divide the church in Acts Chapter 15, the apostles and elders assembled in Jerusalem to consider the matter. After the matter was resolved and communicated to the church, Acts 16:5 says the churches were established in the faith and the numbers increased. Even from a business perspective, companies that are fractured rarely experience growth. However, when there is unity and the mission and vision are clear, the results are positive. This is why one of the main strategies of the devil is to divide the church with false doctrines. With that said, the objective of wolves and hirelings is to scatter the sheep. Hence, by keeping the church divided, it is simultaneously being kept from achieving the maturity of Christ.

Notice that contained within the second target is a more definitive criterion for assessing its accomplishment. Therefore, in bestowing the gifts of Christ, not only is the target maturity but maturity of a certain measure. Based on this premise, the measurement for determining the maturity of the sons of God is in accordance with Christ's standards. Hence, success in this instance can be measured. With that said, how do we determine success in ministry? How is stewardship evaluated? Is it by the size of the congregation? Is it by the popularity of the minister? Obviously, the short answer is no. To be clear, these are certainly not adverse achievements. However, based on the measurement established by the Father, this is not how we gauge success.

Unfortunately, based on prevailing perspectives, these benchmarks seem to be more accepted than others. Nevertheless, included in the concept of measurement is the expectation of a certain quality. If an assignment is given to produce a product of a particular quality, and the numbers are achieved but the product falls short of the quality standard, can we claim success? In comparing this to the work of the ministry, while amassing numbers is certainly not a failure, the objective should be quality and not specifically quantity. For what is the significance of simply accumulating great numbers without the congregation achieving the maturity of Christ?

THE UNITY OF THE FAITH

How do we determine if we have attained the target of the unity of the faith? First, we have to identify what is meant by the term "the unity of the faith." For years, when I heard this phrase, I was of the opinion that it simply meant that the entire body of Christ should believe and speak the same thing. While this position has validity, the meaning is certainly more elaborate than that. Therefore, it requires further explanation. With the term "the unity of the faith," there are two concepts that are being promoted that are also interrelated.

The first one is the notion of unity. However, that unity is based on the principles of the faith. To be clear, when we think of *the faith*, we cannot have a denominational perspective, for there is no unity in that. Therefore, to truly appreciate the dynamics of the unity of the faith, we must first have an understanding of what is meant by "the faith" along with its components. It is this particular faith that produces the fruit of unity. With the definite article "the" preceding the word "faith," it limits the noun "faith" to a particular thing. Therefore, whenever Scripture uses the term "the faith," it is in reference to a single predominant idea. Let us look at several examples from Scripture that speak specifically regarding *the faith*.

> If ye continue in *the faith* grounded and settled, and be not moved away from the hope of the gospel, which ye have heard, and which was preached to every creature which is under heaven; whereof I Paul am made a minister. (Colossians 1:12)

6. As ye have therefore received Christ Jesus the Lord, so walk ye in him:
7. Rooted and built up in him, and stablished in *the faith*, as ye have been taught, abounding therein with thanksgiving. (Colossians 2:6-7)

> Now the Spirit speaketh expressly, that in the latter times some shall depart from *the faith*, giving heed to seducing spirits, and doctrines of devils. (1 Timothy 4:1)

In emphasizing the message of a single principle of truth, Ephesians 4:4 says emphatically that there is, "One Lord, one faith, one baptism." Based on the context of the verse, it should be noted that the phrase "one faith," is synonymous with the term, "the faith." Additionally, even though there are many denominations with varying beliefs, Scripture is clear there is still only one faith. Therefore, with the understanding that as it pertains to *the faith*, there is only one concept, what precisely is this general idea? According to Scripture, what is the one specific purpose that is both evident and pervasive throughout the Bible? Without question, it is the eternal purpose, which the Father predetermined for all humanity in Jesus Christ (Ephesians 3:11). Hence, when the term "the faith" is used, it serves as an encapsulation of all the elements involved in God's eternal purpose. From before the foundation of the world, the Father had an idea and Ephesians Chapter 1 reveals the components of that plan.

- The Father chose us in Him and decided humanity would be holy and without blame before Him in love. This means He made provision for us to be just like Him and possess His very nature and character. He simply wanted to reproduce Himself in humanity. Therefore, when He looks at His sons, He sees Himself, for we are reflections of Him.
- The Father predestinated humanity unto the adoption of children by Jesus Christ unto Himself. This signifies a relationship with the Father in the capacity of sons and being members of His house and of His kingdom.
- The Father made us accepted in the beloved or Jesus Christ. In Him, we are highly favored.
- We have redemption through the blood of Christ, the forgiveness of sins according to the riches of His grace. This speaks of complete

restoration and reconciliation with the Father. In Christ, we have eternal redemption (Hebrews 9:12).

- In Christ, we have obtained an inheritance being predestinated according to the purpose of Him who worketh all things after the counsel of His own will. We are heirs and joint-heirs with Christ. This speaks of an eternal inheritance (Hebrews 9:15).
- The Father sealed us with the Holy Spirit of promise, which is the earnest of our inheritance. Not only did the Father give us an inheritance, but He also gave us the Holy Spirit as a guarantee of our inheritance.

When we combine all of these benefits or what Ephesians 1:3 refers to as spiritual blessings, we have a comprehensive offering of everything the Father purposed for humanity from before the foundation of the world. Therefore, when these are all packaged and taught as a complete idea, we have what Scripture refers to as "the faith." Every promise and covenant the Father has ever made is embedded in the above list. It is what the church subscribes to; it provides us with hope and assurance; it is from which we derive doctrine; therefore, it is what we believe. When we preach the word of faith or the gospel, this is what we are preaching. Hence, there is only one faith. This is what Jude 1:3 exhorts us to earnestly contend or fight for. Various denominations may have their catechism or confessions of faith, but these constituents are the prevailing factors.

Now that we have a better understanding of what is meant by *the faith*, we can progress in our discussion on the unity of the faith. Those who have been bestowed the gifts of Christ are all assigned until the church comes into the unity that is associated with the faith. Therefore, God's purpose is designed to produce unity, and it is the responsibility of apostles, prophets, evangelists, pastors, and teachers to ensure that the church attains that level of unity. Of note, Ephesians 4:13 says until we <u>all</u> or the entire body achieve the unity that the faith offers. Unfortunately, because many do not understand what the faith is about or that it is indeed a single purpose, the unity contained in the faith is not promoted and realized. Recall that when God determined His purpose and chose us in Him, nationalities, ethnicities, denominations, gender, and social status did not exist. Hence, His purpose is for all humanity, which makes it one of unity. As stated in Chapter 5, unity is defined as the following:

- The quality or state of being united or joined as a whole
- Oneness or a condition of harmony
- Having a common purpose, objective, or aim
- Being of the same substance, essence, or character

God's purpose is not intended for a particular group, ethnicity, gender, or denomination. His purpose is that of oneness. Furthermore, the Father's purpose is realized in Christ. Galatians 3:28 says that in Him, "There is neither Jew nor Greek, there is neither bond nor free, there is neither male nor female: for ye are all one in Christ Jesus." Thus, it is impossible to truly teach God's purpose without prompting the message of unity. Those who operate in the leadership gifts and are not advancing unity are promoting an incorrect version of the faith. It is this position that has given birth to denominationalism and marginalization in the body, which are both the antithesis of unity. As witnessed in the example provided by the Corinthian church, division is the offspring of envy and strife, which is fostered by babes in Christ. Consequently, if unity is not being promoted, then the church cannot experience maturity and growth.

As leaders who have been bestowed the gifts of Christ, it is imperative that the gospel or the message of the faith be preserved and taught in its unadulterated form. How is this accomplished? Recall that one of the responsibilities of an apostle is to set the parameters or the structure for sound doctrine. In paralleling this to a natural example, just as a school sets the syllabus for its students, apostles do so in relation to the church. Therefore, in 1 Timothy 1:3, when Paul left Timothy in Ephesus, he gave him explicit instructions regarding what was to be taught. Just as a teacher in a school system is expected to adhere to the syllabus, thereby ensuring consistency, Paul gave Timothy similar instructions to convey to the church. In this regard, he instructed Timothy to command certain individuals that they "teach no other doctrine." In other words, based on the doctrine or the syllabus that has been established, do not deviate from it. Furthermore, to ensure the consistency and continuity of the doctrine that was established, Paul also instructed Timothy to teach others. 2 Timothy 2:2 says, "And the things that thou hast heard of me among many witnesses, the same commit thou to faithful men, who shall be able to teach others also."

One of the greatest challenges to the unity of the faith is the variation of what is believed and subsequently taught. This is why the concept of denominationalism is so destructive to the body of Christ. Keep in mind that God's purpose or the gospel has the element of unity attached to it. However, if various groups have a different interpretation of what God's purpose is, then their perspective of unity will be based on that. In other words, if the doctrine that we subscribe to does not support the concept of unity or being one in Christ, then there will be no unity of the faith. For example, if the tenets of a particular denomination do not support women in ministry, especially in a leadership capacity, then unity in this respect will not be realized. Instead, we will have the marginalization of members of the body of Christ solely based on their gender. Similarly, if the precepts that are espoused make distinctions based on the color of a person's skin, then this perspective does not promote the notion of unity. Rather, the notion of unity will be in accordance with those who share similar traits and characteristics. With *the faith* or the doctrine of the faith being the foundation, and unity being the house on that foundation, if the foundation is faulty, then the house is vulnerable. Again, this is why doctrine matters.

The unity of the faith is critical to the body of Christ; no wonder the devil, through false doctrine and heresy, works to create an atmosphere of disunity in the church. Unity is a formidable force. In Genesis Chapter 11, in recognition that the people were one, the Lord said, "Nothing will be restrained from them, which they have imagined to do." In other words, there are no limits on what they can accomplish. However, the minute the element of division was introduced and the thing that kept them united changed, the work they were doing ceased. As a result of division, their purpose was abandoned. Just how apostles, prophets, evangelists, pastors, and teachers have the responsibility of the unity of the faith, false apostles, false prophets, and false teachers are charged with creating disunity in the body. Armed with false doctrine and heresies their objective is to undermine the unity of the church.

One of the impacts of this strategy is infighting in the body of Christ due to the differences in doctrine that exist. For if the church is preoccupied with internal conflict over various doctrines and who is right versus who is wrong, we will take our eyes off the purpose to which we have been called. Furthermore, this makes it easier for the Enemy to wage war on the church. This is how the gates of hell attempt to prevail against the church. If we are busy fighting ourselves, the Enemy can easily creep in and sow seeds of discord. Can you imagine the impact the body of Christ will have on itself and on the world when we attain the unity of the faith? Actually, Ephesians 4:16 answers this question, which we will address in the final chapter.

THE PROPER STRUCTURE PROMOTES UNITY

To attain the unity of the faith, the right organizational structure must also be in place. One reason unity is absent in the church is because the proper structure based on Scripture has either been ignored or replaced. As I have mentioned on several occasions, the book of Acts provides the record of what the apostles did in establishing and organizing the church. By this measure, it serves as a blueprint of how the church should be structured. Consequently, because the proper structure based on apostolic order was orchestrated, the unity of the faith was evident. Let us revisit several examples of this from the book of Acts.

- First, in relation to the entire body of Christ, there was singleness of doctrine, which promoted unity. Acts 2:42 says that the church continued steadfastly in the apostles' doctrine. They were the ones who established the foundation concerning the doctrine of the church. This was the same message that Jesus taught His disciples prior to His death and even after His resurrection. His consistent message was about the things pertaining to the kingdom of God (Acts 1:3).
- The church had all things common or everything was shared by all (Acts 2:44). Furthermore, the church had singleness of heart; they were of one mind (Acts 2:46). These are all the hallmarks of unity. Hence, as a result of having the proper structure, unity was evident among believers.

- One of the recurring themes throughout the book is that once there was order or proper structure, the Word of God increased, and many were added to the faith (Acts 6:7). Additionally, despite the immense growth recorded in Acts 2:47 and Acts 4:4, the unity of the faith was not lost. The concept of denominations did not exist. In fact, the very concept of denominationalism undermines the structure of the church presented in the book of Acts.
- As a result of having the proper structure, when the dispute of circumcision threatened to divide the church, the matter was properly addressed and resolved by the apostles and elders (Acts Chapter 15). Clearly, once the proper structure is intact, an environment of unity in the church is fostered.
- The consciousness that there is one ministry also promotes unity in the church. In Acts Chapter 8, as a result of Stephen's stoning, believers were scattered everywhere, and they preached the gospel where they went. After word reached the leaders of the church in Jerusalem that many in Antioch had turned to the Lord as a result of their preaching, they sent Barnabas there to support the work. This is what unity looks like. They were not rivals, but rather workers together with God. Also, Priscilla and Aquila, after hearing Apollos preach and realizing he did not have the fullness of the gospel, pulled him aside and expounded unto him the way of God more perfectly (Acts 18:24-28). Again, in this example, we see the same singleness of mind based on the premise of unity.

Notice, that with all these points, the common characteristic was unity or oneness, which was a consequence of having the appropriate church or organizational structure. The Father gave apostles, prophets, evangelists, pastors, and teachers to unify the body. However, before even speaking of the gifts, Ephesians 4:3-6 gives the perspective of unity in relation to the entire body of Christ.

3. Endeavouring to keep the unity of the Spirit in the bond of peace.
4. There is one body, and one Spirit, even as ye are called in one hope of your calling;
5. One Lord, one faith, one baptism,

6. One God and Father of all, who is above all, and through all, and in you all. (Ephesians 4:3-6)

PRINCIPLES OF THE UNITY OF THE FAITH

To attain the unity of the faith, there are certain principles we must adhere to. Three of them are listed below.

1. We do not see or identify each other after the flesh. As new creatures in Christ, we do not subscribe to fleshly identifications. In this regard, 2 Corinthians 5:16-17 conveys the principles of how we should see each other:

    16. Wherefore henceforth know we no man after the flesh: yea, though we have known Christ after the flesh, yet now henceforth know we him no more.
    17. Therefore if any man be in Christ, he is a new creature: old things are passed away; behold, all things are become new.

    As a hindrance to unity, part of the challenge is a lack of understanding the concept of what a new creature is. In the natural, a new species is determined based on DNA analysis and characteristics, which distinguish it from other species. Similarly, the adjective "new" used to describe "creature" in the above passage means that as a species we are unprecedented or of a new kind. Furthermore, as we are born of the Father by incorruptible seed, His DNA distinguishes us from who we were.

    Based on the context of 2 Corinthians 5:16-17, being a new creature in Christ, includes not only being born again, but it also involves how the new creature in Christ is identified. Hence, we cannot use old classifications in identifying the new creature in Christ. Notice specifically that this recognition speaks of knowing or identifying no person after the flesh. This means that in the body of Christ, as new creatures, we make no distinctions based on someone's earthly tabernacle or other fleshly attributes. For example, some denominations do not accept female leaders and hold the position that a woman should be silent in the church. For those who take this position, their recognition of the new creation is still after the flesh.

As new creatures, we no longer fall into the categories of male or female, which carry classifications based on the flesh. The same applies if our identification of each other is based on the color of our skin or any other natural identifier. Additionally, once we have put on or have been clothed with Christ, He then becomes our identification. Therefore, when we see each other, we see Christ. This new creature belongs to one family and has one Father. This in itself is the foundation of unity. Therefore, as we are one in Christ, when we see each other, we should not see nationality, ethnicity, gender, or social status, which are fleshly identifiers. Galatians 3:27-28 provides a wonderful summation to this point by saying, "For as many of you as have been baptized into Christ have put on Christ. There is neither Jew nor Greek, there is neither bond nor free, there is neither male nor female: for ye are all one in Christ Jesus."

2. To attain the unity of the faith, there has to be the recognition that God's purpose is for all humanity. It is not designed for any one particular group of people or a specific nation. As stated, when the Father determined His purpose from before the foundation of the world, it was ordained for all humanity for the concept of nations or nationalities did not exist. Furthermore, to show His consistency, the Lord made a promise to Abraham in Genesis 12:3 that in him *all families or all nations would be blessed*. When we take into consideration the components of this promise, they are consistent with the same blessings in Ephesians Chapter 1 that the Father purposed from before the world began.

When God predetermined these blessings, He purposed them in Himself. However, when He made these identical promises to Abraham, the blessings then became a covenant. Furthermore, Hebrews 6:13 says that to guarantee the promise or make it unconditional, the Father swore by Himself. The promise to Abraham was therefore the embodiment of God's eternal purpose. For this reason, Galatians 3:8 says that when God made this promise to Abraham, He was actually preaching the gospel message to him. Therefore, contained in the promise was the fullness of the gospel message. Furthermore, Galatians 3:16 provides more enlightenment and adds that not only was the promise made to Abraham, but also to his seed: Jesus Christ. Hence, Jesus Christ is the one through whom the promise of the Father is fulfilled. This coincides with Ephesians 1:3 that the spiritual blessings are in Christ Jesus.

Moreover, one of the reasons the Lord chose the nation of Israel was to preserve the seed to whom the promise was made. Additionally, Galatians 3:19 also says, the Law was also added until the seed came to whom the promises were made. Hence, Hebrews 10:1 says that the Law was only a shadow of good things to come. In this vein, the Law served as a schoolmaster to bring us to Christ that we may be justified by faith and thereby partake of the spiritual blessings predetermined by the Father. Finally, in Christ, the designation of what it means to be an Israelite is not determined based on fleshly birth but rather by being born of the Spirit (Romans 9:6-8). This further adds credence to the first point that the new creature is not identified based on fleshly attributes.

Furthermore, the distinction that once existed between nationalities and ethnicities particularly Jews and Gentiles no longer exists. The middle wall of partition, which divided humanity has been removed (Ephesians 2:14). Again Galatians 3:28 says that in Christ, the concept of nationalities does not exist and all those who are Christ's are heirs or inheritors of the promise or the blessings. In addition, based on the Father's ultimate purpose, in the dispensation of the fullness of the times or when time is complete, He will gather all things in one, in Christ. Therefore, in the aggregate, God's purpose is truly one of unity.

9. Having made known unto us the mystery of his will, according to his good pleasure which he hath purposed in himself:

10. That in the dispensation of the fulness of times he might gather together in one all things in Christ, both which are in heaven, and which are on earth; even in him. (Ephesians 1:9-10)

3. Just as the Father has one purpose, there is only one general doctrine associated with that purpose. If there is only one objective, how is it that there are countless doctrines, which attempt to convey the Father's intention? Jesus' primary message was concerning the kingdom of heaven or the kingdom of God. Everything He taught was based on this principle. In fact, even after His resurrection, He spent 40 days with His apostles speaking of things pertaining to the kingdom of God (Acts 1:3). Therefore, in terms of His doctrine, there was no ambiguity. Consequently, once the church was instituted, Acts 2:42 says that believers followed steadfastly in the apostles' doctrine. The apostles' doctrine was the same message that Jesus taught. Seeing that the Father's purpose is one of unity, the doctrine communicating that purpose also has to be one of unity and promote unity.

Having spent a considerable amount of time discussing the components of the faith and the principles of unity in Chapters 2, 3, 4, and 5, this established a platform for understanding the unity of the faith. Now that we have a better understanding regarding the unity of the faith, we will discuss attaining to the measure of the fullness of the stature of Jesus Christ.

THE MEASURE OF THE FULLNESS OF THE STATURE OF CHRIST

Apostles, prophets, evangelists, pastors, and teachers are also given until the entire body of Christ comes into the knowledge of the Son of God, unto a perfect man, unto the measure of the fullness of Christ. What precisely is this target referring to? In essence, this goal is stating that the objective of leadership is to bring the church into maturity and that standard is the maturity of Christ. In other words, we become just like Him. However, to understand what that level of maturity looks like, there must first be an understanding or a knowledge of who He is. In practical terms, to achieve a certain goal, we must know the benchmark.

To improve their performance, many companies engage in what is called benchmarking. A benchmark is defined as something that serves as a standard by which others may be measured or judged. It is an objective standard. Hence, companies identify competitors known for their best practices and use their standards as a reference point to evaluate and improve their own product or service. Similarly, the Father has implemented leadership in the church to accomplish the same objective. However, in this instance, the aim is a measure of maturity based on the standard of Christ. This too is an objective standard or level of maturity; it is not subjective. Therefore, the level of maturity to be achieved is not based on personal opinions, interpretations, or feelings but on a specific benchmark: the standard of Jesus Christ.

In the previous chapter, one of the three leadership objectives we discussed was the perfecting of the saints. Recall that this involves the process of developing the sons of God so we transition from being babes in Christ to full age or maturity. This discussion adds more focus to that objective by providing a specific standard or measure of maturity. Notice that Ephesians 4:13 specifically says, until *we all* meet the mature standard of Christ. Hence, the goal of the leadership gifts is not to create a selection of "superstars" but to ensure the entire body achieves the same standard. How does the body of Christ come into the measure of the fullness of the stature of Christ?

Before answering that question, let us first establish a foundation for this discussion and talk about the church in relation to Christ. For within the body of Christ, there seems to be a great disconnect between who Jesus was while He was on the earth and who we are. To understand what the Father has determined for us, we must first understand who Christ is and what He represents. Indeed, Jesus was unique in His purpose but not in what He represented. On this note, Romans 8:28-29 offers a good perspective on the connection between Jesus Christ and the church:

> 28. And we know that all things work together for good to them that love God, to them who are the called according to his purpose.

> 29. For whom he did foreknow, he also did predestinate to be conformed to the image of his Son, that he might be the firstborn among many brethren.

Notice that the passage specifically says those who are *the called* according to the Father's purpose. Again, the definite article "the" identifies those *called* as a specific or definite group. However, to identify who this group is, there must be an understanding of God's purpose, for it is based on His purpose that they are called. Having spent a significant portion of this book discussing the Father's purpose and understanding it extends to all humanity, the term, "the called" simply refers to those who are now in Christ. It is therefore a designation for the sons of God. Contrary to the erroneous doctrine of Calvinism, which states that God has predestined certain individuals to be saved, the Father's purpose is designed for all.

1 Peter 3:9 says, "The Lord is not slack concerning his promise, as some men count slackness; but is longsuffering to us-ward, not willing that any should perish, but that all should come to repentance." Furthermore, from the introduction of the book of Romans, Paul sets the premise for who are *the called*. In addressing the entire church at Rome, Paul says in Romans 1:5-6:

> 5. By whom we have received grace and apostleship, for obedience to the faith among all nations, for his name:
> 6. Among whom are ye also the called of Jesus Christ.

Hence, the term "the called" is a general classification, which refers to all believers. Therefore, Paul was saying that the entire church in Rome was included in the term "the called." Nevertheless, the emphasis of Romans 8:28-29 focuses on the destiny God had predetermined for *the called* or His sons. Recall, that when God created humanity, His intent was not only to have a family but one that possesses His nature and character. Therefore, Jesus Christ came in the capacity of a Son so that He would be the firstborn among many brethren. Additionally, in His role as a Son, He also came manifesting a certain image or character. Thus, "Jesus being the firstborn among many brethren" is not a statement of quantity but one of quality. The Father determined beforehand, that the destiny of His many sons would be to conform to a certain standard. That benchmark is the image of Jesus Christ.

Even though God is in the numbers business as it pertains to salvation, He is also in the quality business in relation to the character of His many sons. Therefore, the Father provided Christ as the benchmark for how His sons should behave and He made this our destiny. The word "conformed" in Romans 8:29 is the Greek word *symmorphos*. It is a combination of two Greek words *syn* meaning *to be one with* and morphe meaning *form or appearance*. In combination, it means having the same form as another. Therefore, it speaks of having the same form or the same image of Jesus Christ, which refers to His character and mind.

Based on His foreknowledge, the Father predetermined that the many brethren or the church would manifest the same image or character and mind as the firstborn. This is why the statement was made that Jesus was unique in His purpose but not in what He represented. It was never the Father's intent to have one Son of a certain image or standard and the others of a different one. However, to attain this measure, transformation is required. This is why 2 Corinthians 3:18 says, "But we all, with open face beholding as in a glass the glory of the Lord, are changed into the same image from glory to glory, even as by the Spirit of the Lord." The word "changed" in this passage is the Greek word *metamorphoo*. In short, it means to change from one form to another. However, we will discuss that in detail in the next section.

The word "changed," coupled with the term "glory to glory," speaks of a process. Therefore, it is by a process that the sons of God are changed or transformed into the image of Jesus Christ. This is the same measure of the fullness of the stature of Christ mentioned in Ephesians 4:13. Furthermore, in Galatians 4:19, in relation to conforming to the image of Christ, Paul says, "My little children, of whom I travail in birth again until Christ be formed in you." The word "formed" is the Greek word *morphoo*, which carries the same connotation as the other Greek words mentioned above. It means that as an apostle, Paul was laboring until the character and mind of Christ were formed or developed in the people of God.

John 1:14 says, "And the Word was made flesh, and dwelt among us, (and we beheld his glory, the glory as of the only begotten of the Father) full of grace and truth." Jesus was the manifestation of the Word of God made flesh. In other words, He was a visible demonstration of the Father's character and substance in human form. Notice that John 1:14 says the visible manifestation of the Word of God is glory. This is the form or appearance that the Greek word *morphe* refers to. This means that the presence of God's Word is always evident, and the appearance is one of grace and truth. In simple terms, grace is defined as God's influence in the heart, which is then reflected in the life. This is seen as righteous character on display. Truth speaks of the substance or essence of God or simply put, His Holy Spirit. Hence, the evidence or the presence of grace and truth is always seen as glory. To put it another way, glory is produced when grace and truth are present.

Similarly, as sons of God who have the substance or truth of God in us, the operation of grace now has to take effect in our lives. When the Spirit of God writes His Word in our hearts, 2 Corinthians 3:3 says we become visible manifestations of the epistle of Christ. That is to say, we become a representation of His character in human form or the Word made flesh. Additionally, this is also seen as glory.

In essence, the process of the Spirit of God writing His Word in our hearts or minds is how we are transformed. Writing His Word in our hearts means He is making an impression on our minds and having an influence in our hearts. This is His grace in operation, which is then reflected in our lives as glory. When the Lord writes, He changes the way we think. He changes our habits and desires, so we conform to the image of the character of Christ. The more the Lord is allowed to write, the more we move from glory to glory until we are changed into the image of Christ or attain His measure of maturity. On the other hand, the less He is allowed to write as a result of disobedience, then the process of transformation is hampered. As a consequence, we remain babies or conclude that the standard is impossible to attain.

Jesus was a recognizable manifestation of God's character and substance. Therefore, through the process of transformation, the church is also capable of being visible expressions of the Father. For more on this please refer to my book *God's Eternal Purpose Volume 2. The Identity of the sons of God: The Image of Jesus Christ.* Let us examine the transformation process in greater detail and look at the specific components involved.

THE TRANSFORMATION PROCESS

Like most things in life, there is a process involved whether it is a routine before a morning run, the procedure for getting dressed for work, or the method for cleaning the house. There are steps or actions that are followed to achieve a particular objective. Processes are important because they describe incrementally how things are done. Similarly, in attaining to the measure of the fullness of Christ, there is also a process involved. As we have discussed, this process includes the steps associated with transitioning from being a babe in Christ to being mature sons based on the standard of Christ. For each one of us, the actual steps may be different, for the Lord's manner in bringing us to perfection can vary. However, for all of us, the requirements are the same. Romans 12:1-2 explains what they are:

1. I beseech you therefore, brethren, by the mercies of God, that ye present your bodies a living sacrifice, holy, acceptable unto God, which is your reasonable service.
2. And be not conformed to this world: but be ye transformed by the renewing of your mind, that ye may prove what is that good, and acceptable, and perfect, will of God.

In reference to the above passage, transformation to the image of Christ or maturity based on the standard of Christ can be achieved based on a three-step process. They are:

1. Present our bodies as living sacrifices (holy)
2. Be not conformed to this world
3. Renewing of the mind

According to the passage, the word "transformed" is the Greek word *metamorphoo*. Recall that this the same Greek word for "changed" mentioned in 2 Corinthians 3:18 concerning the process of moving from glory to glory.

The word is a combination of two Greek words *meta* meaning after and *morohoo* meaning form. However, the form or appearance is one that is in harmony with the character and mind of Christ. Therefore, in support of the process involved in transformation, it does not refer to the present form but the one that shall be evident afterward. It is from the same Greek word that we get the English word "metamorphosis," which means a striking alteration in appearance, character, or circumstances. In short, transformation or metamorphosis speaks of a change. For example, when a caterpillar becomes a butterfly, it goes through a metamorphosis, and the form that appears after the process is completed is different from the one at the beginning.

Although being a butterfly is the caterpillar's destiny, this is not achieved until the caterpillar goes through the process. Thus, it is the same for the sons of God. Even though Romans 8:28-29 says the Father predetermined that we would be conformed to the image of Christ, we still have to go through the process. Moreover, once the transformation is complete, the butterfly doesn't have the same mindset or characteristics as the caterpillar. It now thinks and behaves like a butterfly. Similarly, once our transformation is completed, the way we think and behave changes. Our characters and purpose are different.

In the previous chapter, we discussed that the church does not have a nature problem but rather, a nurture problem. Therefore, the transformation process is to nurture the sons of God into maturity.

1. PRESENT OUR BODIES AS A LIVING SACRIFICE, ONE THAT IS HOLY

To attain the measure of Christ, the first step involved in the transformation process is to present our bodies as a living sacrifice. If there is no presentation, there can be no transformation. To be clear, when we are born again, the Holy Spirit quickens or regenerates our human spirits. Hence, to attain the measure of Christ's maturity, it is not our spirits or the inner man that is involved in the process, but our bodies and minds. However, the Holy Spirit does strengthen us with might in our inner man, enabling us to accomplish the will of God.

1. And you hath he quickened, who were dead in trespasses and sins;
2. Wherein in time past ye walked according to the course of this world, according to the prince of the power of the air, the spirit that now worketh in the children of disobedience:
3. Among whom also we all had our conversation in times past in the lusts of our flesh, fulfilling the desires of the flesh and of the mind; and were by nature the children of wrath, even as others. (Ephesians 2:1-3)

Despite being born again, we are still familiar with the former lusts of our flesh and the desires of our minds. All the habits and practices we were engaged in were not miraculously forgotten. We still remember the feelings, names, and addresses. Before we were quickened, we were dead *in* sin, but now, the purpose of transformation is to bring us to the point where we are functionally dead *to* sin. To accomplish this, the process begins by offering our bodies to God as living sacrifices. Romans 12:1 figuratively uses the example of a sacrifice because of what it represents.

In the Old Testament, a sacrifice was a consecrated offering made to God for the atonement of sin or for an expression of thanksgiving. In principle, an offering is a gift. Therefore, when we present our bodies to God as a sacrifice or offering, we are presenting ourselves to Him as a gift. In fact, Romans 12:1 calls it our reasonable service. According to *Barnes Commentary*, a sacrifice "implies that he who offers it presents it entirely, releases all claim or right to it, and leaves it to be disposed of for the honor of God." Hence, when we present our bodies as living sacrifices, we are giving our entire selves to God and relinquishing our rights to our bodies. Ironically, 1 Corinthians 6:19-20 says that as the temple of the Holy Ghost, our bodies are not our own, for we are bought with a price. Hence, God is simply requesting that we present to Him what already belongs to Him. This is why it is called a reasonable or rational service.

Notice specifically that Romans 12:1 says we are to *present* our bodies as living sacrifices. The usage of the word "present" indicates that in terms of the sacrifice, the action is personal and voluntary. It is something done of our own free will, and it is based on the willingness of the heart to please the

Lord. Therefore, despite our bodies already belonging to Him, God wants us to freely offer them to Him. According to the Law of Moses, there were various offerings required of the children of Israel. In particular, one was called the freewill offering. This willing offering was voluntary and could be offered at any time. Additionally, a freewill offering could be either a burnt offering also referred to as the whole burnt offering or a peace offering, both were voluntary sacrifices (Leviticus 22:17-23). Specifically, the burnt offering was an offering that was completely consumed by fire (Leviticus 6:8-13). In making the connection to Romans 12:1, presenting our bodies as living sacrifices is a freewill offering to the Lord. This means that it is voluntary and expresses a willingness of the heart to please the Father.

Like the whole burnt offering, which is completely consumed, this sacrifice represents a life wholly dedicated to the will of the Lord. It speaks of us being completely and wholeheartedly devoted to God. Additionally, the sacrifices under the Law had to meet certain criteria in order to qualify as honourable sacrifices. In relation to animal sacrifices, they had to be without blemish; they could not be blind, maimed, or have any deformities. Similarly, in offering our bodies to God as living sacrifices, the requirement is holiness.

The term "living sacrifice" in Romans 12:1 is associated with the word "mortify," which is used in Romans 8:13. Therefore, it adds a practical operation to the process. The verse says, "For if ye live after the flesh, ye shall die: but if ye through the Spirit do mortify the deeds of the body, ye shall live." The word "mortify" means to put to death or to kill. Once we give ourselves wholly to God, we are capable of putting to death the deeds or activities of the body. How is this accomplished? The answer is through self-denial of bodily desires or appetites, the same ones we have not forgotten. In this regard, Romans 6:13 provides a practical operation, which is consistent with this discussion. It says, "Neither yield ye your members as instruments of unrighteousness unto sin: but yield yourselves unto God, as those that are alive from the dead, and your members as instruments of righteousness unto God."

The word "yield" means to present. In relation to fulfilling our desires, it means we have choices and also the power of restraint. Therefore, we can either yield or exercise discipline. The more we exercise discipline and abstinence, the more the passion dies. Eventually, that particular activity no longer has the power to draw us away. In admonishing us regarding self-control, Romans 6:11 warns us not to present our bodies or their parts as instruments or tools of unrighteousness. When we were dead in sin, this was the normally accepted behavior. We were under the dominion of sin and did not have a choice. However, now that we have been made alive, the reasonable service is to present ourselves to God as living sacrifices. Furthermore, we are to present our bodies <u>and all their parts</u> as tools of righteousness unto God. The emphasis of this passage is that we have choices; our bodies can either be used as tools for unrighteousness or righteousness. It is whatever we submit to.

As a member of the body, the tongue is also included in the overall presentation of our bodies as living sacrifices. In fact, it is the stimulus for all the activities of the body. For though it is a little member, James 3:8 says it can defile the whole body. Furthermore, James 3:2 adds, "If any man offend not in word, the same is a perfect man, and able also to bridle the whole body." Therefore, mortifying the deeds of the body begins with presenting our tongues to God to be used as tools of righteousness. The key to restraining and governing our bodies begins with controlling our tongues or words. With this principle of governing our tongue as a backdrop, 1 Peter 2:21-23 provides the example of Christ's suffering and the pattern we should follow:

21. For even hereunto were ye called: because Christ also suffered for us, leaving us an example, that ye should follow his steps:
22. Who did no sin, neither was guile found in his mouth:
23. Who, when he was reviled, reviled not again; when he suffered, he threatened not; but committed himself to him that judgeth righteously:

Notice that all the instances of Christ's suffering were related to Him controlling the usage of His tongue. There was no guile found in His mouth. He didn't speak with subtlety or deceit. He was not duplicitous with His words. Oftentimes it is so difficult to get a straight and honest answer from people. When pressed, they sometimes speak in shadows saying one thing and really meaning something else. This is the opposite of having integrity.

When Christ was reviled, He did not retaliate in kind or use abusive language. Of note, to be reviled is not an act of one person but of many. Therefore, when negative information was spread about Him, He did not reciprocate. When He suffered or was mistreated, He did not threaten in return. He did not issue His own threats but committed Himself to God for vindication. Restraining the tongue allows us to control all of our bodies because the words we use are reflections of our hearts. Matthew 12:34 says, "For out of the abundance of the heart the mouth speaketh." To control the tongue, the mind has to be renewed. The renewing of the mind will be tabled later in this chapter.

In light of the discussion of this section, 1 Peter 4:1-2 provides a great summation of the results of presenting our bodies as living sacrifices or suffering in the flesh:

1. Forasmuch then as Christ hath suffered for us in the flesh, arm yourselves likewise with the same mind: for he that hath suffered in the flesh hath ceased from sin;
2. That he no longer should live the rest of his time in the flesh to the lusts of men, but to the will of God.

2. DO NOT BE CONFORMED TO THIS WORLD

The second step involved in the transformation process is not conforming to this world. However, it should be noted that with transformation being progressive, our bodies never cease from being living sacrifices. In fact, it is a lifetime offering. Therefore, not conforming to this world is only possible on the condition that we present ourselves as consecrated offerings to God. In the previous section, it was stated that if there is no presentation, there can be no transformation. In furthering that point, if there is no presentation, then by default, there is conformation to the world's standards. Hence, for the sons of God, the only way not to conform to the world is to give ourselves to God.

In reiterating Romans 8:29, the image of Christ is the benchmark when it comes to the standard of conformity for the sons of God. However, the world also presents itself as another benchmark or standard of conformity. Two standards serve as objectives to which we can dedicate ourselves, obviously, with varying results. As stated, to be conformed to the image of Christ, the requirement is to present our bodies as living sacrifices. On the other hand, to be conformed to the world, the requirement is indulgence in the things of the world and presenting our bodies as tools of unrighteousness. Interestingly, the word "conformed" used in Romans 8:29 is a completely different Greek word from the one used in Romans 12:2. Consequently, their meanings and operations are also totally different.

In Romans 12:2, the word "conformed" is the Greek word *syschematizo*. It is a combination of two Greek words, *syn* meaning to be one with and *schema* meaning fashion, mold, or external conditions. Whereas "conformed" in Romans 8:29 refers to having the same form or being one with Christ in terms of character and mind, "conformed" in Romans 12:2 means becoming one with the fashion or external conditions of the world. Furthermore, in this context, to conform also means to act in accordance with the prevailing standards, attitudes, and practices of the world. Hence, conforming to the world is not a difficult task but simply requires acquiescing to what is around us. It does not take strength to conform to the world. However, it does take strength and discipline to be conformed or transformed into the image of Christ.

With the world presenting itself as a benchmark of conformity, let us take a closer look at the word "world." The word "world" in Romans 12:2 is the Greek word *aion,* which means age or period of time. It refers to all the opinions, thoughts, cultural norms, behaviors, or phrases that exist in the world during a period of time. It is what is accepted as normal behavior. Therefore, the admonition not to be conformed to this world refers to not becoming one with the nature and characteristics, which define this age. However, this is not to be confused with another Greek word for "world" being *kosmos,* which refers to the principles that govern the world we live in, which Satan is the god of (2 Corinthians 4:4). 1 John 2:15-16 places all the operations of the world (*kosmos*) and all that it has to offer into three distinct categories.

- **The lusts of the flesh** — Lust simply means desires. Therefore, this refers to that which appeals to the desires and appetites of the flesh or

our physical needs. These include the indulgences of sex, food, etc., with the focus being the pursuit of pleasure.
- **The lusts of the eyes** — This encompasses a broad range of items but basically, it refers to coveting whatever we see with the desire to have it. This is the result of a materialistic heart and is also the cause of envy. This is a possession-driven desire.
- **The pride of life** — The pride of life is that which promotes the ego and results in self-exaltation. It is concerned with status, reputation, title recognition, and is also connected to vainglory.

No matter what generation or age we are in, these three attributes of the world system are always in operation. Indeed, every generation may offer different variations of these three, but they are consistent no matter the period in which we exist. The way they are presented may be tailored to the specific generation, but they are the same. Hence, every enticement that the world could ever present comes through these avenues. Therefore, when Romans 12:2 says not to be conformed to this world, this is what it is referring to. Do not allow the dictates of the time in which we live to mold our minds.

> *As obedient children, not fashioning yourself according to the former lusts in your ignorance. (1 Peter 1:14)*

The term "according to" in 1 Peter 1:14 is the same Greek word for "conform" used in Romans 12:2. Therefore, for the sons of God, conforming to past behavior is seen as regressive. On the other hand, conforming or transforming to the image of Christ is seen as progressive and a change for the better.

3. RENEWING OF THE MIND

The final step in the transformation process is the renewing of our minds. Recall Romans 12:2 says once our minds have been renewed, we will be visible manifestations or endorsements of God's will. The word "renewing" is the Greek word *anakainosis,* which means renovation. Therefore, for transformation to occur, the mind has to be renovated. In applying this to the natural illustration of renovating a house, we get the perspective that a process is involved. For example, when a house is undergoing renovation, the procedure includes the removal or demolition of certain items and their subsequent replacement. While the process is ongoing, the site seems chaotic and confusion abounds. However, once the house has undergone the transformation and is completed, then its glory is visible to all.

Similarly, the renewing or renovation of the mind is also a process designed for us to manifest the glory of God. This is the same as being conformed to the image or character of Jesus Christ. As a principle, Proverbs 23:7 says, "For as he (a man) thinketh in his heart, so is he." Hence, who we are is a reflection of the way we think. Therefore, once we can change the way we think, we can experience transformation. Conforming to the world is based on a particular frame of mind. Similarly, transformation requires a specific way of thinking. This is why 1 Peter 4:1 says that in terms of the way we think, the mind of Christ serves as our benchmark. Additionally, Ephesians 4:20-24 serves as another witness that transformation is the result of the renewing of the mind.

20. But ye have not so learned Christ;
21. If so be that ye have heard him, and have been taught by him, as the truth is in Jesus:
22. That ye put off concerning the former conversation the old man, which is corrupt according to the deceitful lusts;
23. And be renewed in the spirit of your mind;
24. And that ye put on the new man, which after God is created in righteousness and true holiness. (Ephesians 4:20-24)

After highlighting the lifestyles and mindsets of those who live according to the standard or benchmark of the world, Paul says in Ephesians 4:20, "But ye have not so learned Christ." As it pertains to Christ, this is not what you were taught. In other words, the standard of conformity or the benchmark Christ presents is the opposite of what the world offers. It then goes onto say, if you have been properly instructed concerning Christ, you have a responsibility. This is why those who have been bestowed the gifts of Christ are so essential, for they are charged with the task of providing the knowledge of the Son of God. However, without this teaching as the benchmark, there can be no transformation to His image. Therefore, the correct teaching is a prerequisite to attaining maturity based on the measure of Christ. Hence, in part, the church is not developing to that level of maturity because the teaching is not in accordance with the measure of Christ.

Nevertheless, Ephesians 4:21 says if you have been properly instructed concerning Jesus Christ, there is a requirement. In this regard, the passage speaks of an exchange. It calls for the sons of God to put something off, but it also calls for us to put something on. To manifest the image or character of Christ, the requirement is to put off the old man and, in turn, put on the new man. One is based on conformity to the world and the other is based on being conformed to Christ. This exchange is the same process as the transformation mentioned in Romans 12:2. Hence, the term "put off" means the same as presenting our bodies as living sacrifices or crucifying the flesh with its affections and lusts (Galatians 5:24).

In highlighting what we are to put off, Ephesians 4:22 refers to it as our former conversation. This speaks of our previous lifestyle, habits, conduct, behavior, and characters. Our old nature had a particular lifestyle associated with it and its passions and desires were corrupt. However, as sons of God and having received a new nature, we are called to put off the lifestyle we were accustomed to. To be clear, Romans 6:6 says that our old man that was a servant of sin has been destroyed. However, many of us are still clothed with the habits of the old man and wear our old lifestyles as garments. Unfortunately, this prohibits us from manifesting the glory of God. The glory of God that is on the inside has the potential of being seen on the outside, but it's being cloaked. It is being covered by the works of the flesh. However, to put off this garment, we have to be renewed in the spirit of our minds. Being renewed in the spirit of our minds is the same as renewing or renovating our minds, which results in transformation.

Ephesians 4:23 uses the term "the spirit of your mind" to emphasize the life the mind is capable of producing. As a result of Adam's transgression, Genesis 6:5 says, "The wickedness of man was great in the earth, and that every imagination of the thoughts of his heart was only evil continually." Due to the nature of sin, every imagination of the mind was constantly evil. This was the spirit or the life the mind produced, and this was demonstrated in their actions. A more comprehensive list of the spirit of the mind includes imagination, will, passion, affections, understanding, emotion, intellect, desires, etc. Based on our old nature, these reflected lifestyles that were consistent with that nature.

Our imaginations were evil. Our wills were in opposition to God, and our lusts or desires were for the things of the world. Hence, the spirit of our mind will always be manifested in our behavior. Therefore, for our characters to change, the spirit of the mind has to be renovated. However, the first step is a change in nature. Hence, having now received the nature of God, for us to manifest the character of Christ, the next step is we must be renewed in the spirit of our minds. Our imaginations, wills, emotions, intellects, and desires, etc. must be renewed or renovated. For this to happen, the Holy Spirit must be allowed to write His word in your hearts.

Recall that grace is God's influence in the heart, reflected in the life, and this reflection is expressed as glory. Therefore, for us to manifest the glory of God, He has to be allowed to influence our imaginations, wills, emotions, intellect, and desires, etc. For example, when we face circumstances where our desires are being tested and we do not use the members of our bodies as tools of unrighteousness, we are allowing God to write His righteous standard in our hearts, thereby impacting our desires. When someone speaks evil of us, and we bless them rather than verbally attack them, God is writing His Word in our hearts, thereby impacting our emotions. This is the practical process of how the spirit of the mind is renewed. At the same time, the Word of God is being manifested in the flesh, grace and truth are on display and we are manifesting God's glory.

This is how we put off the lifestyles, habits, conduct, behavior, and character of the old man. Being renewed in the spirit of our minds results in having the mind of Christ. The bridge between putting off the old man and putting on the new man is being renewed in the spirit of our minds. Therefore, through the process of renewing the mind, we are clothing ourselves with the new man, which according to Ephesians 4:24, is created after God in righteousness and true holiness. Hence, we have put off one garment and put on another. This new garment or the new man bears the image of God. Once we are clothed in this, the glory of God is manifested in our lives. This new man is a visible manifestation or endorsement of God's will operating in our lives. This is what

Romans 12:2 means by proving what is that good, acceptable, and perfect will of God.

As sons of God, the question is what garment are you wearing? Is it the old man with past habits or is it the new man that manifests the character of Christ? The chart below provides a summary of the contrast between being conformed to the world and being transformed into the image of Jesus Christ.

TABLE 6

CONFORMATION	TRANSFORMATION
• Acting according to certain accepted standards. **To be one with the fashion of the world. To fashion one's character and mind after the world**	• To change in form, shape, or appearance. Having the same form or image of Jesus Christ, which speaks of His character and mind
• The world is the benchmark.	• The image of Christ is the benchmark
• Based on a carnal mind (carnally minded)	• Renewing or renovation of the mind (spiritually minded)
• Self-filled	• Proves God's will
• Requires no power	• Requires power
• No glory	• Glory (from glory to glory)
• Walking in the flesh	• Walking in the Spirit
• Regressive	• Progressive

When the Father sees His sons, He sees a representation of Himself. In fact, the reason God created humanity in the first place was to be a reflection of Him. Therefore, He created us in His image and likeness (Genesis 1:26).

Additionally, in reproducing Himself, He crowned humanity with glory and honour (Psalm 8:5), for the reproduction of the Father is always glory. Hence, all humanity, based on creation, is a visible manifestation of God's glory. To this end, Psalm 139:14 says we are fearfully and wonderfully made and marvelous are God's works. However, this is the general image or reflection that is inherent with all humanity. This image is based on our heritage from the first Adam. But based on our heritage from the last Adam who is Jesus Christ, we are capable of exhibiting another kind of glory. Our first image is as a result of our creation; however, the second image is possible because of our recreation.

To restore us, the Father gave us of His nature, the Holy Spirit, thereby once again reproducing Himself and making us new creatures. Recall that the reproduction of the Father is always glory. However, unlike our initial creation, which speaks of being crowned with glory and honour, Colossians 1:26 talks about Christ in us the hope of glory. The glory of God inside us allows us to be visible manifestations of the Father's glory. As a Son, Christ came as the visible manifestation of the Father's glory; it was one of grace and truth. He came as a representation of the glory or character that the other sons are capable of reflecting. However, to attain the measure of Christ, it involves the process of moving from glory to glory (1 Corinthians 3:18).

Despite the specific functions of those who have been conferred the gifts of Christ, they all work in unison to accomplish two collective goals:

1. The unity of the faith
2. To bring the sons of God to a level of maturity based on the measure of Christ

The unity of the faith represents the singular expression of the Father's purpose, which He predetermined for humanity. It is the united message for all humanity that was orchestrated through Christ. Again, it is not subjected to ethnicity, gender, social status, denominations, or any other dividing factors. Additionally, the measure of Christ's fullness represents the benchmark of maturity for the sons of God. However, to attain this standard, the requirement is transformation. Indeed, it is not an easy process, but in the end, it produces the peaceable fruit of righteousness, the character of Christ. Moreover, as we have discussed, these targets are not independent of each other, for without the unity of the faith, there can be no maturity. The message of unity is promoted by those who are mature.

CHAPTER 14

A UNIFIED AND MATURE BODY: A GLORIOUS CHURCH

Everything related to the responsibilities of the apostle, prophet, evangelist, pastor, and teacher has brought us to this point. As a reminder, Ephesians 4:12 indicates that the gifts are given to accomplish the following objectives:

- The perfecting of the saints
- The work of the ministry
- The edifying of the body of Christ

According to Ephesians 4:13, all of the gifts and the objectives are functional until two specific targets or goals have been achieved. These are:

- Until the body of Christ comes into the unity of the faith
- Until a level of maturity measuring that of Jesus Christ's fullness is attained

What then is the reason for setting goals? In short, goals help us to define our purpose. Whenever an organization makes appointments, establishes objectives, and sets a specific target, it is to make its priorities clear or to reveal what everyone needs to focus on. Goals are therefore a reflection of purpose. With that said, based on the goals the Father has communicated to the church, He has a specific purpose for the church as revealed in Ephesians 4:14-16:

14. That we henceforth be no more children, tossed to and fro, and carried about with every wind of doctrine, by the sleight of men, and cunning craftiness, whereby they lie in wait to deceive;

15. But speaking the truth in love, may grow up into him in all things, which is the head, even Christ:
16. From whom the whole body fitly joined together and compacted by that which every joint supplieth, according to the effectual working in the measure of every part, maketh increase of the body unto the edifying of itself in love.

Attaining to the unity of the faith and reaching a level of maturity based on the measure of Christ is necessary so that corporately, the body of Christ looks and behaves a certain way. It is the cumulative purpose of why leaders are appointed and what their ultimate focus should be. Therefore, when the Father predetermined His purpose from before the foundation of the world, this was the goal He had in mind.

NO MORE CHILDREN

Notice that the context of the passage is about the condition of the entire body of Christ. It has a global perspective. The goal of leaders is to ensure the church, collectively, does not exhibit the characteristics of children. The word "children" in Ephesians 4:14 is the Greek word *nepios,* which means a babe, not of age and unskillful. Therefore, as we have discussed throughout this book, the purpose of the "perfecters" is to bring the body of Christ into maturity. In this vein, Ephesians 4:14-16 packages everything we have addressed and says this is what a mature son looks like and this is the effect maturity has on the body. However, to create a contrast, the passage first presents the tendencies of a child or those who have not reached maturity.

In describing the disposition of children, Ephesians 4:14 provides the analogy of a vessel that is out at sea and is constantly tossed by the changing wind. In other words, because of the instability of children, they are directed and driven by every wind of doctrine that comes along. This is the illustration of those who have not attained the unity of the faith. With no anchor in the Father's purpose, they are not yet rooted and grounded in the truth. For this reason, they are carried about by those who traffic in deception. When false teachers and hirelings come along, they are easily persuaded by gimmicks and tactics that claim to have spiritual relevance.

By identifying the tendencies of children, the comparison also provides us with additional characteristics of a mature son. Children are the antithesis of sons who are mature or those who are skillful in the word of righteousness. In contrast, mature sons understand the Father's purpose and are therefore grounded and stable. As a result of this, they are not influenced by the changing winds of doctrine but are established in the faith. Additionally, because they know how to discern both good and evil, they are not easily manipulated by those whose purpose is to deceive. On this point, it is easy to deceive and exploit those who do not understand their purpose. In harmony with this discussion, Galatians 4:1-2 provides a wonderful principle concerning what a child represents:

1. Now I say, That the heir, as long as he is a child, differeth nothing from a servant, though he be lord of all;
2. But is under tutors and governors until the time appointed of the father.

Based on the passage, if the inheritors of estates are children, they are no different from servants even though they are masters of all. Even though it is their destiny to rule, as long as they have not reached the age of maturity, they are subject to the control of others. Maturity makes them suitable to rule and clearly distinguishes them from servants. The potential is there; the inheritance of the father has already been determined; however, the only thing that is required is maturity. Hence, maturity puts us in a position to fulfill our destinies.

The chart below provides a list of the tendencies of children compared to the attributes of those who are mature. Children are susceptible to every wind of doctrine because of their characteristics. In contrast, those who are mature are not vulnerable to such manipulations. Hence, it is the responsibility of those who have been bestowed the gifts of Christ to create an environment, not of children but adults.

TABLE 7

CHILDREN	ADULT/MATURE
• Tossed to and fro and carried about with every wind of doctrine	• The unity of the faith
• Carnal (1 Corinthians 3:1)	• Spiritual (1 Corinthians 3:1)
• On a diet of milk (1 Corinthians 3:2, Hebrews 5:12)	• On a diet of meat and strong meat (1 Corinthians 3:2, Hebrews 5:14)
• Resembles a servant (Galatians 4:1)	• Is a master
• Unskillful in the word of righteousness (Hebrews 5:13)	• Senses exercised to discern both good and evil (Hebrews 5:14) • Skillful in the word of righteousness.

WINDS OF DOCTRINE VERSUS SPEAKING THE TRUTH IN LOVE

Not only does Ephesians 4:14-16 offer a contrast between children and those who are mature, but it also presents a distinction in relation to doctrine. In the first instance, we have winds of doctrine designed by the trickery of men to deliberately mislead the sons of God. They are intended to promote instability through deception. Based on the passage, winds of doctrine have the following attributes:

- They do not provide a firm foundation for believers. They have a destabilizing effect.
- They do not provide a definite course or direction. They are based on changing winds.
- There are no fixed principles of holiness.

Winds of doctrine consist of teachings, which are mainly subjected to changing times and conditions. They are amended in accordance with what is popular, the desires of the flesh, and human interests. Based on the characteristics above, they do not have the substance to assist believers in being rooted and grounded in the truth. Instead, because they are fleeting and shallow, they are specifically manufactured to shipwreck the sons of God. One such doctrine is the teaching that suggests prosperity is an indicator of spirituality. This is what Paul warned Timothy against in 1 Timothy 6:5. In the passage, he says that those who are destitute of truth promote the teaching that gain is godliness. By extension, they also endorse the opposite that a lack of prosperity demonstrates spiritual deficiency. However, Scripture teaches us that godliness or holiness with contentment is great gain (1 Timothy 6:6). Furthermore, it adds that such teachings create hearts of covetousness, and those that pursue them depart from the faith. As previously mentioned, this is a wood, hay, and stubble doctrine that is incapable of providing a defense against the fiery trials of life.

Another example of a wind of doctrine is the acceptance or normalization of homosexuality in the church. Winds of doctrine attempt to relax God's righteous standards by making concessions for immorality and human desires. However, the Lord's righteous standard has not changed despite the changing times. For example, Romans 1:26-27, specifically addresses the practice of same-sex relations and how it is contrary to the natural design and function of men and women. However, based on the influence of the times and the lust of the flesh, there is an aggressive attempt to regularize this behavior in the church. To be clear, the emphasis is not exclusively on this practice but on all acts of immorality; however, this activity to a great extent is seeking righteous endorsement. In a similar circumstance (along the lines of sexual immorality in the church), Paul chided the Corinthian church because one of their members was having sex with his father's wife (1 Corinthians 5:1-8). Additionally, what made it more egregious is the act neither grieved the members of the church nor did they sever fellowship with the individual. In fact, fornication had become so common in the church it became acceptable.

To prohibit this leaven from impacting the entire church and normalizing the behavior, the church member was temporarily suspended from the church. Subsequently, in Paul's second letter to the Corinthians, he petitioned the church to reinstate the man to the fellowship (2 Corinthians 2:7). As a hallmark, winds of doctrine are void of righteousness and true holiness even though they may have elements of it. They are designed to appeal to the temporary and physical needs of the flesh or humanistic interests. Overall, these teachings do not facilitate growth.

Whereas winds of doctrine are subjective, truth, which is based on the principles of the unity of the faith is premised on an objective standard. This means it does not fluctuate based on the changing times, personal feelings, and other conditions. Additionally, winds of doctrine are intended to deceive and consequently mislead the people of God; however, the truth has a different purpose.

- It provides a firm foundation for believers. It is designed to edify the sons of God and bring them into maturity.
- It provides a definite course or direction. No constantly changing winds.
- Is based on the fixed principles of holiness.

According to the attributes of truth, it has the substance needed for believers to attain the measure of Christ's maturity. On the other hand, winds of doctrine are devised to maintain the status of childhood. Therefore, the two classifications of doctrine have contrasting agendas. With this in mind, Ephesians 4:15 says, "But speaking the truth in love, may grow up into him in all things, which is the head, even Christ." The term "grow up into Him," refers to attaining to the measure of the fullness of the stature of Christ. Therefore, this reinforces the fact that truth is needed for the sons of God to come into maturity. Moreover, the truth must be spoken in love.

FITLY JOINED TOGETHER

To explain the concept of unity and interdependence in the church, 1 Corinthians 12:12-26 uses the analogy of the human body. To this end, 1 Corinthians 12:12 says, "For as the body is one, and hath many members, and all the members of that one body, being many, are one body: so also is

Christ." Hence, the communication of the chapter is many members but one body. Additionally, the statement "so also is Christ" reinforces the fact that just like the body, Christ is not divided. In essence, this communication of unity is a continuation of the one discussed in 1 Corinthians 1:10. Recall that in the midst of a divided church, the question was asked, "Is Christ divided?"

In addition to the message of a single body, the illustration of the human body is also used to demonstrate the interdependent relationship the parts of the body have with each other. To emphasize this, 1 Corinthians 12:21 says, "And the eye cannot say unto the hand, I have no need of thee: nor again the head to the feet, I have no need of you." For example, in shaving my head this morning, I required the use of my hands; however, I also needed my eyes to see what I was doing. The point is the members of my body were dependent on each other to achieve the objective of a shaved head. The Lord fashioned the human body so it cannot operate effectively based on division. It is designed to function in unity. The same fundamentals also apply to the body of Christ.

Similarly, in expressing the same principles of unity and interdependence, Ephesians 4:16 also uses the example of the human body. However, in this illustration of the body, the distinction emphasized in Ephesians Chapter 4 is that Christ is the head of this body (Colossians 1:18). Therefore, unity and interdependence are not just with each other, but they are also with Him. We are a single entity or body with Christ. He is also a member of the body, so we are not just reliant on each other but also on Him. As the head, He sets the agenda for the function of the entire body, and there is a single purpose. Thus, the body operates based on what the head decides, and all the members are dedicated to that objective. Additionally, as the head, He serves as the benchmark of maturity so that we can grow into the same stature. Moreover, being connected to the head, the rest of the body is fitly joined together and compacted. This means that the body is properly organized so that every part is in the right place.

The phrase "fitly framed together," used in Ephesians 2:21 concerning a building, is synonymous with the term "fitly joined together" in Ephesians 4:16. One describes the unity and connectivity that exists in comparing the church to a building and the other is used to express the same sentiments concerning the human body. Therefore, when we examine the human body, based on symmetry, each part is in the best place and properly connected to the other part. The foot should not be where the hands are or the ears where the eyes are. According to how the body has been arranged, this design creates unity and harmony in the body. Furthermore, based on how the body has been structured, each part is dependent on the other and supports the other. Thus, this connectivity allows each part of the body according to the effectual working of the part to contribute to the growth of the body. Therefore, no member of the body is insignificant or meaningless. Each part is essential. Hence, to have unity in the body and maturity based on the measure of Christ, every member's contribution is necessary.

The human body does not work against itself. The hands and the legs are not in contention with each other to see who can be the most popular. Rather, they support each other based on the goal established by the head. Additionally, parts of the body are not marginalized, for there is a common and united purpose that all members of the body are working toward. Inevitably, growth occurs when all members of the body support each other and are seen as equal participants. Moreover, when there is a single message rather than winds of doctrine, along with a united goal, this fosters growth.

When we take into consideration the definitive goal of those who have been bestowed the gifts of Christ, we get the perspective of a body that is a representation of the Father's purpose. It is a mature body with a unified objective and each part contributes to its overall growth. Having a church comprising of babies does not meet the Father's objective for the offices. Notice that despite the environment of division, which is so pervasive in the body today, Scripture continues to remind us of the message of unity. Hence, the gifts of Christ are given for the entire body and they all work collectively to accomplish a unified purpose. Maturity creates a cohesive body of believers, who based on being mature, fosters continued growth in the body.

A GLORIOUS CHURCH

To be clear, what is being expressed in Ephesians Chapter 4 is not a body comprised of members who are children and unstable, but rather, those who have the disposition of attaining to the measure of Christ. The passage is painting the picture of the collective growth of the body. However, with each part contributing to the whole, corporate growth is also dependent on individual growth and maturity. With this in mind, the effectual working or contribution of each member has to be based on the unity of the faith and the standard of Christ's maturity. Without these elements, the body does not grow. This is why the Lord appoints apostles, prophets, evangelists, pastors, and teachers. The Father is interested in corporate maturity. He is not coming back for a church that resembles a nursery but for a glorious church (Ephesians 5:27).

The term "glorious church" speaks of a body of mature sons who manifest the glory of God or the character of Jesus Christ. It is the body that reflects who He is. His purpose from before the foundation of the world was to have sons who share His nature and demonstrate His character. He wanted a family that resembles Him. Moreover, the goal of the Father is to have a glorious bride that is suitable for a husband. In this regard, Ephesians Chapter 5 provides the illustration of a husband and wife. However, in using the practical relationship of a husband and wife being one, Ephesians 5:32 says the true communication pertains to Christ and the church.

25. Husbands, love your wives, even as Christ also loved the church, and gave himself for it;
26. That he might sanctify and cleanse it with the washing of water by the word,
27. That he might present it to himself a glorious church, not having spot, or wrinkle, or any such thing; but that it should be holy and without blemish. (Ephesians 5:25-27)

At the beginning of this book, the question was asked, "Why did the Father give apostles, prophets, evangelists, pastors, and teachers?" In answering the question, we took a systematic approach detailing the Father's purpose, the specific responsibilities of the gifts, and their collective objectives. With that said, Ephesians 5:27 brings the purpose of God full circle. Based on Ephesians 1:4, the Father chose us in Him before the foundation of the world that we should be holy and without blame before Him in love. As we have detailed on several occasions, He determined that humanity would be just like Him and possess His very nature and character. He wanted humanity to be a reflection of Himself. In accordance with this, Ephesians 5:27 says Christ gave Himself for us so He might present us to Himself as a glorious church. One that is holy, without spot, wrinkle, or any other blemishes. This is the same purpose outlined in Ephesians 1:4. Therefore, this serves as the cumulative purpose of why the gifts were appointed in the first place.

The diagram below provides a fitting illustration of what we have discussed throughout this book.

EXHIBIT 13

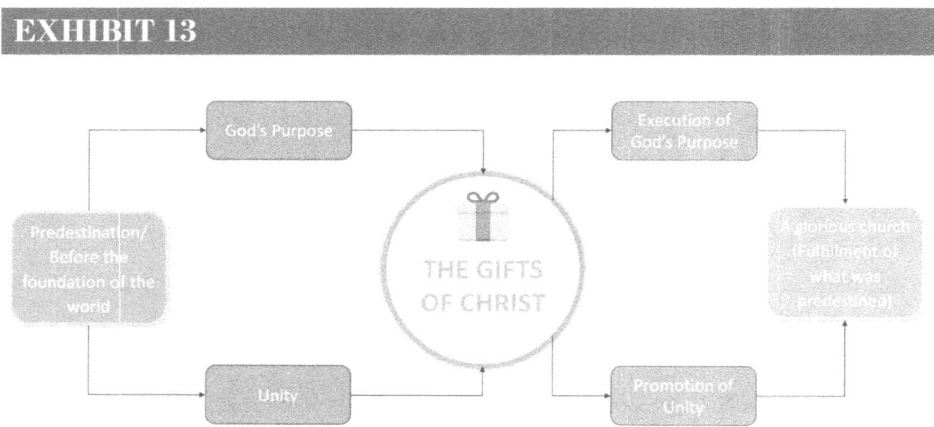

CONCLUSION

Throughout this book, all the information was directed at answering the fundamental "why?" Why does the Lord appoint apostles, prophets, evangelists, pastors, and teachers to the church? The direct answer according to Ephesians 4:12 gives three specific objectives:

1. The perfecting of the saints
2. The work of the ministry
3. Edifying of the body of Christ

However, to truly have an appreciation for these responsibilities and to know what they entail, they have to be understood in the context of God's purpose for humanity. Hence, without an understanding of the Father's purpose, the church cannot be effective in the execution of the gifts.

According to the Father's purpose, before the foundation of the world, He chose humanity to be His sons and to be partakers of His divine nature. Through Jesus Christ, humanity can become members of both the Father's house and His kingdom. Additionally, because His purpose pertains to all humanity, it is one of unity. Therefore, He has conferred His gifts to us to promote His purpose and for the message of unity.

When we take full account of Ephesians 4:13, the gifts and the objectives are geared toward two particular goals:

1. Until the body of Christ attains to the unity of the faith
2. Until it reaches the standard of maturity Christ exhibited

With that said, despite the individual responsibilities assigned to each gift, they also have a collective function. As a whole, they exist to create a unified, mature body that is a reflection of the Father's purpose.

Having read this book, it is my hope that you are now furnished with a more comprehensive perspective of the gifts of Christ in light of God's purpose. Furthermore, armed with this disposition, let us all work to accomplish the Father's purpose.

REFERENCES

- Purpose [Def.]. Free Dictionary by Farlex Online. In the Free Dictionary by Farlex Retrieved March 2, 2019, from http://www.thefreedictionary.com/indentity
- AMG Publishers, The Hebrew-Greek Key Study Bible. Editor, Zodhiates, S. © 1995
- Strong, James © 2009 Strong's Exhaustive Concordance of the Bible.
- Sinek, Simon, Start with Why: How Great Leaders Inspire Everyone to Take Action, "People don't buy what you do; they buy why you do it. And what you do simply proves what you believe."
- Butler, Clement C, ©2017 God's Eternal Purpose Volume 1: The Establishment of God's Kingdom.
- Butler, Clement C,© 2017 God's Eternal Purpose Volume 2: The Identity of the sons of God: The Image of Jesus Christ.
- Dominion [Def.]. Free Dictionary by Farlex Online. In the Free Dictionary by Farlex Retrieved March 12, 2019, from http://www.thefreedictionary.com/dominion
- King [Def.]. Free Dictionary by Farlex Online. In the Free Dictionary by Farlex Retrieved March 20, 2019, from http://www.thefreedictionary.com/king
- Kingdom [Def.] Merriam-Webster Online. In Merriam-Webster. Retrieved April 12, 2019, from http://www.merriam-webster.com/dictionary/kingdom
- British Empire Retrieved April 14, 2019 from https://en.m.wikipedia.org/wiki/British_Empire
- Father [Def.] Strong Concordance with Hebrew and Greek Lexicon Retrieved April 20, 2019 from https://www.blueletterbible.org/lang/Lexicon/Lexicon.cfm?strongs=G3962&t=KJV
- House [Def.] Strong's Concordance with Hebrew and Greek Lexicon Retrieved April 25, 2019 from https://www.blueletterbible.org/lang/Lexicon/Lexicon.cfm?strongs=H1004&t=KJV

- Children [Def.] Strong's Concordance with Hebrew and Greek Lexicon Retrieved April 27, 2019 from https://www.blueletterbible.org/lang/Lexicon/Lexicon.cfm?strongs=G5043&t=KJV
- Butler, Clement C, © 2018 Are There Really Mansions in Heaven? It's a Family Affair.
- Inspiration of God [Def.] Strong's Concordance with Hebrew and Greek and Hebrew Lexicon Retrieve April 30, 2019 from https://www.blueletterbible.org/lang/Lexicon/Lexicon.cfm?strongs=G2315&t=KJV
- Blessings [Def.] Strong's Concordance with Hebrew and Greek Lexicon Retrieved April 30, 2019 from https://www.blueletterbible.org/lang/Lexicon/Lexicon.cfm?strongs=G2129&t=KJV
- Chosen [Def.] Strong's Concordance with Hebrew and Greek Lexicon Retrieved May 3, 2019 from https://www.blueletterbible.org/lang/Lexicon/Lexicon.cfm?strongs=G1586&t=KJV
- Predestinated [Def.] Vocabulary.com Retrieved May 12, 2019, from http://www.vocabulary.com/dictionary/predestinated
- Adoption [Def.] Strong's Concordance with Hebrew and Greek Lexicon Retrieved May 12, 2019 from https://www.blueletterbible.org/lang/Lexicon/Lexicon.cfm?strongs=G5206&t=KJV
- Redeem [Def.] Vocabulary.com Retrieved May 12, 2019, from http://www.vocabulary.com/dictionary/redeem
- Enlightenment [Def.] Strong's Concordance with Hebrew and Greek Lexicon Retrieved May 20, 2019 from https://www.blueletterbible.org/lang/Lexicon/Lexicon.cfm?strongs=G5461&t=KJV
- Earnest [Def.] Strong's Concordance with Hebrew and Greek Lexicon Retrieved May 25, 2019 from
- https://www.blueletterbible.org/lang/Lexicon/Lexicon.cfm?strongs=G728&t=KJV
- Exceeding [Def.] Free Dictionary by Farlex Online. In the Free Dictionary by Farlex Retrieved May 26, 2019, from http://www.thefreedictionary.com/exceeding
- Power [Def.] Strong's Concordance with Hebrew and Greek Lexicon Retrieved May 29, 2019 from https://www.blueletterbible.org/lang/Lexicon/Lexicon.cfm?strongs=G1411&t=KJV
- Unity [Def.] Free Dictionary by Farlex Online. In the Free Dictionary by Farlex Retrieved June 4, 2019, from http://www.thefreedictionary.com/unity

- World [Def.] Strong's Concordance with Hebrew and Greek Lexicon Retrieved June 10, 2019 from https://www.blueletterbible.org/lang/Lexicon/Lexicon.cfm?strongs=G2889&t=KJV
- World [Def.] Strong's Concordance with Hebrew and Greek Lexicon Retrieved June 15, 2019 from https://www.blueletterbible.org/lang/Lexicon/Lexicon.cfm?strongs=G165&t=KJV
- The soreg, Retrieved June 20, 2019 from http://holyland-sites.blogspot.com/2013/11/jerusalem-temple-mount-soreg-wall-of.html
- Nature [Def.] Free Dictionary by Farlex Online. In the Free Dictionary by Farlex Retrieved June 30, 2019, from http://www.thefreedictionary.com/nature
- Type [Def.] Merriam-Webster Online. In Merriam-Webster. Retrieved July 5, 2019, from http://www.merriam-webster.com/dictionary/type.
- Without Christ Retrieved July 10, 2019 from https://biblehub.com/commentaries/barnes/ephesians/2.htm
- Commonwealth [Def.] Strong's Concordance with Hebrew and Greek Lexicon Retrieved July 15, 2019 from https://www.blueletterbible.org/lang/Lexicon/Lexicon.cfm?strongs=G4174&t=KJV
- Access [Def.] Free Dictionary by Farlex Online. In the Free Dictionary by Farlex Retrieved July 20, 2019, from http://www.thefreedictionary.com/access
- Fellowcitizens [Def.] Strong's Concordance with Hebrew and Greek Lexicon Retrieved July 21, 2019 from https://www.blueletterbible.org/lang/Lexicon/Lexicon.cfm?strongs=G4847&t=KJV
- Household [Def.] Strong's Concordance with Hebrew and Greek Lexicon Retrieved July 25, 2019 from https://www.blueletterbible.org/lang/Lexicon/Lexicon.cfm?strongs=G3609&t=KJV
- Dispensation [Def.] Merriam-Webster Online. In Merriam-Webster. Retrieved July 30, 2019, from http://www.merriam-webster.com/dictionary/dispensation
- Dispensation [Def.] Strong's Concordance with Hebrew and Greek Lexicon Retrieved August 1, 2019 from https://www.blueletterbible.org/lang/Lexicon/Lexicon.cfm?strongs=G3622&t=KJV
- Fellowship [Def.] Strong, James © 2011 Strong's Greek and Hebrew Dictionary of the Bible

- Endeavoring [Def.] Vocabulary.com Retrieved August 20, 2019, from http://www.vocabulary.com/dictionary/endevoring
- Measure [Def.] Strong's Concordance with Hebrews and Greek Lexicon Retrieved August 25, 2019 from https://www.blueletterbible.org/lang/Lexicon/Lexicon.cfm?strongs=G3358&t=KJV
- Minister [Def.] Strong's Concordance with Hebrews and Greek Lexicon Retrieved August 30, 2019 from https://www.blueletterbible.org/lang/Lexicon/Lexicon.cfm?strongs=G1249&t=KJV
- Race and the Priesthood Retrieved September 15, 2019 from https://www.lds.org/topics/race-and-the-priesthood?lang=eng
- Religion [Def.]. Free Dictionary by Farlex Online. In the Free Dictionary by Farlex Retrieved September 20, 2019, from http://www.thefreedictionary.com/religion
- Men [Def.] Strong's Concordance with Hebrew and Greek Lexicon Retrieved September 26, 2019 from https://www.blueletterbible.org/lang/Lexicon/Lexicon.cfm?strongs=G444&t=KJV
- Structure [Def.] Merriam-Webster Online. In Merriam-Webster. Retrieved October 2, 2019, from http://www.merriam-webster.com/dictionary/structure
- First [Def.] Strong's Concordance with Hebrew and Greek Lexicon Retrieved October 8, 2019 from https://www.blueletterbible.org/lang/Lexicon/Lexicon.cfm?strongs=G4412&t=KJV
- Secondarily [Def.] Strong's Concordance with Hebrew and Greek Lexicon Retrieved October 20, 2019 from https://www.blueletterbible.org/lang/Lexicon/Lexicon.cfm?strongs=G1208&t=KJV
- Apostle [Def] Retrieved October 20, 2019 from https://www.biblestudytools.com/dictionaries/bakers-evangelical-dictionary/apostle.html
- Apostle [Def.] Strong's Concordance with Hebrew and Greek Lexicon Retrieved October 27, 2019 from https://www.blueletterbible.org/lang/Lexicon/Lexicon.cfm?strongs=G652&t=KJV
- Government [Def.]. Free Dictionary by Farlex Online. In the Free Dictionary by Farlex Retrieved November 1, 2019, from http://www.thefreedictionary.com/government
- Ordain [Def.] Strong's Concordance with Hebrew and Greek Lexicon Retrieved November 10, 2019 from https://www.blueletterbible.org/lang/Lexicon/Lexicon.cfm?strongs=G2525&t=KJV

- Commendation [Def.] Strong's Concordance with Hebrew and Greek Lexicon Retrieved November 12, 2019 from https://www.blueletterbible.org/lang/Lexicon/Lexicon.cfm?strongs=G4956&t=KJV
- False apostle [Def.] Strong's Concordance with Hebrew and Greek Lexicon Retrieved November 15, 2019 from https://www.blueletterbible.org/lang/Lexicon/Lexicon.cfm?strongs=G5570&t=KJV
- Simplicity [Def.] Strong's Concordance with Hebrew and Greek Lexicon Retrieved November 25, 2019 from https://www.blueletterbible.org/lang/Lexicon/Lexicon.cfm?strongs=G572&t=KJV
- Transformed [Def.] Strong's Concordance with Hebrew and Greek Lexicon Retrieved November 30, 2019 from https://www.blueletterbible.org/lang/Lexicon/Lexicon.cfm?strongs=G3345&t=KJV
- Prophet [Def.] Strong's Concordance with Hebrew and Greek Lexicon Retrieved December 5, 2019 from https://www.blueletterbible.org/lang/Lexicon/Lexicon.cfm?strongs=G4396&t=KJV
- Prophecy [Def.] Strong's Concordance with Hebrew and Greek Lexicon Retrieved December 5, 2019 from https://www.blueletterbible.org/lang/Lexicon/Lexicon.cfm?strongs=G4394&t=KJV
- Prophesying [Def.] Strong's Concordance with Hebrew and Greek Lexicon Retrieved December 5, 2019 from https://www.blueletterbible.org/lang/Lexicon/Lexicon.cfm?strongs=G4395&t=KJV
- False Prophet [Def.] Strong's Concordance with Hebrew and Greek Lexicon Retrieved December 10, 2019 from https://www.blueletterbible.org/lang/Lexicon/Lexicon.cfm?strongs=G5578&t=KJV
- Evangelist [Def.] Merriam-Webster Online. In Merriam-Webster. Retrieved December 15, 2019, from http://www.merriam-webster.com/dictionary/evangelist
- Evangelist [Def.] Strong's Concordance with Hebrew and Greek Lexicon Retrieved December 15, 2019 from https://www.blueletterbible.org/lang/Lexicon/lexicon.cfm?strongs=G2097&t=KJV
- Reconcile [Def.]. Free Dictionary by Farlex Online. In the Free Dictionary by Farlex Retrieved December 17, 2019, from http://www.thefreedictionary.com/reconcile
- Redeem [Def.]. Free Dictionary by Farlex Online. In the Free Dictionary by Farlex Retrieved December 17, 2019, from http://www.thefreedictionary.com/redeem

- Preach [Def.] Strong's Concordance with Hebrew and Greek Lexicon Retrieved December 21, 2019 from https://www.blueletterbible.org/lang/Lexicon/Lexicon.cfm?strongs=G2097&t=KJV
- Pastor [Def.] Strong's Concordance with Hebrew and Greek Lexicon Retrieved January 6, 2020 from https://www.blueletterbible.org/lang/Lexicon/Lexicon.cfm?strongs=G4166&t=KJV
- Reagan, David, "Pastor" Scriptural in the New Testament Retrieved January 6, 2020 from http://www.learnthebible.org/pastor-scriptural-in-the-new-testament.html
- Oversight [Def.] Strong's Concordance with Hebrew and Greek Lexicon Retrieved January 7, 2020 from https://www.blueletterbible.org/lang/Lexicon/Lexicon.cfm?strongs=G1983&t=KJV
- Elder [Def.] Strong's Concordance with Hebrew and Greek Lexicon Retrieved January 7, 2020 from https://www.blueletterbible.org/lang/Lexicon/Lexicon.cfm?strongs=G4245&t=KJV
- Maxwell, Dr. John C, Everything rises and falls on leadership
- Bishop [Def.] Strong's Concordance with Hebrew and Greek Lexicon Retrieved January 9, 2020 from https://www.blueletterbible.org/lang/Lexicon/Lexicon.cfm?strongs=G1984&t=KJV
- Overseer [Def.] Strong's Concordance with Hebrew and Greek Lexicon Retrieved January 9, 2020 from https://www.blueletterbible.org/lang/Lexicon/Lexicon.cfm?strongs=G1985&t=KJV
- Lords over [Def.] Strong's Concordance with Hebrew and Greek Lexicon Retrieved January 11, 2020 from https://www.blueletterbible.org/lang/Lexicon/Lexicon.cfm?strongs=G2634&t=KJV
- Rule [Def.] Strong's Concordance with Hebrew and Greek Lexicon Retrieved January 11, 2020 from https://www.blueletterbible.org/lang/Lexicon/Lexicon.cfm?strongs=G2233&t=KJV
- Oversee [Def.] Free Dictionary by Farlex Online. In the Free Dictionary by Farlex Retrieved July 3, 2019, from http://www.thefreedictionary.com/oversee
- Teacher [Def.] Strong's Concordance with Hebrew and Greek Lexicon Retrieved January 11, 2020 from https://www.blueletterbible.org/lang/Lexicon/Lexicon.cfm?strongs=G1320&t=KJV
- Doctor of the Law [Def.] Strong's Concordance with Hebrew and Greek Lexicon Retrieved January 11, 2020 from https://www.blueletterbible.org/lang/Lexicon/Lexicon.cfm?strongs=G3547&t=KJV

- Scribe [Def.] Strong's Concordance with Hebrew and Greek Lexicon Retrieved January 14, 2020 from https://www.blueletterbible.org/lang/Lexicon/Lexicon.cfm?strongs=G1122&t=KJV
- Authority [Def.] Strong's Concordance with Hebrew and Greek Lexicon Retrieved January 14, 2020 from https://www.blueletterbible.org/lang/Lexicon/Lexicon.cfm?strongs=G1849&t=KJV
- False Teacher [Def.] Strong's Concordance with Hebrew and Greek Lexicon Retrieved January 14, 2020 from https://www.blueletterbible.org/lang/Lexicon/Lexicon.cfm?strongs=G5572&t=KJV
- Heresy [Def.] Strong's Concordance with Hebrew and Greek Lexicon Retrieved January 14, 2020 from https://www.blueletterbible.org/lang/Lexicon/Lexicon.cfm?strongs=G139&t=KJV
- Preach [Def.] Strong's Concordance with Hebrew and Greek Lexicon Retrieved January 21, 2020 from https://www.blueletterbible.org/lang/Lexicon/Lexicon.cfm?strongs=G2784&t=KJV
- Teach [Def.] Strong's Concordance with Hebrew and Greek Lexicon Retrieved January 21, 2020 from https://www.blueletterbible.org/lang/Lexicon/Lexicon.cfm?strongs=G1321&t=KJV
- Perfecting [Def.] Strong's Concordance with Hebrew and Greek Lexicon Retrieved January 11, 2020 from https://www.blueletterbible.org/lang/Lexicon/Lexicon.cfm?strongs=G2677&t=KJV
- Doctrine [Def.] Merriam-Webster Online. In Merriam-Webster. Retrieved February 2, 2020, from http://www.merriam-webster.com/dictionary/doctrine
- Reproof [Def.] Merriam-Webster Online. In Merriam-Webster. Retrieved February 2, 2020, from http://www.merriam-webster.com/dictionary/reproof
- Correction [Def.] Merriam-Webster Online. In Merriam-Webster. Retrieved February 2, 2020, from http://www.merriam-webster.com/dictionary/correction
- Increase [Def.] Strong's Concordance with Hebrew and Greek Lexicon Retrieved February 10, 2020 from https://www.blueletterbible.org/lang/Lexicon/Lexicon.cfm?strongs=G837&t=KJV
- Strong [Def.] Strong's Concordance with Hebrew and Greek Lexicon Retrieved February 10, 2020 from https://www.blueletterbible.org/lang/Lexicon/Lexicon.cfm?strongs=G4731&t=KJV

- Ministry [Def.] Strong's Concordance with Hebrew and Greek Lexicon Retrieved February 10, 2020 from https://www.blueletterbible.org/lang/Lexicon/Lexicon.cfm?strongs=G1248&t=KJV
- Deacon [Def.] Strong's Concordance with Hebrew and Greek Lexicon Retrieved February 20, 2020 from https://www.blueletterbible.org/lang/Lexicon/Lexicon.cfm?strongs=G1247&t=KJV
- Edifying [Def.] Strong's Concordance with Hebrew and Greek Lexicon Retrieved February 20, 2020 from https://www.blueletterbible.org/lang/Lexicon/Lexicon.cfm?strongs=G3619&t=KJV
- Aristotle, "The whole is greater than the sum of its parts."
- Conformed [Def.] Strong's Concordance with Hebrew and Greek Lexicon Retrieved February 20, 2020 from https://www.blueletterbible.org/lang/Lexicon/Lexicon.cfm?strongs=G4832&t=KJV
- Changed [Def.] Strong's Concordance with Hebrew and Greek Lexicon Retrieved February 20, 2020 from https://www.blueletterbible.org/lang/Lexicon/Lexicon.cfm?strongs=G3339&t=KJV
- Sacrifice [Def.] Retrieved March 20, 2020 from https://biblehub.com/commentaries/barnes/romans/12.htm
- Conformed [Def.] Strong's Concordance with Hebrew and Greek Lexicon Retrieved March 30 20, 2020 from https://www.blueletterbible.org/lang/Lexicon/Lexicon.cfm?strongs=G4964&t=KJV
- Renewing [Def.] Strong's Concordance with Hebrew and Greek Lexicon Retrieved April 7, 2020 from https://www.blueletterbible.org/lang/Lexicon/Lexicon.cfm?strongs=G342&t=KJV
- Children [Def.] Strong's Concordance with Hebrew and Greek Lexicon Retrieved April 10, 2020 from https://www.blueletterbible.org/lang/Lexicon/Lexicon.cfm?strongs=G3516&t=KJV
- Booth, Dawn, photographer, "Armor of God" [Contenders for the Faith]. Photograph. 2010. Retrieved December 9, 2020 from https://www.google.com/search?rlz=1C1CHBF_enBS731BS752&source=univ&tbm=isch&q=dawn+booth+photo+of+the+whole+armor+of+God&sa=X&ved=2ahUKEwi7yvq-gsTtAhXkAp0JHVPXCNUQjJkEegQIBRAB&biw=1536&bih=755#imgrc=jul37HAxzbtFjM

www.ingramcontent.com/pod-product-compliance
Lightning Source LLC
Chambersburg PA
CBHW081415230426
43668CB00016B/2241